The Paranormal Pop Culture Collection

Rambling and Shambling Through the Entertainment of the Unexplained

Stay Spooky + Keep It Weird!

AARON SAGERS

D1521940

THE PARANORMAL POP CULTURE COLLECTION

By: Aaron Sagers

www.ParanormalPopCulture.com
www.AaronSagers.com
Patreon.com/AaronSagers
Instagram.com/AaronSagers
Twitter.com/AaronSagers
TikTok.com/@AaronSagers
Facebook.com/AaronSagersPage
Subscribe to NightMerica Podcast
Contact: Publicity@AaronSagers.com

.

Thank you to the creators who fueled my childhood imagination and sparked my future creativity: Isaac Asimov, Ray Bradbury, Steve Ditko, Ian Fleming, Jim Henson, Stephen King, Stan Lee, George Lucas, Richard Matheson, Edgar Allan Poe, Gene Roddenberry, George A. Romero, Rod Sterling, Steven Spielberg, and Kurt Vonnegut Jr.

Foreword

Dear 21st Century Reader (Or time traveler, alien anthropologist or post-apocalyptic survivor):

To begin with, greetings from the past! As I write this, the world is but a few days from December 21, 2012, also known as the day, when the feces hit the air conditioning and the world ends.

Humans of December 2012 are currently planning for solar flare- powered zombies with the bird flu who emerged out of a giant crashed asteroid armed with nukes to march on world capitals to launch a new world Illuminati order, which is actually run by a shadow extraterrestrial government that forces us to compete in hunger games to avoid becoming Soylent Green chow to be fed to highly intelligent ape overlords.

Or maybe that's just what I'm planning for because I really am behind on my holiday shopping and would rather not deal with it.

Regardless, if you are reading this, it means you made it through December 21, and either the Mayans were wrong and nothing happened (take that, stupid ancient civilization!) or you need some reading material in the ruins of humanity.

Whichever the case, this volume is the result of three years and change of work. And I appreciate you taking the time to read it - especially since you might want to consider burning this book for warmth. If you're documenting the literary works of planet Earth, well, there's probably a copy of Everyone Poops around here somewhere that you may want to check out first. I mean, it is a pretty epic tome where you find out at the end – spoiler alert - everyone does really poop. But back to this book.

In 2009, this mainstream journalist launched ParanormalPopCulture.com as a spot dedicated to "exploring the entertainment of the unexplained." What I set out to do and succeeded with the help of many supporters and contributors, was a fun little home on the Internet (you remember the Internet, right?) where we could celebrate all the ghosts, vampires, aliens, zombies and monsters in movies, TV, comics, novels, and video games.

I have never wanted to tell people what to believe when it comes to the supernatural and paranormal. I don't need to;

according to a 2010 Pew Research poll and 2009 Harris Interactive poll (and multiple other polls), a large number of Americans have some belief in the supernatural. About 65 percent of the Pew respondents experienced diverse supernatural phenomena, and about 40 percent of the Harris respondents expressed a belief in ghosts. That is a lot of people who believe in something big, and also a lot of people who don't buy into it at all.

Still, though there is disagreement about ghosts and goblins existing, we can all agree that they are fun to talk about. Long before TV, movies or radio shows, people told ghost stories and believed in monsters and magic men. Spawned from mythology and religion, these tales were essentially paranormal popular culture. They tapped into the shared experiences of anyone who has been afraid of the dark and unknown.

And isn't that pretty much all of us?

I count myself incredibly fortunate that that is indeed the case, and that the multi-billion-dollar entertainment industry cannot get enough of the undead, walking dead, haunting dead and creatures from the corners of this world and others. This has led to the PPC site showing up on CNN, Travel Channel, BBC, Playboy, Entertainment Weekly, The Hollywood Reporter and many other great media outlets. We even managed to bring PPC to TV full-time with the entertainment news show Paranormal Paparazzi on the Travel Channel - and that has been pretty rad.

In fact, this gig of mine has been an enormous blessing to the nerdy child of the '80s who grew up devouring pop culture - and not just the paranormal variety. While I could not get enough of old Twilight Zone and In Search Of... episodes or those Time-Life Mysteries of the Unknown books and "true" ghost stories, I also devoured anything I could that involved sci-fi, superheroes, horror and adventure.

As such, this collection is not every article from PPC since its founding in 2009. In fact, not all of it is even paranormal or from the site; it simply reflects a sliver of my work during the awesome journey in the last couple of years, along with the date it was published. I've attempted to leave the pieces herein as untouched as possible to preserve the moment they first appeared. You'll see familiar names pop up a few times to chat about new stuff and hear from people you may not have thought about in a while. I hope you enjoy the voyage.

Finally, speaking of voyages, if you've joined me for this fantastic voyage read my stuff, visited the site, spoken with me at events or over social media and just generally supported me—I thank you. This is for you, and because of you.

If, however, you are a time traveler or alien anthropologist, my real name is J.K. Rowling. Look it up, I'm kind of a big deal. And sorry for Honey Boo Boo; I swear I had nothing to do with that.

And if you are a post-apocalyptic survivor, feel free to toss this on the fire. It burns really nicely right around 451 degrees Fahrenheit.

Aaron Sagers December 2012

Table of Contents

CHAPTER 1

Investigating the Paranormal

10 Things You Should Know About the Paranormal

(January 2011)

Most of us are smugly convinced we live in a fairly defined world where answers to most questions are a few touchscreen taps away on a smartphone (even how to crush those encamped evil green pigs in "Angry Birds"). But when the sun goes down and the house makes unusual "settling" noises in the middle of the night, or we see an odd series of lights flashing across the sky, we become aware there are a lot of unanswered questions in this great big universe and we really don't know shit.

With new paranormal shows, movies, comic books, and video games invading our lives more each day (and stoking our fears at night), it's a good time to get to know a few things about the unknown.

The Word of the Unexplained

The word "paranormal," which means above the norm, was coined around 1920. It generally covers all phenomena not currently explained by science. It's an umbrella term that includes everything from mysterious creatures like Sasquatch and the Loch Ness Monster to vampires, werewolves, fairies, and anything else that that makes True Blood possible. But when a wave of documentary-style reality TV shows premiered about six years ago, the public's main association with the paranormal became ghosts.

It's Above Normal, but Not New

For as long as humans have gathered around to share stories, we've been shooting the bull about the supernatural. Sharing stories about the unknown was a good way to trade experiences, explain the world and come to a general understanding of what's "out there." Plus, the paranormal made for great plot devices in popular culture. In the eighth century BC poem "The Iliad," Homer (he of the toga and not the D'oh) wrote the ghost of Patroclus appears to Achilles and vanishes "as a vapour, gibbering and

2

whining into the earth."

Right around the same time, according to the Hebrew Bible (Old Testament), the prophet Jonah was busy getting swallowed by a monster fish. The "greatest story ever told"-which doesn't feature a boy wizard or Jedi but does focus on Jesus of Nazareth (appeared in the year 5 BC, launched a religion, perhaps you've heard of him?) is loaded with mentions of spirits and demons and the dead returning from the grave.

If You Don't Believe in It, Your Neighbor Probably Does

Science may have answered many questions about the world that stumped our ancestors, but plenty of mysteries remain. What happens to us after we die? Is there life on other planets? How much gel is required to cement Pauly D's hair in place? Although skeptics deride most discussion of the paranormal as silly, 1,500 years after the Loch Ness Monster was first written about by Saint Columba in the 6th century, Nessie received news coverage after she was sighted on Google Earth. More than 400 years after a Swedish folktale emerged about a ghostly hitchhiker in the 1700s, the story is still playing out on YouTube.

A serious, modern belief in the paranormal isn't just limited to other countries where people talk funny and concern themselves with numerology and slaying vampires. A December 2009 Pew Research Center survey found 65% of respondents reported experiencing "diverse supernatural phenomena." Even Bill "The Sports Guy" Simmons recently came out of the paranormal closet as a believer after having a ghostly encounter in the Oklahoma City Skirvin Hotel, which is notorious for terrifying the New York Knicks.

We Live in the Prime Time for the Paranormal

We are in the midst of a paranormal boom, where the unexplained is taking center stage. Whether there are UFOs over New York City (which were probably just balloons), a mysterious swamp monster caught on camera in Louisiana (which was probably just a viral marketing stunt for a new movie or video game) or Lady Gaga paying $5,000 for a ghostbusting kit to purge backstage specters (y'know, that one seems likely), news outlets gobble up stories with a supernatural bent.

The obsession extends to entertainment media where the current primetime TV lineup is under siege by vampires, werewolves, aliens, demons, and ghosts. One new show, *Being Human*, on Syfy - a remake of a popular BBC series - throws together a werewolf, vampire, and ghost as roomies. In movie theaters, two of 2010's top grossing films - *Harry Potter and the Deathly Hallows: Part 1* and *The Twilight Saga: Eclipse* - exist in worlds of the unknown, as does the massively successful franchise *Paranormal Activity*, which mimics the docustyle of shows like the Travel Channel's *Most Haunted.*

On the upside, even if you hate the trend, you're in luck because the world is ending in 2012, according to the internet's favorite paranormal theory.

The Supernatural "Likes" Social Media

Paranormal pop culture in movies, TV shows, video games, etc. provides an entertainment outlet to, and sate the curiosity of, a sizable number of Americans who believe in the supernatural. But the paranormal trend didn't kick into overdrive until the creatures of the dark went online.

Before online social media, the curious believer was limited in finding a paranormal community by social mores and geography. While many Web sites and even investigative groups existed before 2004, it was the wild success of the relatively new networking site Myspace, then Facebook, that permitted paranormal enthusiasts to transcend the borders of their town or avoid potential embarrassment from judgmental PTA members.

A paradigm shift occurred where groups could gather and ghost hunt, and attend paranormal conventions, and feel secure knowing they were with like-minded individuals. Now there are a multitude of dedicated paranormal social networking sites such as LiveParanormal.com. Meetup.com, the online source for finding communities with shared interests, lists 622 "paranormal" groups - which is an amount right in the middle of the 480 "Democrat" and 705 "Republican" meetup pages.

Still, Everything Dead is Alive Again

The modern paranormal boom that encompasses our culture resembles the Spiritualist movement that began in the mid-1800s and continued through the early 20th century. The mainstream

4

acceptance that communicating with spirits was both possible and positive was largely launched by the Fox Sisters of Upstate New York. Kate, Leah and Margaret Fox were mediums (people who could chat with the dead) and would fill auditoriums with crowds wanting to see them perform. They were reality celebrities of the time and sort of like the Kardashians of their day, except, ironically, not foxy.

The pursuit of the paranormal as a worthy academic (and scientific) endeavor was taken up by organized groups of learned men with bowties and waxed mustaches, and not just crackpots. And like our current era of Neo-Spiritualism, this period saw newspapers covering unexplained phenomena seriously as well as the launch of niche paranormal publications. There was a lucrative entertainment mechanism in place, and plenty of scams took root - one of the most popular was the William Mumler spirit photography, which used a primitive Photoshop technique to layer images of spectral dead relatives over family members' pics, which were then passed off as real.

The Paranormal Loves Celebrities ...

Simply put, if we were to anthropomorphize the paranormal, it would be a bit of a starfucker. In the early 20th century, Sherlock Holmes' creator Arthur Conan Doyle was a Spiritualist and believer of ghosts, mediums, and the Cottingley Fairies. His famous frenemy was illusionist Harry Houdini, who was a skeptic and set about debunking those who claimed proof of the paranormal - and the two had a war of words in the media, which culminated with Conan Doyle accusing Houdini himself of having supernatural powers (ooh, snap?).

To this day, many celebrities openly discuss their interactions with the paranormal. Patrick Stewart claims he saw a ghost while performing on stage with Ian McKellen; Nicolas Cage at one point owned, but never slept in, the haunted Vieux Carre house in New Orleans and believed in the ghostly presence; original KISS guitarist Ace Frehley says he frequently sees UFOs. And Dan Aykroyd, who created the modern pop culture mold of the paranormal investigator (outfits, gadgets, logo, car, and team mentality) in his film "Ghostbusters " comes from a long line of Spiritualists.

... But Not Experts

Regardless of the fame attached to figures within the
paranormal, and no matter how many books have been written,
haunted houses visited, or probing by aliens received, no one can
be an expert on the paranormal - although the probing gets you
pretty darn close. Even though his fame has been built by pursuing
spooks, famed ghost hunter Jason Hawes says, "There's really no
experts in this field. How can we be?" When the word "paranormal
" means beyond scientific definition, anyone claiming to be an
expert on the unexplained is either a scam artist or from the future.

But It's Worth Trying to Become One ...

Even though there are currently no experts in the paranormal ¬
there won't be until proof of a phenomena is captured and able to
be repeated under test conditions and explained by science - there
are a hell of a lot of people who read Fox Mulder's poster and
believe the truth is out there. Googling "paranormal investigation
group" nets nearly 12 million results, and it's not hard to figure out
why. It is exhilarating and a little scary to spend your nights on a
quest to figure out if the dead continue to stick around.

Of course, the odds are astronomically against you discovering
and replicating phenomena that turns something from paranormal
to just "normal," but that puts the aspiring investigator in the same
camp as scientists who have changed the world by accident. If you
happen to be the lucky individual that lands an exclusive one-on-
one with a Chupacabra or your dead Aunt Sally, then you
automatically get a chapter in the tomes of human history, a book
deal, movie adaptation and probably an action figure modeled after
you. And don't forget the groupies.

... Although It's Unlikely

The desire to seek out and understand the unexplained seems
hardwired into our brains, although some feel the pull more than
others. You can spend a fortune on the latest gadgets (and iPhone
apps) to seek out creatures and specters, travel the world's
paranormal hotspots and still have nothing more to show for it than
a raging TSA pat down fetish and a lot of stories.

But the stories of personal experience make it almost as
worthwhile as evidence. Unlike edited reality TV or the movies, a

paranormal investigation takes hours and a super-sized amount of patience, but the tales of the paranormal connect us all back to ancestors who tried to understand their worlds still untouched by scientific definition. Skepticism is a good thing; it's valid to have a properly calibrated bullshit meter that hits red anytime someone has a cold chill in a drafty house and calls it a ghost. A good skeptic is less of a sucker and can vet experiences to debunk claims and hold on to the actual unexplained phenomena, as long as they keep in mind that - as either a fortune cookie or Carl Sagan said - the absence of evidence is not the evidence of absence.

How To Speak Apocalypse: A Terminology Primer
(January 2012)

It's the end of the world as we know it, and I feel confused. Instead of a lone doomsday-sayer on a city street corner with a sandwich board, the news media and popular culture have taken to talking about the end being nigh. Especially with the 2012 Mayan calendar predictions, the big one has become big business. But not all end-of-days scenarios are equal within the world of dedicated apocalypse nerds.

There are multiple theories that go beyond the zombocalypse or rise of the machines, and even the words themselves that are used to describe humanity's last hurrah have different meanings, depending on the groups that use them.

To understand the nuances of the language of the end times, we compiled the following key phrases from the nerd set as a glossary to go out on, along with the help of John R. Hall, a professor of sociology at the University of California, Davis, and author of *Apocalypse: From Antiquity to the Empire of Modernity*.

Al Qaeda
An apocalyptic-minded group (or "apocalyptic warring sect," according to Hall) within Islam seeking to bring on the end of this

world and the beginning of the next. Al Qaeda believes that "only through the exercise of violence can God's plan for a new age be realized," and its members see themselves as God's agents, Hall said. The same definition may apply to actors within the Puritan Revolution in the 17th Century (Oliver Cromwell) and the Crusades, he said.

Apocalypse
In Greek, "apocalypse" means something like "disclosure of things previously hidden." "That being the title of the [Christian] Book of Revelation, it's often taken to mean the revelation of the last things before God's final judgment," Hall said. Apocalyptic movements emerge many times through history were profound changes are said to occur and a new world is dawning. But, Hall added, "those movements are not generally about the end of the world in the ultimate sense."

Armageddon
"End times" is simply a popular usage for talking about the end of the world, and the same thing can be said for "doomsday." Armageddon is a specific reference to the Book of Revelation or apocalypse in the Bible's New Testament. Said Hall: "It is the final battle between good and evil that comes just before God's judgment at the end of the world."

Big Crunch
This is essentially the opposite of the big bang. This theory among cosmologists posits that the constant expansion of the universe will one day stop and reverse, and the universe will collapse until it becomes a black hole.

Books of Chilam Balam
These Mayan books from the 16th to the 18th centuries speak about history, myths, medicinal recipes, daily life, war, and politics - along with some apocalyptic predictions. In 1951, astronomer and linguist Maud Makemson, a recipient of the Guggenheim fellowship for the study of Mayan astronomy, released *The Book of the Jaguar Priest.*

The book contained her translation of *The Book of Chilam*

Balam of Tizimin from the 1500s, which presented a Mayan end-of- world scenario on December 21, 2012: "Then the god will come to visit his little ones. Perhaps after death will be the subject of his discourse." Makemson also translates that, "in the final days of misfortune, in the final days of tying up the bundle of the 13 [cycles] ... then the end of the world shall come" and "these valleys of the earth shall come to an end." Then again, the Maya may have believed that the end of one world was followed by the beginning of a new one.

Camping Rapture

Evangelist and religious broadcaster Harold Camping predicted the Rapture would take place on May 21, 2011, which would have righteous believers of Jesus Christ rising up to heaven, followed by a five-month period of torment on Earth brought on by the Four Horsemen of the Apocalypse. On October 21, 2011, the world was then supposed to end. Camping had previously made predictions for 1988 and 1994. "Harold Camping is probably the most successful date-setting apocalypticist the world has yet seen," Hall said.

Catabolic Collapse

A theory by John Michael Greer, an author and *Grand Archdruid of the Ancient Order of Druids in America*, catabolic collapse refers to what happens when civilization can't meet the demands for the stuff it produces. When maintenance needs cannot be met by available resources, societies may cut back for a bit and are impoverished, then return to business as usual, or they could begin to amass even more stuff for the next round.

Greer suggests that we're at the end of a big collapse, largely because of fossil fuel consumption. He is, however, optimistic that as this current cycle of civilization comes to a close, it will re-emerge as a radically different, newly optimistic one.

Eschatology

A belief or theology regarding the end of humanity or the end of the world.

Galactic Superwave

The superwave theory by physicist Paul LaViolette, Ph.D., in the book *Earth Under Fire* posits that as spiral galaxies detonate on a periodic basis, the explosions can expand to encompass our entire outer space neighborhood. Not only would we not know of an impending superwave for thousands of years after it began, but the explosion would probably bring a lot of debris that would cover up our sun.

LaViolette also thinks a superwave might be heralded by a gravitational wave and then a gamma-ray burst. He suggests that the Asian tsunami on December 26, 2004, was actually caused by a gravitational wave and said the largest gamma-ray burst ever recorded occurred on December 27.

Ice age

This doomsday scenario involves the arrival of a new ice age, and perhaps one brought about by global climate change. As ice packs in the Arctic melt, the oceans become less salty, which could prevent the Gulf Stream's warmer currents (driven by salt falling to the bottom) from reaching the North Pole. Things would get very cold, very fast, and the Northern Hemisphere would be covered in ice for quite a long spell. Then again, a recent study published in the journal *Nature Geoscience* said greenhouse gas emissions have delayed the next ice age.

Mayan Long Count Calendar

The 2012 doomsday scenarios are based on the nonrepeating Mayan long count calendar, which was actually used by other Mesoamerican people and originated a significant amount of time before the Maya. The calendar has cycles ("baktuns") of about 400 years, the 13th of which will end, and the 14th begin, on December 21. The long count calendar was used to record time

for periods longer than the 52-year "calendar round." The Mayan "Chilam Balam" jaguar priests eventually switched over to the 260-year short count calendar before the Maya began to abandon their cities.

Nemesis

Nemesis is a red or brown dwarf star hypothesized to orbit the sun that periodically (every 26 million years or so) disrupts billions of comets from a surrounding - also hypothetical - "Oort" cloud, some of which would then hit Earth and lead to a mass extinction event. This "death star" theory was independently published in 1984 in the journal *Nature* by two groups of astronomers after paleontologists David Raup and Jack Sepkoski said they'd discovered a time pattern to extinction over 250 million years (later updated to 500 million years).

Omega Point

Jesuit priest Pierre Teilhard de Chardin elaborated on Ukrainian scientist Vladimir Vernadsky's concept of the "noosphere" (the idea that human thought and the mastery of the physical realm, as during the atomic age, has significantly transformed the planet) to postulate that a planet-wide shared consciousness was emerging between humans. The omega point - which some believe we'll reach in 2012 - is the culmination of evolution.

Humans will be organized in the best possible way, which then will lead to telepathy and a transcendence. In a way, when humankind reaches this point, it is joining God in the Christosphere, where we will be redeemed.

Pole Shift

Within the scientific community, there is an accepted idea of "true polar wander," which states that the Earth's poles readjusted themselves about 800 million years ago. But whereas the poles shifted about 50 degrees over 20 million years, author Patrick Geryl theorizes that the Earth might capsize and dramatically roll over in 2012, thus causing continents to collide, natural disasters and an upheaval of ecosystems.

Technological Singularity

In 1965, Gordon Moore, the co-founder of Intel, wrote that computing power essentially doubled every two years, and he predicted that the trend would continue for at least 10 years. Nearly 50 years later, Moore's prediction has remained true. In his 1993 essay "The Coming Technological Singularity," mathematician and sci-fi writer Vernor Vinge expanded on Moore's Law to suggest this means that computers will gain "superhuman artificial intelligence" and that the human era will be ended.

Futurist Ray Kurzweil is a proponent of the technological singularity theory and supports the concept of transhumanism, which means the singularity could lead to an improvement of our physical state (goodbye, mortality) and a digital-human consciousness - or to a Cyberdyne-esque rise of the machines.

Zombocalypse

A pop culture apocalypse concept introduced by George A. Romero, in the 1968 film *Night of the Living Dead*, that showed the dead being resurrected as flesh-eating, mindless ghouls.

Romero was inspired by Richard Matheson's apocalyptic story *I Am Legend*. While originating in entertainment and enjoying a resurgence because of books such as Robert Kirkman's *The Walking Dead* and Max Brooks' *World War Z*, the zombie apocalypse has taken hold as one of semi-serious conversation and planning.

Paranormal Glossary: Brush Up on Your Paranormal Jargon
(September 2012)

It's a big, wide unexplained world where the dead refuse to go away, mysterious creatures stalk the land and inhuman visitors can't get enough of our company. At least, that is what many believers think, and they have a lot of terminology to keep it all straight. So, whether you are a skeptic who just wants to know what all the talk is about - and know how to argue about it - or you're a believer who needs to know the name of that thing in your closet, here is a basic breakdown of some popular paranormal words.

Apocalypse

A Greek word translated approximately to mean "disclosure of things previously hidden," it is a term most often applied to the end of the world, the dawn of a new world or the revelation before mankind's final judgment.

Bolide

Informally defined as an exploding meteor that resembles a bright fireball.

Cryptozoology

The study and pursuit of cryptids, creatures traditionally considered mythical, folkloric or previously extinct. Example: Bigfoot, Chupacabra, Loch Ness Monster.

Disembodied Voice

A voice or noise that lacks an explainable source.

Elemental

Supernatural nature spirits that include fairies, trolls and banshees.

EVP

The abbreviation for "electronic voice phenomena," which refers to noises of a paranormal nature that cannot be heard with the human ear but are recorded by electronic devices.

Ghost

Typically refers to the soul of a deceased human (or animal) that continues to exist in some form on an earthly plane without "crossing over."

Inhuman Entity

A supernatural being - such as a demon or jinn - that did not begin its existence in human form.

Intelligent Haunting

Activity resulting from an aware ghost or spirit that interacts with its environment.

Mayan Long Count Calendar
The basis for the doomsday predictions, which is a nonrepeating calendar with "baktun" cycles of about 400 years - with the 13th ending, and the 14th beginning, on December 21, 2012.

Orb
An often translucent, circular anomaly (or "ball of light") seen in photography - and sometimes with the naked eye - that may be, depending on your theory, a bug, speck of dust, reflection, moisture or spirit energy.

Paranormal
Literally, "above normal," it refers to anything outside or beyond current scientific explanation.

Paranormal Pop Culture
Term given to paranormal-themed movies, TV shows, comic books, video games, music and literature; also known as "entertainment of the unexplained. "

Paranormal Tourism
The niche within the travel industry where tourists attend paranormal-themed conventions and festivals, investigate famously haunted locations (or camp out to search for Bigfoot or UFOs), and join ghost tours or haunted pub crawls through cities.

Pareidolia
Also known as "matrixing," it is the brain's perception of a meaningful pattern within random sounds or images.

Possession
The state where an entity inhabits and exerts a level of control over a living thing or object.

Prepper
An apocalyptically-minded individual preparing themselves for survival during an imminent societal or global disaster.

Preternatural

Instead of being connected to the spiritual realm, like supernatural matters, the preternatural applies to things that are of the natural world but currently unexplained.

Residual Haunting

Repetitive paranormal activity resulting from the energy imprint of a person or event in time.

Shadow Person

A commonly reported inky black humanoid entity that moves fast, it is often spotted out of the corner of the eye and has been interpreted to be anything from a ghost or demon to an alien, time traveler, or inter-dimensional being.

Spirit

As opposed to a ghost (see above), a spirit is normally the soul of the deceased that has crossed over and exists in a spiritual or metaphysical plane.

Supernatural

Typically referring to spiritual or religious matters, the laws of nature do not apply to this realm.

UFO

Abbreviation for "unidentified flying object" which does not necessarily apply to extraterrestrial or secret governmental crafts but can be anything unknown spotted in the sky.

Zombie

The classic version is a mindless, frequently violent, product of supernatural magic or pharmacology while the modern incarnation is a reanimated human corpse infected with an unexplained contagion that is relentless and aggressive.

Top 10 Paranormal Myths
(September 2012)

Just because the paranormal is the realm of the unexplained doesn't mean there isn't any explaining to do. Humans have always sought to give definition to the world around us, and even to the worlds that may be beyond us. As a result, over the course of millennia, we have developed countless theories and told endless stories within the realm of paranormal pop culture, and there have been a lot of misconceptions that have taken root in the public's consciousness. Believe it or not, even when dealing with the mysterious realm of ghosts, aliens, and creatures, there are some things we can fairly confidently label as false. So, to clear up some incorrect assumptions about the unexplained, let's take a look at the Top 10 Paranormal Myths.

Paranormal Facts Exist

The term "paranormal" applies to anything currently beyond the range of scientific explanation. So, anyone who claims they have access to the rulebook of the paranormal, and that they know a foolproof way of making a ghost go "boo!" is probably a charlatan - or about to be pretty famous. Plenty of researchers - including reputable scientists - have compelling theories about unexplained phenomena and are attempting to apply those utilizing the scientific method, but so far, paranormal facts don't quite exist.

Ghosts Only Come Out at Night

There are a lot of reasons to ghost hunt at night: The world quiets down as the day fades away; some locations only let you enter after the close of daytime business hours; it is much creepier at night; and, most importantly, it's the best time to play with your sweet night vision camera! But if you want to chase ghosts, you can just as effectively do it during the day, according to most paranormal researchers. In fact, it might even be a more effective time because that's when the dead were probably most alive.

There is No Physical Evidence of Bigfoot

While there have not been any bodies found, Bigfoot researchers claim there is quite a bit of physical evidence to suggest the creatures exists - including hair, blood, tissue, tracks and, yes, poop. There is also a growing community of scientists who believe in Sasquatch, including famed primatologist Dr. Jane Goodall and Dr. Jeffrey Meldrum of Idaho State University, among others. Eric Altman of the Pennsylvania Bigfoot Society stresses that, as far as the lack of physical remains (a dead Sasquatch), fossilization requires very specific conditions and Mother Nature has an effective system of breaking down animal remains in about 10 days - so a freshly-dead specimen of the already-rare creature would be hard to find.

Only Old Buildings are Haunted

A decrepit, ancient Victorian mansion with broken windows, creaky floorboards and moldy furniture may be the best haunted house in Hollywood, but it's not where ghosts necessarily hang out. Beyond just old houses, researchers claim to have found paranormal evidence in jails, asylums, hospitals, hotels, museums, battleships, cruise liners, cars, roads and forests. New locations can also be haunted, as can the ground where a new building is established. There doesn't necessarily have to be a death on the property, either. It is widely accepted within the paranormal community that objects and people themselves can be the focus of a haunting.

America's Paranormal Fascination is New

Although the paranormal has become quite popular with the arrival of investigation-based reality shows, America's fascination dates back to the origins of the nation. The paranormal peaked in the US in the mid-19th and early 20th centuries with the introduction of Spiritualism, a religious philosophy that espoused that communication with the spirit world is positive. Mary Todd Lincoln, Mark Twain and Harry Houdini were among the American celebrities who became part of the paranormal conversation, and the public gathered in homes and auditoriums to connect with the dead in seances. Beyond ghosts, future president Teddy Roosevelt wrote of a frontiersman's encounter with a

Bigfoot-like creature in 1893, and other Sasquatch stories would periodically make their way into the news. Long before the Battle of Los Angeles in 1942 or The Roswell Incident in 1947, "airships" were reported in the skies above America - and newspaperman S.E. Haydon wrote about the crash of such a ship in Aurora, TX in 1897, about 6 years before the Wright Brothers' first flight.

Aliens are Little Green Men in Flying Saucers
Actually, the most popular aliens are little grey men, according to believers. In America, "The Greys" are the archetypes when discussing alien encounters and were supposedly found in The Roswell Incident. The creatures supposedly have large, black, buggy eyes and a slit for a mouth on their oversized noggin.

However, aggressive reptilians and blonde-haired Nordic humanoids have also been reported by eyewitnesses, along with dozens of other alien species. As for the flying saucer part, UFOlogists claim we should add flying crescents, cigar-shaped crafts, triangular ships and a V-shaped craft to the classic flying saucer motif.

No One Still Believes in Vampires
The bloodsuckers from folklore have enjoyed a nice comeback in paranormal pop culture in the last few years, but they never completely went away in some societies. Recently, Indian politicians placed a $2,000 bounty on vampires sucking the blood from villagers' cattle in the town of Dharampuri in Tamil Nadu, which called to mind the 2004 exhumation and subsequent staking of a corpse in Marotinu de Sus, Romania. The supernatural ghouls may not resemble the sexy beasts of *Twilight* and *True Blood*, but they are still very much alive (or undead) in various parts of the world. Even within the United States, there are subcultures of individuals who believe they are among a class of vampire - with especially active groups in New Orleans and New York City.

Modern Zombies are Supernatural
The term "zombie" has been in use for well over a century and, before 1968, applied to seemingly soulless slaves created by Haitian voodoo "magic." After 1968, when George A. Romero's

Night of the Living Dead was released, the term was forever changed. Modern zombies are the result of an unexplained contagion but are not supernatural. According to zombie expert Matt Mogk of the Zombie Research Society, the modern zombie is a relentlessly aggressive, re-animated human corpse driven by a biological infection. So, supernatural vampires, mummies, Nordic draugrs, and all revenants need not apply for brunch with this bunch.

Skeptics and Believers Don't Get Along

There are actually many skeptics involved in the paranormal community, and they are normally welcomed by investigative groups. When the two groups operate together, the skeptics can assist in disproving misidentified phenomena. If something cannot be disproven, it then leads believers closer to a possibly legitimate experience. Dave Schrader, host of the popular paranormal radio show Darkness Radio, says paranormal believers are not at war with the "skeptic nation," and he embraces their input because he'd rather be taken seriously when findings are reviewed. Additionally, most skeptics are confused for cynics, but actively want a paranormal experience - and they want it to be real and not just a false positive.

The Paranormal is Bad for Business

Even if the phenomenon is unexplained, the business world is a big believer in the paranormal. Paranormal Tourism, where travelers spend vacation money on pilgrimages to genre conventions and famous hotspots, is an active industry. Instead of shying away from a paranormal reputation, locations are embracing it. Every city seems to have a few ghost tour operations, while haunted house attractions and vampire balls abound, and entire towns in America are defined by their paranormal personalities. The Roswell UFO Festival attracts droves of alien enthusiasts to New Mexico every July. Meanwhile, Point Pleasant, WV, belongs to The Mothman, and Salem, MA, has a tourism industry focused on the infamous witch trials.

Zombie walks, runs and obstacle courses (along with proms, protests and pub crawls) are weekly occurrences in cities across America.

Paranormal Rock Stars
(September 2012)

Sightings of specters, cryptids, and interplanetary interlopers abound on this planet, but who are the biggest stars of the unexplained? I picked some of my favorites - real or not.

Bigfoot
Whether you know him as Sasquatch, Yeti, Wooly Booger, Skunk Ape, Fouke Monster, or Mo-Mo, every region has a name for the big guy (or gal) that goes back generations. In fact, the bipedal primate has been spotted across the world and in each US state except Hawaii. We started calling this wildman of the woods Bigfoot in 1958, and he has a famous following that includes Teddy Roosevelt, Jane Goodall, and Jack Black.

Chupacabra
Spanish for "goat sucker," this relative newbie in the paranormal world only arrived on the scene in 1995 in Puerto Rico. Said to look like a large wild dog with mange - or a reptilian creature with a dog's head - it supposedly exsanguinates livestock in the US Southwest and Mexico but has been spotted in Maine and Russia. Chupey might be related to Montauk Monster-like cryptids (or partially decomposed dogs/raccoons/rodents?) that have washed ashore.

The Greys
When it comes to a race of aliens, you can't get much more famous than the Greys (sorry, Klingons). Believers say extraterrestrials come in reptilian, Nordic humanoid and other varieties, but these telepathic fellas with oversized heads, large black eyes and greyish skin are frequently seen by possible abductees. They have also been connected to the 1947 Roswell Incident in New Mexico, and the 1961 Betty and Barney Hill case in New Hampshire.

Romero Zombie

Variations of the Haitian voodoo zombie drone exist in many cultures' tales of supernatural undead creatures. But the modern, infected reanimated corpses prone to biting and shambling were created in Pittsburgh by director George A. Romero for his 1968 film *Night of the Living Dead*. They now dominate pop culture and can be spotted in every city across America at walks, runs, proms and pub crawls - and in an impending zombie apocalypse.

Nessie

In North America, there's no shortage of river serpent stories. Champy swims in Lake Champlain, in Vermont and New York; Ogopogo in British Columbia's Okanagan Lake; and Native American folklore has multiple tales. But Scotland's Loch Ness Monster, first reported by Saint Columba in the 6th century, and gaining fame in 1933, is the queen of cryptids. Some theorized Nessie, possibly a plesiosaur, died long ago, but sightings continue.

Mothman

No one knows whether it's an alien, demon, angel, mutant, or monster, but the Mothman of Point Pleasant, WV, was first seen leading up to the Silver Bridge collapse of 1967 which killed 46 people. Several eyewitnesses (or more than 100, depending on your source) reported seeing a humanoid creature with glowing red eyes and giant wings. Mothman was connected to UFO and MIB sightings and is celebrated at an annual Point Pleasant festival.

Jersey Devil

Mainly stalking the New Jersey Pine Barrens near Atlantic City, JD is either a cryptid or supernatural scion of Satan. Stories vary, but he's possibly the 13th child of Mrs. Leeds (who wished her child would be a devil) born with a horse's head, bat wings, and tail. Reports date back to the early 1800s and multiple sightings sparked a "week of terror" in 1909. Plus, Bruce Springsteen name-checked him and he's a hockey team mascot.

White Lady

Also known as the Grey Lady, this famous ghost is traditionally seen in Great Britain and Ireland but has become a staple of American ghost sightings. An apparition of a woman in a white gown (often thought to be a wedding dress), she apparently frequents cemeteries, such as Tolomato Cemetery in St. Augustine, FL. She has also been connected to hitchhiker ghost stories, as with the White Lady of Whopsy in Altoona, PA.

Men In Black

Instead of an affable Will Smith-esque character, MIB are dark-suited, ominous agents who appear to eyewitnesses of strange phenomena. Modern sightings began in 1947 after a Maury Island, WA, UFO sighting, and were popularized in 1956 by author Gray Barker. Some speculate they're part of a secret government agency, but because they supposedly behave so oddly, others think they are aliens themselves. Still others say they may be extradimensional beings, time travelers, or demonic manifestations.

Hat Man

Associated with the classic "shadow person," those inky humanoid specters seen in peripheral vision, Hat Man is purportedly more defined (and maybe even solid) and wears a wide-brimmed gaucho hat and long coat. Eyewitnesses claim he materializes out of nowhere, looms and fills them with dread, all while feeding off their fear. He is the Bogeyman incarnate, and some say he's a dark entity or the devil himself - or an observer for extraterrestrials.

CHAPTER 2

Pop Culture Pontifications

'Ghost Hunters' Living Up to The Spirit of Pop Culture

(June 2009)

About halfway through a rerun last week of the Sci-Fi Channel's *Ghost Hunters*, paranormal investigator Grant Wilson began the oft-repeated sentence, "E.V.P. stands for electronic voice phenomenon ..."

As Wilson read off the definition on camera, myself and a few friends watching the show from my living room finished the line with him, following the cadence and rhythm as closely as we might if a red ball had been bouncing across words on the screen.

That's when it struck me that I was witnessing something pretty rare, like the pink albino dolphin.

Wilson and partner Jason Hawes - along with their team, The Atlantic Paranormal Society (TAPS) featuring Kris Williams, Steve Gonsalves and Dave Tango - have become more than just stars on a popular show that draws about 2.8 million viewers a week. It doesn't matter if you believe in ghosts or not because the stars of the four-year-old show are pop culture prodigies.

Since the 2004 premiere, *Ghost Hunters* has re-invented the reality-TV genre by focusing on a topic outside of most of our realities. It's not about contests on an island, weird foods, big families, small families, lousy roomies, bachelor's harems and hot tubs, racing, singing, dancing, or working for, and being eliminated by, a perpetually angry boss. But it is about a group of friends that started a hobby with the intent to help people as well as get answers about the afterlife.

Whether by design or mistake, the show is also unique among its reality-TV brethren for observing the basic formulas present in the best of pop fiction.

The heroes are believably human. From Peter Parker to Homer Simpson, most memorable heroes are flawed but likable with an everyman attitude. Unlike the cocky, overconfident nitwits who populate reality-TV and lack the potential for introspection, Wilson and Hawes (and especially Tango and Steve) achieve this and do it without seeming to take themselves too seriously.

Ghost Hunters has also implanted its mythology into our consciousness. I have known about TAPS since a 2002 *New York Times* article and have interviewed the stars on a few occasions, but most of us can recite a version of the Wilson, Hawes and Co. story from the show alone. After about 80 episodes, even if the names are fuzzy, they're well-known as the Roto-Rooter plumbers with the working-class appeal from Rhode Island who investigate the paranormal. Since the group began in 1990, when a door opens on its own in an old house, they try to find out why; when there is a loud crash in the dark, they give chase instead of running away (except for the one catchphrase-making "Dude, run" incident). And when something truly startling happens, audiences are likely to hear "what the frig?" instead of a scream.

But along with a familiar mythology, *Ghost Hunters* honors a code that we love to see in our pop culture. There are three rules to owning a Mogwai, charge the power ring every 24 hours, observe the Prime Directive, you must reach 88 miles per hour to generate 1.21 gigawatts of power needed for time travel, and always try to debunk ghostly reports before calling it haunted.

Audiences may enjoy surprises, but we also like a framework of rules and expect our heroes to follow them.

In the case of the so-called "TAPS method" of debunking before believing, the show has also redefined what audiences are used to seeing in reality-TV, and haunted house shows in particular. As opposed to the Travel Channel's *Most Haunted* (featuring shaky cams, dramatic psychics and jumpy Brits) or MTV's deceased show *Fear* (featuring head-mounted cameras and a lot of screaming), *Ghost Hunters* places emphasis on the process of investigating instead of trying to deliver scares.

By giving off a CSI: Paranormal vibe, the show allows a sometimes anti-climactic climax. This reduces the audience expectation of a spectral money shot; if there is one, and there isn't always, they get even more traction from it.

Although the TAPS team sometimes catches spooky disembodied EVPs on digital recorders, or amorphous forms on a heat- sensitive thermal camera, or electro-magnetic field anomalies on a gadget called the K-2, much of their show is about something we all relate to: waiting and talking. They talk to scared homeowners, they wait around reviewing hours of evidence, they wait around in the dark while talking. It's compelling television, but it's not always very exciting.

Of course, anytime something new is created and becomes a fixture in popular culture, there will be followers and imitators, as well as detractors and naysayers. That's to be expected as much as the *Ghost Hunters* spin-offs and T-shirts, and the eventual TAPS breakfast cereal, action figures, and video game. Most of the imitators won't last long, and the controversies won't prove to be true, I suspect, but they don't matter anyhow.

Frankly, whether ghosts do exist or don't doesn't matter either. Even if the truth is *not* out there (despite what Mulder believed) *Ghost Hunters* is a very real game changer on the reality-TV scene and has secured a spot in pop culture history.

Monsters Exist, But I'm Not Afraid
(October 2009)

There is a lot to be afraid of out there in the big, bad world; terrorism, swine flu, Lady Gaga, and bad sushi, just to name a few. But of the things that frighten me, vampires, werewolves, zombies, mummies, (which are just antique, gift-wrapped zombies) and ghosts are not amongst them.

Of course, it's not because they don't exist - as I'm certain you're thinking - because they most certainly do. All of the full moon or no moon creepy crawlies that cause the jeepers and the creepers, the heebies and the jeebies, are all real. And by my standards, they're also all right. See, without them, I'd be really freaked out.

As a kid growing up in Central Florida in the early to mid-'8os, I remember the night. Not even a Muppets nightlight penetrated more than a few feet of the inky black that enveloped my childhood home. It wasn't an old home. As was the case with most neighborhoods I knew as a kid, our subdivision seemed to have recently sprung from marshy areas complete with K-Marts and drug stores. The Amityville house at the end of a long, creepy road ours was not.

Yet it terrified me.

My older brothers and sister convinced me our home was haunted. It's still something that is mentioned on occasion to this day, so I guess they believed it to be so. Maybe it was. If so, the logic of them putting me, the youngest child by four years, at the back of the line during a midnight exploration of a mysterious sound perplexes me more so now than it did then. And even then, I knew on some level that it was bunk that I was at the end of the line. Couldn't I be in the middle of the group so I'd neither be first nor last in the row, and the most vulnerable to the creatures of the night? No answer has been provided to me yet.

Anyhow, the children's bedrooms were separated in the back of the house, far removed from the safety of the master bedroom by a long hallway, large dining room and massive family room. The parental units were far enough away that a certain brother or sister could be engaged in a violent throwdown without the sounds of screaming making it to the front of the house.

Needless to say, if a little boy with a throbbing bladder busting at the seams - if a bladder has seams, and since the mental image of mine is an old leather bota bag canteen, it does - needed to go to the bathroom in the middle of the night, it wouldn't be easy to penetrate the dark silence (and overcome a father's loud snoring) and reach the master bedroom with shouting.

So, I had to go it alone. Getting out of bed and heading to the bathroom at the end of a hall was a trip filled with recollections of my oldest sibling's Alfred Hitchcock recorded stories and the albums of Halloween sound effects. It was a walk remembering the scary parts of the "Thriller" video (in a time when Michael Jackson being a potential zombie and/or werewolf was the freakiest part about him). It was a painful pee-encroaching tiptoe where I couldn't help but think about all the monster comics and horror movies seen by sneaking around corners and watching when I was supposed to be in bed.

I couldn't run because I'd wet myself, and I couldn't wait - my bad habit of remaining constantly hydrated was already in effect at that age. So, I let them in. I let them all in.

It started with Frankenstein's monster, followed by Bela Lugosi (not as Dracula but as Bela Lugosi), followed by werewolves.

Freddy, Jason, and the Creature from the Black Lagoon were there, as was, yes, zombie Michael Jackson.

Despite my parents' assurance that these beasties didn't exist in the real world, I decided at that moment that they did. All of the things that go bump in the night became my escorts to the bathroom. What's more, I began to acknowledge, address, and attempt to control them. I distinctly remember telling Frankenstein's monster, who was hiding behind the shower curtain, to leave me be and not watch me whiz.

By becoming aware of my fears, and accepting the reality of them, I could prevent them from controlling me - and avoid a wet and stinky pair of pajamas.

And on some level, by admitting they were real, I steeled myself for taking them out should the need arise. I consumed horror flicks and watched them as research. I thought myself to be a monster hunter and tough kid. The Wolfman could try to bite me, but I was armed with silver spoons and butter knives. Later on, when I read Stephen King's *Salem's Lot*, the character of Mark Petrie - a Universal Monsters-obsessed boy who recognizes the town's vampire threat before others - seemed to be modeled on my estimation of my young self.

Weirdly, by embracing the dark and all the things that stalk within it, I conquered other fears. When you're a master zombie killer in the *Left 4 Dead* video game, or you know in the back of your head that the Ikea coffee table's leg separates into an ideal wooden stake for vampire slaying - assuming vampires are susceptible to particle board - you become less interested in being armed with a bottle of Purell.

So it goes. There's a lot to be scared of in this world, but once you allow for the fact that Imhotep's mummy or creepy corn children might come for you any minute, you put swine flu into perspective and worry a lot less. Although Lady Gaga is admittedly pretty terrifying.

'Lost' & 'Empire Strikes Back': Pop Culture Milestones, Same Weekend

(May 2010)

It is a dark time for the Candidates. Evading the dreaded Smoke Monster, a group of island castaways led by Jack Shephard have escaped the Widmore sub and established a new temporary base on the remote Dharma Island. The evil demigod Man in Black, obsessed with finding Shephard, is dispatching a final plan to kill the survivors and escape the far reaches of the island...

On May 21, 1980, *The Empire Strikes Back* opened in theaters and has been received as not just a great film in its own right, but as one of the best blockbusters and finest sequels in movie history. On September 22, 2004, *Lost* premiered on ABC and has since become one of the most celebrated dramatic shows in television history.

It seems fitting - and worthy of the prologue/plot mashup above - that the 30th anniversary of *The Empire Strikes Back* occurs on the same weekend that *Lost* will conclude with the two-and-a-half-hour series finale. In addition to being personal favorites that blew my mind, earned slavish devotion and launched countless conversations, both are significant pop culture institutions that changed what many of us can expect from entertainment, but also what entertainment can expect of us.

As a child, *The Empire Strikes Back* was a film I loved and loathed. It was my first "What? Aw, hell no!" movie. It ended on a down note where the villains won, the Big Bad made a shocking reveal that stomped the hero's soul, and the audience was left with a three-year cliffhanger. I was too young to remember much about the theater experience of *The Empire Strikes Back*, but I nonetheless consider myself lucky to be of a generation that didn't know about Luke Skywalker's daddy issues before reaching the movie's final act.

As an adult, I've had many of the same reactions while watching *Lost* over the course of six seasons. I don't remember when exactly I became a fan - sometime around the end of the first season, I think - but I remember the impact it had on me. The many cliffhangers, even the ones that spanned only one week as well as between seasons, felt like they lasted for years. The reveals have been shocking, and "What? Aw, hell no!" has been shouted many, many times. Although I've loathed Lost at times, overall, I've enjoyed it pretty much from the beginning.

From the opening credits, where one logo zooms away in space and the other floats through darkness towards the screen, the connection between Lost and the *Star Wars* series has always been evident. Creators J.J. Abrams and Damon Lindelof, along with showrunner Carlton Cuse, have allowed Lost to proudly wear its geeky heart on its sleeve. Instead of trying to hide it, the Lindelof and Cuse team frequently make direct and indirect references to the George Lucas franchise, and have quoted it within the show.

The character of Hurley even attempted to re-write The Empire Strikes Back in one episode. Instead of being merely homage, however, Lost has channeled what made The Empire Strikes Back great.

With two dueling protagonists of the hero complex boy scout and the self-serving lovable rogue, with a strong but conflicted woman caught between, the Lost trio of Jack/Sawyer/Kate is the new trio of Luke/Han/Leia from The Empire Strikes Back. Jacob has the Obi-Wan act manipulating the truth and being noticeably absent when needed the most down pat. Hurley and Miles at times serve the purpose of C-3PO and R2, and Richard Alpert has remained a man of mystery who generates intense curiosity despite very little screen time - not unlike a certain bounty hunter. Finally, Locke has been both a Yoda and Vader figure as a man who preached of faith but was consumed by darkness. And both are steeped in paranormal pop culture aspects of with ghostly guides, psychic powers and monsters.

Beyond the obvious comparisons, Lost and The Empire Strikes Back are alike, and probably so beloved, because they are both deceptively simple stories of ordinary people in extraordinary situations contemplating the questions about - to borrow from Douglas Adams-life, the universe and everything. They revolve around the nature of light vs. dark, good vs. evil, science vs. faith and ultimately about the redemptive power of love and sacrifice.

Moreover, like the Dark Side cave which Yoda tells Luke contains "only what you take with you," *The Empire Strikes Back* and *Lost* both allow the viewer to imprint his/her own experiences, philosophies, beliefs, and theories upon the stories. When fans spend significant time searching for clues and connections, and twist the plots around in their brains, they become involved. The question of "what does it all mean?" becomes quite personal.

OK, so that's admittedly a gooey nugget of a "deceptively simple story" covered in very lofty, convoluted candy coating.

Additionally, faith has been more than a recurring theme within the plots of both stories; it's also part of the viewing experience. Both request the viewer to place trust in them and have essentially redefined what it means to be a fan of something. The Empire Strikes Back and Lost are entertainment that requires the patience of the audience, and as a result, there is a contract with the fans that promises some sort of resolution.

That faith is why many of us have been able to stick with Lost despite Nikki and Paulo (and the Bai Ling episode, which was a hot mess of Jar Jar Binks and Ewoks rolled into one). It's also why the emotions viewers feel are real when invoked by the death of certain characters, or bad things happening to these on-screen people we've accepted into our lives. Frankly, if you ever want to trigger the waterworks in me, show me back-to-back scenes of Han saying goodbye to Leia, and Sun and Jin holding hands in that submarine - then you've got Niagara Falls, Frankie Angel.

So, you don't have to be a member of the congregation to enjoy either, but for the converted, The Empire Strikes Back and Lost are pop culture belief systems that inspire worship. They belong together in my best-of library, and I'm happy to say happy birthday to one, and sad to say goodbye to the other - but I'm pleased I can do both in the same fitting weekend.

Vampires vs. Werewolves: An Immortal Pop Rivalry

(June 2010)

There's no arguing that even the biggest pacifist among us loves a good fight in our entertainment options. Popular culture thrives on rivalries. There's nothing quite like a showdown between epic arch-nemeses to get audiences tuned in, taking sides, and passionately invested in the outcome.

Long-standing rivalry is what drew 28.2 million viewers to watch the June 17 game seven of the NBA finals between the Los Angeles Lakers and Boston Celtics, making it the highest-rated NBA game in 12 years. Also, within sports, rivalry defines relationships between entire cities, as with the New York Yankees and Boston Red Sox, and splits other cities in two (Mets vs.

Yanks, Cubs vs. White Sox). Some rivalries have clear cut winners and favorites (Abraham Lincoln vs. Stephen A. Douglas, Batman vs. The Joker), while others will remain historically open to interpretation, despite the final score ("Marvelous" Marvin Hagler vs. "Sugar" Ray Leonard, King Kong vs. Godzilla).

The hunger for rivalries is such that we even create imaginary scenarios where conflict doesn't really exist, e.g., The Beatles vs. The Rolling Stones, pirates vs. ninjas. The best rivalries are defined by tension and a war of words that's only occasionally - even rarely interrupted by actual encounters.

Though feuds exist in popular culture the world over (Macbeth vs. Macduff, Glasgow Celtics vs. Rangers football clubs), America is especially caught up in a game of "who would win" in a fight. Perhaps because the Civil War left such a cultural scar on the nation's childhood, Americans continue to pit sides against one another, as if in a perpetual adolescence.

Which leads to the current preferred rivalry in American entertainment; it's a rivalry both sides can really sink their teeth into: vampires vs. werewolves. Like a brawl between goths and jocks, or a contest between the couch potatoes and the outdoorsy types, this current battle royale is dominating all areas of paranormal pop culture.

At the moment, the stand-off is famously characterized by Team Edward and Team Jacob in *The Twilight Saga* film franchise- the third installment of which, *Eclipse* opens in theaters across the US June 30. In the book and film series, the vamp and "were" issues go back for ages in Forks, Washington, but mainly begin to flare up in Stephenie Meyer's 2006 young-adult novel *New Moon*, because of—what else—a girl. (Before Twi-hards begin a letter-writing campaign, yes, I know Jacob Black's Quileute tribe are technically shapeshifters, but I'm sticking with werewolves, here.)

Considering the recent plotlines of vampire pop *True Blood*, now in its third season on HBO, or ABC's new summer primetime soap opera The Gates, it's easy to assume the conflict between these two supernatural species was spawned directly from the mega-successful Twilight machine. Yet while the current depiction of this age-old rivalry seems new (and ripe material for a *Pride and Prejudice and Zombies-esque* literary mashup starring the Capulets and Montagues, or at least *a West Side Story and Werewolves* theatre treatment), it precedes Meyer's books by more than 60 years.

This rivalry also predates author Charlaine Harris' first introduction of her Sookie Stackhouse character (who would later be immortalized on *True Blood* often in the nude, by Anna Paquin) to werewolves in the 2002 book *Living Dead in Dallas*, and then to handsome wolfie Alcide in 2003's *Club Dead*. It goes back before Kate Beckinsale and Scott Speedman fell in love as Vampire and Lycan in the 2003 movie *Underworld*, before Hugh Jackman wolfed-out to defeat Dracula in 2004's *Van Helsing*, and before the Sunnydale vampire slayer encountered were-Oz in 1998 on Joss Whedon's *Buffy* series. It even predates the Anita Blake adventures from 1993's *Guilty Pleasures* by Laurell K. Hamilton.

The contentious relationship has some of its modern roots in *The Dark Reunion*, the 1991 installment of L.J. Smith's young adult book series *The Vampire Diaries* - the same one recently adapted by The CW into a show by *Scream* and *Dawson's Creek* creator Kevin Williamson - where the werewolf character Tyler squares off against vampire Stefan.

Indeed, as Eric Nuzum points out in his pop-vampire exploration *The Dead Travel Fast* (an excellent 2007 book begging for an update) the resurgence of the supernatural family feud is largely attributable to the 1991 role-playing game *Vampire: The Masquerade* by White Wolf Publishing. However, even if White Wolf had the most significant impact in popularizing the rivalry in the last 19 years, it existed to some degree in 1968 as a plotline on the daytime soap *Dark Shadows*, and really began stateside in 1944 and 1945 thanks to Universal Pictures.

The most famous vampire and werewolf characters appeared together on screen in *The House of Frankenstein* (1944) and *The House of Dracula* (1945) where Lon Chaney, Jr., as *The Wolf Man*, squared off against the big daddy of bloodsuckers. Due to the success of the monster mashups, Chaney did it again in 1948 when his werewolf battled Count Dracula once more, this time played by Bela Lugosi, in the horror-comedy *Abbott and Costello Meet Frankenstein*.

In the comedy, without the wolfman, the master vampire would've wreaked havoc with Frankenstein's monster's re-energized body (and yes, *Van Helsing* ripped off this yuk-fest). So, what's the appeal of this rivalry that has given it legs for nearly a century, and keeps it going strong?

Well, it's hard not to love a war between the cursed and, well, the cursed, since no matter who prevails, someone bad bites it. Like the zombified Hatfield and McCoy feud on display in George A. Romero's new flick, *Survival of the Dead*, it's fun to watch powerful supernatural creatures who appear pretty evenly matched throwing down in the schoolyard. Neither can easily die so it's a fight that could potentially last for an eternity - long after anyone really remembers why they're fighting in the first place.

That's another reason the rivalry is engaging-and relatable.

Many of the wars waged in the real world are fought because of ancient grievances - over outdated maps, dusty religions, long- ago insults, East Coast vs. West Coast rapping supremacy- and essentially, they curse people to fight, in perpetuity, for fighting's sake. Forgetting the catalyst for the rivalry is a theme that very much applies in reality. Much like conflicts between peoples (past and present), what's most ironic about vampires vs. werewolves is that they have more in common with one another than not.

For example, the previously mentioned Lon Chaney, Jr. While making bank as his most famous character Lawrence Talbot, aka

The Wolf Man, he was also moonlighting as the Count in Son of Dracula in 1943. Now that's close. Further, as The Straight Dope website points out, old Eastern European legends foretold that dead werewolves would rise as vampires. Of course, it's well-known vampires can transform into wolves, as well as bats, but even the Slavonic word *volkodlak*, which means werewolf translates into vampire in Serbian.

Plus, both creatures are fang-driven; they come out only at night; neither are fans of silver; in animal form as bat or wolf, they both are carriers of the exact same scourge: rabies. They are also both damned, and that's a big common bond to commiserate over.

Besides, if pop culture continues to be inundated with vampire/werewolf wars, audiences will overdose and both cadres of the nearly-immortal will receive a lethal injection and will be rendered dead - for a while. As mentioned earlier, the best entertainment rivalries are defined by only occasional battles.

Unless a new element is introduced, all good fights get old (see: Paris Hilton vs. Nicole Richie, Keith Olbermann vs. Bill O'Reilly).

So perhaps it's time to listen to the call for peace, love and understanding as told by Elvis Costello - who walked "through this wicked world searchin' for light in the darkness of insanity". Maybe in order to keep their particular piece of paranormal pop culture fresh, these wicked ones at war should take a break from ripping each other's throats out to resolve their differences.

Or even better, how about a Justice League and Legion of Doom- style team-up? Since neither can really emerge from the darkness of insanity (that would entail burning up in the rays of the sun or going down via a silver bullet to the chest) they can forge an alliance and go after a new enemy - not completely unlike teams Edward and Jacob try doing in Eclipse.

Just a suggestion: Vampires and werewolves vs. the Los Angeles Lakers... and maybe mummies, too? That might net some ratings for the next, oh, 60 or so years.

Harry Potter: The Boy Who Out-lived Luke?

(November 2010)

The "Boy Who Lived" from my childhood is Luke Skywalker. The magic of the Force was taught to the young and powerful sorcery newb by a little green wizard who lived on the swamp planet of Dagobah. And the black-clad, "You Know Who" villain with pale, damaged skin was actually the young apprentice's father, not the one who killed him.

More than any other popular culture masterwork, *Star Wars* defines me. It is a part of my POP-DNA; having been born into it and grown up with it, I am a proud member of Gen X-Wing. Yet I feel the pull of the Potterheads.

J.K. Rowling's first book was introduced to American readers in the Fall of 1998 in *Harry Potter and the Sorcerer's Stone*; it was the second year of college, and my pop culture attention was wrapped up with a movie which wouldn't be released for another eight months - *Star Wars Episode I: The Phantom Menace*, the first of George Lucas' prequels (and no, I'd rather not talk about it). It wasn't until 2000, when book four, *The Goblet of Fire*, was published that I began to read up on the books and take notice of the Pottermania.

While I came to appreciate the books, and the expertly-cast film franchise that began in 2001, the story of a chosen-one orphan against an ultimate evil engaged me - but not enough to label myself a "fan." I presumed there can really be one defining pop phenomenon per lifetime, and I'd staked out mine.

Then I visited The Wizarding World of Harry Potter attraction at the Universal Orlando theme park. It was a pretty balmy October evening in Central Florida, but as I crossed the threshold into Hogsmeade and saw the snow-covered shoppes of the wizarding hamlet - with Hogwarts castle presiding over the entire town - a childlike sense of wonder kicked into overdrive. The experience was not unlike a very early memory of taking in the eye candy of Santa's village occupying the rotunda near the food court in our local mall.

I still don't know if the chimes of John Williams' "Hedwig's Theme" from the movies was actually playing in the park, or if I just heard it in my head, but I do know that I sucked down multiple Butter Beers (a delicious cream soda/caramel cider/butterscotch hybrid beverage), ate chocolate frogs from Honeydukes and seriously considered getting a wand from Ollivander's . Around the same time a colleague asked, "You must be a big fan of Harry Potter, right?" - after riding The Forbidden Journey attraction three times and discussing much repressed trivia about the Potterverse - I realized an inner HP fanboy was hiding in me behind my *Star Wars* nerd.

I sort of have been talking about Harry Potter a lot since that visit. In fact, I think it's making friends uncomfortable. Last weekend's Quidditch World Cup in New York City captivated me more than the Super Bowl, and the tipping point may have been when I recently attended a meal at some fancy joint decorated with the illusion of floating candles all over the room. With more genuine enthusiasm - and far less sarcasm - than intended, I questioned aloud when McGonagall would be showing up with the Sorting Hat.

Speaking of being sorted, I purchased a large, ornate Slytherin stein (with faux-ruby snake eyes on the handle) in Orlando, and I feel deliciously evil when I drink coffee out of it.

Although I'm not ready to cut off my Padawan braid just yet, the wonder and awe I'd discovered in relation to Rowling's creations isn't really shared with the galaxy far, far away. *Star Wars* will always be what defined my childhood entertainment, and molded much of my entertainment consumption habits, but the Harry Potter series just may be what defines my inner kid - the one we are all allowed to indulge over the holiday and with simple pleasures like an ice cream cone or a trip to the zoo. As much as *Star Wars* is cool and fulfills a young boy's hero fantasies, Potter is magical.

I will still take a lightsaber and membership with the Jedi any day over attending Hogwarts with a wand, but there is something slightly more appealing in the idea of a realm of wizarding all around us, in the modern world, that's just a little beyond the view of Muggles.

Like other readers, I know how conflicts are resolved for Harry,

Hermione and Ron, and this Friday I shall join movie audiences to begin the eight-month farewell to the film franchise starring Daniel Radcliffe, Emma Watson and Rupert Grint in part one of the final chapter - I'm still wrapping my head around that - titled *Harry Potter and the Deathly Hallows, Part 1*, which will conclude in July 2011 with Part 2.

But conclusion aside, the Harry Potter phenomenon won't end - at least, not for me. Ten years after my introduction to the magic, I'm still a member of Gen X-Wing, but I've been sorted as a Potterhead.

Summer Goes Supernatural

(April 2011)

When the temperature inches up, most of us strip down to shorts and flip-flops, and take our two weeks vacations in the lower latitudes or perhaps hitting a theme park run by a rodent of unusual size for a little bit of relaxation.

But for pop culture, when the summer hits, it's time to get freaky.

Like a drunken coed who finds *Girls Gone Wild* empowering, pop culture flashes the world with its goods during the summer season and spares no expense on blockbuster events chockablock with special effects. Moreover, when the real world is focused on clear and sunny days, pop trends towards dark, stormy and paranormal.

Within the entertainment world, summer blockbusters have been very good to the supernatural and unexplained. Some of the best installments of paranormal pop culture debuted during the warmer months.

The concept of the blockbuster extends beyond just movies and includes any outperforming entertainment product (novels, video games, etc.).

They existed in some form before June 1975, but it's historically considered the year of the first, and it was just a big fish story about a man and the need for a bigger boat. Even before *Star Wars*

in 1977, Steven Spielberg's *Jaws*, a movie version of a Peter
Benchley's blockbuster book, redefined the event movie.

The cryptozoological Moby Dick tale was the first movie to
open nationwide on the same day, instead of being rolled out
slowly, and it survived through box office staying power. The
overwhelming success of Jaws led to more summer blockbusters -
some which would become cultural events, and many that would
cement actors' careers and make studios a lot of money and not
surprisingly, several of those were anchored with paranormal
themes.

Following *Jaws*, the antichrist romp *The Omen* continued the
paranormal blockbuster trend in June '76, as did *Alien* in '79, and
Raiders of the Lost Ark and *E.T. the Extra-Terrestrial* in 1981 and
1982, respectively. Revisit the most memorable characters and
catchphrases from summers past, and your favorite flicks are likely
littered with ghosts (*Ghostbusters, Poltergeist, The Sixth Sense,
Pirates of the Caribbean: The Curse of the Black Pearl*), UFOs
and aliens (*The Thing, Men In Black, Signs*), cryptids (*Gremlins,
The Descent*) or other unexplained phenomena (*An American
Werewolf in London, The Mummy, Hellboy,* the Harry Potter
franchise).

This summer, the trend shows no signs of abating with 16 films
to be released that deal with the mystical, magical and monstrous;
beings from other worlds and the underworld; or the dead, undead
and walking dead.

To name but a few, Harry Potter returns for the second part of
his last adventure in wizardry in *Deathly Hallows, Part 2* while
Norse god *Thor* sets out on his first; a *Priest* battles vampires and
another vampire battles a teen in *Fright Night; Cowboys and
Aliens* fight, and good robot aliens fight the bad ones in
Transformers: Dark of the Moon while kids with a *Super 8* film the
invasion; *patriotic Captain America* seeks an unexplained cosmic
cube and drunken Captain Jack Sparrow seeks mermaids and
zombies in *Pirates of the Caribbean: On Stranger Tides*. These
supernatural cinematic offerings don't even include paranormal
pop on TV screens and in video games or books, either.

However, the correlation between paranormal blockbusters and
summer isn't as difficult to prove as the existence of Bigfoot.

When a big studio is planning a movie's opening date, it times the ones with the largest mainstream appeal and the films considered bankable "tentpole" vehicles for wide release during months when people have extra free time to flock to climate-controlled theaters. Do the quick math, and you can figure out that an event movie with a few pretty faces, cool effects and centered around a popular paranormal trend equals a good chance of being a success.

But an intriguing side note to these paranormal summers is that while much of the mainstream isn't quite ready to dredge Loch Ness, these mysterious and unexplained topics resonate with people on a deeper level than we may initially think. When a movie makes $100 million and more, and becomes a pop culture touchstone, that means there are a lot of people interested in things like the afterlife or outer space life.

And that's the freakiest part of summer: As people head out on vacations this summer and gaze into the night sky, and inevitably ask what's "out there," the answer may be as close as the local Cineplex.

Swashbucklers in Film History
(May 2011)

The modern archetype of the movie pirate is that of a rum-soaked rock star with braids, eyeliner, staggering walk and swirly, floating finger gestures; but even before Johnny Depp brought Captain Jack Sparrow to life in 2003's *Pirates of the Caribbean: The Curse of the Black Pearl* - and again in three sequels, including 2011's *Pirates of the Caribbean: On Stranger Tides* - swashbucklers sailed the cinematic seas for more than a century.

Pirates, or unaffiliated bands of apolitical sea raiders, are an ancient class of criminals. The earliest mentions of them occur in reports of the Sherden, a group of "Sea Peoples" who attacked the Egyptian coast and were deflected by the pharaoh Ramesses II in 13th century BC. Yet it wasn't until the early 18th century that the most popular image of the pirate began to emerge, in the 1724 collection of nonfiction biographies, *A General History of the*

Robberies and Murders of the Most Notorious Pyrates by Captain Charles Johnson (which some say is a pseudonym for author Daniel Defoe). In addition to telling the tales of Blackbeard, Calico Jack Rackham, and Black Bart Roberts, familiar tropes such as the Jolly Roger flag, buried treasure, and missing eyes emerged. The book covered much of what is known as the "golden era" of pirates between the 1650s and 1720s, and it is this time period most often reflected in pirate films.

It was Robert Louis Stevenson's 1883 book *Treasure Island*, however, that introduced pirates into pop culture and central pirating concepts such as "X" marking the spot; a parrot on the shoulder; the phrase "shiver me timbers"; as well as the pirate lifestyle.

Pirates in the Silent Era

The impact of Stevenson's coming-of-age adventure tale was seen early in the still-new medium of cinema with *The Story of Treasure Island* (sometimes referred to as *Pirate's Treasure*), a 1908 film that has been lost to time. By 1920, the story had been adapted two more times, and more than forty times since, making it popular culture's most prominent scallywag story.

Released in the years before women's voting rights were guaranteed by the US Constitution in 1920, *Daphne and the Pirate* (1916), *Peg of the Pirates* (1918) and *Such a Little Pirate* (1918) showcased female protagonists as worthy adventurers or damsels who had been kidnapped but eventually helped foil their captors. Along with the 1925 film *Clothes Make the Pirate, Peg of the Pirates* is an early example of comedic pirates who are redeemed and educated by the heroine.

The 1920s saw multiple pirate feature films and movie serials, including *Pirate Gold* (1920), *The Road to Romance* (1927), an *Our Gang* serial *The Buccaneers* (1920), the underrated *The Sea Hawk* (1924) and more. But it was 1926 that delivered one of the most important early pirate movies.

While actor William Desmond portrayed a chivalrous but fierce pirate in the 1918 film *The Sea Panther*, it was Douglas Fairbanks in *The Black Pirate* (1926) who gave audiences a romantic high seas hero with noble roots. The silent film - the first widely seen to be photographed with the two-color Technicolor process - revolved around Fairbanks as the son of a slain Duke who embeds himself with pirates to exact revenge. Quick with a sword, and often laughing with his fists on his hips, Fairbanks was a true swashbuckler (much as he was as *Robin Hood* and *Zorro*).

The Black Pirate, adapted from a story by Fairbanks, also included impressive special effects and water stunts, a thrilling soundtrack typical of the genre, and contains one of the most famous scenes in pirate films where Fairbanks slits into the top of a ship's mainsail with his dagger and rides it all the way down.

Additionally, the greedy, conniving group of pirates in the movie wore familiar jewelry and bandanas or tricorne hat and spouted lines like "Dead men tell no tales."

The Swashbuckling Mantle is Passed

After Fairbanks, pirate films enjoyed success and the 1930s were a heyday for the movies, which even came to include musicals such as 1936's *The Dancing Pirate*. However, the next actor to stand out in a crowded genre and leave a lasting impression on pop culture pirates was Errol Flynn.

A breakout hit in his first starring role as the titular *Captain Blood* (1935), Flynn was a charming rogue and buckled swashes in *The Sea Hawk* (1940), *Against All Flags* (1952), and the buddy pirate movie, *The Master of Ballantrae* (1953). Flynn's fight choreography with expert arrangers allowed his sequences to be incredibly fast and realistic, and the 1935 adaptation of *Captain Blood* is also notable for giving the character a formidable adversary in Basil Rathbone, which is perhaps a precursor to Hector Barbossa in the later *Pirates of the Caribbean* franchise.

Interestingly, during the advent of "talkies," Flynn's more "pirate friendly" native Australian accent was eschewed for a standard British one. Later, his son Sean Flynn even got into piracy with the 1962 sequel, *The Son of Captain Blood*. Just as notable for defining the pirate character, but with a lot less screen time: Lionel Barrymore as Captain Bill Bones who first uttered the famous "Arrr!" in the 1934 version of *Treasure Island*.

In the run-up to World War II, pirate films provided movie going audiences with escapist entertainment not connected to current world events. Notable exceptions include Flynn's *The Sea Hawk*, which has fairly obvious references to Nazi Germany, and

The Pirates of the Seven Seas, a 1941 offering filmed in 1938 with the foresight to include a German villain before World War II broke out.

During this era, the pirate-as-hero image gelled, and instead of largely being depicted as a villain, movie pirates were typically fallen men of respectability. *The Black Swan* broke from this pattern slightly. Starring Tyrone Power, Anthony Quinn and Maureen O'Hara, the 1942 film largely involves a Pirate Brotherhood and a band of reformed brigands versus their unrepentant comrades. Working for a fictionalized version of real-life privateer Henry Morgan (Laird Cregar), Power is Captain Waring, a flamboyant pirate and flashy dresser, who sets out to capture "bad" pirates like Quinn's eye patched Wogan. Power plays Waring with a quick wit and passion, and a sense of humor that compels him to kidnap O'Hara's character just to get to know her better. For her part, O'Hara would be a major female player in other pirate-themed movies such as *The Spanish Main* (1945) *and Sinbad, the Sailor* (1947). Yvonne DeCarlo, best known for her later role as Lily on TV's *The Munsters*, was also known for her pirate films in 1950s Buccaneer's Girl and Sea Devils (1953).

Towards the end of the war, through the late 1940s and early 1950s, pirate films were becoming more associated with comedy of errors stories and family fare. Bob Hope disguises himself as The Hook in the 1944 farce, *The Princess and the Pirate*; The Three Stooges pose as pirates and are then pursued by the evil Black Louie in *Three Little Pirates* (1946); Bugs Bunny faces off against pirate Yosemite Sam in *Buccaneer Bugs* (1948); *Abbott and Costello Meet Captain Kidd* (1952) features the duo finding a treasure map and running afoul the villainous captain.

The Disneyfication of the Genre

Walt Disney Productions, as it was known before 1986, affected the film genre with 1950s *Treasure Island* and *Peter Pan* in 1953. The first color adaptation of Stevenson's book, and Disney's first completely live-action feature, *Treasure Island* is not exceptionally faithful to the source material but is regardless seen as close in spirit to the book. Moreover, Robert Newton's over-the-top, campy performance as Long John Silver is considered classic. His portrayal also likely marks the first time a cinematic pirate used the well-known Southwest England regional accent and further popularized the "Arrr!" growl. Newton would return to the big screen as Silver in two non-- Disney-produced films and a TV series.

Peter Pan, meanwhile, also strayed from J. M. Barrie's original work, but the depiction of Captain Hook as a garish fop modeled after a Spanish King has remained an iconic template for silly pirates. In the subsequent years, many films and adaptations - including 2003's *Peter Pan*, starring Jason Isaacs as Hook - have unsuccessfully tried to return the character to Barrie's description of him as evil and feared, handsome yet "disgusting," and a successful pirate feared by even the fictional Long John Silver.

While the 1952 film *The Crimson Pirate*, starring Burt Lancaster as the title character, wasn't initially intended to be a slightly goofy, upbeat action comedy, it ended up being a good move on the part of director Robert Siodmak to make some changes.

Utilizing the aerial abilities of Lancaster and costar Nick Cravat, who had both been circus acrobats before turning to Hollywood, the stunts were exciting - and planned by Lancaster himself. The film is reminiscent of the early pirate primetime in the 1930s, and its lasting legacy is that it is said to be the inspiration behind the original *Pirates of the Caribbean* ride at Disneyland.

Pirate films continued to be produced throughout the 1950s, but their quality and commercial response started to flag towards the latter half of the decade and through the 1960s. To be sure, there were exceptions like the 1965 *A High Wind in Jamaica* starring Anthony Quinn and James Coburn, and Disney's family comedy, *Blackbeard's Ghost* (1968) as the genre was eclipsed by popular Cold War spy films and commando-style war movies. The 1970s were no kinder to pirates, and the 1971 big-budget, Hollywood star vehicle *Light at the End of the World*, was a box office flop despite performances by Yul Brynner and Kirk Douglas. Another failure was *Swashbuckler*, a 1976 film starring a cast led by Robert Shaw. However, disaster films such as 1975's *The Towering Inferno* and *Earthquake* were preferable to audiences.

With a few exceptions, rough sailing for pirates continued for much of the next 20 years despite numerous attempts to popularize the genre again. *Nate and Hayes*, a 1983 attempt to cash in on the

Indiana Jones franchise failed miserably, as did 1986's *Pirates*, directed by Roman Polanski and starring Walter Matthau. Science fiction pirate outings, such as the 1984 adventure *Jee Pirates* and 1995's *Waterworld* were also deemed flops (though *Waterworld* did eventually make a sizable profit, it is still considered a failure).

There were critical and commercial pirate hits in the 1980s and 1990s, however. Although critically lambasted, Spielberg found treasure at the box office with his 1991 live-action *Peter Pan* sequel, *Hook*. And *Muppet Treasure Island* was a successful 1996 pairing of actor Tim Curry and the famous Muppets in yet another adaptation of Stevenson's book.

Regardless of the aforementioned successes, pirate movies were tabled after the disaster of 1995's *Cutthroat Island*. The intended blockbuster film starring Geena Davis cost $115 million to make and was intended to relaunch the already-weak genre. Instead, the film grossed only $10 million domestically and bankrupted studio Carolco Pictures.

Enter Jack Sparrow

For nearly eight years after the *Cutthroat Island* debacle, there was no big budget, live-action pirate adventure on the big screen. Then the Walt Disney Company premiered *Pirates of the Caribbean: The Curse of the Black Pearl* in 2003. The film was a gamble since the genre had been dead for years-and because *Black Pearl* was a movie based off a theme park ride.

However, the formula worked due to Depp's unorthodox performance, and a unique plot that had undead pirates, Aztec gold, and showed pirates trying to return treasure instead of stealing it. Additionally, instead of being the focus of a romantic plot, Depp's character was involved in hatching machinations while the love story was left to the Errol Flynn-esque Orlando Bloom and his love affair with Keira Knightley's character. With a budget of $140 million that allowed for computer-generated effects and elaborate fight sequences, the film was a huge success, grossed $654 million, earned Depp a Best Actor Academy Award nomination and led to three sequels: *Dead Man's Chest* (2006), *At World's End* (2007) and the newest, *On Stranger Tides* (2011).

The success of the franchise hasn't led to a resurgence of pirates in film but has popularized the pirate "lifestyle." There have been forgettable imitations of the films, such as 2006's Pirates of Treasure Island. *The Pirates Who Don't Do Anything: A Veggie Tales Movie* is a 2008 children's film that tried to cash in on the genre by featuring anthropomorphic vegetables who espouse Christian values - while being lazy pirates.

Throughout more than a century of depictions in cinema, pirates have encountered both calm waters and maelstroms when audiences couldn't get enough of the rogues and when the seafaring criminals were as well-received as scurvy. But even when the genre isn't successful, the brigands keep returning to the movies. As a result, it is clear that the pirate genre of cinema is a formidable one that refuses to stay sunk, no matter how much it adapts and changes over time.

The Camping Rapture, Social Media Apocalypse & Doomsday Entertainment

(May 2011)

In case you hadn't heard, the end is nigh. As in, like really, really nigh - if Harold Camping and his Family Radio Network is to be believed.

According to the Christian evangelical, who has previously predicted the end - obviously unsuccessfully - the Rapture will occur on Saturday, May 21, at 6 p.m. (apparently in each time zone so there is less of a rush of the chosen few for the pearly gates). After that, the world has about six months to go to hell, literally, before Jesus shows up for his Second Coming.

The upside to Camping's prediction is that he has been wrong before. The downside: December 21, 2012, is just around the corner, when the Mayan calendar ends and possibly signals yet another end-of-world situation.

But there is still more good news. Pretty much since the beginning, humanity has been thinking about the end. The only thing that makes Camping's prediction unique is that it's really the first Social Media Apocalypse.

His movement gained attention because the message was spread across the Internet. Even when the theory is being mocked, it is still being propagated. Not unlike a "winning" Charlie Sheen clip, auto-tuned "Bed Intruder Song" or hated Rebecca Black "Friday" video, the Camping Rapture has gone viral. It is maligned but widely known and is the topic of many conversations. So, while the revolution will not be televised, the end of the world will be YouTubed, Facebooked and Twittered (in 140 characters or less).

Plus, let's face it, both the Camping Rapture and the 2012 Mayan Calendar theories keep us enthralled because the end of the world is damn fine entertainment. Whether the end really is here or nowhere near, the end to apocalypse porn - like the Camping Rapture - is nowhere in sight.

Apocalypse porn isn't a new thing in the media, either. In a thesis project studying genre fiction from the last 200 years, Chandra Phelan writes the main thing that's changed is a spike in unexplained end-of-world scenarios in the mid-1990s.

As is the case with Cormac McCarthy's book (and the 2009 film adaptation) *The Road*, Phelan wrote in a sci-fi blog on io9.com that, in current pop culture, "It doesn't matter how the world ends, just that it does ... Stories of the End have never been about ending - they're about the beginning that comes after."

The "beginning that comes after" has been the appeal for me following *Mad Max Beyond Thunderdome* in 1985. Before then, my estimation of the future was that it would be pretty relaxed.

There were rockets ships, cool-looking aliens and robots prone to repeating "biddi-biddi-biddi-biddi." Aside from the unfortunate tendency to wear tight, stretchy clothing and occasional Klingon run-ins, the future was set in a good neighborhood - and even Klingons eventually became our friends.

The world Mad Max inhabited was different. The burnt-out, oil-depraved and nuclear-ravaged land was bleak and hopeless. As if marauders roaming an unforgiving, yellow desert wasn't bad enough, the one city to be found was run by Tina Turner in a fright wig.

Even with a "happy" ending (hey kids, we get to live in scenic, decimated Sydney, Australia!), the message was clear: The future sucks. But survive in it, and you earn a Samuel L. Jackson B.A.

degree (Denzel in *The Book of Eli* was only auditing).

Living through the bitter end is the greatest challenge.

Entertainment depicting a sunny tomorrow is fun. Yet the greater adventure is when, if the future's so bright you gotta wear shades, it's because the Earth is hurtling towards the Sun and we're all melting.

A Tomorrowland where the final frontier is so ... final is more intriguing. There's a primal connection to surviving "out there," and trying to find something to eat without getting eaten.

When it comes to the last gasp of humanity, I'm a zombie-head. I prefer scenarios where a ragtag group of survivors fight off hordes of the walking (or shuffling or running) dead craving a little filet o' flesh. Hence the reason I've spent more than a few nights staying up playing *Left 4 Dead 2*, the awesome zombie- killing video game sequel, and why my go-to Halloween costume is Simon Pegg's character from *Shaun of the Dead* (complete with regulation-size cricket bat).

But if re-animated corpses aren't your thing, maybe you'd prefer apocalypse porn to be in the form of the cataclysmic planetary pole realignment, as in *2012*. Or perhaps divine intervention at the hands of a ticked-off deity and an angelic war, like *Legion*, strikes your fancy. Whichever it is, there's plenty to choose from when it comes to dehumanizing the planet.

Whether it's the aforementioned zombie attacks (George A. Romero's oeuvre, *Zombieland*), genetically-altered vampires (Will Smith's *I Am Legend*, Justin Cronin's book *The Passage*), robot uprisings (the Terminator and Matrix trilogies), biological disasters (*12 Monkeys, Children of Men*), nuclear warfare (too many to count), alien invasions (*Mars Attacks, Battle: Los Angeles*), or the rapture (all those Left Behind books), it's easier for us to relate to those scenarios than to Captain Picard's continuing voyage of exploration while wearing a Spandex onesie.

Plus, apocalypse porn can be viewed in a practical way.

It is great training watching the ugly stuff where mankind is crawling towards extinction; where the survivors are few, the good guys even fewer and Charlton Heston is the apparent king of Dystopia (well, based on *Planet of the Apes, Soylent Green* and *The Omega Man*). *Left 4 Dead 2* alone has prepared me to survive decomposing cannibals using teamwork and a sparingly- used flashlight, shotgun and frying pan. Consider it pre- apocalypse preparation so I can fare better when the dead actually walk the Earth.

Be it the fascination with the Mayans, or the Camping Rapture or Armageddon movies, our affinity for end-of-days entertainment definitely says something about us - but I don't believe it's that we're a culture of joyless wretches who have lost all hope in a better world.

In fact, It's open to interpretation, but McCarthy's post-apocalyptic *The Road* sums it up nicely for me. The Pulitzer-winning work - perhaps the bleakest piece of pop I'm aware of - is about a father and young son trying to maintain their humanity while staving off starvation and sickness, and avoiding cadres of cannibals, on a dead highway to the coast.

But at one low point, the father says to his boy, "when your dreams are of some world that never was or of some world that never will be ... you have given up."

To me, this means our dreams of a blissful world where Elroy zooms to school and Rosie the Robot cleans the house is a rose-colored distraction. End-of-days entertainment is a cautionary tale, a scared-straight warning of what could be.

Maybe as long as we've pop culture that warns us the end is near, we will be less interested in having an apocalypse now - or anytime soon.

Aliens Among Us: An Otherworldly Season of Pop

(July 2011)

Zombies I can deal with. They are hungry, relentless and aren't immune to emotional vulnerabilities, but are dumb and slow-witted, and a shotgun, axe, or even a bat can dispatch them. Vampires aren't too much of a concern since they seem mainly occupied with seducing women, acting morose and feeling threatened by werewolves. Speaking of werewolves, their threat level can be monitored via a lunar smartphone app and avoided by simply not wandering any moors just one night a month. Meanwhile ghosts moan a lot and throw stuff, but tend to be attached to old houses, videotapes and the occasional doll.

So, what's scarier than all four? After reading NASA researcher Richard B. Hoover's *Journal of Cosmology* article last March, where he states he's found fossils of bacterial life not native to Earth, the scariest threat out there could be one that can't be dispatched simply with a shotgun, wooden stake, silver bullet or exorcism: aliens from another world.

Within pop culture, 2011 is a year of intergalactic menaces - and it's about time. If movies and TV are guides to an alien threat, then humans should unite, get with the program and realize that when we receive visitors from outer space, it ain't going to be pretty.

First, let's dispel the myth of the good aliens who wish no harm or want to make us better citizens of the universe.

Maybe they exist. In *Smallville* and the alien-stoner comedy Paul, out on DVD August 9, lifeforms from the stars crash land or breakdown in the bad galactic neighborhood that is Earth. But in the tradition of *E.T. the Extra-Terrestrial* and *My Favorite Martian*, they befriend and assimilate with us puny humans. Like Kryptonian Clark Kent from Smallville, July's Autobots from *Transformers: Dark of the Moon* and the Corps from the planet Oa in *Green Lantern*, some even choose to battle evil and save humanity.

Yet for every good Autobot, Kryptonian and Green Lantern, there is a Decepticon, General Zod or evil Lantern Parallax. For every wisecracking Paul or cuddly E.T. that visits Earth to serve man, there are several variations of visiting aliens who wish to serve man - as dinner.

In June, a really giant, pissed-off alien was caught on film in *Super 8*. That one became ill-tempered because humans imprisoned him for decades, so maybe he had a good reason. No such reason for the spidery "skitters" from TNT's *Falling Skies*, starring Noah Wyle. In the summer show, which focuses on a band of surviving humans six months after an alien invasion that wiped out much of humanity, the things from another world just seem to flat-out enjoy kidnapping, and enslaving teenagers while killing the adults.

And what aliens wouldn't want to invade, dominate and dine on us (or even use as incubation vessels for baby aliens after a little face-sucking, ala *Alien*)? Aside from possibly tasting delicious to interplanetary tastebuds, humans take up valuable real estate.

Plus, we are also apparently pretty fun to dress up as.

On the now-canceled series reboot *V*, alien lizards wore human skin and have been hanging out on Earth for years until finally making a grand entrance in the skies. They seem pleasant and benevolent enough at first, sharing their energy source and technology until they reveal plans to breed with us Earthies.

From the original *Invasion of the Body Snatchers* in 1958 (and the '78 remake) and the schlocky *The Faculty*, to the September found footage horror film *Apollo 18* and October's *The Thing* prequel, this doppelganger plot is one of the more unnerving aspects to alien flicks. The infiltrating creatures look like us; they make it nearly impossible to trust anyone and inspire paranoia.

Still, at least with the human doppelganger aliens, there is typically a plan in place. The deception happens for a reason and the endgame can take years to be revealed. That gives the human race time to uncover the plot and fight back, but with the nasty beings that show up in our skies and start trashing the joint, there's hardly enough time to react.

Just like a criminal who doesn't bother to wear a mask, visiting extra-terrestrials who appear in their natural form have no intention of leaving survivors behind. The aliens of *War of the Worlds*, *Independence Day*, *Mars Attacks* are old-school Galactus baddies only concerned with wiping out human insects. They popped up again in more recent entries *Skyline* and *Battle: Los Angeles*.

Other aliens who take time to visit Earth do so just to abduct for experiments, entertainment or forced employment. As seen in the disturbing films *Fire in the Sky*, *Communion* and a few scenes in the otherwise shoddy *The Fourth Kind* - as well as the series and first film installment of *The X-Files* - abductors are the worst kind of alien threat.

The kid flick *Mars Needs Moms* features an unsettling plot where the Red Planet dwellers are in serious need of maternal attention. So, they just visit human homes and take our mommas much like they nabbed Saint Nicholas in the 1964 movie *Santa*

Claus Conquers the Martians. What's more is they even attempt to enslave frontiersman and Apaches in the Jon Favreau-directed *Cowboys and Aliens*, due out July 29.

The idea that a highly intelligent being will enter a home, paralyze and steal a human away whilst they sleep, all so they can satisfy their own pursuits is unsettling. It is so unnerving that even when the abduction is couched in a "good alien" story like *Close Encounters of the Third Kind*, one can't help but feel icky. Tales of torturous scientific exploration on abductees makes it hard to look at E.T.'s probing, glowing finger.

To wit, even director Steven Spielberg - who gave us the lovable E.T. - has apparently changed his tune and decided aliens are more frightening than exciting. After directing or producing films and TV shows in the 1980s which included only friendly off-worlders (**batteries not included*), he made a switch to threatening ones in the late '90s (the *Transformers* and *Men In Black* franchises, *Indiana Jones and the Kingdom of the Crystal Skull, Super 8, Cowboys and Aliens*).

Maybe the latter-day Spielberg is more accurate when it comes to real visit from alien life. Perhaps our "first contact" won't be as fun as sharing Reese's Pieces - at least that's what renowned cosmologist Stephen Hawking thinks.

In his documentary *Stephen Hawking's Universe*, the scientist says he believes life is out there, but it may not like us very much. He predicts they may be nomads, conquerors and colonists.

Yet, with our human track record of encountering, perhaps we're sort of asking for some extreme probing as karmic payback.

Let's face it, in reality, humans are often xenophobic and slow to accept game-changing events. When aliens like Klaatu from *The Day the Earth Stood Still* land on our rock with a mission of peace, our world is so shaken that we welcome them with weapons, gunfire and dissections.

The Doctor from *Doctor Who* is often lamenting this childlike response, but Agent K from the incognito alien police force in 1997's *Men In Black* said it best: "A person is smart. People are dumb, panicky, dangerous animals."

A look at mankind's history (ancient to present) shows we're willing to subjugate the less powerful, and those perceived to be inferior somehow. That's within our own species, so is it reasonable to expect alien lifeforms to behave any different when we're clearly less advanced than any beings able to traverse long distances on a space highway?

Hawking says no.

"If aliens ever visit us, I think the outcome would be much as when Christopher Columbus first landed in America, which didn't turn out very well for the Native Americans," he told the *Times of London* in April 2010.

Of course, even if humankind can fight off or elude the doppelgangers, destroyers and abductors, we may still fall victim to simple "microfossils of cyanobacteria," as NASA's Hoover describes them.

But on the upside, if popular culture has taught us anything, if we get infected by strange bacterium, we'll likely just turn into vampires or zombies - and those are easy enough to kill.

Nerds and Hipsters: The Yin and Yang of American Subcultures

(August 2011)

The pursuits and appearance of both nerds and hipsters change constantly, yet when observed together, they always appear as funhouse mirror reflections of the other: united by their exclusion from the mainstream.

On one side is the form of the cool kid who obsessively pursues the obscure to achieve outsider status; the other side is the shape of the uncool kid whose outsider status is the result of his obscure, obsessive pursuits. Kind of like the Wonder Twins, but not exactly.

"Nerds take things seriously, and hipsters don't seem to take anything seriously; they're sort of natural enemies," Andrew Matthews, a filmmaker living in Austin, TX, said.

The editor for the acclaimed feature documentary *Best Worst Movie*, he also wrote - and will be sharing directing duties on - *Zero Charisma*, a film about a *Dungeons & Dragons* nerd whose gaming universe is invaded by a hipster.

Matthews is a self-described nerd.

Like the main character in his movie, he's a "D&D" player - he created a club for it in high school - as well as a dedicated sci-fi enthusiast and *Teenage Mutant Ninja Turtles* fan. His "nerdery" made it difficult to be popular as a kid, he said. While he may be okay with that now, he said he understands why some nerds may not take well to hipster neo-nerds: Nerds want to be recognized for being experts at their passions, whether it's for science or for gaming. Hipsters, through their self-presentation and interests, want to be part of the excluded uncool kids.

Although he credited hipsters with being curious, he said their interests are more fashion than substance. The nerd vs. hipster animosity - at least in his movie - exists partly because hipsters haven't paid the social stigma dues of being committed to a nerdy passion.

Seeing a hipster wearing a TMNT vintage tee buoyed Matthews' belief. "I got made fun of for having those, and now you're cool and have that. Is that fair?" he said.

Like poles that do not attract

Philip Zoshak, a 23-year-old literacy nonprofit worker in Orlando, Florida, agreed that nerds have to pay social stigma dues. However, he referred to it as his "nerd pride." Zoshak, a history, gamer and fantasy nerd, said when he thinks of nerds, he thinks of the skinny, awkward kid with glasses and adds, "I personally fit that bill."

Zoshak said he doesn't have nerd rage toward hipsters but does attach a negative connotation to them because they are co-opting, not adopting, nerd culture.

"The idea of the hipster is to be passionate about being antisocial," he said. "For nerds, there's no choice but to be on the outside looking in."

This is the crucial distinction between hipsters and nerds, said Lisa Wade, Ph.D., a professor of sociology at Occidental College in Los Angeles, California.

Wade also runs the Sociological Images website and focuses her research on how people create social differences within groups. She examines groups like nerds and hipsters to see how subcultures emerge or are actively cultivated, and to study the experience of being different.

For example, she said a hipster can take off the thick-rimmed glasses, but a nerd cannot shed what they've grown into as an outsider. Compared to hipsters who are self-excluding and could fit with the mainstream if they so choose, this cultural critic calls nerds actively excluded; "authentically misfits."

"They're stigmatized; they're seen as not very attractive, as socially inept and overly interested in things that nobody else is really passionate about," she said.

Even though nerd culture has evolved over the years (computer nerds are only a few decades old, for instance), nerds keep many archetypal hallmarks. But hipsters historically change - often in reaction to the mainstream - and that leads some to question how authentic they are, Wade said.

"There is something entirely genuine in a nerd that you will not find in a hipster," Hayley Smith, a 23-year-old marketing professional in New York City said. She is also, probably, a hipster.

But Smith won't openly identify herself as a hipster. She said to do so, to say you are hip, is the antithesis of the concept - it's used as a derogatory term in her circle. But if one were to look at her and her friends, "we would be called hipsters," she said.

Smith said she finds it appealing to re-appropriate things once seen as lame, such as mustaches, short-shorts, and "grandma shoes" thereby making them cool.

"It intellectualizes something that is not intellectual," she said. "It turns the uncool into the cool; thus, if you have the power to make the 'uncool' cool, then you must really be someone cool."

The context of cultures

Nerds and hipsters are similar in that they tend to obsess over the technical details of a pursuit - computers, fashions, steam punk accessories, etc., said Lee Konstantinou, a new faculty fellow at Princeton University in New Jersey, and Post-1945 literature and culture expert. He finds it "socially relevant" to compare them because of the two groups' differing motivations.

Konstantinou explored the hipster subculture at length in "Hipsters and the New Gilded Age" for Stanford University's "Arcade" website and his "coolhunters" article in Duke

University's "boundary 2" journal.

"Nerds geek out out of a genuine love of - or obsession with - whatever it is they're geeking out about," he said. "Contemporary hipsters - though they may often sincerely love what they geek out about - are also concerned with opposing the mainstream, so they're motivated by a social desire to distinguish themselves, to be quirky or hip or different from everyone else.

Hipsters "geek out" on questions of self-formation in relation to what cultural products they consume, Konstantinou said. Nerds are typically "more interested in things than in people" and are "interested in questions about technology, and questions about scientific information."

Yet he doesn't think hipsters intend to be disrespectful to a community they buy into. They are approaching nerd culture with "authentic but different" motivation. If a nerd is interested in the technical details of the way a computer works for its own sake, the hipster is motivated by a social drive to be distinct.

"Nerds are useful to hipsters only because they are actively stigmatized," she said. "When hipsters appropriate nerdiness, they are saying 'We are so not mainstream that we embrace the very thing that the mainstream rejects.'"

Subcultures as catalysts for change

Melissa J. Daniels, a 33-year-old professional photographer in Newark, New Jersey, sees the hipster experience differently.

Daniels is a hipster nerdy about astrophysics and *Mortal Kombat*, among other things, and views hipsters as more diverse than nerds. She says hipsters are progressive thinkers who want to be seen as unique individuals and "reject culturally ignorant attitudes of the mainstream."

In her opinion, hipsters are activists affecting change through a rally and alter cultural trends, but the nerd is offering change via contributions to government and the sciences or technology.

"It's a way of paying homage to the nerds," she said. "If you're accepting a part of another's counterculture - and you're assimilating it into your own - you're accepting it as a part of you; that creates a common thread."

For Matthews, that homage would have been unwelcome when he was younger.

"Growing up a nerd, you would have loved to be considered cool or would love to be stylish, but it was just kind of out of your realm," he said. "As much as nerds might hate hipsters, there's probably a little bit of envy."

Taboo of The Horror Nerd
(October 2011)

They are outsider fans in an outlaw genre. Even as comic book, science fiction and fantasy nerds are embraced by popular culture for their quirk and charm, the horror fan culture exists on the fringe, left out in the cold and dark - perhaps with a chainsaw-wielding maniac on the loose.

And that may be how horror nerds prefer it.

To be a horror nerd is to celebrate a low-rent, often underground kind of entertainment, even when it doesn't involve Jason Voorhees, Samara, or Pazuzu. It also means being the bad kid playing in the mud when others are allowed in the mainstream sandbox.

Basically, there is no The Big Bang Theory chronicling the lovable foibles of a dedicated nerd who can list his top five cannibal movies and is steeped in a fandom of dismembered bodies and buckets of blood.

But if other groups have become eccentric darlings of the mainstream, horror nerds prefer their passion to be punk. Even with an implied desire for more widespread respect of the genre, there is concern about the mainstream attention that accompanies it.

"It should feel like two steps away from pornography," said Joe Hill, the horror novelist of "Heart Shaped Box" and the comic *Locke & Key*. (He's also Stephen King's son. Yeah, THAT Joe Hill.)

"Let's keep it grubby and dirty and shameful," said Hill, who added he likes his horror to feel like a taboo "private pleasure," and that part of its appeal is delighting in content that can unsettle.

Reigning scream queen and genre heroine Danielle Harris

(*Hatchet II, Halloween, Stake Land*) believes horror stands alone in a "little world of its own" for that reason.

"It's not quite in the mix," said the actress. "That's what makes it special." Harris added part of the appeal of horror as a fan and creator is its ability to force a reaction out of audiences.

As a sociology professor who teaches about the horror genre at the University of Colorado - Boulder, Marshall Smith concurs.

"[Horror] is a genre that is meant to evoke a bodily response - shivers, goosebumps, etc.," he said. "It celebrates what is supposed to be reviled." As a result, Smith said, nerds "derive some sense of identity from reveling in that which others find objectionable."

Exploring horror

Brad "Mr. Disgusting" Miska has built a career out of being an insider amongst the outsiders. The co-founder of BloodyDisgusting.com, launched in 2001, Miska's site attracts approximately 1.5 million unique visitors to his horror entertainment site each month - and up to 2.5 million during October and January, the two most popular months for genre movies. Miska's site serves casual horror fans but also the nerds who like to take ownership of, and share, new genre entries.

He said the culture of those nerds is to be "the discoverers of new, independent horror films - the lower budgets ones friends don't know about."

Miska said another important aspect to the horror culture is the tight-knit community where celebrities such as genre actor Kane Hodder or makeup effects master Tom Savini are accessible.

At horror cons such as Spooky Empire in Orlando, Florida, Miska said fans "can just walk up and talk to these guys and it makes them feel special."

Petey Mongelli, the founder and promoter of Spooky Empire, (which wrapped its ninth year October 9) noted the appeal of the genre to a nerd like himself probably isn't unlike other fan cultures - and that includes the tendency to obsessively collect and categorize details.

"They know every single scene in every movie and every movie each actor has done," he said. "They have the original posters or the first copy of the VHS or Beta autographed by everybody and need every single zombie from *Dawn of the Dead* on their poster—

even if they were in the movie for five seconds."

Hard-gore fans versus loose screws

Mongelli also described the "real hardcore fans" as those who have actor or character likenesses tattooed on them, then "go get that autographed and get that tattooed."

Speaking of those hardcore fans, Harris said a horror nerd is someone who loves the genre and has fun with it, and even wants to be a creator of it, but acknowledges there is an element within fan culture that has a "teeny, tiny, little screw loose" and gets excited to see someone murdered onscreen.

"The guy who can recite every Halloween line and is so into it or has seen the movies 500 times - like the Adam Greens and the Rob Zombies of the world" are the nerds, she said. "Then you've got the guy who comes to a convention dressed as Michael Myers and stands in the corner with the mask on and breathes heavy and stares at me for an hour; there's a difference."

The "screw loose" element Harris refers to is the negative stereotype of the creeper fan that Miska says doesn't really apply to most horror nerds.

"*Hostel* set this precedent that horror fans wanted dark gore and torture," he said. "But people don't want to watch that (expletive); people want to have fun when they watch movies - Even with a horror movie."

Torture porn aside, Mongelli said fans still exist on the fringe even though horror is easily accessible on Netflix and dedicated TV networks such as Chiller.

It is an interesting point. Horror is readily available to audiences, but audiences don't readily take to it. It has never really been uncommon for the general populace to respond to individual horror films when they become part of the pop culture zeitgeist.

The masses have gleefully paid for their screams with commercial hits such as 1931's *Dracula, The Exorcist, Halloween* and *Jaws*.

Action figures of Freddy Krueger can be found on the shelves of a big box toy store, and most people have an awareness of who the character is, but the nerdy pursuit of the genre lacks the mainstream momentum seen behind fantasy, for instance. Even if the average *Entertainment Weekly* reader is aware of the plot of

The Human Centipede, that knowledge doesn't necessarily translate into viewership.

Although he said it depends on the subgenre of horror, Smith said he doesn't see that changing. If part of the appeal of the genre is the "deviant or repulsive," not too many fans from the mainstream will convert to horror nerd-dom no matter how easily you can purchase *Cannibal Holocaust* on Amazon.com.

"Casual fans are more interested in just an occasional scare particularly when a film is somehow registering on the cultural level as a phenomenon," said Smith. He acknowledges the successes of anomalies such as the $193-million box office take of *Paranormal Activity*, but added, "I think of summer blockbusters; horror films will only ever make so much money in comparison to the action, comedy, etc."

Commodity of horror

Besides, *Paranormal Activity* isn't really for horror nerds anyhow.

Harris speaks to a consensus amongst horror fans that mainstream culture doesn't "get" them, but that entertainment media is nonetheless trying to capitalize on the genre - often times through gimmicks, remakes, found footage flicks, and 3-D - without always adding to the art or craft.

"It used to be that horror movies were always thought of as 'B' movies or Grade-Z movies, and now sometimes they're tentpole releases," Hill said before adding, "In some ways things were more exciting when they were riskier, when there was an outlaw vibe."

"We're being played to a wider audience than we used to; that's positive, I think," Hill said. But he added he has "mixed feelings" about mainstream acceptance.

But there might be another alternative for horror nerds that allow them to hold onto their outsider status while also embracing the mainstream, or at least other nerd cultures.

Horror events such as Mongelli's have recently become part of an overall convention culture where everyone mingles together. He calls them "convention fans" and started noticing their appearance two or three years ago. Instead of fans dressed up as horror genre favorite Victor Crowley, or even as a generic monster, there were non-horror characters from *Star Wars*, *World of Warcraft* and so on.

"I was surprised they weren't there earlier," said Mongelli. "You see zombies at the comic book conventions, so why wouldn't we have Iron Man or Spider-Man?"

Mongelli said this is a good development. He and Miska agreed that horror enthusiasts will stay loyal to their specific circle, but that the convergence of fans blends together like-minded people - nerdy about different things - into a more diverse social gathering.

What Harris called "a place where nerds can play," regardless of the common obsession, and what Hill referred to as "genre play" and the "sandbox of the imagination," conventions have become a site of a giant nerd herd merge where - to borrow from Adina Howard - everyone is a "freak like me."

And in the end, those horror freaks can maintain their status as outsider fans in an outlaw genre - or at least as insider nerds with fringe benefits.

Paranormal State Of TV

(October 2011)

It is a lively time for the haunting dead, the undead, the walking dead and the deadly things in the water, forests and outer space.

Especially in the midst of Halloween season, all the creeping, crawling, shambling and stalking amounts to a lot of bumps in the night. And many of them are coming from the television. Scary movies, comics and video games aside, there is a lot of paranormal activity on TV this fall, but instead of slipping away after October 31, there is a trend of the entertainment of the unexplained continuing year-round as part of ongoing seasons. And there are plenty of bogeyman for viewers to choose from. Ghosts, vampires, zombies, werewolves, witches, beasts, and demons are currently haunting in high-def on reality-TV and scripted fare every day of the week.

On Sundays, *The Walking Dead* brings high-brow zombie drama to audiences on AMC. Monday is a good night for the MTV creature comedy *Death Valley*. On Wednesday, Syfy offers its long-running reality-TV show *Ghost Hunters* followed by reenactments of bigfoot, alien, and spectral encounters on Paranormal Witness. The twisted modern ghost story series *American Horror Story* on FX also gets the Wednesday treatment. A Thursday-night trifecta of vamps, werewolves and witches invade The CW with *The Vampire Diaries* and *The Secret Circle*. Friday is guys' night as a trio of reality-TV investigators search for the unknown on Travel Channel's *Ghost Adventures* while two brothers battle biblical forces on The CW's *Supernatural*. Even in the dead zones of Saturday and Tuesday, it's a solid bet that reruns of *Celebrity Ghost Stories, My Ghost Story, Ghosts: Caught on Tape* or some such programming will be airing in the primetime on the Biography Channel.

Of course, paranormal pop culture isn't particularly new. The human race has always told tales about the things in our universe that had yet to be explained (paranormal) and that which existed beyond the rules of nature (supernatural). But why does the fascination remain today?

The *de facto* response of the spiritually-minded was to say the need to believe in something larger than ourselves was necessary in a post-9/11 world. Lately the trend points to an impending shift in 2012 where the unreal is going to get real. Depending on the viewpoint, the end of the Mayan calendar will lead to humanity either getting scraped from the Earth's sole (due to the The Rapture or zombie apocalypse) or experiencing a spiritual re- awakening.

Then there is the "same as it ever was" David Byrne argument: Mankind has always been curious about the unknown and told tales, found religions and created myth to explain it. But old fears persist about what's "out there." Regardless of the answers we learn about our world and universe, there is an unsettling realization that there are things that remain unexplained.

Of course, another way to look at it is that the paranormal is just a fun sandbox of the imagination to play in. Even without any expectation of ghosts, vampires, and zombies being real, they're still as much fun to think about as having superpowers or traveling through time and space in a police call box.

On the still relatively new medium of TV, *The Twilight Zone* - and *The Outer Limits* to a lesser degree - explored the paranormal in the 1960s. In Search Of ... with Leonard Nimoy and *Unsolved*

Mysteries did it in the 1980s and '90s, as did *The X-Files* and *Buffy the Vampire Slayer* in the 1990s and early 2000s.

But instead of just a few scripted or reenactment programs on the air, the midpoint of the new millennium's first decade saw paranormal entertainment shift into high gear on television. In the fall of 2004, *Lost* premiered as a show laden with supernatural phenomena. Also, in the latter half of 2004, the erstwhile Sci-Fi Channel (now Syfy) debuted *Ghost Hunters*. By fall 2005, genre shows *Medium*, *Ghost Whisperer*, *Night Stalker*, *Supernatural*, and the documentary series *A Haunting* had debuted. The list would only continue to grow even as some shows survived, and others got the axe.

Although the big three television networks fairly quickly became gun shy of paranormal programming targeting adults, The WB - emboldened by previous successes *Charmed*, *Angel*, and *Buffy* - picked up the supernatural slack with shows marketed to high school and college students. They then continued the trend as the reincarnated CW network.

The CW programming expanded and toyed with literary tropes from the "dark fantasy" subgenre such as angels, fairies, witches, werewolves and vampires. Those paranormal shows would eventually include *The Vampire Diaries* and this fall's witch coven series *The Secret Circle* on The CW - both based on young adult fiction - as well as *True Blood* on HBO, *Teen Wolf* on MTV, and Syfy's upcoming succubus soap (imported from Canada), *Lost Girl*. However, aside from a few exceptions - Syfy's werewolf-vampire-ghost roommate series *Being Human*, which returns for season two in January - apparitions have been most successful on reality-TV.

Many scripted shows have used ghosts as a plotting technique and metaphor for the unresolved past returning to haunt the present. Lost used them to great effect (or was that just the Man in Black the whole time?), as did the once-successful, now canceled ghost series *Ghost Whisperer* and *Medium*. But the spirit has been weak with rating on ghost-centric scripted shows in the last few years.

Meanwhile, it was two Roto-Rooter plumbers by day, and paranormal investigators at night, who put a spotlight on ghosts on TV.

While the British reality-TV show *Most Haunted* - memorable for the night vision camera theatrics of host Yvette Fielding - preceded *Ghost Hunters* by two years, the Syfy program can be credited with launching the paranormal investigation docudrama where teams set out to explore, prove, or debunk unexplained phenomena.

Perhaps without actively intending to do so, the show breathed life into the characters from the 1984 comedy hit *Ghostbusters*.

Team leaders Jason Hawes and Grant Wilson of The Atlantic Paranormal Society (TAPS) approach their investigations with a debunking-before-believing "scientific method, " and an assurance that the paranormal isn't often something to be afraid of. They combine a blue-collar ethic along with a sense of humor and a "We're ready to believe you" attitude with spooked clients. Like the team led by Peter Venkman in *Ghostbusters*, TAPS utilizes fun gadgets, wears clothing branded with their logo and drive around in a cool signature vehicle. In a 2010 interview with ParanormalPopCulture.com, even *Ghostbusters* creator Dan Aykroyd said the program is "no doubt inspired by us."

After seven years on the air, more than 150 episodes, two spin-offs (*Ghost Hunters International* and the since-canceled *Ghost Hunters Academy*), five live Halloween-night specials and one canine investigator, the show is the network's longest running program and has been renewed for an eighth season in 2012. The two plumbers by day "origin story" even has a recognizable origin story - a unique feat for reality stars to achieve. Moreover, the show has cemented itself in pop culture and encouraged other cable channels to air their own ghost hunting programs.

New paranormal reality-driven shows are appearing constantly - *Paranormal Challenge, Paranormal Witness, Haunted Collector*, to name some recent additions. But there are also enough canceled, or un-renewed, reality-TV ghost hunting and documentary-style shows from the last seven years to fill a TV graveyard; *A Haunting, The Haunted, Ghost Lab, Ghost Cops, Paranormal State, Extreme Paranormal, Psychic Kids, Psychic Detectives, The Othersiders* and *Monster Quest* are just a few that would appear on headstones.

Meanwhile Travel Channel's *Ghost Adventures* is a marked contrast to *Ghost Hunters* on TV. Co-created by team leader Zak

Bagans and Nick Groff, it premiered on Travel in 2008 after a 2007 documentary aired on *Ghost Hunters* network, Syfy. The fittingly-named show is more adventure-based than *Hunters*.

Bagans and his two-man team, which also includes artist Aaron Goodwin, are "locked down" overnight in the locales where they actively pursue the darker elements of the unexplained - namely nasty ghosts and demons (which Bagans refers to as paranormal "bullies). Not surprisingly, by merging the dark fantasy subgenres with paranormal reality-TV, "*Adventures*" tends to appeal to the audience watching *Supernatural* on The CW.

Although ghost hunters, adventurers, explorers and trackers have had a good run-on reality-TV, the paranormal investigation show is poised to be overtaken by new reenactment programs.

Paranormal Witness, another supernatural Syfy show, features new stories of encounters with the unexplained each week.

Produced by documentary filmmaker Mark Lewis, whose work for the BBC and National Geographic has won him multiple awards, *Witness* intercuts eyewitness interviews with reenactment featuring actors. The show premiered in September and highlighted harrowing and inspiring tales involving angels, demons, beasts, UFO and a ghost without a face. The appeal of the shows is it allows viewers to reset their skepticism each week. If you don't believe the account of a helicopter pilot pursued by a flying saucer, then there's always next week to try again.

Paranormal Witness intentionally dips into the scary aspects of the paranormal. While other paranormal reality shows have a habit of sanitizing the topic too much, or assuring people they shouldn't be afraid, *Witness* is happy to terrify. Along with the scares of *Witness*, there is FX's new drama *American Horror Story*, created by Ryan Murphy (*Glee, Nip/Tuck*). Debuting October 5 to a respectable 3.2 million viewers, the series is a about a fractured family in a haunted house and is like Stanley Kubrick's *The Shining* meets *Twin Peaks*. Similar to the zombie survivor show *The Walking Dead* on AMC, *American Horror Story* meshes high production value and top tier talent with the horror genre on a weekly basis.

If the early successes of the plot-driven, horror-based shows are any indication, it would appear that paranormal TV is going to continue heading down a scary street - but the question is whether the trend will be to the detriment of the dark fantasy teen shows or investigative docusoap. Yet there is little question about the enduring power of the undead or the dead-on TV. Whether it is a reality-TV ghost, a dark fantasy teen vamp or a hardcore horror zombie, these beasts don't appear to be dying off.

Holly Jolly Halloween Gives Christmas Heave-ho-ho-ho
(October 2011)

Even with kids jingle belling, and everyone telling you to be of good cheer - when friends come to call - Christmas is no longer the most wonderful time of the year. Instead, with kids trick-or-treating and everyone telling you to have a good fear - when maniac killers come to call - now Halloween is the most wonderful season of all.

Andy Williams may have been right when he sang about Christmas in 1963's "It's the Most Wonderful Time of the Year, " but Pumpkin King Jack Skellington has since taken over as grandmaster because when it comes to the "it" holiday to celebrate, black (and orange) is the new green, and red.

In 2006, ABC News reported the season had become the second- biggest decorating holiday of the year. Plus, retailers have come to rely on the season as a precursor to Christmas and the best chance to improve sales numbers between back-to-school time and December 25 with costumes, candy, party supplies and decorations, reported *The Birmingham News* in 2010.

On the popular culture landscape, October is a primo time for networks and movie studios to get their hooks into audiences with, as Williams sang, "scary ghost stories" and terrifying fare.

On television, FX unleashed its haunted house soap opera *American Horror Story* on October 5. Also, AMC's zombie drama *The Walking Dead* returned for a second season on October 16 with very high expectations, and the new fairy tale-inspired show *Grimm* premieres on October 28. In film, *Paranormal Activity 3* will continue the found footage franchise when it is released in theaters October 21. And the gonzo horror-comedy *Butterfinger the 13th*, directed by actor Rob Lowe and featuring, yes, the candy bar, was unwrapped on October 13.

Further, when the entertainment industry as a whole is hurting for new ideas, Halloween is a season to roll out re-releases, familiar fare, and recaps for easy ratings or box office receipts.

The 1984 hit *Ghostbusters* will be re-released in theaters on October 13, and every *Halloween, Nightmare on Elm Street* and *Friday the 13th* installments get time on the cable channels in October. The Syfy Channel and sister channel Chiller is featuring "31 Days of Halloween" where the networks air new and classic horror films, along with specials such as "Horror's Creepiest Kids" on October 28 which intersperses movie clips with celebrity interviews to allow audiences to reminisce about past scares.

Yet while these facts show an effect of Halloween as an increasingly popular holiday, they don't explain why it has become so. It seems easy to suggest that a season characterized by the supernatural, magic, maniacs and scary good times is so fun because it allows us to find a catharsis for our real-world fears in some unreal ones. Sure, that does sound pretty good; when the economy and environment both seem to be facing disaster - as our government seems to stare on vapidly like a lethargic zombie - entertainment about the devouring undead seems downright light and airy. But the greater reason Halloween might be taking the lead over Christmas is the October holiday is a chance for kids to be kids, and a chance for adults to be even bigger kids.

First off, there's the dressing up. One only need look at any local comic book convention to see that no one ever really outgrows the desire to get into costume. Actual children are allowed to wear a cowboy hat on a Spider-Man costume in their everyday life, but such attire is frowned upon by grown-up society - even though most grown-ups are itching to let their inner Cowboy Spider-Man out. So outside of San Diego Comic-Con or other similar events, Halloween is the only time an adult can rock a cape and latex horror makeup or show some skin as a slutty superhero/vampire/nurse/Raggedy-Ann/etc. The difference is at a con it's called cosplay, but at Halloween it's "seasonal."

Keeping with the big kid theme, Halloween also allows adults to be selfish, indulgent monsters - you know, like most toddlers. Instead of encouraging the spirit of God-bless-us-everyone goodwill and sharing, October is when people can get sick on junk food, party it up and not give a darn about what the rest of the extended family is up to. With the exception of parents who have to take the kids trick-or-treating, there isn't anyone to answer to on Halloween. The costume is a choice; the decision to go out or stay in is yours, as is the number of candy corn you wash down with a UFO Pumpkin beer. Whereas December is about striving to be the best human we can be, October is about unleashing the id and being the worst.

Of course, the elimination of many economic hardships during the Halloween season also makes it an up-and-comer against Christmas. It is far easier to come up with a simple costume and manageable party plan than it is to figure out how to afford gifts for an entire family and social circle, or how to come up with enough money to travel to see them.

The decorations are also cooler. Visiting a Christmas village or festive, brightly lit neighborhood can elicit a sweet "aww" or even a teary emotional response, but that rarely equals the completely authentic screams a good haunted house attraction can cause. The things that bring people joy in December are fairly straightforward, but the things that terrify or unnerve us are deep and unending.

On a recent trip to Eastern State Penitentiary's "Terror Behind the Walls" attraction in Philadelphia, the screaming attendees provided as much of a soundtrack as did the fake moans, growls, and shouts of the funhouse performers. The emotional output at exhilarating attractions like Eastern State's is three times as much as from a Christmas village; the moments of terror are preceded by anxiety and followed by joy, but Christmas cheer begins and ends with joy. Still, at the end of the day, there's less emotional responsibility during Halloween as well. If you never get frightened during Halloween, it's no big deal. But if you aren't feeling the spirit in December, you're labeled a Grinch.

Certainly, the holiday season of Christmas won't be going away anytime soon, nor should it. Halloween is just a simpler, easier holiday to celebrate. As Andy Williams sang, "our hearts will be glowing when loved ones are near" in December, but Halloween fear makes this the most wonderful time of the year.

Putting The 'Con' Back in Santacon
(December 2011)

Santacon may have started off using "con" ironically, but at this counterculture, mischief-making costume party the nerds are making themselves known.

The San Francisco Chronicle reported the tradition - initially dubbed "Santarchy" - began in San Francisco in 1994 by The Suicide Club, "a collection of people dedicated to urban adventure and pranks." When the Suicide Club disbanded, former members formed the Cacophony Society, a San Francisco anarchic performance art group which carried on the Santa antics.

Since then, cities across the world have launched their own variation of the event. Santacon NYC seems to be the best-organized of the gatherings - or as organized as an event can be that is "non-denominational, non-commercial, non-political and non-sensical" and "occurs once a year for absolutely no reason," according to the event's website. The Santacon mob roams the city supporting charities, spreading cheer, singing naughty carols, consuming copious amounts of holiday spirits, and even visiting one strip club.

It is impossible to ignore the irony present in an event initially started to stir up the mainstream by causing mischief - all the while subverting the character of Santa. The origin story of Santacon is just the sort of performance mob art hipsters and hippies alike dig into. This is not the description of a nerdy event.

And yet, at 10 a.m. last Saturday at Manhattan's North Cove Marina, among the thousands of people dressed as Santa Clauses, elves, reindeer, Jesuses and more, were Santa Neo from *The Matrix*, Incredible Hulk Grinch, a trio of Run-D.M.C. Santas,

S.W.A.T. elves, Santa Batman, Victorian Father Christmas, Kurt Cobain Claus, and more sexy variations of holiday tropes than one could shake a candy cane at.

Have the nerds and superfans crashed Santacon? Yes and no.

There is a Christmas nerd subculture, comprised of Christmas fans who indulge in the holiday season yearlong, sort of like post-ghost Scrooge. They may keep an active model of a mini-

Christmas village in their basement, visit the "Golden Glow of Christmas Past" convention in July and various Christmas shops in August or make the pilgrimage to Mickey's Very Merry Christmas Party at Walt Disney World in Orlando, Florida. "Santa nerds" are specialized fans of the Christmas culture who collect the ornaments, dolls, action figures and decorative plates emblazoned with the jolly fat man.

Santacon is probably not the right scene for those people, although a form of nerd culture did emerge on Saturday.

The event is a mainstream party with a geek bend. There was a palpable sense of nerdy joy throughout the day's events. Despite a few slackers who opted for the no-effort Santa hat and beard, a majority of the revelers took pride in their costumes, and others showed appreciation for it. Like a scene out of any nerd con, a couple dressed as hydrogen and oxygen symbols from the Periodic Table of Elements ("H" and "O"), stopped for photos with fans every few feet on Stone Street - as did the man dressed as the Snow Miser from animation trailblazers Rankin and Bass' 1974 Christmas special *The Year Without a Santa Claus*.

The nerds were drawn to each other by the recognition of the obscure, creative outfits. But the larger community of Clauses included the nerds; they moved together, interacted, shared holiday memories and compared notes in typical tribe fashion.

With two starting points, the marina in Manhattan and the Brooklyn Bridge Park, the mass of Santas were fed instructions and destinations through the Santacon Twitter feed that this year led us to at least 10 locations such as the South Street Seaport, City Hall Park, Time Square, carols on the steps of the Public Library, the dance club District 36 and Rick's Cabaret. And this was before the after party was announced in Brooklyn. There are also suggested rules for Santas to follow, such as arriving on the scene with canned goods for the Food Bank for NYC and patronizing bars that donate portions of Santacon proceeds to Toys for Tots.

Other rules stress being creative with outfits, not being sloppy drunk, and tipping.

What's more, the spirit of Kris Kringle thrived at Santacon. Aside from the mountain of canned goods left at the marina, which was then carried by Santas to marines who loaded them into vans, the singing and affability shown to tourists and children (the ones not terrified by the bearded army) proved infectious. The mood was just cheery, and Santas by-and-large dedicated themselves to honoring the mainstream "goodwill to all" mission of the holidays.

And why not? Santa naturally appeals to both nerds and non-nerds. An immortal benevolent, Santa is a paranormal figure many children are actively encouraged to believe in; he is an accessible religious figure (that we can visit at malls!) who is also available to the secular. Depending on your standpoint, Santa is kind of like Jesus or Superman except he embodies the best of what humans can be (kind, charitable, jolly, nice to animals) with a dash of relatable human foibles (bad eating habits and fashion sense).

Perhaps that is indeed the mini miracle of Father Christmas; the character encourages all to take part in varying degrees of geekiness. Intended or not, nerd culture emerged at Santacon in a sincere, un-ironic - albeit bawdy - way. And then the nerds got loaded.

Zombie Apocalypse Preparedness: Are You Ready?

(February 2012)

Look at you, all plump and fleshy, with a quickening pulse and body jam-packed with sweet meats. That brain of yours, with the scrumptious gray matter and thinking cap makes certain re-animated corpses crave a dining bib.

So, what are you to do when the formerly living awaken with a hunger for a little human takeout? Are you ready for the zombie apocalypse?

Probably not. If you have to ask yourself that question, or took a moment before answering, then definitely not. In the time it took you to hesitate, even the slowest zombie could pull a dine and dash - or shamble - on you.

On the upside, you're in luck since most people haven't made the adequate preparations for Z-Day.

Here's the deal: A zombie can be a member of the walking dead or a barely living victim from a curse, virus, etc., and alternately run or shamble. They can be the creation of stupid humans, angry gods, black magic, mad science, cosmic events, or - as is most often the case - comic book/sci-fi/horror nerds. But whatever their origin, they are a problem that must be dealt with.

But not even the Centers for Disease Control and Prevention thinks the masses are ready for the onslaught of the undead.

"There are insufficient people prepared for emergencies in the United States," said Rear Adm. Ali S. Khan of the CDC.

A multi-credentialed doctor, assistant surgeon general, and director of the CDC's Office of Public Health Preparedness and Response, Khan was behind the zombie preparedness guide the organization published online May 2011.

Inspired by zombie-related social media buzz after the Fukushima Daichii nuclear disaster in Japan last March, and released days before Harold Camping's predicted rapture, the preparedness guide is a tongue-in-cheek plan. Its message boils down to the idea that if you're ready for a zombie apocalypse, you're ready for any more likely crisis or disaster. The CDC website received 2 million page views the first week as a result, and the guide went viral.

The CDC has also recently partnered with AMC's zombie drama *The Walking Dead* - based on Robert Kirkman's comic book series - to utilize clips from the TV show and add helpful tips such as, "Clean water is zombie-free water."

Apparently, according to TV Land, another tip to survive the zombie apocalypse is to not work at the CDC, which may have been the last hope for humanity in *The Walking Dead* and went kablooey in a giant explosion at the end of Season One.

Khan reminded us, however, that the real deal is "alive and well" and that even in any scenario where the CDC would be blown up, they would have "contingency plans" to make sure they're still addressing public health - which might be a subtle way of suggesting the government agency has a way cooler underground bunker than we originally thought.

Still, being prepared for a zombie uprising isn't the same as surviving, and thriving, in one.

Author Max Brooks is the father of zombie survival after he

literally wrote the book on it in 2003. Set against recorded attacks throughout history, *The Zombie Survival Guide* gives practical tips on defensive and offensive strategies against the ghouls whether you're at home, in a public space, on the move, or living in an overrun world.

Brooks goes a step further than the CDC (which he toured in October) and gives an extensive breakdown of weapons and combat techniques for life among the dead, but he still equates a zombie apocalypse to a natural disaster or - more likely, he said - a viral outbreak.

"People prepare for the obvious threat," he said. "It's the ones they underestimate that kill them."

Also the author of *World War Z* - the book about a global undead pandemic which will be released as a film starring Brad Pitt in December - Brooks gives zombie self-defense lectures that he said remain packed with a diverse crowd of teenagers, middle-aged housewives and other hopeful survivors.

As an esteemed member of the advisory board of the Zombie Research Society, (alongside director George A. Romero) Scott Kenemore (author of *The Art of Zombie Warfare*), describes members of the zombie survivalist subculture as "super Boy Scouts" who will be armed head-to-toe and skilled at hunting, fishing and camping.

"Zombie enthusiasts have been preparing woodland hideouts, remote bunkers and treetop deer stands where they can use their skills to live zombie-free well into the apocalypse," he said.

"Accordingly, the zombie apocalypse nerd is likely to be wearing a combination of protective gear to shield against zombie bites, and half the winter section of an REI to facilitate their outdoor survival plans."

If you haven't been training since 1968 when *Night of The Living Dead* debuted, or since 2003 when Brooks released his book, there's no need to panic - even if your name is Barbara and they are indeed coming to get you.

For about $100 and a plane ticket to England, you can attend Wish.co.uk's Zombie Boot Camp in Droitwich, Worcestershire, for training with military instructors. Utilizing body armor and weaponry, you learn battle tactics and unarmed combat and sniper skills as you train for an attack on a zombie den. Tea, coffee and light snacks are available for non-zombies to eat during training.

A little closer to home for American survivors-to-be is the Run For Your Lives "zombie-infested 5k obstacle course race," which advertised on *The Walking Dead* midseason premiere February 12. After launching in Baltimore last October, RFYL is hosting races across the country, with the first of 2012 taking place on March 3 in Atlanta.

The American Red Cross and CDC will be present at the race, as will IronE Singleton ("T-Dog") from *The Walking Dead*. And Dr. Khan from the CDC will also be running. He said he plans to stay with a large group of buffers.

But really, to survive zombies is to understand zombies. Education is key and learning the difference between an enchanted Voodoo zombie and flesh-eating monster could be tough for newbies not already prepped.

Luckily there are resources such as Ross Payton's *Zombies of the World: A Field Guide to the Undead*, which gives a handy visual reference to everything from the Common Gray Shambler to the Nordic Draugr and Chinese Hopping Corpse. He also provides a helpful guide of types of humans not to trust when the dead begin to roam. For the more scientific minded, Harvard psychiatrist Steven C. Schlozman, M.D. has documented the biology of zombies in *The Zombie Autopsies*.

So at the end of the day, or at the end of human existence as we know it, if you're unprepared for the zombie apocalypse, it's your own fleshy fault. There are resources to build muscles and train your tasty brain for when corpses come back to life.

'Run For Your Lives': 5K Puts Racers In The Middle Of A Zombie Apocalypse

(March 2012)

When it comes to the zombie apocalypse, popular culture has taught us that everyone falls into one category or another: infected or survivor.

You're either running away from an undead threat, or you're running, and shambling, after your next human snack. Yet the role that's so rarely discussed with zombie pop is that of a maker.

That has now changed. Instead of an act of God, nature or mad science, the zombie apocalypse has been orchestrated by one man, Derrick Smith

Smith is the co-creator of Run For Your Lives, a 5K race and "zombie-infested" obstacle course that officially launched last October in Darlington, Maryland, and is launching a nationwide roll-out in cities across the country, beginning with Atlanta on Saturday.

A fan of AMC's *The Walking Dead*, Smith said he and childhood friend Ryan Hogan planned on creating an event similar to intense races Warrior Dash and Tough Mudder to raise the profile of Hogan's athletic clothing line, Warwear. But then, they were trying to decide on something to run "from," and the idea of zombies emerged.

Although he doesn't classify himself as an "avid zombie fanatic," Smith said he's always enjoyed the movies and specifically prefers the zombies of *28 Days Later*.

"I definitely appreciate the quick-moving zombies and the vacant city setting where there's strategy involved," he said.

As a result, the 5K RFYL course (3.1 miles) is not a straight shot from start to finish. Smith and Hogan opted for a race where each course is unique and unpredictable.

"All of our course locations are designed based on the existing terrain with about 10 to 12 man-made and natural obstacles included," Smith said. Furthermore, "there's multiple routes to the finish line, and there might be a couple dead ends, or you might hit a fork in the trail, and one way is going to be a little bit longer."

He added that the course maps and obstacles are kept hidden, but the Darlington race included a 20-foot-tall cargo net and a "blood pit" filled with red liquid. The "Event Day Info" sent to participants warned of strobe lights and 3 feet of water. Smith also gleefully acknowledged that the Georgia red clay would leave a lot of opportunities for mud at the Atlanta race.

As for the zombies, Smith said they're actually volunteers recruited through Facebook and Twitter. On race day, runners traverse this wasteland populated by slow and fast volunteer brain munchers.

The runner "survivors" wear a flag football belt with three flags that signify their health. If zombies pick off all the flags, runners are infected by the end of the race and won't be eligible for prizes.

Meanwhile, the living get a survivor medal and a chance to win swag.

"We actually have health bonuses hidden throughout the course," Smith said. "So as you're running through, you could lose all your flags, but - kind of like a real-life video game - there's going to be opportunities for you to snag a little health pack that would ensure you cross the finish line as a human."

The attention to detail and strategy involved could position RFYL to capture the zombie zeitgeist and expand it into the real world as it spreads to 11 more cities in 2012 - including Boston, Los Angeles, Toronto and Pittsburgh, where director George A. Romero's *Night of the Living Dead* was shot. Smith said the Darlington event attracted approximately 10,000 spectators and participants between the ages 14 and 55.

Smith described the runners as a weird mix of hard-core zombie nerds, first-time runners and running enthusiasts looking for a new challenge.

He added that he's received feedback from people who say they finally have an excuse to run, and that the strategy of the race allows the less athletically inclined to slow down, move with packs of survivors and avoid the next pack of the "dead" walkers.

"I'm athletic, and I participate in recreational sports. But actually, just, like, running from point A to point B, or running around a track, never really interested me," Smith said. "So that's why we took this direction; the obstacle course race, and then throwing in the zombies, makes it all a little more exciting."

As far as what attracts people to the idea of running the race, Smith said RFYL attracts different levels of zombie fans, including those who view it as survival training.

"You have those people who have a plan, they have an arsenal, they have the water, the canned food, that whole bit," he said. "Then you have the people who are more about just thinking about what an apocalypse actually would be; it's definitely an entertaining thought in my mind to think."

But he added that he thinks the analysis of the meanings behind zombies has gotten "a little too deep" when "just in general, I think you're dealing with death and what happens after death."

The Run For Your Lives obstacle course is apparently one hell of a party. Once the race is over, zombies, survivors, infected zombies-to-be, and even spectators join in the apocalypse after-party in the "safe zone." With involvement from the American Red Cross, the Centers for Disease Control and Prevention and an appearance by lronE Singleton of *The Walking Dead*, Atlanta's all-day event will offer live music, food and drink, an awards show and games (knock the stacked zombie heads over with a baseball).

Smith said this party is nearly as crucial to the experience of surviving the "apocalypse" as running the race.

"We really try to put as much effort into the after-party as we do the race itself," he said. "If it's the end of the world, you're going to want to have a good party."

When Hollywood Gets in The Way of a Perfectly Good Myth

(April 2012)

Remember how the half-god Perseus flew on the winged horse Pegasus to save Andromeda from Hades' Kraken, and then later battled the chimera, minotaur and titan Kronos? If your basis for Greek mythology is the 2010 *Clash of the Titans* remake and the new sequel *Wrath of the Titans*, that's how you might remember the pursuits of Perseus. But that's not how it happened.

Right, so technically none of it "happened," but the Greek myths of titans, gods and men that have existed for more than three millennia are the stuff of ancient religion and part of our pop culture pantheon. Many myth geeks like me were exposed to the tales - which live at an intersection of history and storytelling - at an early age when we craved adventures about monsters, violence and valor (and were exposed to, incidentally, sex, betrayal, and heinous acts).

Personally, I remember seeing the original 1981 version of *Clash of the Titans* with the Ray Harryhausen visual effects when I was about 4 years old. While not so much obsessed with Harry Hamlin as Perseus, I couldn't get enough of the Medusa the Gorgon, the Kraken, and Pegasus.

I even had a few of the action figures from Mattel's very limited toy line that never took off. But more than the winged horse toy whose wings kept falling off, my prized *post-Clash* possession was a tattered 1957 copy of W.H.D. Rouse's *Gods, Heroes and Men of Ancient Greece* that was kicking around my house for some reason.

Written in a spry tone I'd later associate with John Hurt in *The Storyteller*; Rouse's book became a preferred storybook for me. Along with dinosaurs, animals and superheroes, I memorized and categorized the names of the major and minor players of myths. Although the stories themselves didn't change as I grew older, the way they were told and interpreted did.

And then I saw the *Clash* remake in 2010. Though I tried to keep it in check, my nerd rage began to boil over.

More so than in the original, this version took pretty exceptional liberties with the Greek myths (and the original wasn't totally faithful either). Perseus' mom Danae is now Acrisius' wife, not daughter? Hades killed Perseus' adoptive father and controls the Kraken? Zeus gives Perseus his sword, and is then punked by Hades and needs human help? Perseus bails on marrying Andromeda?

What happened there? It was like the screenwriters hadn't even read the myths and simply co-opted a hodgepodge of stories with mixed-and-matched familiar-sounding names to create an origin-story flick where the bad guy from the beginning is responsible for creating the hero that will destroy him. Yep, that's exactly what happened.

And the liberal alteration of mythology continues in *Wrath of the Titans*, when Perseus hops back on Pegasus to cozy up to Andromeda and get an assist from Hephaestus to stop Hades and Ares (who had already killed Poseidon because gods can die) from sacrificing Zeus to the recharged Kronos. That's in addition to the aforementioned battles with the minotaur, chimera, and big-daddy titan.

Okay so let's put aside the matter that Hades - who was never all that evil in myth - actually aided his nephew Perseus in defeating the Gorgon by loaning him the Helm of Darkness. We'll also forget that Perseus wore Hermes' winged shoes instead of riding Pegasus and that the Kraken was actually Poseidon's beast the Cetus - and that Theseus defeated the Minotaur and Bellerophon took out the chimera (while riding Pegasus).

I should just ignore the mythological alterations in these movies as well as *Hercules: The Legendary Journeys, Disney's Hercules,* the Percy Jackson franchise and others, right? These changes should simply be chalked up to Hollywood rewrites for smoother storytelling?

Then it also shouldn't be a big deal to make Spidey's webshooters organic and have Greedo shoot first?

These myths are the focus not just of much academic study but are tales that inspire imaginations and dedicated passion in some people.

To significantly alter them is to toy with the source material many of us came to love in our childhood. And lest we forget, they are also at the core of a religion - one that is still being worshipped by Hellenists. I can't help but speculate about the ensuing outrage if a movie about Jesus was released where he decided to team up with the three Wise Men and his Uncle Moses to kick some butt in ancient Rome.

Then again, maybe the flip side is that, by watching movies like the *Clash* remake, people will be inspired to pursue that source material and read the correct versions of the stories - much like the original Clash of the Titans prompted me to discover Rouse's book and begin the transition into a mythology geek.

But that may be as likely as Sisyphus getting that boulder to stay on top of the hill in Hades. It could happen (and Sisyphus did get a break when Orpheus visited the underworld), but my concern is that, after enough changes, the stories themselves might begin to change.

Myths that lasted for millennia may not withstand a century or so of cinema.

'Avengers' Vindicates Geek Community

(May 2012)

So yeah, I loved *The Avengers*.

Let's simmer on that word for a few: love. Love for a movie is a pretty significant emotion, and yet I stand by it. While not perfect (the gripes are ridiculously minor), the film was a pure joy. It delivered on the promise of a Marvel-ous adventure with Captain America, Thor, Iron Man and (finally) an awesome, Incredible Hulk.

But this isn't a movie review.

Instead, it's more of an "I told you so," to Hollywood power brokers locked into the philosophy that audiences crave dark heroes and sober plot lines, and that the geeks who grew up loving the source material could not be trusted to make a blockbuster.

Nerd favorite writer and producer Joss Whedon assembled *The Avengers*, who stormed the box office last Friday. There was a sense by Sunday that everything had changed for superhero movies.

On Sunday night, Walt Disney Co., which owns the Marvel Comics characters, announced the new flick had debuted to $200.3 million (later updated to $207.4 million) - the largest all- time opening weekend for a movie (and yes, a sequel is coming). But for fanboys and comic geeks like me who had been tracking the super-group superhero movie, this was no big surprise.

Okay, so it was a little bit of a surprise - a pleasant one - but we geeks had been waiting for this.

In fact, we've been debating, discussing and having fantasy casting sessions for the movie for years. Geeks have been so patient, waiting for a movie that could pit Earth's (and Asgard's) mightiest heroes against themselves before teaming them up to battle a common, villainous threat.

This goes for all superhero groups and coincidental team-ups. For comic book nerds, these ultimate matchups are fueled by years of imagining what would happen if comic book universes faced off (Superman vs. Thor, Captain America vs. Batman, etc.).

The Avengers is a supergroup movie on an entirely new scale. Outside of animated features, the only time we've really seen team-ups has been in disappointing franchise films like *The Fantastic Four*. Additionally, Marvel has taken its time by slowly building their universe through stinger scenes and Easter eggs in their other movies, beginning with 2008's *Iron Man*.

Moreover, there is this desire within the nerd community to share their love of these fantastic characters and the infinite possibilities of a team like the Avengers. Whedon's the one who has been able to help us communicate to all our friends and family, "See? This is what I have been talking about!"

I spent my comic book collecting youth wishing that a fellow nerd would create a movie for us. Be true to the material, we all thought, and others would fall in love as well. And now that it's here, it is as if the clouds parted and our new, four-color mythological gods of the funny books had sprung to life on the movie screen just as we'd always hoped.

The Avengers movie feels like an Avengers comic.

This isn't to say that comic books haven't spawned some truly visionary films.

As much as I've enjoyed Christopher Nolan's take on the Caped Crusader in *Batman Begins* and *The Dark Knight* - and actively look forward to the conclusion of his series in *The Dark Knight Rises* - I never walked out of the new Batman movies feeling the elation I felt after *The Avengers*.

Dark Knight was great and masterfully executed, and I remember chatting on the way out of the theater with others also impressed with the serious film, but my fanboy glee was absent.

Exiting *The Avengers* was another matter altogether.

It is a popcorn-movie, not a film, but people were excited, inspired, giddy, animated as they walked out of the theater. There even seemed to be a few newly converted geeks. I have caught glimpses of this before in varying degrees - during moments of *Superman Returns, Spider-Man 2, X-Men 2, Iron Man* and the other Marvel precursors to *Avengers* - but never like this.

The joy I felt after watching *The Avengers* was enlightening: I think I've had my fill of "gritty realism" when it comes to comic book heroes. Nolan has done a great job at showing that a man can become a symbol in an ultra-realistic world, and he did it with an epic scope and without CGI effects, but I would still like to believe a man can fly.

Likewise, I think audiences would like to believe a demi-god alien can crash to Earth, a super soldier clad in stars-and-stripes can survive being frozen for 70 years and that a Hulk can smash. A little magic and a fantastical adventure are as good for the geek as it is for the muggle; perhaps it is no coincidence that the last biggest opening weekend record holder was another magical adventure: *Harry Potter and the Deathly Hallows - Part 2*.

Hollywood should listen to the geeks more often - if only to ensure the superhero genre continues to go up, up and away in quality and box office receipts.

Comic-Con Wrestles Business Out of Chaos
(July 2012)

If you don't have some reaction to San Diego Comic-Con International you're not participating in popular culture.

What began more than four decades ago as an intimate gathering of comic book creators, fans and legends has become a packed entertainment event. Although it doesn't have the same ring to it, Comic-Con could more appropriately be called the Transmedia Pop Culture Con where buzz for a year's worth of projects is created, prolonged or squelched.

Yet, despite the awareness that the con is a giant marketplace where producers sell directly to customers, there has been shockingly little analysis of the business of the event before Rob Salkowitz's new book, *Comic-Con and the Business of Pop Culture*.

Seated at a conference table at the McGraw-Hill building in Manhattan, Salkowitz delved deep into his nerd-business theories.

A futurist and business writer, Salkowitz approaches "The Con," as it is known in nerdy circles, as more than just a meeting ground of Hollywood suits and 130,000 fans. Instead, he calls it a "laboratory in which the global future of media is unspooling in real time," where people participate in their entertainment instead of just consuming it.

Salkowitz writes that Comic-Con can actually teach some important lessons about challenges facing all creative endeavors in our globalized, digital world, but he does so from the perspective of a comics nerd who attended his first con when he was eight.

"In fact, I learned to read and write from comics, and I learned, basically, the fundamentals, of visual communication," said Salkowitz. He strayed from the church of comics for a time as an adult but returned to it and attended his first San Diego Comic-Con in '97. After he ended up in a game of Five Card Nancy (based on the Ernie Bushmiller strip, and created by Scott McCloud) with McCloud, Kurt Busiek and Will Eisner, you could say he was back in the congregation.

Salkowitz's nerd cred makes him the ideal candidate to examine The Con's moment of "Peak Geek," where comics culture is at a maximum saturation level, and to make some educated predictions of what happens next.

Without slipping into a dull business discussion about something like a Trade Federation dispute, Salkowitz acknowledged that Comic-Con's environment consists of consumers who are simultaneously fans and co-creators in a business fueled by talent.

"At the highest level, this is a book about this industry that started out at the fringes of culture and of business, and over 25 years, it came to inhabit the center of both of them," he said. He called The Con a "triumph of the nerd story," but added "the 2011 Con felt to me like Europe in 1914, right before everything blows up."

He added there is always the risk that Hollywood might move on from The Con, because that industry is interested in making hits - a hard thing to manufacture. Even if a movie like *Scott Pilgrim vs. the World* connects with fans, and is true to the source material, it may not connect with the mass media (it didn't). Even if lesser-known characters like Iron Man can be the focus of a successful franchise - and lead into the mega-successful *The Avengers* - that doesn't make *Green Lantern* a sure thing (it wasn't).

"Maybe popular culture gets sick of this and the moment passes, and in a few years, comics are like disco," he said. "A lot of people looking back are going to say, 'Wow, that's really strange that was so popular' and comics either go back to being this nerd niche ... or become just like jazz."

That's why Comic-Con has decided to embrace brands like *Twilight*, he said. If Comic-Con can get a younger generation to build memories that way, it could guarantee fans return to the convention 30 years from now for nostalgia's sake.

Salkowitz sees Comic-Con in a state of mid-jump over the shark. Much of the event's celebrity component lacks "meaningful activity," he said, but there is also a "very authentic, historically-focused" aspect of creators trying to do real work.

Enter "nerd media." While companies want to attract the raving comics fans who attend The Con, those fans are not zombies, Salkowitz said. They talk back and participate and can't be taken for granted.

Having someone like Chris Hardwick or Harry Knowles behind an entertainment company's project adds credibility - unless it begins to look like those nerds are so integrated into a marketing and publicity machine that they've been corrupted. If that happens, there will be at least 10 other grass roots websites ready to emerge from the basement and take their place, Salkowitz said.

Looking forward, Salkowitz the business writer wants to observe the impact of digital comics at the 2012 Comic-Con more than anything else. He said he's interested in seeing if the direct comics market can survive, and if retailers will be able to participate. Also, in a situation where anyone can be a publisher now, but the value is placed on the distribution, he is curious how things play out when everybody has an incompatible format.

Salkowitz the nerd, meanwhile, is excited about the "deluge of good vibes" that comes with walking into a room filled with 130,000 people having the time of their lives. He added that that's the side he really wanted *Comic Con and the Business of Pop Culture* to be about.

"There's always going to be the terrible commercial aspect," said Salkowitz. "At the end of the day, people are interested in this stuff because of the stories, because of the characters, because it captures our imagination, because it's well told and well executed ... It's people that are doing that, and not the people at the top of the companies."

'Make Them ... Love Zombies Even More' with Bruce Campbell
(July 2012)

If Comic-Con is "nerd Christmas," then speaking on a panel at the con feels like taking Santa's sleigh out for a spin. I have been fortunate to speak at large cons like New York Comic Con and Dragon*Con, but San Diego is the "really big shoe" - so obviously I didn't want to crash and burn.

When Matt Mogk, founder of the Zombie Research Society, invited me to join him and zombie intellectuals, authors and experts on the *History of the Modern Zombie* panel, nerdy giddiness overcame me. That was then immediately followed by an "Oh, crap" moment.

Sure, I've written and spoken quite a bit about zombies, but these were dudes whose work I followed, like Max Brooks, Steven Schlozman, Scott Kenemore, Bradley Voytek, and Dan Drezner. Speaking in front of a crowd didn't freak me out and I have confidence in my knowledge. But I'm also a fan and very aware that the ZRS has legit legend George A. Romero on the Advisory Board.

So, to prep, I did what any good journalist would do: call in an expert. Actor Bruce Campbell is con royalty and if he didn't attend San Diego, it could be considered a harbinger of doom in some nerd cultures. Instead of deep, philosophical advice about my first SDCC panel appearance, Campbell kept it simple.

"Don't get too serious," he offered. "You're going to be speaking in front of a thousand people; you got to play to the whole room and speak with enthusiasm and fun and get them involved somehow. "

The people in the room are clearly fans of zombies, but Campbell pointed out that I was on the panel for a reason, and it was partly my job to create a dialogue that extends beyond the hour spent on a stage.

"Make them, by the time they leave, love zombies even more," Campbell said.

My arrival at Room 7AB of the San Diego Convention Center humbled and excited me. I was greeted by fans and colleagues, and a long line had formed - which eventually led to people getting turned away. Admittedly, most of the crowd was there for the zombie rock band of Brooks, Mogk, Scholzman, and Kenemore (sort of the zombie equivalent to Crosby, Stills, Nash & Young).

By comparison, I was a garage band act, although I did break news about my new Travel Channel show *Paranormal Paparazzi*, debuting September 28, which I'll be hosting and had the support of these dudes.

As the moderator and leader of the merry band of undead experts, Mogk introduced his panelists and threw a few softball questions before clearing out of the way and letting the fans take over.

What makes zombies unique is the fact that these Hollywood-created monsters have been transported through popular culture into the real world. Most fans don't prepare for an encounter with Modok or the Borg as they do for a potential zombie apocalypse. Like many things discussed at Comic-Con panels, the audience clearly thought a lot about the topic and had questions to ask and anecdotes to share.

Some of the questions came faster than others, but it immediately became clear that when a panel is executed correctly, like this one, it becomes a conversation and not a professorial lecture to students.

I have no doubt that many fans asking the questions had as much of an encyclopedic knowledge of the genre as us authors and "experts." But they just wanted to get our take and engage us in a discourse. That's the spirit of Comic-Con on display: Let's chat about the stuff we love.

There was a moment - or several - when I fretted that I'd forget years' worth of passion about zombies and somehow slip into an analysis of vampires. But no, not only did I remember this stuff, but I was able to geek out about it, and disagree about it, with my compadres.

It was about 45 minutes into the hour-long panel that I suddenly recalled the advice given to me by LeVar Burton about being on a panel.

"Savor the moment. It'll go by incredibly quickly," Burton said. "It's like your wedding day and it's over way too fast so, consciously remind yourself, take mental snapshots of the experience and when you go to relive it, you have the materials that you'll need in terms of imagery, sights, sounds, smell."

Although the reality in my head may not mesh with what actually happened, the way I now remember the panel is that I was able to fire off a few smart comments or funny zingers. My role as a journalist who has written much about the genre was served, and it was fun as hell. But more than that, I remember being with "my people." I felt at home, the ultimate emotion to experience at Comic-Con.

But after the panel, a piece of advice had rung the truest for me. Deborah Ann Woll of *True Blood* advised me to eat the chocolate on the table that's put in front of me, and I did do so to calm me down.

"Bring your camera with you and take a picture," she also told me. "It will definitely be a sight."

And it was. I was honored to be with my colleagues and the fans, and as my fellow panelists sat to have dinner afterwards, I didn't remember much of it. As Burton warned, it was over fast, and I'd reached my geek pinnacle. The photos I took during the panel were my cognitive trigger. It had happened, and I had lived in a nerd spotlight.

So, in the end I don't think I crashed Santa's sleigh: here's hoping for another shot at the reins.

'Being Human': Comic-Con's Next Big Thing
(August 2012)

After writing about pop culture for a while, attending a dozen San Diego Comic-Cons, and observing - as well as being a part of -

fan culture, you start to notice the signs of a growing movement.

Comic-Con has always been a litmus test for pop culture's appeal. How the hordes of attending fans react to the convention's exclusive presentations often dictates a more mainstream success for comic books, TV shows, movies or collectibles. But predicting a franchise's Comic-Con pH is tricky, since there is always an intangible element to what nerds adopt or reject.

But when you're a nerd and the nerd world is your business, you start to feel like Buffalo Springfield singing, "there's something happening here ... everybody look what's going down" about tribal movements. And after this year's Comic-Con, my gut tells me such is the case with Syfy's *Being Human*.

Already a favorite of dark fantasy fans, the show stars Sam Witwer, Sam Huntington, and Meaghan Rath as a vampire, werewolf and ghost (respectively) living together to achieve a sense of normalcy.

If a group of supernatural roommates sounds like a soapy set up, that's because it is. What beloved ongoing story line in nerd culture isn't? Hook ups, break ups, deaths, resurrections, addictions, arch nemeses, memory loss - not to mention occasional mutations, undead infestations and body switching; this is the stuff that fans cheer for at Comic-Con.

And cheer they did. The trio drew a larger crowd to their end-of- day Saturday panel this year than last. The audience in the Hilton Bayfront Hotel's Indigo Ballroom was full of fans who sat waiting there for hours, specifically so they could see the *Being Human* stars.

The excitement around *Being Human* reminds me of the groundswell that started the current *Doctor Who* craze. The show has been around since 1963 and always enjoyed a solid fan base, but the franchise was never a dominant force at Comic-Con until relatively recently. A noticeable uptick in Whovian cosplay during David Tennant's tenure as The Doctor (2005 - 2010) started a pattern of excitement.

By Comic-Con 2011, *Doctor Who* had arrived. *Doctor Who* cosplay evolved that year to include not only an army of women fans in cute Dalek dresses, but also nerd culture mashups, like a zombie Doctor. Ultimately, the Hall H appearance of cast members Matt Smith (the current star of *Doctor Who*) and Karen Gillan in

San Diego was a watershed moment for the franchise, moving it into the mainstream.

Currently filming its third season for a Winter 2013 return, *Being Human* also has roots in *Doctor Who's* home turf. The show is the American reimagining/reboot of BBC's original, eponymous and also popular show. Reflecting on the success of Syfy's version of the franchise at Comic-Con, Huntington said he thinks it is a show that "views real world scenarios and issues through a supernatural lens."

"Were you to take the words 'vampire,' 'werewolf,' and 'ghost' out of the scripts, the stories would still work," Witwer added.

But the supernatural element doesn't hurt; these types of shows are already a hit at Comic-Con (see: *Supernatural*). *Being Human* fits neatly into a crossover-friendly territory between younger-skewing, more romantic *Twilight* and the naughtier, older *True Blood*. And it certainly helps that the lead actors are attractive twenty-somethings. Even so, eye candy alone isn't enough to keep nerds coming back.

Most importantly, a genuine nerd pedigree accompanies Being Human, which primes it for a huge showing at future cons.

The actors have a geeky chemistry with one other that's endearing to fans. They dodge the actor trap of being too cool for their fans, and never come across as just playing a nerd on TV. At Comic-Con, I've seen this cast earnestly interact with fans, even waiting long past the scheduled end of their appearance for fans. The cast moved around the convention together, emphasizing their support of the show and the characters they play, rather than their own celebrity.

It's a formula that works.

"I can't think of a more appropriate place to promote the show than Comic-Con, " said Huntington. "Nerd culture, and the content with which it was born, relies almost 100 percent on suspending belief, while at the same time creating characters that are inherently relatable. I think - hope - that that's exactly what we do."

Witwer agrees. "That's why we seem to be developing an audience with our 'nerd culture' brethren," he said.

It's easy to see the nerdy kid in the grown-up Huntington, an erstwhile Jimmy Olsen and star of *Fanboys*, and Rath is a confessed bookworm.

Meanwhile Witwer, the one who has been elevated to heartthrob status, has built the most geek cred of them all after long stints voicing characters for George Lucas on *The Clone Wars* show - he is Darth Maul, for Pete's sake - and in *The Force Unleashed* video games (not to mention his work as Crashdown on *Battlestar Galactica*, and as Doomsday and the voice of Zod in *Smallville*).

Even the show's first season boss villain Bishop, played by Mark Pellegrino, who re-appeared in season two, is a power broker in the nerd community after his major roles on *Lost* and *Supernatural*.

If the *Being Human* cast continues to embrace being nerds, they might be the focus of the next con craze.

Shark Week: I Believe in Monsters

(August 2012)

I believe in monsters because one bit me on the foot. OK, it was a small one.

I grew up on the beaches of Florida and was literally in over my head one day. It isn't as if I was in that deep of water for an eight- or nine-year-old, but it was deep enough I was bouncing up and down, launching off the sand below, to keep popping my head up for air. Adults were all around me, but none of that mattered when I bounced down and something clamped on.

There was a tough, alien feeling below my feet immediately preceding the pain that sunk in. Right underneath the part of my brain that was processing that pain - a lot of it - was a thought of "shark, shark, shark!"

This was happening probably two years before Discovery Channel launched Shark Week in 1988, more than a decade after Jaws made America afraid to go into the water - but still probably a year before *Jaws 4* made it personal (and personally helped to ruin Michael Caine's career for another decade).

A kid who wanted to be a marine biologist well into high school, and who attended "sea camp" with his eighth-grade class, I have always been a bit of an ocean nerd, and specifically a shark nerd.

And Shark Week, launching its twenty-fifth year on August 12 on Discovery, has been one of my holidays. Referred to in my home as Sharkmas, Sharkmukkah, and Shar-kwanzaa, it is a yearly celebration of Mother Nature's ultimate predators.

Previously hosted by Adam and Jaime from *MythBusters*, Craig Ferguson and Andy Samberg, the event is part of our pop culture lexicon. Nearly 27 million people tuned in to watch Shark Week in 2011 to see half-crazy (or "passionate") scientists drop themselves in cages underwater, or on sleds above water, to gather data on the beasts - and to introduce us to new phrases like the leaping great white "Air Jaws," which explodes out of the water for a seal meal.

The emphasis of Shark Week is on understanding and education. Yet over the course of eight specials - including a new "Air Jaws" entry, a special *MythBusters* episode, an examination of the impact of *Jaws* on sharks and interviews with shark attack survivors - there is definitely an acknowledgement that, yeah, these things can eat us up real good.

This is something I can personally relate to every time I go to a beach, snorkel in deep water, watch *Jaws*, or even listen to Jimmy Buffett's "Fins."

Again, I probably should have been born with gills for as much time as I spent in the ocean. I was snorkeling in the Florida Keys with a conservationist family friend involved in the "Save The Manatee" movement at such an early age that images of coral, colorful fish, freaky fish, rays, manatees, and even sharks are among my earliest.

The ocean was not something I was raised to be afraid of. Respect it, yes, but not fear it. But when you're a kid and a monster from the world below you is literally reaching up to grab you, things feel different. The thing unlatched from me right away, and although I bled what looked like a lot, I was fine. I only caught a glimpse of the shape, and I believe it to have been a nurse shark. But at the moment of the bite, that thing may as well have been an extinct megalodon coming for me.

Humans are not obviously equipped to survive in the water for long, and when our meaty legs are dangling under the surface - or our plump, meaty midsections are floating around, seal-like - it is difficult not to think about how vulnerable we are. And when a shark is encountered "out there," in the water, an alert part of brain helpfully reminds us that the water is the domain of this thing, and we don't belong.

When I'm underwater, my mind still sometimes wanders to the scene in *Jaws* when Richard Dreyfuss' Hooper discovers Ben Gardner's corpse while on a night dive. It still startles the little kid in me (and maybe the bigger kid, too). Deep down I think about how my sister would read about sharks and shark attacks - on the way to the beach. It was like reading ghost stories around a campfire, except we had no evidence supporting the existence of the Amityville ghosts but the creature from Amity Island was another matter. And the crew of the *U.S.S. Indianapolis* also occasionally enters my thoughts.

But the larger point here is that I kept going back in the water after my little incident. That's the message of Shark Week.

Despite the horror stories of attacks - despite how good they are at eating everything - sharks may seem like monsters, but they aren't out to get us and don't pose a real threat. And obviously the dwindling shark population has more to fear from humans than we do of it.

The ocean is a perfect place to be humbled by Mother Nature, and only education and respect (or blissful ignorance) can prevent one's slide into terror. But that is another reason why shark nerds love Shark Week; it is a chance to appreciate the raw, bloody, brutal beauty of nature outside of us.

Beyond the buckets of chum that are spilled and the amazing slow-motion footage of sharks getting chompy, Shark Week is an opportunity to confront primal fears of our own weakness or insignificance, fears of something so perfectly designed to kill.

'Doctor Who': 'He Doesn't Like Endings,' But Ultimately Whovians Don't Mind

(October 2012)

Amy and Rory couldn't travel with The Doctor forever. Not that fans suspected they could - the Doctor's past includes many companions. But now we have to wait until the special Christmas episode, possibly beyond that, to see the next stop on the epic TARDIS hitchhike.

In Saturday's *Doctor Who* mid-season finale, "change" and "endings" were as thick as the fog that attends the sneaky, predatory weeping angels. For a show about an alien who travels through time saving Earth and thwarting evil across the universe, the message got a bit heavy-handed at times. It was almost as if executive producer Steven Moffat was trying to prepare himself, The Doctor and the audience for the inevitable.

Even Matt Smith (the eleventh man to play The Doctor) was emphasizing that theme in an interview before last month's New York City season premiere screening.

"The show is about change," he said. "Like Steven likes to say, it can never be predictable, it can never be cozy - It's got to feel like it's sort of marking new territory, I think, every season."

But why belabor the point? This is a television show that for nearly 50 years has established the fact that the characters on the show are always coming and going - including the titular main character, The Doctor (who?) Even relatively new fans (and certainly, American fans fit that bill) of the show have gleaned that time travel is a limited engagement.

That started in 1966, when the show's original Doctor, William Hartnell, needed to retire due to health issues. The show's producers devised a clever plan to transition to a new actor, Patrick Troughton, in the main character role.

The alien nature of The Doctor provided the fix: As a species known as a Time Lord, The Doctor can regenerate instead of dying in the traditional sense. Once regenerated, The Doctor is essentially a new person: he retains memories from his previous life but has a fresh personality.

This prevents a classic Dick York/Dick Sargent quandary where a new actor is installed, and no one is supposed to notice the change. Even better, when an actor takes over the Doctor's role, they aren't trying to mimic their predecessor's performance, which allows them to put a unique spin on the character all while adhering to the show's canon.

Doctor Who fans, or "Whovians," are unique among television show fandoms in that each fan can point to a favorite version of The Doctor without also having overwhelming disdain for any particular actor in the role. A popular T-shirt cheekily states, "You never forget your first Doctor," and it's spot-on; a Whovian's fan identity is typically established with the first incarnation of the Time Lord (or his companion) they fall in love with.

By comparison, Trekkers can debate about who their favorite captains from the many iterations of *Star Trek* were, but there generally isn't much disagreement over which specific version of Kirk they love the most (sorry, Chris Pine).

Newer *Who* fans might have joined the party with the debonaire tenth Doctor, David Tennant, but many thirty-somethings within the fandom have a particular fondness for Tom Baker. Baker, with his iconic scarf of many colors and sandy blond afro, was the fourth Doctor and the first whose tenure received an extended run in the US on PBS in the late 1970s (although selected episodes of third Doctor, Jon Pertwee, did air stateside prior to that).

For decades, *Doctor Who* targeted families and garnered solid ratings in the United Kingdom before it was suspended in 1989 due to dropping viewership. Russell T. Davies revived the series with the ninth Doctor, played with edgy fury by Christopher Eccleston, in 2005 following a 16-year absence (save for a 1996 TV movie).

Tennant's Shakespearean flare helped establish a quirkier vibe and romantic core for the show, while Smith's bow-tie-clad turn has transformed the show into an American pop culture staple.

The current season's September 1 premiere earned 1.6 million viewers, a series best since the show moved from Syfy to BBC America in 2009. The numbers represent a 23 percent increase in viewership from the show's 2011 premiere, and the sixth season was the most downloaded show on iTunes in the US last year.

The Doctor's companions, too, are expected to be swapped out with some frequency. Following the Ponds/Williams' TARDIS retirement, The Doctor flew off with their daughter - also his wife - River Song. The comfort of seeing a familiar face helped lessen the blow for fans: River Song has crossed paths with the Time Lord many times over the last five seasons of Doctor Who.

Certainly, Karen Gillan, the actress who played Amelia (Amy) Pond, wasn't entirely ready for the end of this companionship.

After learning her character's fate in this weekend's episode, "The Angels take Manhattan," she sank into sadness.

"I was crying for pretty much the entire two weeks we were shooting that episode. In between takes. Just, in life. Little things were setting me off. I was sensitive," she said at San Diego Comic Con during the *Doctor Who* panel in July.

In a pre-panel interview, fellow companion Arthur Darvill (who played Rory Williams, Amy Pond's husband) said he has enjoyed being one-half of the first married couple on the TARDIS as well as the longest-running modern companions.

"We're so close to it at the moment and I think it will take a few years to be able to actually realize what we've done personally, but also kind of how it is on the show," Darvill said. "Hopefully we've added something quite exciting to it."

Fans have known since March of this year that Amy and Rory would leave the Doctor's side and newcomer Jenna-Louise Coleman will end up riding shotgun in the TARDIS. Fans may remember her as the crashed spaceship survivor from the first episode of this season.

"If you look at the history of the man, he picks up hot chicks and travels around the universe for two years and then goes, 'eh, see you later, Rose," joked Smith. The character of Rose Tyler established the possibility of a companion who was also a love interest - she captured the heart of the tenth Doctor, who still somehow managed to end up with two more companions before his regeneration.

Doctor Who executive producer Caroline Skinner admitted in September that she wasn't "quite ready" to see Gillan and Darvill leave the show. When asked about Smith's departure, she joked, "We're never going to lose Matt!"

"I think that everyone, including the US fans, also seem to really get and love the fact that *Doctor Who* is kind of all about change and change is its essence, and it must never stop moving because that way the show won't really be at its full strength," Skinner said.

And yet, there is a big change in the near future that poses a challenge beyond finding a new companion or actor for The Doctor to regenerate into. According to show lore, a Time Lord can only regenerate 13 times, and Smith is currently the eleventh incarnation.

"They'll have to invent something then where they can keep it going because why would we want to stop making it?" said Smith. "I'll be old news by then, so I don't know, really, but it's a show that isn't afraid of change and I embrace that."

Chasing the Ultimate 'BOO!'
(October 2012)

You're fumbling around in the dark, and unless you have the twisted pleasure of taking the lead, you may be gripping onto the person in front of you as the group makes its way from one room of horror-made-real into another. It is a haunted house attraction, or haunt, and you can feel it in your bones - just around the next corner, someone is going to jump out and squeeze a scream right out of you.

And your scream might just be the highlight of that person's night.

Welcome to the world of the haunt nerd, whose obsession is crafting the best scare he can as an actor or effects artist through homemade and professional haunted houses. Halloween is his Christmas, a season where screams are the gift that keep on giving.

There are a lot of screams to give, according to Hauntworld.com an unofficial haunted attraction industry website. The site estimates there are more than 1,400 for-profit attractions and amusement parks charging admission in America, 3,000 charity attractions and 10,000 "home haunters." Moreover, a recent study by horror site and cable network FEARnet reported that nearly 50 percent of Americans would decorate their home or yard for Halloween and that about 23 percent of people would be visiting haunted houses this season.

These facts add up to a lot of interest in scares by the public, which is no surprise. But who are the people behind the terror? Who are the haunt nerds?

"There is this through line of passion" between haunters and other nerds, said Michael Stephenson, director of *The American Scream*, a documentary about three families behind neighborhood haunted houses.

The show, which premiered on October 28, is set to re-air today at 5:00 pm Eastern on the Chiller network, examines why people dedicate so much time and money annually to the business of fear.

"You watch horror to be scared and have an emotional release," said Stephenson, and the appeal of going to a haunted house is not dissimilar. But those who then choose to provide the scares are seeking to transport people out of reality for a few minutes, just like hard-core fans of fantasy, sci-fi, comic books, etc.

And like other nerd cultures, the haunt nerds are also fairly organized and commune in forums online and at conventions. In addition to the Hauntworld site, which has an active following, home haunt websites such as GarageOfEvilNetwork.com, HauntForum.com, and HauntProject.com all provide a community for haunters to trade tips to create the best scare experience. The nerds are also served by the popular HauntCast online radio, and by the TransWorld and Monsterpalooza cons, just to name two.

And, obviously, there are the costumes. Like cosplayers, "many of these haunters ... share this ability to create a new sense of place and magic," said Stephenson. Unlike cosplayers, they want to use their transformative powers to scare the bejeezus out of people. He called them masters of a "temporal art form" - since their efforts are essentially all for one night - who gain empowerment from creating enough of an altered reality that they can make adults and teenagers scream at the top of their lungs.

"It is the greatest joy of my life," to hear people scream at his attraction, said Robert Frey, CEO of horror director Eli Roth's Goretorium, the year-round haunt in Las Vegas that just opened last month.

"They want the adrenaline rush of being scared within a safe environment, and to be taken away from their daily routine," said Frey, and he's more than happy to provide the experience for patrons. According to Frey, more than 40,000 visitors have walked through since its September 27 opening.

John "Johnny Mischief" Heaukulani, who plays the character of Health Inspector at the Goretorium's fictitious Delmont Hotel & Casino, shares Frey's love for delivering fear. Heaukulani said he experiences a build-up of anticipation and excitement right before he launches into a scare, followed by his own adrenaline rush.

"It gives me joy to see the terrified looks on all their faces," he said.

If the haunt nerd's delight in eliciting screams sounds twisted, it is shared by well-regarded horror creators.

"We scare others for our own enjoyment and for theirs," said R.L. Stine, author of the Goosebumps book series, as well as the adult horror Red Rain and the creator of The Hub network's Haunting Hour children's series.

Stine added he views it as a compliment when people get frightened by his creations - in much the same way it was a compliment when he was terrified in a New York City haunted attraction where he passed through a completely darkened corridor.

He also thinks that the emotional responses evoked by fear and humor are so closely connected that "it's funny" to scare and be scared. As someone who has written more than 110 Goosebumps books, he can relate to the haunt nerds.

Peter Block agrees. Producer of the Saw franchise and president and general manager of FEARnet, Block said he loves to scare other people, and considers it part of his "everyday job" as a dad. He also equates the motivation to scare others to the reasons behind telling a joke.

"There's nothing funnier than watching someone else get scared," he said. And whether you're telling the joke or hearing it, there is a shared relief and release as part of a social experience. He points to *America's Funniest Home Videos* as a similar example where "half the videos are about scaring people."

Stephenson emphasized that giving scares isn't some morbid exercise and that haunt nerds, especially home haunters, are actually quite committed to giving back to their community each

October.

Halloween is a community holiday, he said, and the haunters are inviting a thousand strangers to come through their house or yard on one night to have fun. Likewise, he said the sharing extends to the online community of home haunt nerds, where there is no real sense of competition.

Whether they work as amateurs or professionals, haunt nerds are like most other nerd cultures in that there is a strong desire to collect. But instead of rare issues, replicas, or toys, haunters collect scare stories.

Stephenson relayed the prized story from Victor Bariteau, one of the home haunters from *The American Scream* who has since gone pro with his Ghoulie Manor attraction in Taunton, Massachusetts, Bariteau's giant "Gourdzilla" Pumpkinhead monster scared a grown man so severely he "ran backwards, fell down and did a reverse-backward crab walk all the way down the street."

Meanwhile, Heaukulani, who calls screams the "money shot" of his job, said he had a man who was "roughly 6'8" and had a macho presence" to shriek like "like a little girl."

"That was by far the best moment to date!" he said.

So, although they resemble other nerdy cultures, in the October world of the haunt nerd, tricking people into being afraid is the biggest treat.

Apocalypse Believers' Big Finish Varies

(December 2012)

When the Mayan "Long Count" calendar ends on Friday, December 21, some people predict it could mark the end of the world as we know it. But despite the attention that December 21 is garnering, many apocalyptic believers don't actually give much thought to the hype surrounding the Mayan calendar.

Some doomsday believers pinpointed 2012 as a pretty good

year for disastrous solar flares, giant asteroids, or global pole shifts that could likewise signal the apocalypse. Other theories that may or may not happen this year involve the Rapture, the catastrophic collapse of civilization or even a zombie uprising.

There is diversity among apocalyptic "prepper" groups, and to paint them all with a broad stroke of the crazy brush is to ignore the nuances in what these various groups believe.

John Hall, author of *Apocalypse: From Antiquity to the Empire of Modernity*, said groups organized around 2012 end-of-world predictions - driven by pseudoscientific or numerological predictions - are "more fanciful" than some other doomsday believers. That's because they look toward dramatic external events, as opposed to others that approach theories with a "fair amount of scientific basis," such as the disappearance of natural resources.

Although Hall and his colleagues have spent years trying to define or connect them, the groups can be as hard to explain as their disparate beliefs.

"It's not like a pie of apocalyptic stories that can be divided up so much as it is a story where people coming from many different places can ... express the urgency of the crisis they foresee," Hall said.

For instance, Hall said the survivalists - both those of the fundamentalist religious persuasion and the nonreligious - are looking to opt out of post-apocalyptic strife.

That analysis applies to Dan Martin, a survivalist living off the grid and author of *Apocalypse: How to Survive a Global Crisis*, a book that teaches skills for living a self-sufficient life after what he perceives to be an oncoming collapse of civilization and governments. He said his readers are "normal middle-class" soccer moms and teachers who read about world events and "connect the dots."

"Most of my readers aren't die-hard, end-of-the-world subscribers or enthusiasts," he said. "They don't want things to change but aren't ignorant to the fact that they most likely will within our own lifetime, so preparing for such a strong possibility isn't desperation or ignorance or naivety, it's just another insurance policy."

Insofar as civilization's collapse is something we're bringing upon ourselves with a little help from world powers, Martin and his readers might relate to radical environmentalists or peak oil environmentalists, who subscribe to the theory that there is a date when petroleum production will max out and decline rapidly.

Hall sees a connection between the survivalists and religious rapturists who "look at themselves as missing out on the agonies of the apocalypse because they're going someplace else."

Jerry Jenkins, co-author of the *Left Behind* book series about the Rapture within the Christian Bible's end-of-days Book of Revelation, doesn't completely agree with Hall's assessment.

He said the media has incorrectly portrayed his readers as triumphalists who boast "We're going, you're not, too bad for you." The whole point of the Left Behind books, Jenkins said, was to encourage people to read the Revelation prophecies because religious rapturists want all people to have a better life in heaven.

"[We're not] saying 'good' people go and 'bad' people are left behind," said Jenkins, who believes the key to being raptured (or taken into heaven before the Apocalypse happens on Earth) is to receive Jesus Christ. But Jenkins added that even those "looking forward to being rescued" are still dedicated to improving life for everyone on terra firma before they go.

Interestingly, Jenkins said Christ himself said he didn't even know the day or hour of the Rapture, so the ilk of Christian radio broadcaster Harold Camping who attempt to predict its timing are "crazies" engaged in folly that "make us all look like idiots."

Camping claimed he was able to use the Bible to calculate the exact date of the Rapture (most recently it was supposed to be May 23, 2011, and before that in 1994).

Those who point to science instead of Biblical lore to predict the end of the world are another apocalyptic subculture, according to Hall. These groups are comprised of theoretical physicists and futurologists - such as Michio Kaku - whom Hall calls "optimistic utopian prophets."

These people believe in the Technological Singularity theory: The possibility that technologically augmented intelligence will change human life as we know it or possibly wipe it out completely. There's even a think tank of sorts formed around this logic.

The Singularity Institute is comprised of scientists, philosophers and philanthropists from places such as the Research Triangle and Silicon Valley, and universities such as Harvard and Stanford, said Michael Anissimov, media director at The Singularity Institute.

Their goal? Constructing a smarter-than-human intelligence that has the values of humanity. Instead of avoiding the growth of artificial intelligence, the Singularity Institute is trying to manage the risk.

If peak oil theorists believe we're rapidly running out of a major resource, the institute postulates that technology itself is advancing so rapidly that society will have an overabundance of it - and an artificial intelligence is set to emerge that will not necessarily pursue mankind's best interests.

"We do think it's possible, if not probable, that it could actually lead to either the marginalization or end of humanity," said Anissimov.

Whereas religious and scientific apocalyptic subcultures converge and diverge on various points, there is one end-of-world scenario that manages to reflect all their anxieties: the zombie apocalypse.

The zombocalypse of popular culture has become something of a Rorschach test of apocalyptic fears. Depending on the point of view, zombies may result from an act of God, the irresponsible use of science, an environmental disaster, a cosmic event and so forth.

Scott Kenemore, author of *The Zen of Zombie* and a member of the advisory board of the Zombie Research Society, said the zombie apocalypse can represent a validation of sorts for people awaiting their particular extinction event.

Hall agreed that the pop culture connection of zombies to apocalyptic groups is "a shared motif of a dystopian world emerging." He added that zombies are a stand-in for "The Other," an alien group, process or force that is "almost always" the basis for apocalyptic developments.

Zombies can be a substitute for a corrupt government, an oil-based economy, foreigners or even a Sodom and Gomorrah society itself.

"[H]ow you deal with the threat is an open question," he said.

Whatever the route to the end (or new beginning), Hall thinks the very diversity of subcultures underscores the fact that we have reached an apocalyptic apex.

"In this moment, people are seeing the old ways of life recede," he said. "That's the occasion when all kinds of different people from all kinds of different directions come forward with one or another apocalyptic scenario."

CHAPTER 3

Fit to List

Does the Suit Make the Iron Man, Or Vice- versa?

(May 2010)

As General Thunderbolt Ross pointed out at the end of *The Incredible Hulk*, Tony Stark always wears such nice suits. With the armor wars heating up in this week's Iron Man 2 release, it looks as if Stark will be wearing even more suits as his "Shellhead" alter ego and will even have extras to hand down to friends and foes.

Yet make no mistake, while it's Iron Man who gets top billing, the Golden Avenger is billionaire playboy Tony Stark's alter ego - not the other way around. So, what about the getups of other famous characters? Do the movie men make the suits, or do the suits make the movie men? Here's a breakdown - costumes, outfits and uniforms aside (with apologies to Batman, Harry Potter, and James T. Kirk).

Dr. No

The tux is as much a part of the Bond film series as the vodka martini and Walther PPK, but since his onscreen debut in 1962's *Dr. No*, six different actors have worn the tux with varying success. Bond the man transcends his snazzy threads. After all, even when Sean Connery was wearing a ridiculous terry cloth romper in *Goldfinger* he was the coolest dude in powder blue.

Besides, if you can't look good in a tux, you simply can't look good. Although George Lazenby's frilly cravat in *On Her Majesty's Secret Service* almost unmade Bond, this is a case where *The Man Makes the Suit*.

Star Wars

Before you witness the stranglehold of the Dark Side, or his slice- em/dice-em lightsaber skills, it's Vader's suit that makes the impression in 1977's *Star Wars*. Sure, his chest plate looks like the outdated ATM at the questionable bodega down the block, but at the time, those buttons and lights looked like they had a purpose. Add to that the hissing sound of his breathing, the all-black pleather outfit complete with cape, and the domed head and featureless faceplate that made him look like a robotic Cenobite biker, and you've got one helluva suit. Let's face it, it was a little disappointing when Vader's mask came off to reveal Anakin, a mere, pale California Raisin of a man. Too bad, as well, we saw him pre-cybernetic suit as a pod racing rug rat and obnoxious adolescent in the prequels. Because no one can really believe it's Hayden Christensen under there, this is a case where *The Suit Makes the Man*.

RoboCop

Alex Murphy (Peter Weller) is the police officer resurrected into Old Detroit's cyborg cop, but it's RoboCop who serves the public trust, protects the innocent and upholds the law in the 1987 film. RoboCop possesses Murphy's face, Swiss-cheesed memories, and gunslinging flair (and KITT's "eye" scanner), but the new combined consciousness of the robot and the man exists inside the hulking blue-steel frame only because Murph was a little too vulnerable to bullets. Since he is more tin than man, this is a case where *The Suit Makes the Man*.

Beetlejuice

Michael Keaton may be most famous for his caped crusader costume, but it was as "Betelgeuse," the ghost with the most, when he wore his best suit. The black-and-white striped suit worn by the bio-exorcist in the 1988 movie is an immediately recognizable pop culture set of threads, and he has worn it in a video game, an animated series of the film, and at the Universal Studios theme parks. He apparently loaned the design to Tim Burton's other undead character, Jack Skellington to adapt, but even when he switches to flannel or a violet tuxedo, the Juice is still loose and ready for showtime. Because Beetlejuice's mayhem isn't contingent on his funeral garb, this is a case where *The Man Makes the Suit*.

The Blues Brothers / Reservoir Dogs / Men In Black

Will Smith always well dressed for the role - in this case, a sequel The classic combo of black suit and tie with white shirt and sunglasses is the de facto clothing for a simple, cool look. It's what to wear when on a mission from God, while pulling off a heist, or when policing aliens for secret agencies, as with the characters in these 1980, 1992 and 1997 films. Even though Will Smith's Agent J claims he makes the suit look good, aside from Rod Serling who did the look sans shades, few men have been able to make this suit work when traveling solo - probably since it's also the standard uniform for butlers and servers at fancy restaurants. So this is one is a toss-up: When alone, the suit makes the man, but as a team, this is a case where *The Men Make the Suit.*

Austin Powers

While James Bond shouldn't be caught dead in a lace cravat, an International Man of Mystery can rock it along with crushed velvet. When he first went with the blue suit in the 1997 movie, Austin Danger Powers (Mike Myers) was irreverent, chauvinistic, very cool, and all British swagger. Powers wasn't tied down to just one fashion, and even said, "If it looks groovy, wear it man." Wear it, he did. Even when he shed the suit and was left with a hair sweater-vest chest and gold medallion, he was still all that. While the same cannot be said about his Nehru-loving nemesis who has a one-note wardrobe, when it comes to Powers, this is a case where *The Man Makes the Suit.*

Godzilla

When the King of the Monsters was unleashed on American soil in the 1998 blockbuster flop, he was a giant computer-generated mutated iguana. This iteration of "Gojira" may have been scarier or more in line with modern movie tastes, but the Roland Emmerich-directed Godzilla wasn't dressed right. Instead, the "real" Godzilla that arrived in Japanese cinemas in 1954 and continues to be loved today with his last on-screen outing in 2004, has always been about the rubber monster suit. Sure, there's a man inside the rubber monster suit, but it's easy to forget that since it's the suit that trashes Tokyo and takes on Mothra and does it better in that rubber suit than any CGI- generated character could. Clearly, when it comes to the big "G," this is a case where *The Suit Makes the Man.*

Halloween

The one-piece jumpsuit is apparel for getting dirty and down to business. Whether it's the business of ghost removal or mass murder, however, depends on the wearer. When Venkman and the boys don their grey Ghostbusters jumpsuits, it's a sign of team solidarity and you know they're ready to believe your ghost story - and thus prevent disaster of biblical proportions. When Michael Myers is wearing his workman blues, however, he's traveling solo and painting the town red. Since we see the busters cracking jokes and being likeable characters when they're not wearing their jumpsuits, it's easy to assume they're feeling good even post-bustin' in the 1984 movie. However, the original 1978 Myers from *Halloween* is never really out of his boiler suit, but he'd probably not be the same terrifying hulking force had director John Carpenter shown him hanging out in a parlor wearing a tweed jacket and khakis. The contrast of leisure suit and work suit is everything, so with Myers and the Ghostbusters jumpsuits, this is a case where *The Man Makes the Suit but the Suit Makes the (mad) Man.*

The Man in the White Suit
In the 1951 sci-fi satire *The Man in the White Suit*, Alec Guinness plays a young scientist who invents a glowing white suit made of a resilient fabric that won't absorb dye and can't get dirty. The suit proves to be a bane to the textile industry since the need for replaceable clothing will disappear. After corporations attempt to manipulate Stratton into signing away rights to the fabric, he dons the suit and takes off in style with a new sense of purpose. Like Tony Stark, the man Stratton literally made the suit, but unlike Stark, this is a case where *The Suit Makes the Man.*

How Does One Beat the Heat? Try Descending Into Icy Madness
(July 2010)

The thermometer icon on Web browsers and smartphones are all deep red; wafts of steam float from the very devices. Every 24-hour news outlet is breaking out special graphics featuring melting ice cubes and a flame-throwing, menacing sun. Air conditioners are defiantly fighting against a weakened power grid and temperatures top 100 degrees. Every moment spent outdoors reveals a new batch of previously undiscovered sweaty pores, and it seems like any second now, the collective faces of American people may melt clean off, revealing a grimacing network of bone and muscle.

The heat wave continues, and it's hot out, darn hot.

To cope with the heat wave, advisories are being issued to visit cooling centers, indoor malls, public pools, or my favorite, movie theaters.

However, while those may all be good ideas, there's also the psychological benefit of simply thinking about cold weather, to help one cope with the rising temps. To beat the heat and achieve a chilled-out state of mind, observe this diet of cool pop culture (along with a second-place scoop) that not only features wintry weather, but makes you actually feel like the iceman cometh.

Some Positively Chilling Flicks

The Thing

When it comes to film, there's no shortage of great cold-weather candidates to make you feel positively icy. *Dr. Zhivago, Fargo, The Ice Storm, A Simple Plan, Groundhog Day* and the first act of *The Empire Strikes Back* all feature Old Man Winter prominently. The cold is never more palpable though, as when it's dead scary, which is why John Carpenter's *The Thing* makes for the best wintry cinematic mix to combat the heat. When a team of researchers in Antarctica discover an alien spacecraft - and are then infiltrated by the mimicking parasitic alien - paranoia sets in amongst the humans isolated in the bitter wasteland. The 1982 film still injects ice into the spine with some of the best monster effects in movie history (R.I.P. Stan Winston). After watching this one, and listening to Ennio Morricone's theme music, you'll be running outside into the glaring sunshine, seeking warmth.

Second scoop: The eerie 2008 Swedish vampire flick *Let the Right One In*.

T... T... Text That Will Make You Shiver

The Shining
Although the 1980 film adaptation directed by Stanley Kubrick definitely feels cold with cool blue visuals and imagery of an iced-over hedge maze and a frozen solid Jack Nicholson, it's Stephen King's 1977 novel that truly chills to the bone. For more than 400 pages, readers are treated to the descent into icy madness as loving father and struggling writer Jack Torrance is tormented by the ghosts of the Overlook Hotel (which was based on Colorado's famous Stanley Hotel after King's stay there). With Jack and family, including his psychic-medium son Danny, voluntarily snowed-in at the hotel as winter caretakers, the weather serves as an imposing, forbidding character that prevents escape from the haunted locale. The movie is a classic, but the book is more satisfying; it's a long, frightening read that will distract you from the heat and turn that sweat trickling down your back icy cold.

Second scoop: The White Witch's snowy domain in C.S. Lewis' 1950 book, The Lion, the Witch and the Wardrobe - before the meddling Pevensie kids thaw it out.

Draw the Curtains, Crank Up the Fan (So Long as the Power Holds) and Bask in the Cool Blue of the Boob Tube

The Simpsons: "Mr. Plow" episode
The ninth entry of its fourth season, "Mr. Plow" ranks as perhaps the best *Simpsons* episode. Ever. Chronicling the epic battle between competing snow plowing personas Mr. Plow (Homer) and Plow King (Barney), it also features a creepy/fantastic Adam West cameo (long before *Family Guy* thought it was cool, natch), and a great Linda Ronstadt appearance. Plus, the 1992 episode is bursting with well-known and obscure pop references. Set against a snow-white background (until God gets involved), the show especially cools off the hot mind with a finale set on the frozen Widow's Peak. As the temperatures rise, it's best to chill out with repeated singing of this famous jingle: "Call Mr. Plow, that's my name. That name again is Mr. Plow."

Second scoop: The holiday classic, *The Year Without a Santa Claus* (1974) starring the supernatural snowflake-man, Snow Miser.

Close Your Eyes, Open Your Ears, and Chill

The Beatles Revolver

To channel music to make you feel cold, it's helpful to create a playlist of depressive, somber or lovesick tunes (preferably with piano-driven ballads) that cool the soul. Coldplay's album XY and Modest Mouse's *The Moon and Antarctica* can have that effect, as well as Radiohead's In Rainbows. Despite the heat wave appropriate "I Melt With You," Modern English's album *After The Snow* belongs with most of the music by The Cure, Joy Division, The Smiths and solo Morrissey. Sufjan Steven's "Sister Winter" song fits, and to battle Katy Perry's "California Gurls," include The Magnetic Fields anti-Cali winter anthem "California Girls." Despite certain tracks with an over-the-top sunny disposition ("Yellow Submarine," "Good Day Sunshine"), The Beatles' 1966 masterpiece *Revolver* provides the best soundtrack to combat the heat. It features some reflective, quiet or sad songs-- "Eleanor Rigby", "Here, There and Everywhere", "For No One"-   that make it a solid chilling-out album that doesn't depress.

Second scoops: Vanilla Ice's "Ice, Ice Baby" and Foreigner's "Cold as Ice."

Ice 'em in Shooter Games

Fallout 3.

The third installment of this popular first-person shooter video game series takes place 200 years from now in "retro-futuristic" Washington, D.C. The city lay decimated after a brief nuclear war between the United States, China and other countries. Released in 2008, the game focuses on an inhabitant of an underground fallout shelter who searches the surface world for his missing father. The character must battle mutants and evil humans in a world of decay, not unlike those of *I Am Legend*. While not technically taking place during winter, the gameplay gives you a good, icy scare.

Plus, there's enough action happening to take your mind right off the heat. If it's a post-apocalyptic winter setting you crave in video games, just download the "Operation Anchorage " add-on for *Fallout 3* where the player must re-enact a famous battle with the enemy in Alaska.

Second scoop: The satellite control station levels in Severnaya, Russia, off the coast of Siberia, in one of the coolest games ever, the 1997 first-person shooter James Bond adventure *GoldenEye 007*.

Zombies Vs. Vampires: Celebrity Undead Death Match

(October 2011)

Within pop culture, there are a lot of monsters, ghouls and maniacs out there that want to terrify us. Especially around Halloween, werewolves, demons, ghosts, mummies, maenads, fairies and half-dead men with hockey masks or razor claws make their presence known. But let's face it, these beasts that go bump in the night lack a certain bite.

For the true masters of horror pop, one need look no further than the two reigning champs of chomps, vampires and zombies. More than any other, these creatures capture the imagination and inspire ferocious loyalty. Zombie lovers corpse-up, congregate in flash mobs and hijack constructions signs to read "Caution: Zombies Ahead." Vamp fans wear molded ceramic fangs, make pilgrimages to New Orleans and Transylvania, and drink Tru Blood.

But really, which beast is best? The walking dead or undead? The brain eater or blood sucker? In order to settle the Zombie vs.

Vampire debate, we've collected notable films of both genres from the last 25 years and arranged them in different categories (emphasis on gore) to determine who each might triumph.

Although judgments on winners are completely subjective, I tried to channel George A. Romero and Bela Lugosi for guidance since they were incredibly influential in both genres. Lugosi starred as the Count in the first official version of *Dracula* in 1931; he also gave the world the grandfather of the zombie movies, *White Zombie*, in 1932. Meanwhile, Romero remains the reigning genius of the zombie genre after directing 1968's *Night of the Living Dead*. Romero also contributed heavily to vampires on screen with the underrated deconstruction *Martin* (1978).

Supernatural slayer, man
(Ash vs. Blade)

From the Sam Raimi-directed *Evil Dead* franchise (1981, 1987, 1992), Ashley J. "Ash" Williams (Bruce Campbell) is a wisecracking, S-Mart housewares employee who uses a chainsaw attachment for his missing hand and double-barreled, 12-gauge "boomstick " to fight zombie (ahem, Deadite) hordes. Ash is a good fighter and inventive, but pretty dim-witted. The title character of his own film series (1998, 2002, 2004), *Blade* (Wesley Snipes) is a half-vampire "daywalker" who possesses speed, strength, healing powers and basically all the powers of a vampire - including blood thirst - but none of the weaknesses. He is a martial arts expert, and makes use of glaives, silver stakes, machine guns, anti-coagulant weapons, and an acid-tipped, double-edge sword. Being half-supernatural and completely tough, Blade has the clear advantage and could kick Ash's ash.

Winner: Vampires

Supernatural slayer, woman
(Alice vs. Buffy)

Alice (Milla Jovovich) is a rugged, superhuman zombie-killer in the post-apocalyptic world of the Resident Evil quadrilogy (2002, 2004, 2007, 2010); she combines occasional telepathic and telekinetic powers with martial arts skills, munitions and a curved "kukri" knife to dispatch enemies. Buffy The Vampire Slayer Summers of the 1992 film is a cheerleader - with valley girl slang and wooden stakes. Not to be confused with the TV Sunnydale version, this Buffy was played by Kristy Swanson, and although she eventually saves the day, Alice could have done it in half the time with far more bloodletting.

Winner: Zombies

Rodriguez/ Tarantino Terrors
(*From Dusk Till Dawn* vs. *Grindhouse*)

Filmmakers Quentin Tarantino and Robert Rodriguez have collaborated on six films together, but the most well-known are the duo's work on the 1996 vampire flick *Dawn* (written by and starring Tarantino and directed by Rodriguez) and 2007's double-feature, *Grindhouse*. In the latter, Rodriguez directed the *Planet Terror* zombie segment, which includes Tarantino as zombified "Rapist #1." Both films sport over-the-top action, plenty of bared flesh - as well as gory flesh-eating. *Terror* features a stripper who kills zombies with a prosthetic machine-gun leg, *Dawn* has mutated vampire strippers. The helicopter kill scene almost clinches it for *Terror*, but the fact that a bank-heist flick successful turns into an unapologetic popcorn bloodsucker movie earns *From Dusk Till Dawn* the win.

Winner: Vampires

Classic remakes of classics
(*Bram Stoker's Dracula* vs. Zack Snyder's *Dawn of the Dead*)

The famous Transylvanian Count created by Bram Stoker in 1897 has been portrayed more on film than any other villain. In 1992, Francis Ford Coppola's contributed his take, which was meant to adhere closer to Stoker's tale. The result had some problems (Keanu Reeves' English accent, anyone?) but is so visually arresting that it's one of the great Dracula films. Specifically, Gary Oldman' s portrayal of the Count as both an old and young man stands out, as does Anthony Hopkins as the grizzled Van Helsing.

Meanwhile, Zack Snyder's 2004 remake of George A. Romero's 1978 celebrated zombies-in-mall sequel solidified the transition from the walking dead into the sprinting dead started by 28 Days Later. Snyder's version starts fast and stays fast and gives excellent gore and a pregnant zombie birth. Dawn fares better when viewed less as a remake than as a standalone zombie flick. Because the first 20 minutes borders on brilliance and the ending is so open-ended, Snyder narrowly snatches victory from the dude that gave us The Godfather.

Winner: Zombies

Man-made monsters
(*28 Days Later* vs. *I Am Legend*)

Before he was the Oscar-winning director of *Slumdog Millionaire*, Danny Boyle was the man who popularized the fast-moving zombie in *28 Days Later* (2002). Along with the first *Resident Evil*, the film helped change movie zombies from reanimated corpses to humans infected with a virus. As soon as the character of Jim (Cillian Murphy) wakes from a coma to find London decimated, the film is an unsettling and unrelenting drama that helped redefine the zombie genre - and make it cool again. With its eerie scenes of an abandoned Manhattan, *I Am Legend* is the 2007 Will Smith film about primitive viral vampires and a scientist who may be the last living human. *Legend* could have been great if it remained focused on Smith's character surviving and combating loneliness, but the CGI virals look cheesy and the film flounders when more humans arrive.

Winner: Zombies

Scary Scandinavia
(*Let The Right One In* vs. *Dead Snow*)

Whether it's Sweden or Norway, Scandinavia is home to cold, quick corpses. In the 2008 film *Let the Right One In*, a 12-year-old borderline sociopathic, bullied boy befriends a vampire who appears to be a young girl. The vampire scenes are violent and scary in the cold environs, but the relationship between the two outcasts shines. The film frightens the most when things are quietest. Meanwhile, the 2009 Norwegian film *Dead Snow* about Nazi Zombies is successful because it's so loud, unsubtle, and schlocky. In the grand old tradition of horror movies, college students go to a remote cabin and battle monsters - this time they happen to be walking dead Nazis. Although it's an excellent addition to the zombie genre, Let the Right One In is an excellent film. Period.

Winner: Vampires

Forget the future
(*Land of the Dead* vs. *Daybreakers*)

When it comes to vampire and zombie movies, the future looks pretty bleak. In the 2005 George A. Romero film *Land of the*

Dead, it's the "not too distant future" and humans are outnumbered by zombies and forced to live in an extremely gated community called Fiddler's Green. The rich live inside a modern skyscraper, the poor must fend on the street, and the zombies outside are becoming self-aware and evolving. In the equally bleak 2010 film *Daybreakers*, vampires outnumber humans in the near future, and blood supplies are running low. Ethan Hawke plays a vampire scientist trying to create synthetic blood while the remaining humans are hunted and harvested in blood banks. *Daybreakers* possesses a nifty concept with futuristic aesthetics similar to The Matrix, but it never captures the attention like *Land of the Dead*. In *Land*, Romero returned to form in a big-budget way and the audience is actually inspired when the dead begin to use tools and decide to work together.

Winner: Zombies

Postmodern monster mash
(*Shaun of the Dead* vs. *Fright Night*)
The postmodern zombie/vampire movie is one where characters encounter monsters as real and proceed to draw on their pop-culture experience to dispatch of them. As such, the 2004 zombie homage (zom-mage?) *Shaun of the Dead* stars Simon Pegg and Nick Frost as low-wage and no-wage worker bees who lead friends through an undead uprising by drawing from the world of George A. Romero and *28 Days Later*. Although the movie is comedic, it treats the creatures as serious threats and actually stands out as one of the best modern zombie films (with the slow- moving variety at that). The 1985 comedy-horror *Fright Night* revolves around Charley, a horror-movie obsessed teen who tries to enlist an aging actor from vampire movies (Roddy McDowell with spray-painted gray hair) to dispatch of a "real" bloodsucker living next door, played by Chris Sarandon. The pair apply all they've learned from vamp movies to destroy the undead. Even though *Fright Night* was successful at the time, it's more cheesetastic than scare-rific compared to *Shaun*.

Winner: Zombies

The Most Evil Books Known To Nerdkind

(April 2012)

Print isn't dead, but it can be deadly.

Within popular culture, there exist guides with the express purpose of wreaking havoc and unleashing hell on humanity. While the Kindle, iPad and Nook might have a killer effect on the book industry, these are books that are very industrious at killing.

For instance, in the supernatural comedy series *Todd and the Book of Pure Evil* - now in its second season on cable horror network FEARnet - a group of teens at the Satanist-controlled Crowley High battle the forces of a mysterious tome that grants wishes with sinister twists.

After witnessing the dark powers of the book and the control it holds over the weak and needy, metal head Todd (Alex House), Jimmy the Janitor (Jason Mewes of *Jay and Silent Bob Strike Back*) and a gang of high schoolers become determined to end the *Pure Evil* plague. The result is a series that has the charm and wit of *Buffy the Vampire Slayer*, but with more of a raunchy, at- times awkward humor that appeals to die-hard horror nerds.

But *Book of Pure Evil* is far from the only one that sits in the devil's stacks. Therefore, what follows is a list of the most harmful books of verisimilitude within pop culture that contain information not to be checked out. After all, while reading is fundamental, it can also be fundamentally dangerous.

Necronomicon

A creation of horror writer H.P. Lovecraft, the *Necronomicon* is a book of spells that first appeared in the 1924 short story, "The Hound." Purportedly written by the "Mad Arab" Abdul Alhazred, it appears in various forms in Lovecraft's work, but is typically leather-bound with clasps. (Descriptions of it as being bound in human skin are likely confused with a separate portfolio described in the same short story.) An unabridged version exists at the fictional Miskatonic University.

Lovecraft's *Necronomicon* is perhaps the most famously evil book that inspires entertainment. Many "real" versions of it have been published, including the controversial "Simon" version in 1977 that was accused of inspiring a cult murder.

The Hitchhiker's Guide to the Galaxy
Although this electronic repository for all knowledge and wisdom suggests to any reader "Don't Panic" in "large, friendly letters," there is indeed a good deal of reasons to panic if you consult it.

Introduced in author Douglas Adams' sci-fi comedy series of the same name in 1978, "The Guide" is riddled with devastating typos, errors and gross understatements. To rely on it is to ensure destruction since most of the editing staff remain on permanent lunch break - even though its advice on towels has proved helpful. Published by Megadodo Publications, "The Guide" itself has a sarcastic tone and looks like a small, thin, flexible laptop computer within a sturdy plastic cover.

Naturan Demanto/ Book of the Dead
A cabin in the Tennessee woods is not normally where you may expect to find an ancient Sumerian text with resurrection spells, but so it goes in the 1981 horror *The Evil Dead*, starring Bruce Campbell and directed by Sam Raimi. When Campbell's crew of twenty-something friends vacation at the cabin, discover the book, and accidentally play an audiotape incantation, demons spring forth to cause trouble and kill them off.

While the sequel *Evil Dead II* and *Army of Darkness* were comedy-tinged sequels that referred to the book as the fictional *Necronomicon Ex-Mortis, the Book of the Dead* was a real Egyptian collection of funereal rites to facilitate a person's journey into the afterlife and popped up as a magical text in other films, such as 1999's *The Mummy*. There is also a Tibetan *Book of the Dead*.

To Serve Man Kanamit cookbook
The danger of *To Serve Man* - from the 1962 *The Twilight Zone* episode of the same name - lies in shoddy, incomplete translation. When the alien race of the Kanamits land on Earth, they do the human race a solid by transforming deserts into oases, ending

world hunger, providing cheap energy and eliminating nuclear weapons.

But when one of the Kanamit race leaves behind his plain black, space-leather bound book at the United Nations, a group of US cryptographers working to decipher the alien language (and apparently the only ones in the world doing so) give up after decoding the title of the alien book: *To Serve Man*.

It is only after much of the human race is zipping off to the Kanamit home world "paradise" that one lone decoder figures out the book is actually a cookbook that reduces humans into "an ingredient in someone's soup."

The Grimoire

Appearing in the 1998-2006 supernatural soap *Charmed* on The WB, *The Grimoire* is a compendium of evil magic and information. *The Grimoire*, which is actually a name applied to textbooks of magic, provides a counterbalance to *The Book of Shadows* used by good witch heroines, the Halliwell sisters. A brown book emblazoned with a skull and upside-down pentagram, *The Grimoire* is a destructive force that can reject the powers of white magic. Even though The CW, the network that replaced The WB, featured grimoires on its current soaps *The Vampire Diaries* and *The Secret Circle*, neither have quite developed the same punch as *The Grimoire* or *The Book of Shadows*.

Book of Vishanti / Eternity Book

Within the comic book world, the *Book of Vishanti* and *Eternity Book* essentially both operate as the same source of magic. Within the Marvel Comics universe, the *Book of Vishanti* is a golden collection of white magical source currently owned by *Doctor Strange* that appeared in 1964 in *Strange Tales*. It was dictated to human magicians by the magical collective of the Vishanti and has been possessed by Atlanteans and Babylonian gods. The good spells can backfire with dangerous, even evil, results.

Meanwhile, the *Eternity Book* exists within the DC Comics universe and contains the secrets of existence.

Seen first *in The Demon* in 1972, it is depicted as red with gold clasps and a red seal and is the personal spell book that once belonged to Merlin. To use it is to know the history of the universe and to gain immense magical powers.

Grays Sports Almanac
Seemingly innocuous while on sale at the Blast from the Past antique store in 2015, the *Grays Sports Almanac: Complete Sports Statistics 1950-2000* was used to upset the balance of the entire space-time continuum. Introduced in the 1989 film *Back to the Future Part II*, the softcover, red almanac contained 50 years' worth of results from football, baseball, boxing, horse racing and more. Used by a time traveler motivated by greed, the almanac can be the key to fame and immense fortune, but also creates a dark alternate timeline. Grays had been publishing sports almanacs since 1923, the 1950-2000 volume was the first to alter reality.

Vampires Are Undead and We're Loving it: An Ultimate List of Pop's Best Bloodsuckers

(June 2012, with Larissa Mrykalo)

Although there have been predictions they'd return to ground for a while now - perhaps so the undead could make room for the walking dead zombies - vampires have yet to be staked by pop culture Van Helsings. In fact, the trend shows signs of immortality, and more vamp-related projects are seeing the light of day every year without turning to ash.

Just this summer, the bloodsuckers have hypnotized us with *Dark Shadows*, a fifth season of *True Blood* and *Abraham Lincoln: Vampire Hunter*. Even the trailer for *The Twilight Saga: Breaking Dawn - Part 2* captivated the Internet when it was released this week. To celebrate the continuing trend of vampires as they dominate the season of sun, Paranormal Pop Culture vampette nerd Larissa Mrykalo set about creating an ultimate list of the undead. Because we want you to have a stake in what we do here, let us know what you think we got wrong, what we missed and what categories need to be added.

BEST DRACULAS

Max Schreck
Nosferatu (1922)
We know his name is Count Orlok and not officially "Dracula" in this movie, but it is based on the popular Bram Stoker novel. The studio wasn't able to obtain the rights so the names were changed. Nevertheless, Count Orlok is one of the creepiest vampires in the history of film.

Bela Lugosi
Dracula (1931)
Lugosi's portrayal of Count Dracula is arguably the most recognized and duplicated. The hair, the accent, the hypnotic eyes are all super iconic. He was a vamp ahead of his time.

Frank Langella
Dracula (1979)
This was probably the Dracula a lot of our moms had a crush on. Super sexy and handsome, Langella made women in the late '70s wish they were one of his victims.

Gary Oldman
Bram Stoker's Dracula (1992)
Francis Ford Coppola's interpretation of the novel and the Count himself is a fan favorite. Great cast, excellent storytelling, and visually stunning, as well as gruesome scenes, make us want to watch it over and over. Oldman is haunting, sad and terrifying.

SEXIEST WOMEN

Countess (Lauren Hutton)
Once Bitten (1985)
Sexually charged and in need of virgin blood, Hutton's performance left teenage boys in the '80s probably more confused than they already were. Hutton was 42 when she made this film. 'Nuff said.

Santanico Pandemonium (Salma Hayek)
From Dusk Till Dawn (1996)
Long name, long snake, sexy dance. A short but memorable scene with this Queen Vampire showed what a stand-out the stunningly beautiful Hayek really was.

Selene (Kate Beckinsale)
Underworld series (2003, 2006, 2009, 2012)
A gorgeous brunette with piercing eyes wearing a leather bodysuit who could kick ass? Yes, please! Beckinsale rocks this role as an icy cool vampire you'd never want to mess with.

Jessica Hamby (Deborah Ann Woll)
True Blood (2008-present)
Jessica starts off as an unwilling, Christian virgin who gradually emerges as the fiery hot redheaded vamp we know today. She's loyal, she's fun and looks great dressed as a naughty Red Riding Hood!

SEXIEST MEN

Eric Northman (Alexander Skarsgard)
True Blood (2008-present)
Eric may be over a thousand years-old but he's one hunky bad-boy vamp. Yes, he's arrogant but he occasionally shows that sweet side (and those abs) that makes women weak in the knees.

Damon Salvatore (Ian Somerhalder)
The Vampire Diaries (2009-present)
Uncomfortably gorgeous, dangerous, adventurous and, well, a tad evil describes this TV blood sucker with brother issues that the ladies swoon over. What it is about these bad boys?

Aidan McCollin/Waite (Sam Witwer)
Being Human (2011-present)
There's something vulnerable about recovering (and lapsed) blood addict Aidan, and even though he's a seasoned vamp, he's kind of sweet and sarcastic, and makes you want to offer up a vein

to him. His dark good looks don't hurt either.

Jerry Dandrige (Colin Farrell)
Fright Night (2011)
Charming, down and dirty, devious, handsome - sure, come on
into my home! Chris Sarandon was pretty hot as Dandrige in the
1985 original, but Colin has added a more modern dimension of
sexuality to the role.

KID FRIENDLIEST

Sam Dracula a.k.a. Grandpa Munster (Al Lewis)
The Munsters (1964-1966)
Grandpa Munster is wily, deathly sarcastic, picks on his poor
son- in-law, and likes to invent things in his basement - sounds like
a lot of our grandpas, right? But can yours shape shift into a bat?
Probably not ... that you know of.

Count Von Count (himself)
Sesame Street (first appeared in 1972)
Even the bats and thunder that accompany this lovable Muppet
make him a non-threatening and iconic teacher of numbers for the
past 40 years. Fun fact: Old folklore spoke of vamps being
obsessed with counting things. Ah ah ah!

Bunnicula Bunnicula: A Rabbit Tale of Mystery
(book debuted in 1979)
The original juicer machine, Bunnicula is a harmless, fanged
little bunny rabbit who uses sucks the juice out of veggies. He also
has vampire powers as shown in the TV special, including the
ability to hypnotize, sprout wings and fly. Adorable!

Rudolph (Rollo Weeks)
The Little Vampire (2000)
What lonely, newly transplanted kid doesn't want a best friend
who is a cool vampire like Rudolph? This family movie is a fun
adventure that proves vamps can have your back instead of just
your neck.

MOST EVIL

David (Kiefer Sutherland)
The Lost Boys (1987)
Sutherland had a knack for playing jerks in the '80s and David is one hell of a bully. He's the leader of a blood thirsty, California-based vampire gang that makes psychopaths look like saints.

Claudia (Kirsten Dunst)
Interview with the Vampire (1994)
Precocious angelic children have a strange creepiness to them, especially when they have no qualms about killing you or their "maker." Dunst was a fantastic child actor and made Claudia's evil soul evident in tandem with making us feel just a tad sorry for her character.

Queen Akasha (Aaliyah)
Queen of the Damned (2002)
Sure, this centuries-old Egyptian vampire queen is sexy and beautiful, but her megalomania and icy cold soul demands world domination. She'll stop at nothing to get it but is finally turned to dust by the vampires she has spared.

Russell Edgington (Denis O'Hare)
True Blood (2008-present)
Russell is crazy, super old (2,800 years!), multilingual and one evil king who chews scenery like it's human flesh! He's fun to watch though, so True Blood fans are no doubt excited to see that his cement and silver grave didn't cause him the true death.

MOST GROTESQUE

Kurt Barlow (Reggie Nalder)
Salem's Lot (1979)
Nalder's portrayal of Kurt Barlow mimics that of an amped-up Nosferatu - bald, glowing yellow eyes and beyond horrid teeth. This terrifying make-up produces a look that's the stuff of nightmares.

Peter Loew (Nicolas Cage)
Vampire's Kiss (1989)
Loew is a yuppie (ewww) who gradually goes insane - and even eats a cockroach (which real-life vamp Cage actually did on camera) in this super dark '80s comedy/horror film. We get to watch his decline and the behaviors that are associated with it, until his death at the end.

Marlowe (Danny Huston)
30 Days of Night (2007)
30 Days of Night features some truly horrifying creatures, with their pin-sharp teeth, black eyes and relentless bloodlust. Huston's interpretation of the hideous and excruciatingly evil leader, Marlowe, makes this one of the most terrifying vampire films ever.

Eli (Lina Leandersson)
Let the Right One In (2008)
An odd, little girl vamp who requires an adult familiar to help her dispose of bodies, Eli is pretty gross when she goes too long between feedings or if she enters a home uninvited. But despite being kind of grody, she's a good friend to bullied kids.

BEST HAIR

Count Chocula
General Mills' Count Chocula cereal (debuted 1971)
Silly, we know, but this sweet Count's hair is deliciously styled and puts all other cereal mascots to shame.

Lestat de Lioncourt (Tom Cruise)
Interview with the Vampire (1994)
Those perfect waves, that lustrous shine, the lovely shade of reddish-brown. How many ladies took a pic of Lestat into their stylist in the mid-90s and asked for this look? Damn him for all eternity for making it look so effortless!

Spike (James Marsters)
Buffy the Vampire Slayer, and Angel (1997 to 2003)
Bleached-out fabulousness best describes Spike the Slayer Slayer' s hairstyle. Vampires with an edge are super cool but the dark eyebrows give away his secret!

Angel (David Boreanaz)
Angel (1999-2004)
Angel may suffer because he has a soul, but at least he has a thick, trendy, head of hair to make up for this punishment. It's the kind of hair you want to sink your fingers into!

MOST ROMANTIC

Count Dracula (various actors)
Dracula
The Count's heartbreaking love for his deceased wife, Elisabeta - and subsequent obsession with her lookalike, Mina - is probably most romantically depicted in Coppola's film version. But most incarnations of the Count show him as a hopeless mush. His love and sadness are painfully evident, and we even feel sorry for this "monster."

"Do you believe in destiny? That even the powers of time can be altered for a single purpose? That the luckiest man who walks on this earth is the one who finds ... true love?"

Barnabas Collins (Jonathan Frid)
Dark Shadows (1967-71)
Even though he does okay with the ladies, he's forever obsessed with former fiancée, Josette. He also manages to put an old-old-school romantic swagger into his sometimes-awkward demeanor.

"A man should be willing to wait for a beautiful woman through all eternity if necessary."

Bill Compton (Stephen Moyer)
True Blood (2008-present)
Bill's long-suffering, undying love and commitment to Sookie Stackhouse (Anna Paquin), and even the backstory around the wife and children that he left behind, make this southern gent majorly

swoon worthy.

"Vampires are always in some kind of trouble. I prefer to be in it with you."

Edward Cullen (Robert Pattinson)
The Twilight Saga (2008-present)
Ahh, Edward, every teenage girl's dream vamp (as well as some middle-aged women's). The 111-year-old man-boy-vamp always knows the right thing to say and will fight until the end for the love of his life, Bella.

"I thought I'd explained it clearly before. Bella, I can't live in a world where you don't exist."

BEST MALE SLAYERS

Peter Vincent (Roddy McDowell)
Fright Night (1985)
Late-night horror movie host, Peter Vincent, is a reluctant vampire hunter to say the least. He is a B-list boss who knows all the traditional tricks of the trade and ultimately saves his young friends from certain doom.

Blade (Wesley Snipes)
Blade series (1998/2002/2004)
Even though he is a half-vampire Daywalker, Blade is a gruff protector of humans from the vampire threat (and raves).

Originally based on the Marvel Comics character, he's a superhero who doesn't have the weaknesses of a traditional vampire and this makes him extra badass.

Van Helsing (Hugh Jackman)
Van Helsing (2004)
This vampire hunter has been played by several actors and first appeared as Abraham Van Helsing in Stoker's 1897 novel.

Jackman's Gabriel Van Helsing is a sexier, kick-ass version working for the Vatican with some nifty gadgets in tow.

Abe Lincoln
Abraham Lincoln, Vampire Hunter (2010 novel)

If your mother was murdered by a vampire, what would you do? Dedicate your life to secretly hunting and slaying vampires, of course! And then become the 16th president of the United States to eliminate a bloodsucker plot to use slaves as food.

BEST FEMALE SLAYERS

Anita Blake
Anita Blake, Vampire Hunter (book series, 1993- present)

Based on the 21-book-strong series by Laurell K. Hamilton, Blake is a St. Louis-based necromancer - a raiser and controller of the dead - and licensed hunter of homicidal vampires. She's a no-nonsense martial arts expert who knows her weapons and has the skills to put vampires in their place.

Buffy Summers (Sarah Michelle-Gellar)
Buffy the Vampire Slayer (1997-2003)

Even though she begins as a beautiful and stereotypical cheerleader, Buffy Summers is "The Chosen One" in the fight against the evil undead. Over the course of seven seasons (and even more in the Dark Horse comics), Buffy evolves into a tough icon with depth. The show featured other sexy female slayers - Justine Cooper, Vi, Amanda, Dana, Kendra, and Faith Lehane - but Buffy is the sexy, kick-ass original.

Anna Valerious (Kate Beckinsale)
Van Helsing (2004)

This family-oriented gypsy and vampire hunter is out for revenge against Dracula after he kills her father. She wants to fight for herself and doesn't want Van Helsing's help. Even in death, she gets revenge; she and her family are accepted into Heaven.

Rayne
Blood.Rayne (video game series, 2003-present)

This video game huntress works for a league of vampire killers called the Brimstone Society, despite herself being a half-vampire

"Dhampir." Redheaded and impossibly sexy, Rayne's mission is to discover the identity of her father - who she ultimately kills along with her other vamp-siblings. She's pretty obviously a ruthless, bloodthirsty killer, which is how we like her.

Pop Culture's (And Humanity's) Best Leaders in An Alien Invasion
(June 2012, with Larissa Mrykalo)

Don't panic but our planet is in dire need of saving - from alien invaders. At least, that's if the impending summer blockbuster movie season is any indication.

The immensely successful superhero supergroup movie The Avengers, directed by Buffyverse maestro Joss Whedon, was not only the beginning of the 2012 summer movie season, but it also signaled the potential end of Earth unless a super-powered resistance can fight off godlike aliens. Then Peter Berg's Battleship - an alien invasion flick based off the board game and starring Liam Neeson - came ashore on May 18. Memorial Day weekend unleashed Barry Sonnenfeld's Men In Black III with Will Smith before Ridley Scott's Alien-esque prequel Prometheus opened up on June 8. The fallout of the alien invasion on Falling Skies is particularly nitty-gritty: The post-apocalyptic world of the 2nd Massachusetts human resistance regiment returned to the airwaves this month with the show's second season.

So, what does all this potential destruction of humanity mean?

Well, we humans certainly love to watch films and television shows where our lives and planet are put in danger, but the appeal goes deeper than that. Audiences can deal with humankind on the verge of an extinction event as long as there are a few good men and women willing to put up a fight to the finish. We love to watch a kick-ass leader emerge even if his efforts don't ultimately stop an invasion. To borrow from Bonnie Tyler, we need a hero who's got to be strong, sure and larger than life—and being smart and funny also helps to cope with the stress of saving the planet and inevitable whining of weaker characters.

With those characteristics in mind, we give you Paranormal Pop Culture's best human resistance leaders to face off against otherworldly threats.

Dr. Miles Bennell (Kevin McCarthy) from *Invasion of the Body Snatchers (1956)*

It is a sure bet most fans of science fiction have seen this classic film or one of its remakes/variations. The original begins with Dr. Miles Bennell in the hospital after he was found ranting and paranoid in the highway. He relays the tale (to a psychiatrist) of what has been happening to everyone around him: Alien plants are replacing everyone with doppelganger pod people devoid of any personality. Bennell is determined to warn everyone but like in many invasion films, no one believes him at first. He's certainly an intelligent man who selflessly goes on a mission to save us all from doom - but he's also a bit nuts. Luckily, he's eventually believed when the doctors at the hospital see the results of the pods for themselves. The authorities are alerted, so everything will be okay, right? Right? The invasion would have been discovered eventually, but Bennell demonstrates qualities of an admirable leader. However, he could've used a sense of humor and some Xanax.

Steve Andrews (Steve McQueen) from *The Blob* (1958)

This classic film (remade in 1988) depicts more of an accidental vs. deliberate alien invasion. An amorphous alien lands, compliments of a meteorite, in Phoenixville, Pennsylvania. He (if blobs have genders) likes to dissolve and consume the unsuspecting townsfolk. And let's face it, the bigger the Blob, the more difficult it will be to destroy. In Steve McQueen's film debut, he's local teen Steve Andrews. Right away, he selflessly interrupts a hot date to take the Blob's first victim to the local doctor. (Warning: never poke at a gelatinous substance that falls from space.) Serious Steve starts to discover that strange things are afoot in his town and rounds up his buds to help warn the skeptical adults. That's great that he has the confidence and organizational skills as a leader, but he is also not thinking through that his pals may get dissolved. Steve remains tenacious and eventually discovers, when hiding in a store's refrigerated area, that the Blob hates the cold. This knowledge ultimately results in the Blob's demise from CO_2. Or does it?

Ripley (Sigourney Weaver) from *Alien* (1979)

While Alien is not technically about an Earth invasion, it surely would have been without the bravery and quick-thinking of one of the strongest women leads in the history of science fiction.

Ripley is a member of the 7-member crew of the Spaceship Nostromo, and during its return to Earth after a mining mission, it picks up a distress signal from an abandoned ship on a nearby planet. They check it out and things go downhill during the investigation and after a "face-off." Oh hey, and they end up bringing a parasite back onto their ship. Hilarity then ensues!

Well, not really, since everyone - including the corporate stooge android (Ian Holm) - ends up dying horribly except for Ripley. She is scared out of her mind but her will to survive (while looking hot in her undies!) is inspiring. In the closing scene, the terror on her face shows her vulnerability but heroes are allowed to be afraid. Ripley's determination to survive and kill the alien result in its demise outside of the craft and prevents it from reaching our planet via the Nostromo. She then takes a long, much deserved, nap.

R.J. MacReady (Kurt Russell) from *John Carpenter's The Thing* (1982)

This gory and "chilling" remake of the 1951's The Thing From Another Planet is more accurately based on a short story by John W. Campbell called "Who Goes There?" A group of scientists are in the Antarctic and one-by-one, their bodies are violently invaded by an unknown organism. MacReady is a loner helicopter pilot who enjoys his whiskey. While having a vice can be a hero trait, a loner doesn't typically have a lot of philanthropic intentions. But his suspicious nature and speculation about the nature of the alien's intentions keeps him alive and determined to destroy the alien. Clearly an intelligent leader, he figures out this particular organism has a defense mechanism that kicks in when threatened. MacReady's initial motivation is his own survival, but when he discovers the alien's horrific nature, he knows it's in humanity's best interest to kill it. The camp is ultimately destroyed by fire - and MacReady survives with one other, but suspects their time is limited.

Elliott (Henry Thomas) from E.T.: The Extra- Terrestrial (1982)

This 30-year-old blockbuster by Steven Spielberg turned on our heart lights when an extra-terrestrial - who was helping his fellow aliens collect samples of our plant life - was left behind on our giant marble when G-men spooked his spaceship driver. The confused E.T. makes his way to the home of a needy little 10-year-old boy. Elliott is an unlikely leader, but we find him to be intelligent; he has geeky toys and is selfless in that he sacrifices his Reese's Pieces to lure the alien into his home. He is also funny, especially when he refers to his jerky brother as "penis breath." Elliott is also brave to take in an unknown being. This bravery, however, jeopardizes his family's lives and potentially the lives of all of mankind. (After all, why were the aliens stealing our plants? What was their intention? Plus, don't you just love how E.T. captures not only Elliott's heart, but the hearts of those around him?) The psychic connection between Elliott and E.T. did reveal the alien's vulnerabilities at the risk of the boy's own life. But hey, maybe being a sweetheart to the alien was an elaborate scheme on the part of Elliott to disarm the long-necked buggers. Eventually, Elliott secured E.T.'s return to his people which led to them leaving our plants, and planet, alone. Thank you, Elliott, for your courage and ingenious plan to capture and mind-bend this creature with your employment of the Stockholm Syndrome.

Juliet Parrish (Faye Grant) from V (original miniseries 1983)

The 1983 two-part miniseries about reptilian aliens who want to deplete our resources and consume us spawned a second miniseries in 1984 (V: The Final Battle) and a television series that same year (V). A remake of the original series also aired for two seasons in 2009-11. The Visitors were friendly and even helpful at first, but their true nature was soon discovered. A resistance eventually formed to fight the Visitors and regain our planet. Fourth year med student and researcher, Juliet Parrish leads the group in Los Angeles, California. Her initial lack of confidence and modesty makes being called a leader difficult for her, but her courage and ability to organize resistance raids, earns her the title. She ultimately aids in discovering Red Dust, a bacterium that is used as a deadly weapon against the Visitors. Girl Power!

John Nada (Roddy Piper) from *They Live* (1988)

As if aliens who want to control our world aren't bad enough, this breed disguises themselves as upper-class a-holes and politicians. Our fearless leader in this film is drifter John Nada, who discovers these rad sunglasses that reveal the aliens and their true intentions. He is also savvy enough to discover they're controlling us through subliminal messages sent through our media. He's not as dumb as he looks and better yet, he's hilarious! One of the most quotable lines from a science fiction/horror movie comes from his lips: "I have come here to chew bubble gum and kick ass ... and I'm all out of bubblegum." Not only does he have a wicked sense of humor and good detective skills, he bravely takes one for the team (a.k.a. the humans of Earth) in the end but only after he destroys the mind- controlling broadcasting antenna.

Captain Steven Hiller (Will Smith) from *Independence Day* (1996)

The plot of this movie is pretty simple: An alien mothership sends its little baby ships out there to help take over our planet. Captain Steven Hiller, USMC, turns on the "hell, no!" and springs into action, ultimately aiding in implanting a computer virus and detonating a nuclear device in the mothership. He does display obvious intelligence with his problem solving, and selflessness and bravery in risking his life - but he also has a hot girlfriend and her son to protect. His sense of humor rocks this movie and helps break up the heaviness of the planet's certain doom. He is confident but possibly to a fault that mutates into cockiness and recklessness, which potentially puts his comrades in danger.

Tom Jones! ... and Richie Norris (Lukas Haas) and Byron Williams (Jim Brown) from *Mars Attacks*! (1996)

The title of the absurd comedy based on the '60s trading card series sums up the premise. Freaky looking Martians come to our planet "in peace," which apparently means taking over and shooting us with disintegrating ray guns. Pretty ominous for creatures that sound like ducks and are perverts. There are a few characters in this Tim Burton cult classic that seem like obvious leaders, like say, President Jack Nicholson or "Chairman of the American Academy of Astronomies", Professor Pierce Brosnan.

Even TV reporter Michael J. Fox seems a likely leader, but they're all too obvious and fail miserably. The true leaders of the human resistance is an employee of a Kansas donut shop; a retired boxer dressed as an Egyptian pharaoh working in Vegas; and eternally sexy crooner, Tom Jones. Richie Norris is your average teenager who loves his grandma. He risks his life to save her during a deadly attack and serendipitously discovers that the Martian's main weakness is the vocal stylings of Slim Whitman. He pretty much saves the planet because of his courage and selflessness. Byron Williams is a determined and humble family man who puts his life on the line by boxing the Martians so that Tom Jones could fly (of course Tom Jones knows how to fly a plane) a small group of survivors to a cave in Tahoe. In the end, the alien's heads turn into the slime that is used for the Nickelodeon Kid's Choice Awards and Richie and his grandma receive the Congressional Medal of Honor from First Daughter Natalie Portman. Byron returns to his ex-wife and two sons in D.C. and Tom puts on a concert for the forest animals with new squeeze, Annette Bening.

Captain Jack Harkness (John Barrowman) from *Torchwood* (premiered 2006)

Brits enjoy their science fiction just as much as we do and this *Doctor Who* spin-off TV series is the perfect example. Torchwood is about a team of alien chasers, led by Captain Jack Harkness and based out of the Torchwood Institute in Cardiff, Wales.

Captain Jack was first introduced to us in the *Doctor Who* episode "The Empty Child." Like the Doctor, he is a time traveler. He is also a former conman who happens to be immortal. As the first bisexual character in the *Doctor Who* series, he has become a positive role-model for British gay and bisexual youth. Jack is a tortured soul who has experienced great loss, but these traits make him a brave and strong leader in combating the alien threats and monitoring a spacetime rift running through Cardiff. He is a cunning problem-solver not afraid to take action where needed, even when there is great risk.

Tom Mason (Noah Wyle) from *Falling Skies* (premiered June 19, 2011)

This Steven Spielberg-produced science fiction television series takes the viewer six months into the aftermath of an alien invasion that not only has wiped out the Earth's power grid and technology, but also the majority of life. The invading "Skitters" are insect-like creatures who kidnap the youth to "harness" and control as slaves. Tom Mason is a Boston University history professor who is an integral part of a group of invasion survivors known as the Second Massachusetts. His confidence and knowledge of historical militia tactics helps him lead in the resistance, but his main goal is to protect his growing sons - and at one point even re-capture his kidnapped son Ben (Connor Jessup). Not much of a sense of humor emanates from Professor Tom but hey, can you blame him? He displays some deep anger towards the cocky aliens (obviously), but he does show key characteristics of bravery when he boards an alien ship to learn more about the uber-aliens controlling the show.

It's A Paranormal Christmas

(December 2012)

Move over, Halloween, because with all its ghosts, goblins, sorcery, and cryptids, Christmas is the ultimate supernatural season. Belief is mainstream at Christmastime, when skepticism is considered crass, and the ambient magic of the season can infect even diehard humbugs. Religious observances aside, these are the best paranormal phenomena from folklore and pop culture that stuff our stockings each December.

Santa Claus aka Father Christmas, Saint Nicholas, Sinterklaas and Kris Kringle

This immortal elfin being has the power to manipulate time and space and leads a cadre of other elf minions who watch children and visit them while they sleep. An amalgam of the 4th-century Greek Christian Saint Nicholas of Myra and the Norse god Odin, Santa is a jolly home invader who can slip down chimneys to give gifts to the "nice." Claus' existence is supported by the North American Aerospace Defense Command (NORAD), which has tracked his journey on radar since 1955.

Krampus
A companion of Santa's, the Krampus is a hairy goat-like demon with horns and cloven hooves who punishes the "naughty" children. Emerging from pre-Christian Germanic folklore, he is sort of an anti-Claus that carries chains, sticks, or whips to beat children with, and he may dish out coal, depending on the culture. But if he's in a bad mood, he'll stuff children in his sack or bathtub, and carry them to hell for cooking. Krampus night is typically celebrated December 5 in Europe, where people celebrate by dressing as the beast and roam the streets drinking schnapps.

North Pole
Based on late 19th-century contributions by cartoonist Thomas Nast and poet George P. Webster - and seemingly supported by the NORAD Santa Tracker - we believe Claus lives on a hidden landmass in the icy waters of the Terrestrial North Pole in the Arctic Ocean. Sort of like Atlantis, but with a toy workshop, the North Pole is also home to the icy giant Hyperboreans of Greek myths. The exact location of Santa's home isn't known but a recent pop culture contribution from the movie Elf suggests it is in close proximity to 7 levels of a Candy Cane forest, near a sea of swirly-twirly gum drops, and not far from the Lincoln Tunnel.

Whoville/Mt. Crumpit
Another hidden city with a Christmas connection is Whoville. Talk begins anew each holiday season about the species of roast-beast-eating "Whos" - discovered by the renowned Dr. Seuss in 1957 - terrorized by a green, cave-dwelling, bipedal humanoid that resides on Mt. Crumpit. The so-called "Grinch" domesticates dogs, and under the right circumstances, it possesses the physiological ability to grow its heart by 3 sizes.

Black Peter aka Zwarte Piet
A character who accompanies Sinterklaas in the Netherlands, Black Peter joins the jolly man on a boat from Spain (where they

live instead of in the North Pole) and assists in distributing goodies to nice children. Peter has alternately been a conquered devil forced to help Santa, a Moorish slave, and a soot-covered chimney sweep. He will punish bad children but is not normally as mean as the Krampus - although he also has a bag for stealing kids for transport back to Spain.

Flying Reindeer

Santa travels the globe in a sleigh led by supposedly immortal flying reindeer, which have evolved in the North Pole. At least one of these cryptozoological wonders possesses a bio- luminescent red nose. According to a story by Robert L. May in 1939, and sung about by Gene Autry in 1949, their adaptation allows survival in the hidden landmass' foggy Christmas Eves.

Kallikantzaros

A goblin of Greek legend, these monsters live underground until Christmas day, where they can then emerge and stir up mischief until returning January 6. Unless a home is protected - with a basil sprig, wooden cross and bowl of water - they will swarm, wreaking havoc. Connected to vampire and werewolf lore, they can appear half-beast and half-human with glowing red eyes.

Some men, especially those born at Christmas, can transform into Kallikantzaroi.

Bumble

It was discovered in the 1964 stop-motion animation TV special, *Rudolph the Red-Nosed Reindeer* that the flying reindeer have socialized with a fellow cryptid, the Bumble, a yeti-like creature known as the Abominable Snow Monster of the North. The large, white Bumble has the ability to bounce, but is prone to sinking. It is enraged by glowing red noses and all things connected to Christmas but can be domesticated by removing its teeth.

Magic Snowmen

A certain level of sorcery is at play during Christmas, where - according to a 1950 musical account by Gene Autry - snowmen are reanimated due to potentially possessed items such as a felt hat.

The snowmen can also grow legs to assist with walking through traffic stops. One incarnation of the magic snowman, which appeared at the North Pole along with the red-nosed reindeer in 1964, prefers to offer moral guidance and sing about silver and/or gold deposits, and holly/jolly Christmases.

LaBefana

The holiday witch of Italy, Befana delivers gifts to good children on Epiphany Eve - the night before The Three Wise Men were said to arrive at Baby Jesus' manger. The stories vary, but she is an old woman who turned the Wise Men down on an invite to join them on the quest (she was too busy sweeping). She has a change of heart, and tries to find Jesus, but is unable. Now she travels on a broom, still searching, and visiting children in the meanwhile.

Time Traveling Ghosts, Inhuman Entities

During Christmas, entities conspire to teach important lessons to the morally bankrupt. As Charles Dickens detailed in his 1843 novella *A Christmas Carol*, the spirit of a doomed business partner might appear, followed by a shapeshifting being with a flame as its head. This androgynous spirit will transport a "Scrooge" into the past, while a jolly giant with a green robe teleports the individual through present events. Then a foreboding Grim Reaper of a future yet-to-come zips him to the future and portends of misery and death. Dickens also dabbled with moralistic Christmas goblins and ghosts in tales such as The Chimes and The Haunted Man and the Ghost's Bargain. At least one other story featured an inter-dimensional angel who slipped a man into a parallel 1946 to show him a world where he doesn't exist, and that he had a wonderful life.

CHAPTER 4

Interviewing the Investigators

Josh Gates' Travels And Terror Of 'Destination Truth'

(September 2009)

Are you hunting Yeti for business or pleasure? Do you have any Chupacabra or Sloth Monsters to declare? Have you accepted any gifts from Swamp Dinosaurs, Bat Demons or Devil Worms while traveling?

The questions Josh Gates encounters when flying across the world for fun and adventure are slightly more exciting than what the rest of us have to answer at the airport. Still, even though the third season of his hour-long show *Destination Truth* premieres Wednesday, September 9 on the Syfy channel, the gig of monster-hunting host hasn't become mundane.

Since June 2007, Gates has traveled to remote, off-the-grid locales with a small crew to investigate claims of encounters with beasts that could take a bite out of Bigfoot and Nessie. As if that wasn't enough, his repertoire has recently extended to exploring curses and ghosts - and his adventures with the unknown all occur after he deals with known dangers. But Gates is an affable guy who, at 32 years-old, sports a professorial-meets-adventurer look. Not completely unlike another such explorer who favors a whip and fedora, Josh Gates has learned to take life-threatening work environments in stride.

"There are two different types of scary occurrences on the show," says Gates. "There's the scary occurrence where you're looking for whatever creature or phenomena that you're looking for where you think, 'wait a minute, maybe this thing is here.' And then there's the scary occurrence when you're doing something that's sort of physically perilous.

"This year we had a very close call on a very old plane in Romania," he adds. "Whether or not you think that there's some sort of unknown creature lurking in the jungles in the Amazon or wherever we happen to be, there's certainly plenty of other things that we know are there. And so we're always very mindful of, 'what if a tiger comes out right now?'"

Gates also admits that a reality of off-the-map exploration is that he often finds himself in very local political systems in tribal communities surrounded by "dudes with machine guns."

"There's a lot of assessing, you know, 'Who am I with and who's that guy with the AK-47?'," he says. "We try really hard to not get in over our head in those kinds of situations because those can get sticky quickly."

But Gates acknowledges that sometimes "scary stuff happens," and when it does, it's pretty mind-blowing. During the second season, Gates was in the Himalayan Mountains in Nepal on the trail of the "Abominable Snowman," aka the Yeti, when he found a rather large set of three footprints. The sets were considered legitimate and non-human by Bigfoot expert Jeffrey Meldrum of Idaho State University.

The find was an exciting one for Gates and he'll be heading back to Nepal to continue the search in the third season. He also describes a fairly freaky experience that happens to a crew member in "Haunted Forest" in the season's first show.

"Evan is one of these guys who's a road warrior; he's shot on a million reality shows. He's shot in war zones," Gates says. "He got really shaken up by something unseen in this forest. It's a really compelling moment where a member of the crew has an experience that fundamentally physically knocks him around."

The footage of the event even leads Gates to pay a visit to Jason Hawes and Grant Wilson, hosts of another Syfy paranormal investigative show, *Ghost Hunters*. Gates asking the duo for some spiritual guidance on the ghostly forest incident is yet another installment of what he calls the "the Flintstones meets the Jetsons routine" on the similar shows. Gates, who has previously hosted two live Halloween shows for the *Ghost Hunters* and is appearing on their show on Wednesday as a lead- into the Destination Truth premiere, hints there are more crossovers to come.

However, Gates stresses that his show complements the *Ghost Hunters*, but he wouldn't want to duplicate them.

"They're really great at what they do. They have great hit shows because they have a very specific way of doing things that really works. And we wanted to be something different. "

That something different is the show's heartbeat as a globetrotting adventure program. Monsters aside, *Destination Truth* is a travel show with a comedic element and an "If it can go wrong, it usually does" attitude.

"We really try to blend into every episode some interesting and really comedic travel up at the top of each show. So you'll see a taste of the cities and the people and the culture and the food of the places we go. Then we clearly, on the show, are kind of going off the beaten path to look for these creatures or to experience these phenomena.

Gates says the travel "full of mishap and full of the unexpected" is actually more important to him for the show. "That's the part of the show that I think pulses the best for me, he says. "People really respond to it."

During the adventures, Gates' reputation as a "big movie guy" pops up often. *Jaws* is referenced in watery episodes, and he says that when recently filming a werewolf episode that "it's hard not to hearken back to some of the classic monster movies."

But it's his well-worn passport, not movie pedigree, which landed Gates the job. An accomplished traveler, he is a SCUBA diver with a degree in archaeology (and drama) from Boston's Tufts University and was just getting back from a trip to Africa when he met to discuss the show.

"They didn't want someone that was necessarily an advocate for these creatures or these stories," he says. "They wanted someone who seemed authentic as a traveler ... someone who had been out there."

Gates' sense of adventure and wanderlust comes honestly, he says. His father, a commercial diver, was always coming back from someplace exotic with gifts from the other side of the world.

Add to that the fact Gates was "fixated on Indiana Jones" and you have a natural explorer with a dream job.

But Gates' tenure as a creature seeker hasn't been without grief from a very visible, if unwieldy beast, the Internet. A handful of forums and bloggers have accused the show of being culturally insensitive or condescending to the villagers and locals from remote areas featured weekly on the show. However, Gates dismisses the accusations.

"Nothing could be further from the truth in terms of the kind of respect that we have for the people that appear on the show."

"People sometimes look at other cultures around the world and there's something sacrosanct about them," he says. "They get this idea that you can't have fun with or fool around with people in the developing nations or people in other cultures because it's somehow insensitive."

He adds that the fun is mutual and shared, and "when the cameras turn off, we go have a drink with them ... they cook for us, and they introduce us to the people in their community."

As for this season, Gates is heading to the ruins of Chernobyl in the Ukraine for an investigation, as well as conducting the show's first United States investigations in Alaska and Florida.

Destination Truth will also have an episode set in King Tut's tomb in the Valley of the Kings in Egypt - which is the world's first overnight paranormal investigation of the tomb.

Regarding future investigations, Josh Gates says he always "has a whole list cooking" for *Destination Truth*.

"I'm really kind of intrigued by a lot of these small Pacific island nations," says Gates. "From Polynesian curses to cursed or haunted islands, there's shipwrecks, there's all sorts of amazing things that are floating out there in the middle of nowhere ...

Maybe we [can] do a season where we take the show on a boat, and we go around the Pacific or something.

He then adds, "I'm of course always secretly plotting to take the show to places that I've never been to before."

Syfy '*Ghost Hunters*' Talk Life, Living And Dead

(October 2009)

After dealing with demons, ghosts and poltergeists, you wouldn't think the stars of Syfy's *Ghost Hunters* would be bested by group of Colorado kids. Still, while investigating the case of a little boy haunted by dead celebrities, Jason Hawes wet his pants - and Grant Wilson, Hawes' co-star of the supernatural reality-TV show, experienced much, much worse incontinence issues - before running out of the house screaming, all the way back to their homes in Rhode Island.

Jason Hawes and Grant Wilson, meet Matt Stone and Trey Parker, the creators of Comedy Central's South Park. In the October 7 episode, the two co-founders of The Atlantic Paranormal Society (TAPS) - the paranormal investigative group around which the Syfy show is based - were spoofed.

Far from being offended or incensed, Hawes and Wilson say they loved being made fun of alongside Michael Jackson and Billy Mays by a show notorious for taking the pulse of a zeitgeist before giving it a shot of adrenaline. Although the ghost hunters weren't involved with the making of the episode and didn't lend voices to their animated counterparts, they helped promote it through their very active Twitter feeds and TAPS fans responded by pushing "#ghosthunters" to a popular "trending topic" of the day.

For two guys with day jobs as Roto-Rooter plumbers who spent more than 20 years of free time in the company of scared homeowners with spectral squatters, this not-insignificant spoof by South Park is another indication that Hawes and Wilson, and the show that premiered in 2004 (on the erstwhile Sci-Fi Channel), have transcended the paranormal entertainment niche, become lasting pop culture mainstays - and are the busiest men in the ghost business.

The show, which received 3.1 million total viewers for the fifth season's October 22 episode, is touted by Syfy as the top paranormal investigative series on TV due to the fact that it more than doubled the audience totals for last week's new episodes of the competing paranormal series *Ghost Lab* on Discovery and Extreme Paranormal on A&E. Numbers aside, the success of the *Ghost Hunters* franchise also includes: two series spin-offs, *Ghost Hunters International* and the new *Ghost Hunters Academy*, premiering November 11; the flagship show's one-hundredth episode, which is filming in November; live speaking engagements and ticketed investigations that draw upwards of two hundred fans; upcoming appearances on October 30 installments of *The Today Show and Larry King Live*; a second book, *Seeking Spirits: The Lost Cases of The Atlantic Paranormal Society*, the follow-up to the 2007 *New York Times* bestselling *Ghost Hunting: True Stories of Unexplained Phenomena from The Atlantic Paranormal Society*.

As far as how they manage to fit so much into a production schedule of 27 episodes a year, Hawes just jokes, "It's a balancing act ... but isn't there like 28 hours in every day?"

"We never thought we'd make it this far," he adds, speaking over the phone from his home in Rhode Island.

"We're living the paranormal investigator's dream," agrees Wilson, also speaking from his Rhode Island home. "We're investigating these great places and you don't necessarily have to foot the bill all the time."

These comments set the tone for much of the interview. Like brothers from another mother, Hawes and Wilson typically agree with, harass, and finish one another's sentences and both maintain a gee-whiz awareness of the long, strange trip it's been from plumbing to ghost hunting on a major cable network. But there is still plumbing to be done.

"We still plumb. It's just when production goes on hiatus, we go back to our normal lives," says Hawes.

Those normal lives include wives and a combined ghost-hunting brood of eight kids. And the duo both say those families are what all the work is for.

"That's what happens when they're requesting 27 episodes a year, it's nonstop. It looks like we're at a place for six hours, we're there numerous days."

While neither is complaining, the grueling schedule takes a toll on how and when they can be with their kids. That's the background to the decision to not take part in a live Halloween night investigation this year. Instead of six hours of watching the TAPS team investigate, beginning at 7 p.m. on October 31, EST, Syfy is airing a five-episode "interactive best-of' - as Wilson describes it - with members of *Academy*, hosted by Josh Gates of *Destination Truth* and supplemented by pre-recorded segments of Hawes and Wilson.

"We've been asking for four years to be able to stay home with our families," says Hawes. "Finally, we're going to be able to. So I'm super-psyched about this."

Adds Wilson, "I'm so tired of telling my son, when he asks, 'What are you going to be for Halloween, Dad? ' and I say, 'Gone.' Not cool."

These problems of dealing with cable networks and live investigations are definitely different than what their TAPS group experienced in its infancy. In Seeking Spirits, Hawes and Wilson, along with co-author Michael Jan Friedman, paint a picture of a young investigative group that travels long distances through blizzards to assist clients in need. Along the way, Hawes and Wilson developed theories, tested new equipment and grew into the televised group millions of viewers now know.

But they never became experts in the paranormal field.

"There's really no experts in this field. How can we be?" asks Hawes, who takes great pains to explain that the word "paranormal" means outside the ordinary, and currently beyond scientific definition.

Besides, says Wilson, what they do is not just about interacting with spirits.

"It's not so much about learning about ghosts as much as it's more learning about the human psyche and how to debunk. I mean, ghosts are a big unknown."

In that statement, Wilson explains the now prevalent mantra among paranormal investigative groups that explains if you go into a supposedly haunted location looking for evidence of a ghost, everything will lead you to believe just that. However, if you try to debunk and prove there is no ghost, what's left unexplained just might lead to proof of the supernatural.

In that regard, *Seeking Spirits* sums up the parallels between ghost hunting and fishing, where you cast a line, wait and eventually try different lures to get something to bite.

"It's not all a waiting game because you're trying different techniques," says Hawes. "If you're in a house that has a child or somebody who believes they're being attacked, scratched, whatever, a lot of times you need to change your investigation methods. At that point, you're trying to instigate, you're trying to provoke something to at least prove to you that it's there so you can give validation to the family and also figure out your next step.

"That's such an important part of investigating that people always seem to forget," agrees Wilson. "They think it's all about the catching. Once you have that, you still have that worried mother or worried family on the other side of the table. You can't just be like, 'Yeah, I caught a fish. Here.' You have to then console them."

Although they've the fanciest equipment a ghost hunter could hope for, like FLIR thermal cameras that detect heat signatures,

Hawes and Wilson admit that they still find themselves on perplexing and frustrating cases like the demonic, elemental (nature spirits) and even perhaps alien cases mentioned in the new book. As such, TAPS frequently has to re-define a paranormal theory they've come to rely on for a long time.

Hawes discusses a recent case referred to them by a church that wasn't filmed for television. Apparently, a family believed they were plagued by an inhuman entity - meaning not an earthbound, deceased human still sticking around.

"We went in believing that 'Alright, the family believes it's an inhuman entity,' and during the entire investigation it led to our belief that it was human entities, but they were moving much larger objects than we had always thought possible."

"At one point," he adds, "they were sliding the kitchen table across part of the floor or things like this which really changes our belief system."

"We'd been under the impression for the last 20 years that a human entity can move an object 10 pounds and under. What gave this human entity the ability to move much larger objects is still unknown. Everything you do is based on theory and you hope to get evidence to solidify that theory ... well, this kind of threw what we believed that last 20 years out."

While the experience was a new one for Hawes and Wilson, the interaction with clergy is not. Not featured prominently on the show, but mentioned often in the book, is the fact that TAPS works with churches and religions to assist people. Wilson also says that sometimes helping to rid a home of an entity can be directly related to a client's belief system.

Says Wilson, "We work with a lot of clergy. We work with many different religions and many different churches. We have a whole abundance of cases that fall under a confidentiality agreement."

Hawes adds that, on the show as opposed to in a book, names and faces are harder to change.

"We've done cases of so-called possession since our show has been on, but we've never wanted to put that on television for the mere fact that we want to protect that person ... the minute we'd do that, everyone online is either going to embrace them and understand them or destroy them.

Within the book, however, Hawes says he and Wilson worked with Friedman to tell compelling stories that all took place prior to the show's premiere. They also wanted to pass along practical investigative tips while being true to themselves and TAPS.

"We sat outside in my camper, went over a lot of old case files - the ones that were prior to the show - and decided which ones would be best suited for the book. We went over the cases with Mike as he wrote them. So we were right there."

"We helped shape it. It's really a collective process," says Wilson.

"Mike's got the talent and we've got the stories."

"Yeah, because Grant and I can't write for crap," jokes Hawes. Still, there might be more writing in their future. Hawes and Wilson have been speaking with Jane Stine, wife of *Goosebumps* author R.L. Stine, about working together on a series of children's books.

Additionally, they were pitched the idea of a Saturday morning TAPS cartoon. The idea never came to fruition, but Hawes and Wilson say they'd "love to do something like that."

In the meantime, Hawes and Wilson say they're happy for the moments when they can hang out with their family and friends, watch *Dexter* on Showtime, and play with iPhone apps. And like two brothers who can be so similar, yet completely different, Hawes digs *Sons of Anarchy* on FX and relaxes to Ozzy Osbourne, Otep, and Black Label Society whereas Wilson is more of an Iron & Wine, Jack Johnson and classical music guy who watches the Japanese manga *Death Note*.

They both agree on the point that while the *South Park* spoof was cool, being lampooned on fellow Rhode Islander Seth MacFarlane's *Family Guy* would be more appropriate.

It looks like Macfarlane has time, though, because Hawes and Wilson will be continuing their ghost hunting on Syfy for the moment.

But they add that they do see an end in sight where they can tend to The Spalding Inn, the joint venture in New Hampshire.

"Jay and I talk about that all the time," says Wilson. "Sitting in the rocking chairs on the front porch of the Spalding ... look at the views and then once in a while, go do an appearance or something."

He adds that "the plumbing days are there for a reason. I'm sure the show is not going to last forever, so we'll go back to that and be happy to go back to that."

'*Ghost Hunters Academy*': Steve And Tango, Paranormal Professors
(November 2009)

Combine an education of science, philosophy, psychology and history with a little electrical and plumbing vo-tech training and the result is a well-rounded, multi-faceted curriculum that many institutions of higher learning would be proud of. Add in ghost hunting and it's the school of The Atlantic Paranormal Society (TAPS), also known as *Ghost Hunters Academy*.

Premiering tonight at 10 p.m., EST, on the Syfy channel, *Ghost Hunters Academy* is the second spin-off from the popular *Ghost Hunters* brand, which began in 2004 with the flagship show starring plumbers Jason Hawes and Grant Wilson. Following the 2008 travel-themed *Ghost Hunters International*, the new Academy is a unique reality-TV paranormal series which focuses on training and selecting new members for the TAPS team.

Led by *Ghost Hunters* investigators Steve Gonsalves, 34, and Dave Tango, 24, the group is comprised of five college-aged "cadets" who travel around the country in an RV to favorite haunted hotspots visited on the main show such as the St. Augustine Lighthouse in Florida, Eastern State Penitentiary in Philadelphia, PA, the battleship USS North Carolina in Wilmington, NC, and the Buffalo Central Terminal in Upstate New York.

During the initial six-episode run of the show, which begins at the Revolutionary War-era Fort Mifflin in Philadelphia, Gonsalves and Tango test and occasionally eliminate recruits who can't live up to the TAPS standards. Along with being a shot across the bow at the other college-focused show *Paranormal State* on the A&E Network, *Academy* is a chance for the *Ghost Hunters* and TAPS team to educate fledgling investigators about what goes into the often-tedious, several-night waiting game of ghost hunting.

Gonsalves and Tango, who both had their own paranormal investigative groups before joining TAPS, spoke over the phone about their new roles as leaders on the show, and what it is like to bring their experiences to the amateur recruits.

What makes for a good cadet and potential TAPS member?

Steve Gonsalves: The passion - that it's there, it's in them and that they love it and want to do it forever. If you join our team, we don't investigate in the same capacity as any other team on the planet. We're much more involved with much more equipment. We do multiple investigations a week where most teams do one a month. If your heart's not completely in it, you're going to fizzle out after six, seven, eight months.

What's a common misconception your cadets, and even some viewers, have about paranormal investigative shows?

Dave Tango: These people come into the show and a lot of them think it's just like they see on TV. That it's like 20 minutes in a room, and that's not the case at all. There's a lot more to it and I'm glad Steve and I were able to show them that. It can be rough sometimes, but that's the way it is. It's not as easy as it looks. Yeah, we're sitting down and we're pointing a camera but there's a lot more to it with the setup and the procedures and protocol of investigating.

SG: You have to have a lot of knowledge. Not that we all have degrees in it, but you have to have a lot of knowledge in the paranormal: the current theories, the past theories, the energy theories. You have to know all this stuff and they all came in not knowing any of it but boasting as if they did. One person says, "I love it, I love it, it's my favorite." She's so happy that it's what she's wanted to do forever, but yet has never read one book, never been to one lecture, never done anything. How can that passion be in you for as long as you can remember but you've never bothered to pick up one book?

DT: Don't just say, "I read this on the Internet, I read that on the Internet." You need to get real books from parapsychologists and true investigators. A lot of these students say, "Well I read this on the Internet so it must be true." Maybe it is, but we don't know that.

SG: We have one girl who says it's been her lifelong dream to be a parapsychologist. I finally asked her, "How do you plan to do that?" She says she's going to go to school for it. It made me realize she had no idea what she was talking about. There is no accredited course in the United States for that ... These are people who think they know everything but are quickly finding out that they don't really know anything.

While you have to train the cadets, do you also have to break bad habits picked up from watching TV, and even from watching the main Ghost Hunters show?

SG: It would be breaking bad habits, but there's only one or two of them that have any investigation experience coming into it. Those people we definitely had to break bad habits. The other people we had to break bad habits because they did see these things on TV, but it was a little easier because they didn't have any prior experience. It was frustrating, it really was. There's this one that just claims to be the queen of the paranormal, but yet... well, you'll see on the show. But it was an experience they all loved. Afterwards, they say, "This was amazing."

DT: You do see progress. Whether it's a little bit or a lot ... a lot of it is just common-sense stuff. I think, for Steve and I, that was the most frustrating - things that you don't have to have any knowledge about. That's the stuff that bothered me the most.

At Fort Mifflin, there's an instance when cadet Susan Slaughter is overcome with sadness and the situation becomes really emotional. The TAPS team stresses not forcing people to be uncomfortable, but do you find yourself rolling your eyes at that drama?

SG: One hundred percent, man. Without a doubt. It's hard to watch. She hid some important stuff from us, like that she even has those feelings ... there's five qualities we're looking for during this show. One of the qualities is composure; another one is professionalism. What she does there doesn't show either one of those.

DT: Or even honesty.

SG: Right. In that circumstance, she blew all of them.
There's nothing wrong with having feelings you can't control or needing to get out of the investigation site. But you say, "Hey guys, I'm feeling uncomfortable. I need to excuse myself; can somebody walk me outside the premises?" You don't just break down and take off. If there are clients there, can you imagine how they're going to look at us now?

There's an excellent moment in the premiere when Steve intentionally misleads cadet Chris McCune to test how susceptible he is to the power of suggestion. Why did you screw with him like that?

SG: (laughing) Yeah, we do that quite often. One of the big problems in this field - and it's not just with new investigators - is to let what other people say suggest what you are seeing and experiencing. You become very impressionable. We do test them continuously throughout the episodes.

Steve, I know you like reality-TV competition shows like Top Chef and Hell's Kitchen. As a viewer of those, you know there are contestants you immediately like or dislike, and people you don't think will last long. Did you have the same experience in the leadership role?

SG: You do find yourself thinking that way, but what I did was treated it like an investigation. When you go on an investigation, you get those feelings at first like, "Oh, we're not going to find anything here." But you have to put all that aside and do a thorough investigation no matter what you think because you never know. That's sort of the way I approached this. I may think this person is never going to last; I may think this person is goofy or whatever, but I have to put all that aside and give them the best training and experience I can.

DT: It's like a big roller coaster ride. You think you know this person, or that person's not going to last, and they come out of their shell and it gets interesting.

SG: It's going to be an interesting show for people because it is an extreme roller coaster. Just when you think they're doing awesome; they end up doing a horrible job. When you think they're going to do bad, they end up killing it. There hasn't been a reality show like this. Ever. It encompasses every element of reality shows, plus you're ghost hunting and in haunted places.

Is it tough being the boss?

SG: What's funny is we all become friends. We're all on the road, we investigate every week, and we spend 12 hours a day with these people ... so it gets a little tough.

DT: They're all great people, and it does get kind of tough, but we have to do what we have to do.

SG: Like I said to one guy, "Hey, I'd be friends with you ... but it doesn't necessarily make you a good team member." You have to sort of separate that.

You don't get rid of cadets every episode, so how do the eliminations work?

SG: If we see somebody is at the point where we've done all we can, and they're just not going to get it, we have to get rid of them and bring in somebody we can potentially use. We do that quite often. That will be fun. What's nice is the recruits are around long enough that the audience will be able to connect with them ... so it's not like you'll see this person for just one episode or half an episode, and you're like, "Aw man, I was just starting to like this dude and he just got kicked off." You'll get to experience each cadet. And then we kick them off! Just kidding.

Since Steve used to be a police officer, who is the good cop and bad cop between you two?
DT: It's kind of both. Certain things will bother Steve, and certain things will bother me more. When they start dilly- dallying, for some reason I can't deal with it. If they're talking away and not doing what they have to do, I just can't stand it. I don't know if it will show on camera, but I get tense and I just snap at them.

Does it frustrate you that you worked for years as paranormal investigators and becoming part of a hit TV show was a result of that, and now you have a group chosen by video submissions dropped into a spin-off without experience?

SG: I know I shouldn't be, but I am. I find myself thinking sometimes, "Wow, I had 15 years in the field before I got a TV show." Now, everyone nowadays looks at ghost hunting on television as a reward system for being in the field. That's why they're in the field - to get on a TV show - which sort of bothers me a little bit. But what I like about it is if it isn't us choosing the people, it's going to be somebody else. At least we're there filtering appropriately.

On the main show, you two are known for pranking one another and exchanging dares. Does that dynamic have to change now that you're the leaders?

SG: It's still there ... but these first six episodes we're still trying to figure out the show and what it's exactly supposed to be. We didn't really have much time to be walking around, investigating and just come up with stuff like that. You're going to see a different side of us, a more authoritative side with a jokester sense as well.

Steve, your fear of flying (along with heights and spiders) is pretty well known. Was that the reasoning behind the RV?
SG: That's funny. No, I showed up the first day on set when we

filmed at Fort Mifflin, and they were like, "This is your RV." We told them we'd be on board, because we wanted to take care of the paranormal aspect of it, but that's all we really cared about. They didn't really tell us about the other mechanics of the show. To show up and find we had an RV was pretty cool.

DT: Steve, you're an excellent driver, by the way. I don 't know if I've told you that. If I drive that thing, it will drive off a cliff, believe me. I could not do that. Seriously, everyone would die a horrible death.

Wouldn't that make for a great season finale?

DT: If they could recover the tapes!

Syfy's 'Paranormal Files' Team On Facts And Faking It
(July 2010)

There was a time when you'd gather around the campfire, and everyone had a ghost story to tell. Now, thanks in large part to the reality-TV paranormal genre, it seems everyone has a story with accompanying video.

When *Ghost Hunters* premiered on the Syfy network in 2004 it popularized the notion anyone could pick up a video camera and possibly find evidence of the paranormal - and so they did. Along with the dozen other similar programs that dominate cable, seemingly thousands of amateur ghost busters and monster hunters launched Web sites and YouTube channels to show off their proof of the supernatural. And it would seem just as many set out to spoof or goof those serious-minded investigators with hoaxes.

That's where former FBI agent Ben Hansen and his team on Syfy's new show *Fact or Faked: Paranormal Files* comes in.

Premiering tonight at 10 p.m. EST, the show is a paranormal *MythBusters*; as opposed to other programs in the genre that look into claims, this one switches it up slightly and essentially investigates the investigators.

Instead of seeking their own evidence or taking on clients, per se, Hansen's crew of supposedly three years - which includes scientist Bill Murphy and journalist/Destination Truth alum Jael De Pardo along with an effects specialist, photography expert, and stunt expert - explores video submissions and famous paranormal footage to determine which can be validated or debunked through experimentation.

For instance, in the first episode, the team tears through a few appetizer videos before selecting two to investigate: The viral "ghost car" video from Georgia that shows a motorist evading police at "supernatural speeds" before phasing through a solid fence, and a collection of extraterrestrial lights over Phoenix, AZ.

The team travels to the spots where the events happened to interview eyewitnesses and recreate the video events.

In a recent interview, team leader Ben Hansen, scientist Bill Murphy, and Executive Producer John Brenkus spoke about Paranormal Files.

When did you know that you wanted to investigate ... was it when you were with the FBI or earlier in your life?

Ben Hansen: Okay, well I actually was about 10 years-old, my father got me kind of interested in this. We used to watch sci fi movies, we used to watch like The Thing and The Fly and those types of things late at night. And he got me interested in UFOs, he started bringing me books to read on it.

I wasn't really aware at the time, but he had a connection with his father, my grandfather. He worked actually at Wright Patterson Air Force Base, I don't know if you know about that base, it's where supposedly some of the wreckage from Roswell was sent.

Well, my grandfather worked there as a civil engineer and throughout the years of talking with him he always kept his oath of secrecy that he made with the projects he was working on. But in so many words he let my father know that we're not alone. So this kind of piqued an interest in my father and in turn he and I kind of bonded on this level where we became just tremendously interested in mostly UFOs.

I remember seeing *E.T.* when I was younger and really becoming interested in the possibility of life on other planets. So to kind of go back, no, I was not, per se, investigating the subject in any professional or official sense when I was working with the Bureau or with any other agency. But I always kept it as kind of a hobby until I developed a group and we kind of got into the ghost hunting and other aspects of it.

Bill Murphy: I'm just going to comment quickly about what really attracted me to the show. First off, I should state that Ben and I had been operating in the same circles for years ... and so when Ben and I met we developed a very quick rapport and we realized we're on the same page but maybe taking it from different angles.

Ben's formal experience has been in law enforcement. Myself, I've been involved in the paranormal for a couple of decades, it kind of goes way back with my family.

And with my family and growing up as a child with it I was very skeptical. It was almost like I'm listening to the older folks talk about the tales and just about sort of skipped through it without necessarily putting a whole lot of weight into it. Until I got old enough to see that these things were kind of going on around us, but I wasn't satisfied with just hearing the tales nor was I satisfied with what I thought my own perceptions were.

I thought I needed to be able to validate these experiences through technology. And so I set about to begin the documentation process. So when Ben and I met, and we spoke it was just like instant connection. And so I felt that this opportunity for me was a really good fit because I had been the skeptical believer, if you will.

... And sometimes that isn't a popular position to take when you're entrenched in the paranormal community. The community looks for gratification from evidence but is it the evidence of the paranormal? Is it misidentification? Is there an explanation that science more readily accepts? Well, this show takes a look at all those things and all those possibilities, and we come up with the best possible answer.

What is the most convincing evidence that you've picked up off the show that viewers will not see? Also, have you had a moment where you or any of your team, has encountered something that really couldn't be proven through evidence, but you just had to believe it; you just bought into it even though you couldn't support it?

BH: That's a good question. Two questions. Bill, do you have something off the bat? I've got a few.

John Brenkus: Let me actually just jump in first ... I think that one of the first things is in the debut show you'll see that we investigate some mysterious lights in Arizona and we genuinely - I was there on the shoot - we were all there on the shoot and genuinely we caught something that we simply can't explain.

We all witnessed it and we were extraordinarily fortunate to capture it on tape and you know it's one of those things that we caught that we can't say for absolutely certain that it is something paranormal but it's certainly something that's unexplainable as of today.

I'm really excited to share it with the audience, that was definitely one of the highlights of the series so far.

BH: And that's really big for John to say that. John is actually one of the biggest skeptics ever. I could bring him a UFO on his lawn, and he'd say it was fake.

BM: You know, I have to agree with John. John, that was an amazing moment to have happen and it was ... to be there while it occurred, it's one of things where you know, can you believe your own eyes? Because seeing is supposed to be believing and in that case, we had to believe our eyes. But what I've learned since then ... is that sometimes seeing is not believing.

Sometimes you can't believe what you're seeing and there's an alternate explanation but in the case of what happened in Arizona, that was a truly phenomenal occurrence to have happen. And I'm glad it did, to that point it was early in the morning, we were all damp and cold and I think nobody was aware of the environment once our eyes were on the sky and we saw what we saw.

It was quite a sight for us.

BH: Talk about something that maybe that you've seen not on the show; the best evidence of something you've experienced that wasn't on the show.

BM: Yeah, that was one of the questions. Well, something that has happened - and again, I think everybody here on the show is focused on looking for an explanation that you can personally accept easier as opposed to moving it into the category of being paranormal. But with that being said, I went to a location in Colorado where there were reports of some sort of - it wasn't necessarily TK (telekinesis) what was happening there, it was people were being - reporting being touched and shoved by an unseen force. And I found that to be interesting because I kept hearing things from a lot of people. So when I was there, I was going through the location and yeah, it's a beautiful historic place.

Although I was enjoying the architecture, I walked through this area of the hall, and it was like I had dozens of vibrating cell phones in every pocket. It felt like all of a sudden, everything vibrated on my body. And I stopped, I was like, "Hey, what was that?"

And I backed up, took a couple steps back and I felt it a second time but wasn't as strong as the first time. And I had to sort of just not laugh but I shook my head in disbelief in going these reports have a validity. There is something here but what is it? As it turned out, there could be an explanation for what people described as being touched by an unseen force and it has its roots in hard science. It has its roots in the geology of a location and sometimes there are enough characteristics of a locale that when they come together, they can cause a phenomenon that can be perceived as being paranormal.

If you took an interdisciplinary approach to it and combined sciences, then you can come up with a rational explanation that can be considered paranormal because it's hard to duplicate that and that is one of the requirements for something to move from theory to fact. Can you replicate it? Can you replicate this effect?

Paranormal phenomena aren't always repeatable even in a lab and that's what makes it confounding. Because you can't deny the existence of these events, but they don't adhere to the protocols that are in place for something to move out of the theory range. But

159

you have to look at people's trendsetting of this thing to happen. If something happens over and over and over, you know there's a certain credibility that comes from the accumulation of witnesses.

And if you can sort of demonstrate how it can happen scientifically then voila, we've done our job from a science perspective.

For me, having the experience of an unseen force seeming to press against you, was quite astounding but it wasn't what we thought it was. You weren't being touched by an external force, it was a shape change to the skeleton and to the skull as a result of piezoelectric activities of the minerals in the location. So you feel your skin moving but it's happening under the skin as opposed to on top of the skin.

That still leaves the question of something that you just really had to believe even though you couldn't back it up with any evidence or any science.

BH: Let me give you an example of something, well, my two examples. The first one was when I was recently out of college, this is actually the very first time I tried doing an EVP session. I had seen there's a local ghost hunter group that would play their clips on the radio and things, and you kind of take it with a grain of salt, just as everyone else who listens to these things. And you may even somewhat believe, but you just put it in the back of your minds because you get up and go to work the next day ... it doesn't really change the impact of your life until you actually hear one of these things yourself.

I was in a memorial - a war memorial park with my sisters and a couple of friends - and we were kind of doing the Halloween thing and going there and doing some recordings. And we're standing next to this war memorial, and I've got two recorders going and I was telling my friend I really wish I could have brought them there before they had cleared out a lot of the trees because it looked a lot spookier, and I could have showed them something that would really scare them. Well, nothing really happened during the whole investigation until I got home and played the set.

And this was one of the old analog recorders and I played it back and I didn't even need to slow it down the first time; very clearly, I heard the voice of either a small child or a woman. It sounded like it was whispering right against the microphone which really creeped me out because you're thinking if this were like a person, they would have to have been right at my hip.

That's where the recorder was and it says, "Get brother. " I knew where the women were in the group and my sister was about 15 feet away; we went through every elimination, it couldn't have been this person, couldn't have been that person. It gave us the chills.

I played it back for my family over and over and I had to face the realization that quite possibly I had captured something that was not a living person ... there are many theories on what EVPs are, but the phenomena are real in the same sense I've witnessed objects in the sky that - I myself am a licensed pilot, I love going to air shows and things - I've seen aircraft that have done things that conventional crafts do not do. And beyond that, I can't say what it is, but the phenomena are real.

So, I think I forgot the original question!

Just what would make you a believer even though you couldn't back it up with evidence.

BH: Not just in a paranormal sense, but there's a lot of things like Bill was starting to say. You know there's this dichotomy of seeing and believing. Can we believe everything that we see, and if we don 't see something does that mean we shouldn't believe in it? So I think a lot of people, especially the viewing audience may never have had an experience of their own but there's a lot of people who believe. And kind of, by proxy or vicariously, you're able to see through the eyes of what these people are seeing and that's the great thing about our show.

Many people would not be able to go out to the places we've been to. And by bringing them our experience through our eyes I think there is a way that you can believe without actually seeing yourself.

So, it's the absence of evidence is not the evidence of absence scenario then.

BH: Correct. I think all discoveries, major discoveries started out with a phenomenon that they couldn't quite explain. Look at electricity and how it was discovered, well, you saw the effects of it, but did you actually see electricity - what it was doing? And so people started setting up controlled experiments to find out well, how can we test that. And I think that's where we're at in the paranormal field a lot of times.

We believe it because we know something has happened, has affected one of our senses. Whether we're able to capture it on film or audio or some other way to demonstrate it to somebody else may be another question.

So, what's the challenge with the tools you have in the field to spot something that could be faked?

BM: Okay, well one of the criteria that we have ... is a strong eyewitness. And so if there are multiple witnesses ... that makes for a really strong case because you're talking about something that is not just a piece of video ... where they shot it but something that physically is there those other witnesses have come forth and said they've seen.

And there could be 911 calls or news reports or whatever it takes, reporting an object or a sighting or some sort of event that's happened. Those are strong cases, so the video is bolstered by multiple eyewitnesses or if there are limited eyewitnesses then there's a credibility you have to look at.

What are the motivations for this video being posted? And if we get there, we really don't pull any punches to try to replicate the video. So the challenges are something that I don't think we've had stop us. Generally, we try to stop at nothing once we're there to demystify the video. I mean we stop at nothing. Really extreme stuff and it's a lot of fun.

BH: When we do come up against those cases that are very difficult, either they're done very well in CG, we're just not sure, that's where I like to use my experience and focus on the poster or the witness who shot this video or provided this photo.

For me, it's a lot easier sometimes to find the signs of deception through the person themselves, and with my experience, I've conducted thousands of forensic interviews. On the show, it's no exception. I like to isolate the witness and use the neutral questions and everything that I would do in a real criminal investigation and try to see if there's deception there. More likely than not, when people are pinned down and asked if they faked something, most people are not good liars.

So, I rely more on that. Bill usually heads up the clarification of images and things like that. I focus on the human aspect. When you finally encounter someone that is faking and you pin them down, I mean you kind of need these people to do your job, they make you sharper and they help put the truth out there.

So are you kind of happy when you find the fakes? Are you happy when you encounter the people that are trying to pull off fake fraud because you need them?

And have you examined other paranormal shows and looked at what they consider evidence? Have you made judgments based on that?

BH: That's a really good question ... I've seen on blogs, I've read people saying you guys should investigate this show or this show, kind of funny.

No, we're not in the business of telling other people how to investigate or what to do. And as far as being happy about catching a hoaxer, I think sometimes the initial discussions I've had with people and the title of the show, sometimes they're a little confused that we are just trying to evaluate hoaxes or not.

And that's not the case. When we say fact or faked, faked could also be not that they purposely faked it but that it was a phenomenon that is naturally occurring that they captured. In fact ... I'm not going to throw a percentage out there but there's a great amount of cases we've gone out on where I find that the witness is very credible. Even from the start I'm not out trying to prove that they faked this video. More so, I'm trying to find out what it was they captured on video. Does that make sense?

So it's not always was the video hoaxed or not, it was the situation a fake situation in that was it natural or other explanation or not.

But yes, if you do find someone who's purposely gone out of

their way to try to pull the wool over your eyes and you're able to show them that it's not real, it is kind of satisfying because I think in the professional community of people who really give their whole professional life to investigate the paranormal, it's disheartening. It really detracts from the real work that's going on when someone wastes someone else's time doing this.

I love the fakes if people add a disclaimer: "Look what I was able to produce!" But that's where the responsibility and accountability come in, so I think it is kind of fun to maybe catch someone every now and then if they really had that intention.

JB: I think when you see the structure of the show, we have this situation room where we sit around and discuss clips. That's really where you find a lot of the blatant fakes ... When we go out to investigate it, we have the cooperation of everybody involved with that case from the people that shot the tape to the eyewitnesses to everybody.

So, I think that unearthing something that was intentionally faked is probably going to be the rarity because we have the cooperation of everybody involved with the case. It won't rise to the level of being a case that we're going to investigate if we can determine that it's fake before we ever go out in the field.

There are just too many cases out there that meet our criteria that we wouldn't really waste our time going out into the field and investigating it if we already know that it's fake. So the cases that wind up being the meat of the show are the ones that we feel are compelling footage with a credible eyewitness and something that is testable.

BM: Many occasions evidence of paranormal activity is recorded by accident. Somebody is out there shooting the birthday party in the backyard for example and then something happens, and the camera was rolling. They capture that, so those people, they're looking for either validation of their material or they're looking for an explanation. So there are many times, just as curious as we are ... it's not like a lot of people that are out there just trying to fool the team.

I mean I'm sure the Internet is full of that, but we do use that filtering process that John mentioned and those are kind of fun to look at but they're easily dismissible.

Kris Williams Takes 'Bait' As 'Ghost Hunters International' Lead

(October 2010)

Like the Lara Croft of paranormal investigations, Kris Williams is adventurous, strong, sexy and steeped in the shrouded world of the supernatural. And with a nickname like "Bait" - given because of her enthusiasm to be the first to enter reportedly haunted locations alone - the 29-year-old TAPS member and *Ghost Hunters* cast mate since 2007 is an inspired choice to be the new team leader on *Ghost Hunters International* alongside Barry Fitzgerald.

It is early October and Kris Williams is about to hit the road. I have just broke news that Buffalo Central Terminal would serve as the site for the live Halloween *GH* episode. But that wasn't Kris' big announcement, after all. When she speaks with me, it's still weeks away before anyone will know the secrecy she's been teasing since August that Bait has gone *International*.

Congratulations on GHI. How does it feel being able to reveal your "big secret"?

I don't know; I'm worried I won't have anything to tweet about now! I guess there's always The Doors (laughs).

What excites you most about GHI?

Outside of getting out of the country and seeing the world, it's that it's different for me this time around. I'm not coming in as the new girl with absolutely no investigative experience. This time, I might be new to the group, but I'm not new as an investigator. Fans has watched me grow over three years, and I'm really proud of how far I've come and what I've learned since my first trip out with

TAPS to Seattle.

Plus, I'm really honored not to just have the position, but to be the first female in it. Women have so much to offer this field, and I'm proud to have the opportunity to show what we can do.

Finally, it's just wild to check out places older than our entire country.

Women are smart, strong, brave, and I hope I do the ladies watching proud.

What's it like being a leader now?

I just want to say that to be lucky enough to be asked to help lead with Barry still humbles me. When they [the production company Pilgrim] asked me if I wanted to go to GHI, I was like, "umm...YES!" It's the coolest experience and I honestly couldn't be happier.

As far as being a leader, good leaders admit they don't know everything, aren't afraid to get their hands dirty, give credit where it's due, rely on the strengths of the team, allow teammates room to grow, and cop to it when they're wrong. These are all things I'm striving to live up to on GHI.

What's the team like out there right now?

We have an awesome team. Everyone contributes something unique and makes us successful as a whole. And Barry just knows so much about the paranormal, and he has all these very cool theories. People have started calling us Mulder and Scully out there because I'm more of the skeptic, and he's a really brilliant believer. Plus, Britt, Joe [Chin], Paul [Bradford] and Susan [Slaughter] are seriously a kick ass team and excellent travel buddies.

Now that you're international, where do you want to investigate?

Well, some people - or everyone - knows I'm a huge Doors fan, so I always joke about investigating Jim Morrison's grave. But honestly, I want to investigate Italy and the catacombs in Paris.

What do you love and hate about travel?

I hate flying, but mainly just like security, luggage and the issues that come along with it. I'm willing to travel anywhere for any adventure, I admit I really care the most about beds. You have got to have a good bed. If the hotel has a fridge, it's amazing. If they have laundry, it's heaven. You really appreciate the smallest things you wouldn't think about normally.

Is it difficult being away from friends and family for several weeks at a time?

Sure, it's tough being away from family, being away from friends. At the same time, I'm seeing things I wouldn't have an opportunity to otherwise. I am insanely fortunate. I mean, I'm hanging out in castles - a bunch of them. How cool is that?

I heard a rumor about you having an adventure streak. Are you an extreme athlete?

Um, not so much. I don't think my sense of fear is developed enough (laughs), which explains the nickname "Bait." But I love adventuring. That is probably because I grew up getting bruised up as a tomboy and athlete, and a girl that always running around competing with guys. I'm into doing stuff outside: camping, kayaking, hiking, whitewater rafting, horseback riding. And I'm up for trying new things; I was recently out in California and tried surfing with a friend.

How'd you do on the board?

I sucked! I am in this wet suit, walking around with the board. I look like I know what I'm doing but get out there and the waves are insane. I was getting knocked all over the place, the board was going one way, I'm going another. When I finally picked a wave, a good one, I'm paddling and paddling. When it's time to push up, I couldn't get my arms to work to save my life. I want to do it again, but I will have to go to the gym and probably do some weights. I'm definitely not going to be a pro surfer.

How is that like ghost hunting?

Beware of ghost sharks? I'd definitely rather be ghost bait than shark chum. No, I guess it's that I try to just challenge myself and chase after the adventure, whether it's a ghost or wave. That's one of the main things I enjoy about my job: I get to learn a lot about myself through the situations I put myself into.

You're one of the very few women leaders in the paranormal reality-TV genre, and perhaps the most well-known, so where do you see yourself as a role model?

When I was growing up, in horror movies or on TV, the females are always screaming, crying like a little girl, running around or freaking out. That always made me so mad. I thought they edited something out because not all women are like that. And I've never been one to scare easily. Women are smart, strong, brave, and I want to inform people about that. If there's some young girl watching me on TV, I hope she gets the idea it's OK to get scared, but also OK to be tough. I mainly hope I do the ladies watching proud.

'Paranormal State's Ryan Buell: Explaining an Unexplainable Life
(October 2010)

Paranormal investigator, 28-year-old reality-TV star, author, former Penn State college student, bisexual celebrity; chances are good that however you choose to label Ryan Buell of *Paranormal State*, you're partially wrong.

Like the paranormal, it is hard to define and explain Ryan Buell. Long before Buell was a TV ghost buster, he was a college student from Sumter, SC, at Pennsylvania State University, where he studied journalism and anthropology. Then, in December 2007, the founder of the college's Paranormal Research Society became a celebrity when *State* premiered with 2.5 million viewers. Since then, the show has remained a contender amongst the reality-TV paranormal docudramas, and began its fifth season October 19 with 1.4 million people tuning in.

The success of *Paranormal State*, which airs Sundays at 9 p.m. on A&E, is attributable to a variety of factors such as adept cinematography, high production values, creepy settings and a rotating cast of compelling characters that has included twentysomething investigators Sergey, Heather and Psychic Kids star Chip Coffey.

Yet the main focus of the show has always been on Buell. That focus on a brooding young man who has had a lifelong fascination with the supernatural and has been investigating since age 15, and with personal demons - as in a literal demon he believes was stalking him - has earned Buell countless fans and more than a few critics.

Now it's his chance to respond. In his new biography, *Paranormal State: My Journey into the Unknown*, Buell discusses, in his own words, his upbringing, Catholic faith, and the beginning of PRS and the show - as well as his revelation as a bisexual man, which has earned the book coverage in the mainstream press. But for Buell, who sits down after a book signing to chat at the Stone Rose lounge in Manhattan's Time Warner Center, it's a chronicle of his backstory and the show's first season. He says the book is less of a memoir and instead largely documents a life transition between college and adulthood.

"It's really only a sliver of my life," says Buell. "I was graduating but was still in school for another degree. We were starting to realize we are getting older and about ready to leave college in another year or so; that's when the show comes along."

Buell adds that his life changed right at the moment when he "was contemplating having a normal life for a change."

Of course, the "normal" that Buell refers to is subjective; although he once described himself as "ordinary guy trying to make sense of this crazy world," most people aren't haunted by "bunnies" (the PRS word for demons), such as the one he says plagued him for years after a case in 2005.

However, the investigator says there's more to him than his very popular demon problem.

"I think there are a lot of misconceptions about my beliefs about the demonic," he says. "I understand that the show kind of makes it seem like I jump whenever I hear the word 'demon ' but I'm actually extremely skeptical - but I do believe in the demonic."

As far as Buell's beliefs, his also includes the Loch Ness Monster, the Jersey Devil, bigfoot and other "undiscovered creatures." He says he's open minded, but raises an eyebrow when people talk to him about leprechauns or fairies.

"The moment I hear that I start to smirk and go, 'yeah, OK,'" he says before acknowledging, "But people do that about ghosts."

On that point, Buell isn't naive about the fact that his paranormal profession is seen as slightly outside the mainstream, even if a recent survey from Colorado-based research firm Resolution Research found 30% of its 2,028 respondents reported having a paranormal encounter. Still, there is an element of crackpottery connected to paranormal investigations he isn't shy about addressing.

"I'm very self-aware at how crazy some of the s--t I say sounds sometimes, and it is crazy," he says. "We just did a case about puckwudgies - little demon leprechauns, if you will, that try to knock you off a cliff. Sounds fucking nuts, but it makes sense in a weird way, and what I love about my job is that it is nuts."

Yet Buell's love of the nuttiness of his job, which he describes as a mix between journalism and detective work, doesn't extend to the human element. In fact, he says he's less frightened by the unseen world than some of his own clients or fans.

"I've had a couple of clients threaten me; one threatened to stab me at one point. So when I deal with cases of possible spirit influence - or they claim there is spirit influence, and it may be mental illness - they're acting with violence ... Or you know, some trailer park where literally they're shooting guns. They have a couple of guns and they're just shooting on a makeshift rifle range they made in the driveway. That kind of stuff scares me a little more."

Buell says he has heard from celebrity admirers of *Paranormal State*, such as Natalie Portman, Demi Moore, Kirsten Dunst, and Kevin Kline - and along the way he mentions he's gotten word of famous people who "had an exorcism performed on them privately" - he professes appreciation for his everyday fans.

Although, he says his own celebrity leads to many odd fan interactions.

"I've had some people claim that I had astrally projected to them and they had 'relationships' with me astrally. I'm trying to be very neutral because they may be reading this; I don't want to insult them - but some really crazy s--t. I've had a lot of people use the demon thing to try to get me in bed with them, and why they think that's a good pickup line, I don't know ... I'm an investigator and they are trying to sleep with me. Why? Because I have a TV show? That's just so bizarre."

The sexual solicitations involved with having a show aside, Buell does realize that his position in the public sphere allows him to affect positive change by speaking about his own bisexuality.

After *Entertainment Weekly* reported on September 13 that Buell "came out" in his new book, he says he heard it was reported positively on CNN, NPR, MTV and other outlets.

Buell's decision to come out, in a span of approximately five pages of the 372-page book, was related to his own awareness at age 13 while living in an intolerant Southern town. His family were practicing Catholics, as is Buell even today, and homosexuality seemed a sin greater than even murder - even to the loving paternal grandfather he looked up too. Added to that were the wounds inflicted by a fellow investigator and minor para-celeb "who got his start through PRS" and established Catholic church connections, only to use them to discredit and betray the *Paranormal State* star once he came out to the friend.

He sums up his choice by pointing out "we live in a world where gay teens are still committing suicide," and that his announcement wasn't because of a desire to sell more books.

"To be honest, it would be more beneficial for me to just continue to lead a normal life," he says. "My audience is predominantly female; so, even though I'm bisexual, it's still kind of a knock. It's still something I am going to take heat for." He adds that there may be additional challenges because the paranormal world lacks diversity and "needs some work."

"I believe the majority of the field is Middle-American white people; everyday, blue-collar workers. There are very few minorities in the paranormal field."

Buell goes on to say, "There's no official statistic on the community of paranormal investigators, but it's also a well- known fact Paranormal State does well in Middle America and in the South. These types of shows resonate well over there, in those types of areas - so, in those areas, where there's a lot of prejudice, there's a lot of homophobia and a lot of racism still.

Regardless, Buell says he realizes the admission has led to more publicity than the book might have otherwise received, but that he never intended" to make this big deal about me coming out."

Instead, he describes the process as giving *Entertainment Weekly* a review copy, "and of course, that's what they decided to focus on."

Since Buell's book is just a "sliver" of his life, and includes behind-the-scenes insight on many *Paranormal State* cases, what might the next book contain?

Buell says he can't rule out future collaborations with former castmate Chip Coffey, the psychic/medium currently starring on *Psychic Kids*, also on A&E, on Sundays at 10 p.m.

"He [Chip] and I grew together; in some weird way we are always going to be connected," says Buell. "You know, I have a big distrust for psychics but, having said that, Chip has impressed me beyond belief many times. Would I work with him again? If the opportunity is right, of course I would."

However, Buell says he has no interest in being on paranormal reality-TV forever, or even when he's 30 - "so I guess two more years max" - but that he'll always be involved in the field.

Moreover, he has been taking over co-executive producer duties on his show, and he'll be producing, but not starring in, *Ghost Prophecies*, a special he hopes will be picked up as a series.

The special, which airs November 28 at 11 p.m. on A&E follows the team of filmmaker and "American Ghost Hunter " Chad Calek. Buell calls this next project very "edgy and rock 'n' roll" because it's evidence based and follows "real " investigators who have been in the field for years.

Between starring on TV, authoring a book and producing shows, it somehow makes sense why Buell would like to encounter the ghost of Alexander the Great. "A young man who did extraordinary things," Buell says Alexander approached things differently and changed the world - a goal perhaps he plans on striving for himself.

But whatever Ryan Buell chooses to do next, whether within or without the supernatural world, it's a safe bet that any label applied to him might continue to be partially wrong and leave the man - like the paranormal field he investigates - indefinable.

You Don't Know Zak: Uncommon Questions With The '*Ghost Adventures*' Leader

(April 2011)

Typically, when a brick is thrown at you, it is a sign of bad things in your life. For Zak Bagans, it was just the start of good things to come.

In the summer of 2007, the Sci-Fi Channel (in the days before Syfy) aired *Ghost Adventures*, a 2004 documentary that showed Bagans and friends Nick Groff and Aaron Goodwin investigating Virginia City, NV, with Goodwin sitting out the second act at the Goldfield Hotel in the same state. It was at the once-revered hotel where a brick appears to be lifted by an unseen force from debris and propelled at Bagans - and in turn, propelling Bagans' career.

Slightly more than a year later, his crew was on a new network, the Travel Channel, with the same *Ghost Adventures* name. Four seasons later, with Bagans serving as executive producer, the 33-year-old (until his April 4 birthday) has driven the show to success, picking up new viewers each week in its timeslot of Friday, 9 p.m.

But what do we really know about the investigator?

There are many assumptions about the man based on the show and his investigative methodology, yet it merits an investigation of the investigator to dispel rumor and uncover truth.

Preparing for back-to-back ticketed events in Colorado and Ohio, and speaking from his home in Las Vegas, the leader of GAC agrees to a little Q&A.

To begin with, do you consider yourself from Washington, D.C.?

No, no. I was actually born in D.C. and moved from there at a very early age - like two years of age. I moved to Clearwater, Florida, with my mother and grew up there for 15 years - then to Chicago, Detroit, Vegas, back to Detroit, then back to Vegas.

You've covered a lot of ground, but I guess you prefer sunny areas over cold spots?

No, not really. I just happened to end up here. I'm completely opposite of that, actually. I like the dark skies; I call it Dracula weather. That's my kind of place but I don't know why I always end up in the sunny, beach places or the desert of Vegas.

When it comes to locations like Bobby Mackey's Music World in Kentucky - supposedly infested with demons or evil ghosts - why keep going back if you have these negative experiences?

Well, Dale Earnhardt, J r., knows his father was killed racing cars, but deep down inside that's in his blood. That's what he loves to do. He knows there' s risk in his job, but people like him know that that's their passion. That's what they love. That's the same concept with us.

What do people ask the most about what you do?

Is it real?

And you say ...

Then I say, "Come with me, I'd like to show you." That's the only way. I asked the same question. Why wouldn't you ask the same question? This isn't scientifically proven. I don't think it will ever be because you can't ever make it happen on cue. It is a great question. You have to really experience this for yourself.

You don't want to persuade people?

It's not our job to persuade people to try and make them a believer while they are sitting on their couch in their living room. They're going to make their own decision. But the thing we like to do is - when we can - is get out there and do events, and stuff like that. That's the biggest reward. That's when I can answer that question for people, let them experience it for themselves. I know it's real. I didn't audition for a spot as a television show host. This is something that fell into my lap. This is something I think happened for a reason. It all started because I wanted answers for myself. And that's what this is about. This is about me going out there and finding answers for myself. Whoever wants to watch and wants to believe with me can, and I hope they do.

And for the skeptics out there?

For all the skeptics out there: I understand. I welcome that. I didn't know if it was real or not either until I had my experience about 10 years ago. Again, that's why we really like to try and do as many events as we can. But you know. Like our last event, we had a lot of crazy stuff happen there. You know, you were there.

Some scary stuff can happen. I mean, is it a coincidence a lady dropped and had a seizure at the same time another lady passed out - at the same time another lady was vomiting, and she says she never does that? And. At. The. Same. Time. In the same jail cell, everyone saw a bunch of dark figures cowering around? We can only supply so much and at the end of the day you're going to make up your own mind. Or not. That's not our job.

What questions do you ask of yourself about all of this?

I have so many questions in my own mind. The longer you do this, the more evidence you find, the more questions you have. My mind doesn't sleep. Every piece of evidence we find is just a snowball effect of questions.

The show also has an entertainment perspective because you're exec-producing this and want people to tune in. What is the entertainment appeal of Ghost Adventures?

Our personalities. Aside from the seriousness of what we're searching for, Aaron, Nick and myself - we're a bunch of friends. We're funny, we have big senses of humor, and that's how we are as people. And we're not going to change. We have a passion for what we do, and we appreciate the people, the fans, who like us as people, and our personalities - and feel that we are entertaining.

What about the behind-the-scenes appeal?

Our show has a very strong production value. And we have a great crew that helps us in the opening act of the show when we portray the history. We present that in a very entertaining fashion. But when it comes down to it, in lockdown, it's just the three of us - and hopefully the ghosts.

You used to be a wedding DJ?

Yeah, yeah. I had a DJ business here in Vegas before all of this. I was deejaying weddings and birthday parties, and all that kind of stuff. That's how I met Nick; he hired my company for his wedding. It's kind of crazy.

If you ever get married, what songs are on your "no play" list?

"Dancing Queen" by Abba. I can't stand that song. I've had to play that song more times as a DJ, and when I play that song, I just - it's like Chinese water torture. I just want to jam a nail through my forehead. I don't like that song "Barbie Girl," either. I've had to play that for some birthday parties and that's torture, too. They should just make our enemies listen to that stuff.

Any similarities between deejaying and paranormal investigating?

When you're a DJ, you have to be able to read the audience, read the energy of the room and be able to try and get those people to interact with you, to dance. You have to be able to use your body to sense that energy. As a paranormal investigator, you try and sense the energy in the room to get those spirits to interact with you. You know, to dance with the devil in the pale moonlight.

Nice Batman reference.

One of my favorite movies.

Do you read a lot of comics?

I used to. I still have a whole box full of comics. My favorite was Ghost Rider. Before I even got into this, I liked Ghost Rider and Batman.

OK, connect poker and paranormal investigations.

You know what's weird? I was watching poker last night and was thinking the same question. I came up with this: Poker is sitting at a table with a bunch of demons trying to steal your money and cheat you out of your money. They're going to try to take from you, lie to you, trick you. That's how demons are. They'll try to take everything you've got; they'll try to trick you and play games on you. You, as the player, have to be very cautious. You have to use all your senses, look for signs of the presence of these demons trying to trick you out of yours, out of what you have and what you own.

Why do you think ghosts like to scratch so much? Why aren't there hugging ghosts?

There are. I think we get the wrath of that because we particularly provoke the spirits that [scratch]. We don't provoke all spirits.

We try and narrow down that spirit and call that spirit out personally. But a lot of times we do feel that loving sensation. Goldfield Hotel with the ghost of the prostitute Elizabeth? I felt very loved in there and you can see a ball of energy go down my arm. A lot of times we feel just touches and when we feel those goosebumps, that's very soft, intimate. That happens at almost every investigation.

So then, when you guys shout a lot or get scratched ...?

We had a pair of sisters in their fifties that were weeping, shaking uncontrollably and wouldn't even go inside the [Villisca Axe Murder House] because when they lived there as children, they saw their father being attacked by this entity. They were literally in tears. Those are the people we are trying to help. We try to get them closure, and fight in their defense. When that happens, all hell can break loose.

Any other paranormal things you're into?

I'm very big into vampires. I have a tattoo on my right wrist that signifies Vlad, the real-life portrayal of Dracula. And when I was a little kid, I used to dress up like Dracula, when it wasn't even Halloween. I still have pictures of that. It's a part of me somehow. I've always had this fascination with the macabre. I want to investigate Italy and some of the real-life vampires; the bodies that we're finding with the bricks in their mouths.

Any favorite little-known ghost memories?

I remember once on Halloween night; I was a little kid and was looking out my window. It was probably about one in the morning, and I lived in a creepy little neighborhood, and I remember seeing there was nobody on the street. All the trick-or- treaters were gone but for some reason I wanted to look out that window. And all I remember is seeing this guy. It was like the one from *Scream*, but without the white mask. There was no face. I get chills - I haven't told this to anybody for a while - and I just saw this thing just show up on the sidewalk. It just disappeared right in front of my face. It was weird man. It was creepy. I'll always remember that.

And that's a favorite memory?

Yeah, it is. It's one of my favorite memories. I always think about that.

Kane Hodder: 'Friday the 13th' Jason's Scary, Horror-filled Life

(June 2011)

Despite being 6-foot-3, and having been in show business for three decades, most casual audiences wouldn't recognize Kane Hodder, but they know his work. The stuntman and actor has appeared in more than 100 films and TV shows and has left a mark on popular culture - and more often than not, it has been a big, bloody mark.

Although he has worked on blockbuster thrillers (*Se7en*), superhero flicks (*Daredevil*) and Oscar-winning films (*Monster*), Hodder's most enduring legacy is his time behind a hockey mask hacking through fornicating teens.

He portrayed killer Jason Voorhees in the classic slasher flicks *Friday the 13th*, parts seven, eight, nine and ten, and is the only actor to play the undead, deformed maniac more than once. More recently, the actor's role in the Hatchet films - as Victor Crowley, another undead, deformed maniac - has allowed Hodder to originate his own character in a cult franchise, the third entry of which was just greenlit in March. The result is a spot in the pantheon of actors who repeatedly left their mark on horror, alongside Robert Englund, Anthony Hopkins, and Anthony Perkins.

But what's a guy to do after making a killing in Hollywood? Hunt for ghosts, naturally.

While filming the 2006 supernatural horror film *Fallen Angels* at the reportedly haunted Ohio State Reformatory in Mansfield, Hodder and fellow stuntmen Rick Mccallum (*Hatchet, The Devil's Rejects*) and R.A. Milhailoff (*Texas Chainsaw Massacre 3, Hatchet II*) - all of whom who portrayed demons in the movie - decided to form the Hollywood Ghost Hunters paranormal investigative group. The team appeared on a January 2011 episode of Travel Channel's *Ghost Adventures* and also organize events where fans and amateur investigators can join the hunt.

Like other ghostbusters, Hodder's crew ain't afraid of no ghosts, but as "horror film professionals stalking the supernatural," the ghosts may just be afraid of them.

On June 10-11, 2011, Hodder will get a chance to spook the spooks at Rolling Hills Asylum in East Bethany, N.Y., where he'll be leading ticketed investigators through the famous haunted site, which has been featured on numerous paranormal programs.

A big, grizzled dude with intense eyes who looks too comfortable wielding a machete or with his hands around someone's neck, Hodder is actually a likable man who's just hacking and strangling for a scene or fan photo and joined us to talk about his upcoming investigation and his work in the entertainment industry.

On Horror

To begin with, you starred in a movie called The Rapture and May 21 was supposed to be Rapture Day. So, what did you do on the possible Rapture Day? Were you concerned and afraid of not possibly floating up to Heaven?

No, of course not. There's a couple of things. First of all, I think it's very funny when people predict the end of the world. I think it's ridiculous and you know, I laugh about it. And then, at the same time, I know based on the way I live my life and the work I've done, that I wouldn't go to Heaven anyway. I'm already resigned to going to Hell, so it doesn't matter when.

Speaking of your work, you've had a lot of onscreen kills. What number are we at now?

Coincidentally, my biography (KILL!: The True Story of the World's Most Prolific, Cinematic Killer) comes out October 1 and we document the first 100 kills. These are one-at-a-time, hands-on kills, not like somebody gunned down 30 people with a machine gun. This is one-by-one-by-one. But it's up to 140 or so.

You've been a busy boy.
That's a lot of killing when it's one-by-one, and the first 100 are just eight movies. So that's a pretty good average, I think.

You've been asked this question a lot and it might change over time, but what's your favorite kill?

For years and years, my favorite kill was the "sleeping bag" in *Friday the 13th, Part VII*, just because I killed somebody with something that isn't even a weapon. For the creativity of it, that was always my number one kill. Once I did the first *Hatchet*, that kill dropped down to number two. In the first *Hatchet* movie, I grab a woman and rip her head apart by her jaw. That is now my favorite all-time kill.

Speaking of Hatchet, it has a cult following. The Victor Crowley character is very popular for horror movie fans. Have you noticed any kind of shift where people are starting to think of you more as Victor Crowley than Jason?

Well, I wouldn't say necessarily more, but after we did the second *Hatchet* movie, I think it's pretty well equal now between Jason fans/Victor fans, or Jason questions and Victor questions. Which is great because I love the Victor character, too. People already know that I always loved playing Jason. I never wanted to stop. But with Victor, I played the character from its inception. Instead of taking over from six different guys that had played the role before me, once each. You know, that's a little trickier. But when you devote a character from the beginning, it's really rewarding to be able to do that and it's nice. Even though I think I developed my own type of Jason, I didn't originate him. It's nice to originate a character.

So, are you going to come back as Victor Crowley in Hatchet III and maybe number four?

I believe so, yes. If it has anything to do with me, yes. I will be back. I love the character, and now I've done it in two separate movies; it would drive me crazy to have somebody else play the character again. Yes, I would do it and I would hope Danielle Harris continues in three and possibly four, too, because we are very good friends. We've done a lot of stuff together. She's a tremendous actress and I think we could make another really good

181

movie.

If you come back for two more, this is suddenly going in a section on your resume where you created a character, saw it through to the end of the series - and it will match the number of Friday movies you've done.

Right. If I could do equal the amount of movies that I did as Jason and knowing I'm the only person to play the character, that would pretty much override the Jason stuff. Although I will never be ashamed that I played Jason; I'll always be proud of it, and always be very thankful because I realize how lucky I was to play that character. As most of these other guys do, too, to have played a character that is known all around the world. I fully understand how lucky I was.

If there was another Friday the 13th movie and they approached you, would you ever want to go back to it? Or do you just feel like that's a chapter in your life that you are ready to close?

Oh no, I'm not ready to close it. I would definitely put that fucking hockey mask back on and rip some people up. I always loved it and never wanted to quit. If for some reason, I did have the opportunity again, I would bury the hatchet so to speak and just play the character again. I think I got a pretty raw deal on the whole thing, but it would be more important for me to play the character again than have an ego about it, you know.

You do so many conventions and then you go to paranormal events, what is the question that you get asked the most?

Oh there are several that are so common and that are, so you know, obvious, but basically, "Did you like playing the character?" whether it be Jason or Victor. Also: "Was it hard playing the character." I don't think anyone understands how difficult it is to do physical things in that make-up. And, coincidentally, "If you had the chance to play Jason again, would you?" I don't mind answering it because if the right person hears it one day, maybe I will.

On Acting

Is there a question that you never get asked that you wish one day someone would throw it at you?

Well, there's one that I don't particularly want to have asked but I'm surprised no one has asked: "How do you take a shit when you are wearing that make up, when it's a full body suit?" The answer is: You don't, because you have to take the entire thing off to do it.

Well, I guess that leads to better growling, right?

Yeah, it does. More anger for sure. "Are you ever going to get the girl?" That's another good question.

Will you?

I doubt it. Although in other characters, I have had love scenes and sex scenes. I mean, I had a sex scene in *Hatchet II*. I actually had my first kissing scene in a movie that isn't out yet, called *Exit 33*. Maybe things are turning around that maybe I'll be able to play some characters that aren't necessarily so horrible - although I'll always love playing those. It is nice to try a challenge of something else. I mean, [*Hatchet* director] Adam Green has me dancing in a movie called, *Chillerama*. I did a movie called *The Afflicted* with Leslie Easterbrook, and I play an abused husband, which was very cool. And I just finished, just as of last month, a movie called *Tag*. Believe it or not, I play a bisexual sadist who gets the tables turned on him by Christopher Mintz-Plasse, the actor who played McLovin. We have a very, very tense, almost like sexually-tense scene together. His character is posing as a male prostitute, and I pick him up in an alley and it's a pretty creepy scene. He turns the tables on me, and I get the worst of it. It is interesting playing characters like that and I'm having a meeting today with a director on doing a comedy. I will never move away from playing the bad guy because I will always love it, but it's fun to do something else from time to time as well.

As an actor, you are craving new roles where you are able to stretch out a little bit?

Yeah, any actor would. Like I said, I don't want to move away from the characters that I can play in my sleep. I can play the brutal character and the scary guy pretty easily. I will always love it. I'm just saying it's nice to have the challenge of something that you never expected to do. Because I went into this business to be a stuntman, I never expected to be an actor; I just got lucky and started getting opportunities and was able to pull it off, I guess.

Speaking of stunt work, it's not as if you ever stopped doing stunts just because you started acting. Was there ever a time when you'd walk on the set to do some stunts, and you find yourself being recognized as the actor?

Normally, if I'm going to be a stunt person on a feature, then I almost always end up being cast in a role before we ever start. Because it makes sense. You've got the stunt coordinator there every day, so you might as well utilize him in a character. In features, I don't really come across as a surprise with other actors but on TV stuff, I do. For instance, I've done several episodes of the show *Chuck*. I went in to just do some stunt things, just a little stunt role on an episode and realized that the main bad guy was being played by Lou Ferrigno. He and I are friends just from conventions and actually, I used to be one of the stunt men on *The Incredible Hulk* TV show. I've known Lou since the early '80s and I didn't know he was playing a part because I was just called in to do some stunts. He didn't know I was coming in, and so that was kind of a surprise. And Zack Levi and I have become friends and we've done a movie together since then.

Any times when others knew who you are, but maybe the "celebrity" doesn't?

Every once in a while, I'll go and just be an "ND," what they call a Non-Descript stunt man and I'll come across some actors I've known in the past and were kind of surprised to see me. In fact, I'll give you a good story. It doesn't happen much, but it does happen from time to time. I was one of the stunt men on a movie called *Under Siege* and we were shooting on a battleship down in Mobile, AL. I was working with Steven Seagal, Tommy Lee Jones, Gary Busey. I was just one of the stunt guys on the movie for about three weeks, and there were some visitors, some kids - like a boy scout group or something that came on the ship to visit the set. One of them recognized me from the Jason stuff and asked me to sign something. I didn't want to seem like an asshole; he had a piece of wood he was carrying around and so I signed it for him. That's the least I could do. He knew me from the Jason stuff. I signed it. Then, maybe half an hour later, I was looking, and the kids were all talking to Seagal, and I saw the kid give Segal the piece of wood to sign also. Seagal took it and looked at it and said, "Who the fuck is Kane Hodder?" I heard him say it, and now I'm going to get fired because I'm signing an autograph on his movie! But nothing became of it. It was just funny to see him do that.

That is funny. After that, did you guys get along or was there just not any interaction with Seagal?

I've done three movies with him. That was the second one, actually. I've done Out for Justice and I did Fire Down Below after that. So we got along fine. I fought with him quite a bit in different scenes. He's a little more for the realism than I am even. I think you have to have some realism in the scenes to make them look authentic, but he wants even more so sometimes it gets a little rough.

Speaking of getting rough, you suffered some burn injuries as a result of some stunt work. How did that impact what you would do for the job?

There's nothing I avoid except horses. I still do a lot of fire stunts. By the way, I'm not sure how that information became known on the Web, but I got burned in 1977. On July 13th. I know it says on IMDB I was burned in the early '80s but it was 1977. It was my first year in stunts, actually. So it wasn't a great way to start my career. I did avoid fire stunts for a little while but then I thought, what the fuck, you know, get back on the horse, like they say.

They I ended up kind of specializing in fire after that. I've never had an incident with fire ever since because I learned so much on that bad one. The only thing I avoid doing is horses because I never really learned how to ride a horse well, so I leave it up to the cowboy stunt guys.

Any movies in your career that you wish you could take back?

I've done some movies that ended up not being very well received but I would never say, "I wish I never did it." Every single movie I've ever done, whether it be big budget, small budget, I've always enjoyed it because of what I did in the movie. Whether it be a cool stunt or whatever. I think it's kind of shitty for people to say, "I wish I never did that movie." You know, fuck you. You should have known that ahead of time. If you knew that it was a small movie, don't do it then if you're going to have a problem with it. I'll never be embarrassed of anything I've done. In fact, with the characters I think are the most embarrassing I've played, I'll be the first one to tell people that they can get a good laugh out of it. Like a movie called, *Hardbodies*. I played a ridiculous character that's embarrassing as hell, but hey, that's part of your process of expanding your career. You do some things that you look at and say, "Oh my God, that's embarrassing. You've got to see this." If you have any confidence in yourself, you make sure people know that.

Give me an example of a movie you're proudest of.

One of the movies I'm the proudest about doing the stunts in was *Monster* with Charlize Theron. She won an Oscar for it. I was the stunt coordinator on it, and I also played the cop that arrested her at the end of the movie. I'm really proud of that because it is so well done, and I think the action is good. There wasn't that much of it but what there is, I think was pretty well done and pretty scary. That's the movie I learned the most about acting. I have never been trained as an actor in any class or in any school or anything like that, but if I can pull off any kind of acting talent, it's because of watching people like Charlize Theron. I watched her for six weeks, every day - how she prepared and how she got to certain places. That's the best training an actor can have: observing.

If I remember correctly, Monster came out in 2003. So we're talking about a couple of decades into your career is when you learned the most about acting?

Oh, for sure, for sure. Even watching other actors, too, but that's the one that stands out the most. I didn't have all that much action to do so I could really sit and watch her work. And it was just invaluable.

On Investigating

What's the real story with how Hollywood Ghost Hunters was founded? I've heard it emerged while filming at Mansfield Reformatory.

Yes, with my buddy Rick. Rick McCallum and I were doing a movie called *Fallen Angels* there and we would have the entire facility to ourselves for the movie. Whenever Rick and I had a chance, we'd go investigate wherever there weren't people, and there was only probably 25 of us in the whole place. It's a big facility, and if you're shooting on one end of the cell block, you could go on the other side and not even know anyone was in there. We just realized, at that time, that each of us was so much into the paranormal and ghost hunting. That's when Rick thought it was a good idea, we form a group. Having a group of ghost hunters that are all involved with horror movies in some way, or another is kind of a cool group because we're all used to being the ones to scare people - and now we're going out there to become scared ourselves. Also, we know all the tricks to making something look real when it isn't. There's nothing that can be staged that we wouldn't see through, you know.

The story is that you saw a shadow person at Mansfield. Was that your paranormal experience?

I've always been interested myself but never, even to this day, have encountered or seen something that is so incredibly paranormal that it freaks me out. I always tend to explain things away scientifically. I'm a skeptic but I'm an open-minded skeptic. I think a lot of ghost investigators tend to get carried away with the smallest things wanting it to be paranormal and making it into more than it really is. I just am very aware that I don't want to do that. So I'm very objective about everything. But my interest in the paranormal goes back to when I was a kid -which is the same with Rick. It's just that we never had the opportunity to investigate something so completely as we did with Mansfield and that's when we really got started.

Has there been any activity on other sets you've worked on?

I've heard of activity on other sets. Rick and I were shooting a movie at a studio, and he did some investigating and encountered some things. He's one of those guys that a lot of stuff happens to. I'm not sure if he makes too much out of things or if he's just one of those guys that attracts the spirits - which I guess I've heard could be possible. I have really never seen anything on a set.

Other actors I've worked with have told me stuff. Danielle Harris, who is also in our group, tells me all kinds of stories that happen to her in her apartment.

When speak to your investigators at Rolling Hills, what are the main tips you try to pass along?

One main thing for me is for that I believe - and I think you probably will too if you are skeptical: I believe the power of suggestion is huge within ghost hunting. What I try and ask people to do is if they see something or hear something, do not specify what it is they saw or heard. I would rather have someone say, "Did you just see that?" and then have somebody else say, "Yes, I did. I saw this." Then let's see if it matches what the first person saw. So many times, I've seen somebody say, "Did you just see that shape go across the hall real low?" and then because somebody has suggested that other people think they saw it. The power of suggestion is huge, which is why in police work, when a crowd or several people witness a crime, they will try to spread those people out immediately. If one person says, "This is what the person looked like," it will suggest that in the mind of other people and they will agree with it without even realizing that's not what they thought they saw ... That's the biggest habit I want people to break themselves of. Don't say what you saw. Even write it down before you talk to each other and then compare it. Then, to me, that's more meaningful.

With your own investigative style, do you prefer your own instincts or technology and gadgets?

I like a combination of both. I may think I hear or see something, but if it's corroborated with technology, that's the best of all possible worlds. I like both. You know, I've never been a big fan of the EMF meters or never was much of a fan of the voice recordings. But then when I caught that one during the *Ghost Adventures* episode, it was the only one that's ever been convincingly clear to me what someone was saying. I am such a skeptic that if I had heard that recording and somebody else said they were holding the recorder, I would have sworn somebody whispered into it.

Zak Bagans Creates 'Paranormal Challenge' For Ghost Hunters
(June 2011)

They call him the "Chairman" but there's never been a boss like Zak Bagans on reality television before.

Clad in all black, military-esque fatigues, he nearly blends into the cave like surroundings. Like a hybrid of Batman and Captain Kirk, Bagans possesses an intense sense of calm, standing with hands clasped behind his back as he peers at the nerve center, the setup of scaffolding and audio/visual equipment. Occasionally he looks over the heads of his "Chief Judge" and celebrity guest judges at a bank of monitors and calls out directions to "listen in" to the onscreen figures, illuminated only in night vision.

Bagans deliberates with his judges, listens thoughtfully and asks questions, the most important of which is not, "Do ghosts exists?" but instead, "Which paranormal team is the best at finding them?"

Zak Bagans is a true believer of ghosts, and this is his world of *Paranormal Challenge*, a new reality series premiering tonight, 9 p.m. ET, on Travel Channel which merges the popular paranormal investigation programs with competition shows.

Serving as executive producer and star - similar to the double duty he performs on Travel's *Ghost Adventures* - *Challenge* pits two ghost hunting teams against one another for bragging rights at some of the nation's allegedly "most haunted" locations.

For the 34-year-old former DJ, ghost hunting is a way for the living to find answers about the afterlife, but also "allows the dead to find their answers" through communication. His pursuit garnered him millions of fans since he co-created the *Ghost Adventures* documentary with Nick Groff in 2004 (where he appeared to catch on film a brick lifted and hurled at him by an unseen force), which aired on the erstwhile Sci-Fi Channel (now Syfy) in 2007 before Travel Channel picked up the show about a year later.

Now, although Bagans is a leader in a crowded field of TV investigators, he insists he doesn't have a monopoly on the paranormal community.

"Just because I'm on television - or other people are on television - doesn't mean that this is our community and that we lead it; this is something that belongs to the world," says Bagans - hence his idea for *Challenge*.

Not only is the show a unique evolution in the paranormal-TV genre, what makes the new program especially notable is that Bagans hopes to share his fame with regional investigation teams who often pursue evidence of the afterlife but may not have a venue to show off their work - and lack access to these well-known haunted hotspots.

"*Paranormal Challenge* was created to spark unity- to not just showcase *Ghost Adventures* guys, not just showcase all these other shows, but to allow these other teams that have been researching the paranormal for so long and allow them now to come into the spotlight."

While Bagans emphasizes that *Challenge* is a small way to give back to fans and give props to other spook seeking organizations, he acknowledges it is still a competition show, which means there has to be judging criteria to determine a winning team.

"We do not tell [contestants] how to investigate," he says before adding, "I've come up with the categories that are essential building blocks of the fundamentals of paranormal investigating which are the use of history, teamwork, technology, and the evidence ... those are things that can easily be judged."

Plus, Bagans points out that winning the challenge doesn't mean "big cash prizes." He says he tells all of his teams it's all about having fun and taking part in a shared goal to "find answers."

That's why he says the victors only get bragging rights. Even with the categories the teams are analyzed on, he says he can't claim to tell a group that there are right and wrong ways to investigate.

Besides, he adds, he already respects and appreciates every team who shows up to pursue the unknown.

Along for the ghost ride with Bagans is "Chief Judge" Dave Schrader - the host of the *Darkness On The Edge of Town* Internet radio show and paranormal tourism event organizer - as well as a rotating stable of notable figures within the paranormal community, including authors, journalists, historians, psychics, inventors, and personalities from other reality shows. As established in the premiere episode at Rolling Hills Asylum in East Bethany, NY, and followed by an investigation at Philadelphia's Eastern State Penitentiary, Bagans and his judges monitor the competing teams live through a system of robotic and static cameras, as well as one cameraman per group.

Compared to the small *Ghost Adventures* investigative crew of Bagans, Groff and Aaron Goodwin, who get "locked down" alone in haunted locales, *Paranormal Challenge* is a larger production. But Bagans says it is necessary to avoid an illusion that competing teams were alone in a building.

"I'm not a big fan of paranormal television with tons of camera crews unaccounted for because audio evidence is one of the most important things, we are searching for ... to have unaccounted crew members in a location where investigators are is like going to a homicide scene, having a bunch of kids walk around without gloves on."

In addition to a larger scale, another difference between *Adventures* and *Challenge* is that Bagans isn't in the midst of the action. He says he's used to the excitement of investigating but relishes hanging back as the Challenge Chairman where he oversees the judges and observes the teams in action.

But, he adds, he does occasionally have the temptation to join the investigation with the groups.

"I'm like a little kid sitting on the other side of a chain link fence watching my friends go ride a Ferris wheel at the fair. It's hard as s--t for me not to get out there."

Statements like this perhaps reveal how much of a big kid Bagans really is. Though a serious enthusiast of the supernatural, and despite his reputation as the guy on TV who runs down dark halls shouting at demons, Bagans isn't afraid to have fun and goof on himself. He's lampooned his persona - and host Joel McHale's - on E! Entertainment Television's *The Soup*. He also thinks the paranormal community would benefit from relaxing a little and dismisses critics who claim a competition show will compromise the credibility of paranormal investigations.

"We need to get away from the seriousness of paranormal investigations; there's people in this industry so protective of it that they think they own it - And that's not right."

In fact, Bagans says anyone can and should research the paranormal and ignore haters who try to claim it or dictate how it must be done.

And though he says he's been dealing with his own paranormal challenge of executive producing and appearing on two shows - as well as working on his September 2011 biography *Dark World: Into the Shadows of the Lead Investigator of the Ghost Adventures Crew* and being a main attraction at paranormal conventions - Zak Bagans can't think of a better way to live.

"It's what I love to do," he says. "And the biggest gift is that the audience loves what we're doing."

"I wish I could go out and hug every single one of them ... Those are the people I'm here to work my ass off for."

The *Paranormal Challenge* and *Ghost Adventures* star Zak Bagans pauses for a moment before continuing with a now-classic, Chairman-appropriate joke: "Winning."

Animal Planet's 'Finding Bigfoot' Believer and Skeptic Sound Off

(January 2012)

One is a believer, one is a skeptic, but both are in pursuit of answers about a missing link myth. On Animal Planet's *Finding Bigfoot* (Sundays at 10 p.m.), research biologist Ranae Holland is the voice of scientific doubt regarding the Sasquatch while Matt Moneymaker, founder of the Bigfoot Field Research Organization (BFRO), needs no convincing but does want more proof. Along with James "Bobo" Fay and Cliff Barackman, each week the show finds Holland and Moneymaker recreating supposed evidence, testing theories, and investigating "Squatch" hotspots.

On the surface, Holland and Moneymaker's relationship seems like it should be confrontational; the church of the proven fact versus the unproven faith normally don't mix so well. However, the pair says they've mutual respect for each other's mission despite disagreements and debate between them - and they finish each other's sentences about as much as they cut one another off.

Paranormal Pop Culture recently brought the believer and skeptic together over coffee in Bigfoot-neutral New York City for a conversation about their relationship on and off camera, the dangers of reality-TV and how Bigfoot fits into the scientific and paranormal communities.

The believer and skeptic, how did you get together?

Ranae Holland: I was raised in South Dakota. My special time with my dad, quality time out alone, would either be testing stunt gear - because he was this crazy daredevil, jack of all trades - or watching Bigfoot movies or *In Search Of...* He was a really into the paranormal, especially Bigfoot. And that was our special time. So, I move out to Seattle, and I'm becoming a research biologist. Thirty some-odd years later, I'm working and contracting for NOAA [National Oceanic and Atmospheric Administration]. In 2003, my dad passed away, and I was going through his things, and I run across some Bigfoot stuff - and I have vivid, vivid memories of wanting to find those Bigfoot stories where I'm doing my field work.

So, I jump on the Internet, I find Matt and the BFRO in 2003, 2004. I tell him, "With all due respect, I personally don't believe in Bigfoot, but I love Bigfoot stories." So we developed a relationship where I could contact him, get access to the database. Meanwhile I'm on the Olympic Peninsula and in the location that's one of the hotbeds of sightings reports, so I can run out there for him. I was actually out there three times a week anyway. He wanted to know about elk, Coho [salmon] and the conditions out there. So we had that relationship for about seven years, and I continue working at NOAA. My contract was ending and there was this window where I'm waiting to head off on a different project and get more schooling, pick up on my funding - and at that point, the universe working its magic, Matt calls me and tells me [the show] was looking nine months for this final person, and that was me. And there you have it.

Matt Moneymaker: That was in 2004 and so if I was already doing [paid Bigfoot expeditions] then, I met you and then you finally called back and said you think something's going on over in "The Twins" [Twin Harbors Washington State Park].

RH: I remember our initial conversation like it was yesterday. Matt's this passionate person, and this is a controversy that's been going on as long as Bigfoot has been around. In all due respect, I don't believe it and Matt does and Matt's seen one.

Have you heard anything, have you smelled anything, have you seen anything? - I just with fondness remember this conversation of theory or belief. Matt said something like, "women have a better advantage of being out there ... men are more intimidating and you're a woman, you're out there driving the same vehicle ...

MM: We had gone out there, gotten engrossed in these things so many times that we knew, just from having a mixed group with us, that these things come closer to females. They just do!

RH: So, I think Matt's thinking it's a great opportunity.

MM: I think they're less afraid of females.

RH: And Matt's got this opportunity. He's like, here's this female biologist on the Olympic Peninsula, this hotbed of activity. She goes out there and stays out there, so he's on fire for that reason.

We have this great relationship and I think we met one time because he happened to be coming in as I was going out, so one time we actually met. But I did see a flash of fur. Which, to me, I don't know what that is. You know, I didn't see Bigfoot ... I see an opening of canopy, I see a flash of fur, but at that point, a combination of bat, or...

MM: Wait wait, it looked like it might. Have. Been. Legs! Not just a flash of fur - it's something that made you think it could have been possibly a Squatch. Right?

RH: Hold on, let me finish, if I may? So, from there, Matt was wanting to find a ridge, find a ravine, and I think from there - really close to my field sites - is where the expeditions started. Now what I've been doing is I've looked over my shoulder, and truly, this is the first time. What was really great is we were going to locations nobody has a reason to go to. We have to sample.

And I've looked over my shoulder, one of my crew members had cracked his knee. So as I look over my shoulder, about 60 or 70 yards, there's an opening in the canopy. But it was up high! It wasn't like down low on the ground, and it's an opening that's more oblong this way, and I just see black movement. So the question becomes, the canopy opening was a certain shape. But it was jet black, it was moving quietly, I don't know what it is. I mean, you're ...

MM: Something gave you a reason that it might not be a bear.

RH: No, well I'm just saying, for you, the opening was, at your assumption as we reviewed it, was that it could be an arm. Your belief because it was moving that way. Because it wasn't an elk, because elk I would have seen the rest of the body, I would have seen the top, or the tan part.

MM: I mean, usually, you can ID something. Why couldn't you just go, "oh, that was a ..." whatever it was?

RH: Because it's at 70 yards and it's just an opening in the canopy. You're only seeing part of something. So I saw something move quick and quietly. To me, I saw a black animal and it's right in the area where there's a hotbed of sightings, and it really spurred Matt to go on, too. That's a great place for locations and your expeditions on "The Twins" had a lot of success.

What drives you nuts about one another?
RH: Well, all four of us are very passionate and very different.

MM: We're put in a very, very tough situation - very frustrating. We're kind of ideological; we have to be pitted against each other because I'm like the leader of the group. I have had a very close encounter with one of these things. I speak in terms of them, like "I know they're real." Obviously, her position, which we want, is somebody who's going to be able to look from the scientific perspective and know that protocol and see what everyone is doing that can fit better in there. She thinks in terms of finding objective evidence to turn around and persuade other scientists.

That's great, and somebody should be focused on that, but if you only focus that way, you're not even going to follow the leads. The leads are anecdotal if they're not even scientific - they're witnesses talking about seeing them there, and kind of piecing together things in a very hypothetical way. You have to have that if you're going to be led to some kind of physical evidence. You know what I mean? It's not that we need the scientific community to confirm for us that these things are there. We do want to get stuff so that they know and so that we can have our big "ha ha, so you were wrong, we were right" moment. We love that!

She kind of comes at it looking at it from that eye. And more importantly, she's been doing field stuff for a long time. I've been with a serious club, and with [the show] Mysterious Encounters.

We had a lead female, Autumn Williams, and it was too brutal for her going out and doing this. You're out in the cold through most of the night, every day and just out exposed to the elements a lot. I knew Ranae could handle that.

How does editing come into play with showing off the skeptic/believer opinions?

MM: She understands exactly where I come from, and I understand where she comes from. We're put in a difficult position where we're given a narrow window to give our responses to a situation. It's really hard to deliver what you have to say about something - especially when you have a few of the people who want to deliver what they have to say about something - and she'll say something I'd want to counter to make sure we have the validity. But we know that it ain't going to fit in the 20 seconds that they're going to give us on the show.

RH: And it's more than that. Here's what it is - you take anybody who is passionate about something, and you've got to be a strong person to do this type of work. You've got to believe in the work. And you've put them on the road for four months with those grueling type hours, and anybody's going to fight. But one thing to look at the show is, I'm not in the BFRO.

MM: She's the infidel! (laughs)

RH: (laughs) I come from a different approach, and it's good that I understand the anecdotal stories and problem solving and being objective. I bring something that Matt doesn't bring. And Matt brings something I don't bring, and Bobo [James Fay] brings something, Cliff [Barackman] brings something - we all bring that. We don't have a leader as a group. We're four pieces to this group and I think that we really need all of us.

MM: We try not to act like somebody being the leader when we're all out there. I wouldn't like that.

Do you view Bigfoot research as an arm of science or as part of the paranormal?

MM: It's definitely an arm of science. There are very prominent scientists in Canada and one in the United States. There's [Dr. Jeffrey] Meldrum, a respectable guy in the United States, [David] Daegling, and then there's Jane Goodall, and there's a few other top-notch scientists who are really analyzing and evaluating and explaining in non-opinion and biological terms what this may be. I don't think you have the same thing with ghosts. I don't think you have a high level of professors in universities in Canada and the United States who are like, "listen, we have ample, a lot of residual evidence to explain that there is a spirit world." You know what I mean? I don't think you have that, and with UFOs, you may have scientists who say yes, it's possible, but they don't really have a grip on whatever it is people are seeing. The Bigfooters are much closer to science, and we've got tons more witnesses, there's tons more sightings, there's interactions - everything falls under a little bit more control and it's really a predictable thing. But we've got a lot more scientists involved in Bigfoot stuff than I think anything other paranormal categories have.

Ranae, as a biologist, do you think it fits within the paranormal community or the scientific community?

RH: Well, I think it's both, but it starts in the physical sciences. Grover Krantz [physical anthropology professor at University of Washington] was the first physical anthropologist to step forward. You've got Daegling, you've got Meldrum, you've got all these scientists who were there, just as Matt said previously. It's something tactile. It's supposed to be something physical, right? It's supposed to be this animal, but as you further delve in, you start to see the reason why it overlaps. There are people whose belief system, whether folklore or not in Native American culture, say it's a shapeshifter or it's this, that - that's where it starts to be paranormal.

MM: But have you heard a model of the paranormal ...

everything you heard come together, does it make sense as a biological entity or does it make more sense as a paranormal entity?

RH: My personal opinion, and the reason why I'm out here with these guys, is I'm within biological sciences, so where is the evidence? Gathering that physical evidence, that's how I interpret it. But generally speaking, I understand how it overlaps into the paranormal realm because there are a lot of people who have reports, beliefs, etc. where it goes into that gray area of the two. My personal belief - if I'm approaching it in a physical science aspect would be a biological animal - if it has behavior, the size of reproduction, the migration routes, caloric intake required, habitat required. Hair, body, blood, you know? All of that. That would be my approach.

Ranae, keeping with the scientific question, how are you received in the scientific community now that you're doing this?

RH: The people that I work with in the core group - being fortunate enough to work with the professional mentors that I have - they all understand my relationship with Bigfoot is the connection to my father, first and foremost. But the more I learn and the more time I spend, I start gathering evidence that isn't easily explained away. I start meeting my academic peers above and below me who, ones who have known me for years, tell me a story that they can't explain away. And I've had that all throughout my career.

MM: They tell you sighting stories, don't they?

RH: No, they'll tell me people who have either heard things, or seen a glimpse of something, and maybe not people that I know in my academic inner circle, but I met some of the few on the periphery who tell me, straight up, that they've seen one at close range. So, do I get the ribbing? Yes, from people who really don't know me. I mean, if you are going to enter the Bigfoot realm, be prepared. I mean, you have to be thick-skinned. And yeah, I get the ribbing, but people who know me professionally and personally know what my connection is and how I remain - and everyone that I know within the academic community feels the same way very much.

When this is all over, when the show ends or when you move onto the next thing, do you think there'll be any resistance when you try to re-enter that academic field?

RH: That was the first question I had when this whole thing came to Matt. I think I said "You know how I feel about this, Matt! Absolutely not." Then it was finally Todd Miller from Discovery who said, "What is your hesitation?" I went to every professional person who mentored at University of Washington, NOAA and everybody was like "Why not?" Now, had I not had a decade of field experience and already worked my niches - and maybe had those openings where I could go back - I probably would never have done it. It honestly was an alignment of many things to make this situation right for me, personally.

How does your role as a skeptic and scientist mesh with the challenges of reality TV where you have to be so brief!

RH: There are people there who see the few things I say on the show - which, of course, are edited - and think that I'm not skeptical at all! You can ask the guys. I am incredibly skeptical to the point where you talked about where we get annoyed, where Bobo just looks at me like, "How can you not believe?" People really need to take the confines of television into account.

Matt, what's your take on the production process? Is there a moment where you wish you had been given more time, or that the editors had cut something a little bit differently to show off more of a situation?

MM: I should say I understand what they're trying to do when they edit - to keep it moving and exciting - and I guess they kind of need to do it. We, of course were hoping and thinking they'd edit in such a way that it would appeal to our own peer group. But of course, we're a small minority and we know too much. We're people who already know the subject. And so the things that are going to interest us aren't necessarily appropriate for the people who don't know anything about the subject.

The example I'll give is the Marble Mountains footage. There's this thing walking along the ridge line. We could have spent a lot more time talking about that footage, but they didn't even show the parts of that that are most compelling. We couldn't get back up there to the site to do a recreation, but there was footage from two different recreations showing how titanically tall that thing was by having people really just stand next to the same tree.

When you show those comparisons, it just like, it just can make you shiver. They didn't show that. We could have spent a lot of time analyzing that, but that's not, that's too documentary-ish, from their perspective. That's what we'd want to do, that's what we want to see! But they want Scooby Doo, man, and so that's why they're having us run around. Again, I guess it makes sense we should try and be appealing not necessarily to our own peers who know everything about this stuff already, but to people who don't know anything.

Television is a different medium. It does require different things. These aren't stupid people who are making the decisions on how the show should go. I think they're right about this. And all the stuff that we can't say - we know if we can't say in this segment this thing about this incident - we've got a lot of episodes in the future where we can communicate that idea. So if we're just throwing out little bits here and there in the context of an action show? Then fine. You know, that's the way they want it, and it isn't necessarily the right way to go after a Squatch, but it's apparently the right way to do a show about going after a Squatch.

RH: Matt made a really good point. What we do want to do on these expeditions is within the confines of television. One thing that is interesting to know is if we're out there and we have something happen over the course of the evening - but we don't catch it on video - it didn't happen, as far as the wrap up of the show. What people fail to understand is how 100 hours of filming on average for a 43-minute show is a lot of waiting and a lot of work and a lot of cold and a lot of elements, and if you don't catch it and capture it on the video part? It didn't happen for the show.

Are you concerned at all about the technology that allows people to create really lifelike creatures with their computers trickling into your work?

MM: I know people who do digital effects, and if someone came up with footage like that that was in clear daylight, looked really real - but still you're wondering, "I don't know, could that be digitally animated?" If we showed [effects experts] that footage, I guarantee you they would be able to look at it and tell you. There is something about the way those composites and images blend in with the background if you really look closely. They can see the telltale signs of the digital calculations done for the composite.
They can tell the difference.

So you're not too worried about a hoax culture?

RH: I am.

MM: Well, it hasn't happened yet! It hasn't happened where somebody has made a convincing piece of Bigfoot footage that turned out to be digitally animated thing. There's always been a guy in costume, and I think there will always be because that's a hell of a lot cheaper!

RH: Technology is a double-edged sword. It has given us thermal imaging, night vision, longer battery life - just when you're out there with the equipment to be out in these areas where it's remote. Technology is on our side but at the same time, technology is against us to people who could potentially build the better costume.

MM: But digitally, that hasn't happened.

RH: But I'm talking - well I'm not saying it has or it hasn't. I'm just saying, in all aspects, just the broad scope of technology is against us. We are constantly fighting the battle. We are constantly taking into account and looking for hoaxes. We're constantly taking [hoaxes] into consideration when we do these expeditions. I'm going to tell you the lengths we go to ...

MM: And they don't show that on the show.

RH: Again, a double-edged sword! Whereas we gain popularity, we're going to get more feedback, people coming in and sharing their stories, sharing their video footage. But at the same time, as we gain popularity, were going to get more hoaxsters.

Speaking of famous hoaxes, the 1967 Patterson-Gimlin film - which really launched the modern fascination with Bigfoot - do you buy it?

MM: Oh yeah, that's a real one.

RH: I love me some Bob Gimlin. (Matt laughs)
Going there to that spot, meeting that man, watching his eyes - I'm still torn, but there is nothing I've encountered that I can just *snap* and say, "Oh, that's not it." Now, you see this video and unfortunately, you're not seeing the original generation of its 1967 film when it's in the distance because the video will put it further away. I hear people talking about it saying, "I see the fingers moving and the muscles bulging" but I don't see that as easily.

You look up at clouds and you get that confirmation bias. You see what you're looking for. But come on, I mean, I do have difficulty writing it off that that's a guy in a suit.

I mean, I am on the fence on that one. I can't wrap my head around that whatever is in this film remains undetected, but at the same time, I don't know how someone was able to fake that. I mean, there was a catastrophic flood the winter before, which was really interesting. I didn't know that. It looks like a lunar landing, and that explains that situation. As far as someone getting down there and walking in some type of suit, it would have been maybe a lot easier - that's why it's so flat. The substrate is very simple, not complex. But putting all those pieces together ... nobody has been able to come forward, explain exactly how they got the suit, produce the suit. I'd love to see someone step forward and show the public how that was done, because I mean there's the Zapruder film, the Bigfoot, there's a lot of controversy that persists to this very day. Passionate people on both sides.

And yet Patterson confessed it was faked right before he died in 1972, right?

MM: Isn't that funny he thinks that! I mean, we're talking about the Surgeon's Photograph. It was a photo of Loch Ness, or the guy who got that photo and as he was dying - the surgeon on his deathbed - said, "yeah I faked it." And a lot of people already suspected it. That story about dispelling got translated into the Patterson footage. It started almost like an urban myth that Patterson had died and that he said on his death bed, but no, he never did. In fact, he said himself, no, there was a few people that Bob Gimlin knew were there. He actually confirmed yeah, it was the real thing. People were trying to encourage him to get better so he could go back down there and get more footage. So, it was the Loch Ness story that got translated to Patterson. So no, that never happened!

RH: If you could look at that film to this day, I mean that's where it all started for me. I'd sit with my dad going, "There is a monster in California!" Well, if that's not real, then how did they do it?

Here I am, 30-something years later, still wondering. You speak to all these special effects people you were talking about; I don't know. If it's not real, then how is it done? That's another part of this whole thing. Where are all those continued reports coming from? I mean, this phenomenon is fascinating.

Josh Gates' 'Destination Dinner' Serves Up Travel to Fans

(April 2012)

To paraphrase Indiana Jones, it's not the years that matter, it's the mileage. And adventurer and TV host Josh Gates has a lot of miles - frequent flier miles, that is. In fact, the star of Syfy's travel and monster-hunting show *Destination Truth* has so many that the confessed miles hoarder will begin dishing them out as part of a new project called "Destination Dinner."

Announced at last week's C2E2 in Chicago, Gates (also the author of *Destination Truth: Memoirs of a Monster Hunter*) will begin advertising dinners to be held across the world as a way to give back to fans, and to expose them to the adventures of travel. Once a location is revealed via social media, Gates will foot the bill for the meal and guide a short tour to anyone who chooses to hop on a plane, train or automobile to get there. Moreover, he will select a random fan and use his miles to cover their flight.

According to Gates, people are looking for adventures and want to get out into the unknown, and "Destination Dinner" is his way of providing that for his supporters. The project will be launching Summer 2012, which is when Season Five of *Destination Truth* premieres, but Gates said this is a standalone, side project not affiliated with Syfy.

Josh Gates sat down for an exclusive with Paranormal Pop Culture to discuss the inspiration behind "Destination Dinner," as well as provide some hints at where dinner will be served.

First off, how many miles do you have at this point? Are we at the George Clooney/ "Ryan Bingham" Up in the Air goal of 10 million?

I don't know that I'm quite at the "Ryan Bingham"/George Clooney "I'm going to get on a plane and never come home" point. But let's say it's a healthy round number.

In the millions?

Uh... healthy round number [laughs]. A lot.

This is really going to put a dent in those miles, right?

It really is. I'm really a hoarder of those miles. Just like in that movie - which really struck a chord in me. He has that really great moment in the restaurant where he's with the girl, and he says it's about the miles, not about using them. It's something to collect, almost.

So I really approached it that way. I've collected them just for the sake of collecting them, and even had opportunities to use them but bought tickets instead just to not dip into the collection. But I have reached the point where I came to a realization that I have a lot of these miles because of the show, because of the fans. It sounds a little saccharine, but I really believe that, and I feel like I want to share them.

But how did this particular idea come about?

One of the questions I get all the time is, "How can we be on the show, and how can we get involved to travel?" and "Do you take applications?" It's something we've known for a long time that people wanted to do but we just haven't been able to make it happen as part of the show. So I'm just thrilled to be able to announce it as something I'm doing personally.

Why now?

For me, I've had an unusual bit of downtime. I've been traveling nonstop for the past four years, but we had this little hiatus between Season Four and Season Five, and I've had more time to meet fans and more time for hearing and reading what they're sending us.

One of the things at the core of *Destination Truth* is to make people excited about the idea of travel. We always say we want people to feel like they're out in the field with us. But reading all this fan feedback, I realized - as much as people really love the show - there is an opportunity here to actually get them out in the world. The time just seemed right for it.

You're obviously passionate about travel, but why is it so important to spread that passion to fans to the point of, "Hey, here's a dinner on me"?

To me, travel is something people should think of as vital. I think of travel the same way as I think of diet, exercise, education. It's a muscle people need to exercise. If I can get people excited and physically out there in the world, then I'd love to keep doing it.

So, you are going to be the Richard Simmons of travel?

[laughs] That's a funny way of putting it! My goal on Destination Truth has always been for people to come away from episodes feeling like they had been exposed to a story, place, culture they didn't know as much about before. I'm also trying to plant that seed for people to have their own adventures. So if I can do that in a very literal way and actually break bread with someone overseas, show them around, that would be an immediately gratifying way to accomplish that.

When is the first dinner?

It will happen sometime this summer; I don't know exactly when. That will be part of the fun of it. I have to figure out where we do these things. I have some really good ideas, and I wanted to do it in a way that anybody could come. I don't want it where just one person wins this thing, so it's not a Golden Ticket kind of situation. If people are really serious about travel, really excited about going out in the field, I want to give them the opportunity to have a really unusual travel adventure - and then give them the benefit of my knowledge and experience of the places they're going to happen in. We'll share a meal with them - give back- to them and guide a little tour for them. I recognize not everyone will be able to afford that, so I'm going to use my miles to bring someone out to each dinner as a way of saying thank you to the fans.

Logistically, how will you get the winner to the destination?

The way this will work is I'll advertise over Twitter with a time, date and place. Depending on the venue, it will be anybody that can make it there is free to come. Or if it's a limited venue - at a restaurant or something like that - we'll figure out a registration.

Before the trip happens, I'll do a draw based on followers on Twitter for one person. We'll have to figure out that lottery system. I'll publish the dates, and if people can commit to those dates, then we'll do a draw and whoever gets drawn at random will have an opportunity to fly out there.

How much notice ahead of time will you post details?

It will depend. We also have to see how successful this is, but my aim is to do a couple different things. I'd love to do a long-lead dinner where we advertise the date well ahead of time so people can figure out vacation time, booking a ticket, things like that. It might also be, "Hey, this is going to happen in a week." It may also be domestic. Maybe I'll try to organize some things in the States so it will be more accessible to our fans in America. It will be a combination of those things.

One of the real fun aspects of *Destination Truth* is the fun, wacky, improvised nature of travel. That's something I hope to replicate. In order for people to come to these things and have that experience, they'll have to put themselves in the position of taking a leap and doing something unconventional.

How many dinners will there be?

My initial goal is to do at least one very exotic location, then something a little less exotic, then something domestic. We'll see how those three goes and play it by ear. I have a real passion for travel, and a real passion for sharing my experiences in these places with our viewers. If I can organize something like this, and people show up - if people grab a passport, get on a plane, go to an exotic location to get out of their element and experience something different - I'll keep doing it.

Will the destinations be mainly from the show or from your own personal experiences?

It will be a combination. Certainly, it won't be part of *Destination Truth*. I won't be able to bring people out in the field as part of the show. But we've made really terrific contacts over the years from *DT* and have certainly steered the show to places very special to me. So there will be some overlap there in terms of locations.

But this isn't the Josh Gates Supernatural Experience Tour? It is less about paranormal and monsters, and more about travel?

Yes, for sure. If I can arrange a paranormal/ghost-hunt

experience, I'd love to do that. But if people are going to get on a plane and go overseas, and put themselves in this totally new environment, they need to be in it for the travel. I think they will be. If they decide to go halfway around the world for dinner, they need to be someone willing to take a risk, and excited about having an unconventional experience. The idea of tying it into a monster hunt is interesting, and I'd love to be able to do that.

Maybe down the road, we will.

What will the menus actually be like?

In a general sense, when we travel for the show, there's been all sorts of gross foods and challenging foods - but what we don't film often is the crew just having dinner. We have had these amazing nights over the past four years where you just end up - whether it's in a city or in the middle of nowhere - with the locals, sitting down and breaking bread.

Those are some of the most special moments in my memory from my travels. So I'd like to find places that are unique, beautiful settings and interesting places. But not gross foods. I don't want to invite people around the world just to gross them out. I want them to eat amazing foods and dig into these local cuisines around the world.

And I hope to have people at the dinners who are friends of mine from around the world. If we're eating in the deserts of Jordan, I hope that we have some locals and Bedouins to talk about the food, and to guide us through the experience. That's some of the most special moments of travel: When you get to the local level where you're just experiencing what the people who live their experience.

Will you announce cuisine in advance so people can decide whether they want to throw their hat in the ring or perhaps wait for a menu more suitable for them?

I don't know; if people are that picky about eating, they may not be the best candidate for this project. Any sort of travel requires a degree of openness to the location, people and food. Wherever it is, we'll have lots of options, but we're looking for people who are ready for a good adventure.

You're a big movie buff, so will there be any pop- culture-centric locales? Will there be dinner on Martha's Vineyard where Jaws was filmed?

Man, you should start planning these things with me. You're full of great ideas! [laughs]. I hadn't really thought of that angle, but now that you bring it up, I think it's a terrific idea. For me, my first instinct is to find a really special destination. Finding some neat destinations locally might tie in really well with that.

Are you pitching this as a show, and will you be filming this to put together a show?

Initially I'd like to ask the people who come to document it themselves. I'm not pitching it as a show, and I don't have an ulterior motive to get it on the air as a project. This is very experimental. The feedback in the last less-than-24 hours has been unbelievable. People are contacting me, left and right, saying how excited they are about it. I've had so many people say, 'I'm doing this, I'm saving my money, I'm putting together a travel fund." I am really hopeful that it is successful. If it is, and people have special experiences that come out of it ... then maybe. I'm certainly open to that because there's nothing more fascinating than exposing people to travel and new experiences outside their comfort zone.

Erin Ryder Changes 'Destination' To 'Chasing UFOs'

(June 2012)

If the truth is out there, a team from the National Geographic Channel might be the best shot there is of finding it. But the network's new docuseries, *Chasing UFOs*, ups the ante in the search for answers from *The X-Files* believer/skeptic duo of Mulder and Scully, and adds a third character - the "skeliever."

Enter Erin Ryder. Hailing from Upstate New York, Ryder has an extensive resume of producing shows that range from topics such as parkour to Pussycat Dolls to, most recently, the paranormal. She is a skeptic who wants to believe - and might have enough reasons to do so after the first season of the NatGeo show, which premieres with two back-to-back episodes tonight at 9 p.m.

Ryder is already known to fans of the unexplained by her work as co-executive producer and on-camera adventurer on the Syfy monster-hunting show *Destination Truth* (which debuts its fifth season on July 10 at 10 p.m.). But in *Chasing UFOs* - also from *Truth* production company Ping Pong Productions - Ryder takes the lead as her team looks to the skies and into the shadows.

Along with UFOlogist James Fox and skeptical scientist Ben McGee, Ryder serves as co-executive producer and field researcher in a pursuit that often takes them into a dark territory of extraterrestrial sightings, alien abductions and government conspiracies. In the first episodes alone, the team heads to Texas and encounters a town where more than 30 residents claim they saw mysterious lights flying above them. Then there is the retired military brass who warn that a large-scale cover-up is in place - a warning that hits close to home when the team believes they're being followed. And yes, there is a lot of investigating and running around in the dark - which is a fun draw of the show.

But instead of only pursuing theories and eyewitness accounts - and playing with lots of cool gadgets - *Chasing UFOs* also attempts to pursue the science behind E.T. experiences. For instance, the show is working with SETI (the Search for Extra-Terrestrial Intelligence) to send an outer space, crowdsourced reply to the "Wow! Signal" of 1977.

Erin Ryder joined us to discuss her leap from monsters to aliens, and open up about the science, skepticism - and lots of bleeped- out swear words - of Chasing UFOs, along with some inside info on the new season (and future) of Destination Truth.

I know your work on Destination Truth, but how do you go from producing sports shows to chasing UFOs?

I've had a love for travel and adventure since I was younger. Anything that's allowed me to do that, in terms of producing, has been fantastic. That's why *Destination Truth* has such a place in my heart. I've been fond of UFOs since I was little; I'm definitely a sci-fi geek at heart. I'd say the [mass] sightings in the Hudson Valley were kind of something that affected my family. They would talk about sightings. It was so intriguing, and I wanted to see something for so long. And I actually saw something. You'll see it this season on *Destination Truth*. We saw something in Kazakhstan that I really cannot explain. And that just kind of revved up this love again.

Since Chasing UFOs and Truth are produced by the same company, did this sighting in Kazakhstan lead you to pitching them a show or was this already in the works over at Ping Pong and it was just serendipitous?

It was serendipitous. It was one of those things where the guys are heavily into cryptozoology and paranormal. UFOs are just an extension of that just in the field of mystery. Those guys are kings of it. They had wanted to do something. Josh Gates [the host of *Destination Truth*] and I calling from the road saying, "We saw something" - who knows if that sparked anything? I do know that the timing just couldn't have been more perfect.

You grew up in New York and then went to school in Syracuse, so did you ever see anything in the skies above the UFO hotspots of the Hudson Valley?

I wish I did. The mass sightings took place, around '82 to, people say, '95. That is definitely while I was there. I had my uncle who saw things and my grandfather, and it was something that I wanted to happen. Obviously, it doesn't always work like that.

What is the transition between pursuing these creatures on DT to UFOs?

Luckily, there's a lot of similarities so it wasn't something that took a lot of changes - aside from the better vehicles because we are in the United States. And luckily, we were renting vehicles that actually had heated seats. If you've seen the *DT* vehicles, they barely run. The way we do things is very similar. What Josh and I do, and what James and Ben and I do, is going out and saying, "if this does exist, is there some sort of scientific way to prove it?"

And that's deep down what we're trying to do. There are a lot of similarities. On DT, we jumpstart getting in a little bit more into UFOs and aliens this season. So I did have a little foray into that. But staring at the sky is definitely something new for me. The lenses and the telescopes we had at our fingertips were incredible.

As a producer, is there ever this moment where you're like, "Okay, we got to make this more exciting because we're just looking up into the sky?"

You know, in the beginning before I went out, I will say that was something I was nervous about. But when you go out there - and you film as long as we do and then you have to cut that down into 42 minutes - you realize that a lot of that boring stuff hits the cutting room floor. Once it's not diluted, it is action packed.

How would you say the show is overall different from a lot of other paranormal investigative shows out there?

I would say the one thing I hope people see that sets us apart is that we do have three completely different points of view. Ben is an open and honest scientific skeptic. Deep down he does want to find something but, until we do, he does have to take a real strong scientific look at everything when we go out there. James is on the other end of that spectrum, and he is a true believer. He's had sightings of his own. He's spoken to government officials and astronauts and collected so many sightings and stories that it's hard for him not to believe. Then I kind of land somewhere in the middle because I have had a sighting, I have talked to these people and felt that they did see something. I want to believe same as all three of us. We get these ranging points of view, and we don't come to one conclusion at the end of an episode.

You go to a town hall, talk to an entire community, and then get a lot of eyewitness accounts. Is there a concern people are just telling you the coolest stories and saying they saw something just to get on TV - especially when the elements of eyewitness stories are so familiar and easy to draw from?

Absolutely. Absolutely. The one thing that we pride ourselves on is that we seek these people out. Very rarely do we talk to anyone that has sought us out because we want to speak to the people that have a lot to lose. We don't want to talk to these people who want the fame and attention by getting their story out there. We want to talk to the people that have been hiding for years and years and years. And we have to pry the story out of them.

Because for me, there's real honesty in that. In Texas, the town hall meeting that we threw, yeah, you have to worry that these people are coming because they want to be on TV. But at the same time, once you're there, you realize the comfort level changes once one person shares a story. You see the other people nod their heads, and then stand up and say, "Well I didn't ever want to share this, but now that other people are sharing these stories, I don't think I'm crazy anymore." ... But yeah, you're going to always have to be wary.

When you encounter overenthusiastic believers of any phenomena, does it sometimes make you more skeptical? Like you're less likely to buy their story?

Sometimes. You know, I think you just have to take it case by case. There are some times where that enthusiasm and that love can really taint a point of view. You just have to be careful of that.

That's what I love so much about James. Yes, he's been studying this forever, and yes, he will come out and say he believes UFOs exist. But at the same time, he doesn't let it taint his point of view. When we go up and speak to someone, he's almost the first-person that will call, "bullshit." And he'll be like, "I don't believe that guy." And I think that's what makes me so fond of him - he's not going out preaching.

Well, speaking of bullshit, you like to swear - or maybe it's just natural ...

214

I tease that I was raised by longshoremen in a fraternity. My mom isn't too fond of that. I would fill a cuss jar in a minute. It's just something that's a part of me. I feel bad that people are offended by it. I'm so happy that I get bleeped because I know there are a lot of kids watching. And I do want to be a role model. I don't want them to follow that behavior. But when I hit a certain level of excitement, it's just, I can't contain it. A lot of times it's just a streaming cuss line that comes out.

A recurring theme of the show involves government cover ups, and that people should be allowed to talk about these experiences openly without fear of reprisal. But when a witness like a retired colonel goes on camera, talking about cover ups and how the government wants to take him out, does that not, in fact, destroy the notion of a cover up? He's talking and hasn't been taken out by a sniper rifle, you know?

I thought that, and I was always kind of suspect of that. But when you talk to people around the time the government stopped being involved in the search for extra-terrestrial life - when they closed Project Blue Book - what happened was they turned to this new method of making fun. So anyone that believed was immediately crazy. It was so wild and so out there. I believe that's what they do with people that come forward now. They don't need to silence them. They let them talk. But they just promote the fact that they think that they're crazy.

In the second episode you pretty much trespass on an airfield. If you guys were really coming close to something real, wouldn't they want to shut you down? We wouldn't even be having this conversation because the show would never get picked up or would never air, right?

Right, and that's the thing. That's why I walk away from Fresno, and I wonder if there really is something to the underground bases conversation [in the second part of tonight's two-hour premiere]. When you do get too close, you know that you get too close. You know. Anyone who's tried to get too close to Area 51 knows that. There were times that the Coast Guard would come out after us.

There were times that the military would send out warnings and helicopters and cops, flashlights, all that kind of stuff. There's always that first level warning. We know to be careful, as producers, as investigators. We know not to push it because we have National Geographic's reputation on the line, we have our reputation on the line. We don't try to go much further than we really have to. But yeah, you know when you do. You know when you've crossed the line.

In episode four, you visit Roswell, right?

We do. We headed to New Mexico. We were at White Sands Missile Range and throughout the area. And I'm happy to say we found something there. We found physical evidence there that defies anything I thought that this project could come up with. You have expectations, and what we found superseded those expectations. It was just beyond words. I'm really excited for people to see that episode. I think Roswell is a famous site for a lot of reasons and something happened there. I've always believed something happened there, and now I'm believing that there may really have been a cover up.

I often think everybody knows some of the classic stories - the Travis Waltons, the Roswell, the Area 51 stories. Have you encountered people that are like, "No, I don't know the story of Roswell"?

I think Roswell's a difficult one, but we do meet with Travis Walton this season. And yes, because it wasn't of their generation, [people] didn't really know who he was, what potentially happened to him. And yeah, I think this is something that is a part of our culture, of everyone's culture. You can go to any country, and everyone has their sightings. I think that that's what is fantastic. It's one of those things that's a common thread.

Did Josh Gates give you advice as you set out for this?

His one piece of advice was, "Try not to fall too hard." He knows that I'm an extreme klutz and I think that was one of his biggest concerns. No, he was really happy and just said to go out there and give it my all. That was really important for me to hear from him because *Destination Truth* is where my heart is and doing this without him was really hard in the beginning. There's no one that does it better than Josh Gates. Getting his blessing and going out was really important to me.

So, does that mean that your time on DT, if it returns for another season, is officially over?

No, Absolutely not ... I wouldn't want to part with that because it is so close to me, it has everything that I love. It just really does, and I think no one does it better than we do. It's just a feeling that I have. I truly hope that this isn't the end of Destination Truth.

You said you were a sci-fi geek growing up. What were the kinds of things that you were into?

Ray Bradbury, God bless his heart, who just passed, I have every one of his books. That's been a major passion of mine since I was younger. *The X-Files* has always been something that just - everything that I could want in terms of a producer, an investigator, that's everything. That has it all. That show is incredible. But, comic books, oddly enough, I've fallen in love with that. I don't keep up with it as much as I probably should. Now that the Green Lantern is coming out gay and whatnot, I feel like I need to get back into it. But it's definitely something that a lot of people don't know about me. But it's definitely something that has made me who I am in terms of someone who wants to explore this particular genre.

What's your favorite alien movie or favorite episode of The X-Files?

Well, my favorite alien movie, and it's not fair because Travis Walton is going to think that I'm cheating, but *Fire in the Sky* is a pretty well-done movie and it's really creepy. If you haven't seen that one in a while, watch that movie. It's very, very eerie.

Favorite *X-Files*: There's so many because I love all of them ... "Fallen Angel" is incredible. Deep Throat's back in that one. I especially love the UFO fanatic guy in that, too ... But it's hard to pick favorites. I really don't have favorites in terms of anything. The fact that David Duchovny and Gillian Anderson could do that for so long and keep us interested for so long is beyond me. They're magicians at their craft.

'Haunted Collector' John Zaffis Is Syfy's Own Godfather

(June 2012)

He is the "Godfather of the Paranormal" because of his knowledge as an investigator, researcher and expert on religious demonology. Yet, it might be more appropriate to call John Zaffis of Syfy's *Haunted Collector* an American paranormal picker.

Premiering its second season tonight, June 6, at 9 p.m., *Haunted Collector* follows lead investigator Zaffis as he tracks down and examines haunted objects and possessed possessions which may be the source of ghostly activity. The task is uniquely suited to this paranormal pack rat who has - over the course of nearly four decades in the field - acquired enough of these items to establish his own haunted museum near his Stratford, CT home. Within the museum, he stores the items to keep their alleged powers at bay and does so with the help of items buried in its foundation which supposedly neutralize their negative energy.

Of course, none of this is news to those within the paranormal community where Zaffis and his museum have become pretty legendary. But non-ghost hunters also became familiar with Zaffis last year after the first season of *Haunted Collector* scored the network its most watched reality debut of 2011.

Now Zaffis returns for another season of investigating claims of the paranormal. But this season, he expands his investigations to include previously unheard-of locations and utilizes new gadgets. In addition to airing 12 episodes compared to last season's 6, there is also a switch up with the HC team. While his adult children Chris and Aimee Zaffis return - along with tech specialist Brian

Cano - new additions Jesslyn Brown and Jason Gates will join the haunted collector as he attempts to answer questions of the unexplained and assist terrified clients, and maybe even pick up a few new items along the way.

In tonight's season premiere, Zaffis and his team head to Warsaw, KY, where two steamboats crashed in 1868, killing more than 60 people - and a woman whose house stands near the crash site says she's suffering hauntings as a result. Then the team travels to Huron, OH, where an abandoned grain silo is scheduled to be destroyed in 48 hours, sending them on a race against the clock to identify and remove any potentially dangerous energy.

John Zaffis spoke with Paranormal Pop Culture about the new season of *Haunted Collector*, as well as about the changes he has seen in the paranormal community and if there are any famous objects he'd like to collect.

How is this season different from the last?

Well, we have a lot of new equipment that we're actually using and implementing into the investigation. I'm looking at it from the perspective that the investigations we are doing in this season are locations that really haven't been investigated before; they're brand new. So we're able to dig into more history of the geographic locations and some of the items.

And you have two new investigators with you this season. Was it difficult training new people to adapt your style and welcoming them into the group, or were they just natural fits?

Actually, there were a pretty good fit. Especially Jason. He's really involved with it. He's really interested in the technical end. He's very much interested in digging into the history of a lot of the things that are going on. Jesslyn is fitting right in. She's had a lot of personal experiences in things. So again, it's the process of pulling in and working and getting involved with them. They were both very excited about the opportunity to work with me. They would ask a lot of questions. And that's what's important about it. They're trying to get a good understanding of how I investigate in some of the different things I do because, Aaron, let's face it, I believe in looking at things from a spiritual perspective. But I also believe that if we can get some type of evidence, if we can get EVPs or cold spots, hot spots, or EMF off something in a particular area, that's important to focus on.

You've been involved with paranormal investigations for so long, and there's a lot of new technology coming out all the time. Is there any type of new toy or gadget that, even after all the years that you've been doing it, you're just impressed by?

Actually, it's this helicopter. It has a whole bunch of cameras that are attached to it. And we're able to use it on a couple of investigations. I'm hoping that it makes it into the episode. It was hysterical as they were unpacking the equipment and pulling things out. I see Chris and Brian putting this helicopter together and getting everything set up on it. I'm like, 'Why are they flying a helicopter around? What does this have to do with anything?' But once they explained it to me ... with especially a big piece of property where there's reports of shadow figures and anything like that, and it's wintertime and you can see down through the trees, and everything ... I was extremely excited about using that.

Do you ever just long for the days of simpler low-tech investigations?

Well, not really. The reason for that is, Aaron, I still investigate the way I always have. I keep it very simple. Going through an area - am I gifted or psychic? No. But you can usually feel if there's something weird in a room. It can feel heavy, it can feel light. And again, those are the areas I will always recommend the guys go in and set equipment up and everything. I get very excited when they do capture something with the EVPs or cold or hot spots or they are getting high EMF. And I think it's important ...

When you can actually get something and get it documented in an area where people are telling you, 'there's a sighting of a shadow form' or 'something moved over in this area and this is where we're having a lot of activity,' it really ties in. I get very excited by it when one of them will pipe up and say, 'John, we actually got something in this area where the reports are taking place.'

After doing investigations for so long, is it ever difficult for you to maintain that amazement or 'gee whiz' factor? Do you ever just sort of approach the paranormal as 'ho-hum'- not as exciting as it once was?

I still pay very close attention if I'm walking through an area and people are telling me that they have reported activity, and then we bring equipment in, and things are occurring and we're getting things documented and getting a piece of evidence. I still get very excited. A lot of times these people think they're crazy, they think they're nuts because they are experiencing these things. But when you can actually show them some type of proof on what's happening or what's occurring, that makes a person feel better.

And I still get excited, especially when working with new people because they are intrigued, they're interested, they're trying to figure the field out. And they're trying to get a better comprehension of why things occur, how they occur.

In the first episode, you investigate a building scheduled for demolition in 48 hours. It's like a deadline investigation. That's sort of a new concept, as far as I'm aware of for these shows. Was that new for you?

I've never been to a point where there was that type of a crunch. I've been restricted, especially when you deal with businesses and you can only go in at night, but you'd have multiple times that you'd be able to go back. In this situation, it was 48 hours. That was it. We did not have that window of opportunity of that building still being there once it was imploded. That was it. It was done and over with. So we needed to figure out what the heck was happening as quick and fast as you could possibly think of. So we were spending a lot of time in there. A lot of people were digging into research and history. There was so much going on. It was extremely fast and quick. And what's interesting about that is we were in there investigating, we went back the next day and staircases we gone. So many things were already removed because they had a deadline. They had a schedule they had to stay on. So the pressure was on, and it was probably one of the most unique environments and investigations that you're going to see.

It seemed like an intimidating challenge. Did you have to remind your investigators, even yourself, to not get so rushed that you start getting sloppy with the investigation?

No, because everyone was really much on the same page. It was where everybody basically knew that we had to get in there, we had to do our baseline sweep. We had to try and figure out and target where some of these areas were where they were claiming a lot of the workers were petrified to go in ... everyone went in with that perspective that we had 48 hours to come up with some type of conclusion for why some of these things were occurring.

So Jason and Amy really were digging into the history to see what they could find out. And the information, as it was flowing, it was coming in quite quick. People were volunteering very easily to give us information. So a lot of it fell into place very quick and very fast ... And finding out some of the information about the land itself, the only thing that kept going through my mind is, 'Is this one of these situations where we are going to have multiple locations within that site where the activity occurred and there could be substantial reasons that it occurred?' That was one of the key things that kept going through my mind.

We are at this point now where people have seen so many ghosthunting shows and maybe are out there investigating on their own. When you encounter a client, is there a concern that they may know too much about the paranormal investigative process, and think they're experts, and that they know the right things to say to get you and a TV crew to investigate?

Absolutely. Today, due to all our TV shows and the radio shows, and all the paranormal conferences and everything that goes out there, a lot of people are more knowledgeable - but it's like a double-edged sword. With that knowledge they can figure things out and get a better understanding of what might be happening in their home. But on the other hand, we have to be extremely careful. That's why our research is so important.

Digging in to finding out anything we can about the property, the home - and finding out about the people because a lot of people are interested in just being on TV. People view it a lot differently today. Years ago, people didn't want to talk about their hauntings.

Syfy is also home to Hollywood Treasure. Think any of those items could be haunted?

Well, there's a lot of memorabilia that I'd love the opportunity to investigate. I've heard from many different people that do collect these types of items that there is paranormal activity associated with some of the items. One of the classic things that I always go back to is the Hope Diamond, and that predates us being on TV with any of these collectibles or things like that. Energy can attach to these items. It can remain with them. And can it pick up energy from a prior owner? Absolutely. There's no doubt about that. I mean, look at a lot of the items that people collect from the movies and movie stars. Have I heard stories? Yeah.

Anything that's on your investigative wish list from the Hollywood world?
Oh, gosh. I particularly like *Hollywood Treasure*. I was very intrigued with Debbie Reynolds' collection - Marilyn Monroe's dress and things like that. I'd be very intrigued to see if there's any type of energy associated with those items ... I'm sitting here trying to think of items and there's so many things going through my mind. I would love the opportunity to be able to check out James Dean's car. They say that's cursed and there's a lot of energy associated with that ... I would be very interested in the opportunity to go in and investigate them and see what's actually attached to them. Are there remnants of the person - energy of the person - that is still associated with some of those items?
And speaking of the Hope Diamond, if you had the opportunity, would you like to investigate that despite the really infamous curse associated with it?

Absolutely. Just to see if there's anything actually getting recorded off it. Being able to do EVPs around it. Setting up EMF detectors. Doing different things from our experimental

223

perspective around items like that. Yes. Because I'd be very intrigued to see if there is anything associated with these things.

You have your own museum of haunted objects, and we see a little bit of that on the show, so is there any museum you'd like to investigate or that you've heard is just crazy with paranormal activity?

Well, most of your museums are. You have to remember with a lot of the artifacts that are brought in, they continuously, continuously have activity in most museums out there. But I think that if it ever presented itself and I had that opportunity right at this point in time, what I'd like to see is Ripley's Believe it or Not museums investigated.

Jason Hawes Keeps the Ghost Hunt Alive
(September 2012, with Erin Wolf)

For Jason Hawes, the hunt continues. The Roto-Rooter plumber- turned-celebrity from the reality show *Ghost Hunters*, Syfy's longest running series, has navigated his way through the entertainment industry and managed to carve out a niche for himself over eight years and nearly 200 episodes.

Of course, his journey as a paranormal investigator and leader of TAPS (The Atlantic Paranormal Society, as if you needed the clarification) has been one that he's taken with the help of his co-leader Grant Wilson. *Ghost Hunters* has become a pop culture mainstay, and is a forerunner within the paranormal reality genre, so ever since Wilson announced his retirement from the show last winter, fans have speculated what will change about their beloved series when its eighth season returns September 5, 9 p.m., ET.

As it turns out, Jason Hawes - who is also an executive producer on the show - assures fans that, to quote his catchphrase, he and the TAPS team are simply "onto the next case."

But that doesn't mean there won't be changes with the show.

Hawes announced last week that a new investigator named Ashley Traub (incidentally, a Paranormal Pop Culture model) would be joining TAPS on the September 26 episode, and that the audience will be able to watch her grow amidst what he calls one of the "best seasons ever." For instance, the show returns with a block of "Southern Spirits"-themed episodes which will have the team heading to Charleston, SC, in search of paranormal evidence of America's first woman serial killer, Lavinia Fisher, as well as tackling the French Quarter in New Orleans.

In the interest of full disclosure, I've known Hawes for several years, worked at TAPS-sponsored events and guest-edited two issues of his *TAPS ParaMagazine*. During that time, I've interviewed him multiple times, and gotten to know him personally and professionally. So I'm admittedly biased in my conversations with him. If you've got a problem with that, this may not be the article for you.

But I digress. Jason Hawes joined us to chat about the show's long life dealing with the afterlife - and offered thoughts about how his approach to the paranormal has changed over that time, how the team has changed without Grant and where he sees things going next.

Wow, Season 8.5? You guys are rolling along there!

Man, who would have thought? I remember me and you talking years ago and me saying, "Man, I can't believe this show's made it this far."

Overall this time, what do you think has changed as far as how you do things, or how you think of the paranormal?

Well, I think I still fall under the same belief system - that 90 percent of these claims can be disproved. And of course, you know I pick all these investigations and Syfy is the one that makes the choice on what airs on their network - which is fine. There's a lot of cases that never air with debunking and disproving, but we're bringing some new equipment in this season, and people are also able to see - with Grant gone - how the whole dynamics of the team have changed.

People start trying to figure where they fit in best, where their new spot is. We brought in a new investigator, and people are going to see how she works out, if her position is going to work out with the rest of the team. You know TAPS; we're a family. We've always been this way, and sometimes people feel like they have a hard time getting into the circle.

Do you find yourself still being surprised after all the evidence you've caught?

No, I can't tell you that things don't surprise me anymore. Of course, some of the evidence we got coming up is incredible. I am left speechless, and at one point, one of our production people gets dragged into our investigation. That person really didn't want to get dragged in, but it became a traumatic experience. So there's a lot of high excitement; some of the best evidence we've ever caught is going to show up this season.

Yeah man, it's wild. It's been an interesting year. And I'm really having a lot of fun with it.

How tough was it to adapt to the investigations without Grant?

Honestly, it wasn't that tough at all because I still deal with Grant daily on other things and he's still there. He had to take a leave of absence from the show but we're … our families are extremely tight and we're like brothers. And, for many years, I investigated without Grant being there for many years of our friendship ... of course it's a little odd not having a guy I refer to as my brother standing beside me all the time. But, you know, I think it wasn't an issue for me at all.

Now that Grant has left, do you see an end in sight for your involvement with the show and when do you think that would be? And do you think Ghost Hunters could continue without you?

You know, I don't - I'm never looking that far ahead to wonder when I'm leaving or if I'm leaving or anything of that nature. To be honest with you, every time I go to do a season, every time I'm requested to do another season, I sit down with my wife and children and it's a choice that we make as a family ...

I remember my oldest, who's 21, she used to come downstairs as a little kid and see Steve and me and Grant and everybody sitting around trying to figure out cases, so she sees how this whole thing has grown and how it's become this international thing now. So, yes, I will stay as long as my family wants me to stay.

And if the show can survive without me, I think it could. I don't know, I guess that would have to be from the viewer's standpoint.

You know, I know that if I was to step back, Steve - who is 100% adequate and able to - could easily run what is going on. I don't know how we would feel about doing that on his own though. So, I don't know, time will tell.

Are you bringing your daughter Hailey back?

Hailey will be on a bunch of these episodes. Actually, today's her birthday. I just moved her into her dorm last week. That's one of those heartfelt moments. I'm used to always having her right there, right around, seeing her car in the driveway and knowing she's there. Now, it's like, she's at college. But she'll be on a bunch, and when she's not in school, she'll be heading down to investigate with me.

You know her, she's a really smart kid and highly intelligent, and really wonderful to have her around. She's at school right now for forensic science and criminal psychology, so she's really trying to get into that area where she's able to understand the mindset of the client you're trying to help out.

You've brought a lot of people onto the team over the years, and guided them to become better investigators, so what's the piece of advice you gave to Ashley, the new investigator?

Honestly, I try to get her in the mindset of investigating and debunking. But also, it's one of those things where I can bring somebody on, and then the team has to decide if that person is working out. They have to work with her and teach her all their ways. She'll pick up what she thinks is best suited for her.

But yeah, of course we try to keep her in the mindset of, "Don't automatically assume it's the paranormal." Let's try to figure out an explanation and figure out where that high magnetic field is coming from. Let's try to determine where that sound is originating from and go from there.

Like me, you are a huge zombie fan. Have there ever been any thoughts on a zombie involvement with the show?

Well, I am a huge zombie fan, but I don't really think I could connect the two, but we've been asked by a couple people from *The Walking Dead* if they could come on and investigate with us. So we'll see.

I know Norman Reedus is a fan. Who knows, it could be the first time TAPS has an investigator toting a crossbow.
I'm also a huge fan of his from The Boondock Saints, right?

Spinning off that, TAPS is really a pop culture entity now. I know you're a fan of Dexter, so if you were to use that pop culture power to be on a show, what would it be?

I wish The Shield was still on, but I'm a huge fan of Dexter, Sons of Anarchy, Californication, those shows. And Breaking Bad? Phenomenal. But Walter is starting to look more and more like me, which has become a problem! [Laughs]

That would be a pretty awesome crew: Heisenberg and Hawes.

[Laughs] That would be. I'd love to make an appearance on it.

CHAPTER 5
Speaking of Celebrity

Dan Aykroyd, From Ghostbuster to Spirit Maker

(April 2010)

Dan Aykroyd looks like a cop in a crowd of Ghostbusters, Blues Brothers and Blues sisters. The shades are reminiscent of the erstwhile Elwood, but the black button-up shirt with insignia above the breast pocket and black University of Maryland Police ball cap reminds one of a police officer, secret service, or DEA agent arriving to survey a scene. It makes it somewhat fitting, then, when the celebrity's first actions at the Joe Canal's Discount Liquor Outlet in Iselin, NJ, in late March include shuffling off overzealous press photographers in an officious "show's over" manner and getting a snaking line of bedecked fans moving for an afternoon of photos, autographs, meet-and-greets - and skull signings.

Despite Aykroyd's physical similarities to a police officer - a comparison he'd likely appreciate considering his longstanding fascination and relationship with law enforcement agencies in the United States and his native Canada - the skulls he's signing aren't human bones that hold forensic clues, but are instead connected to legend, made of glass and contain quadruple- distilled, triple-filtered, additive-free Crystal Head Vodka.

But aside from being just another premium vodka that retails for about $50 and happens to come in a wicked cool glass bottle, CHV - as Dan Aykroyd tells it in between each Sharpie marker signature applied to fans' alcoholic acquisition - is inspired by the crystal skull myth popularized in the last Indiana Jones flick and is the imbibable incarnation of his work as an entertainer and lifelong association with the paranormal and mysticism.

"All my life I've been giving people recordings, radio shows, television broadcasts, sketch comedy, film," he says. "Now I'm actually making something that I can put in their mouths - a tangible, tactile experience."

Launched in Southern California in 2008 (with a viral video some were convinced was an elaborate joke) before rolled out to other regions throughout 2009, the CHV "experience " is the latest endeavor of a man who has created, written and performed as several iconic comedic characters from the past 35 years. Since graduating from Chicago's Second City improv comedy troupe and joining *Saturday Night Live* as an original repertory member in 1975, the lines Dan Aykroyd has penned or spoken could alone fill a sizable volume of pop culture quotable quotes - and no true fan of '80s movies could call his DVD collection complete without at least owning *The Blues Brothers, Trading Places* and *Ghostbusters*. And under the auspices of his cool man-in-black alias Elwood Blues, Aykroyd created the House of Blues restaurant and concert hall chain and educated newcomers to the music genre through his House of Blues Radio Hour.

But Aykroyd is also well known as a Spiritualist and paranormal pop culture icon who holds the belief that spirits, and ghosts communicate with the living - a family tradition covered in his father Peter's book, *A History of Ghosts*, for which he wrote the foreword - and has extensive knowledge on UFOs. His openness on such paranormal topics makes it all the more engaging when he describes the pure Newfoundland deep aquifer vodka filtered through Herkimer Diamonds, polished crystals that are supposed to emit positive energy.

The positive energy is a recurring theme with the crystal skulls legend, which involves 13 ancient, quartz rock human skull carvings that supposedly possess mystical properties that, if brought together, will usher in a new era, or cause the end of the world - possibly all happening on December 21, 2012, which of course marks the grand finale of the Mayan calendar. The British Museum and Smithsonian, both of which possess a skull, determined the objects aren't as old as the tales suggests, but Aykroyd isn't as easily convinced; he claims other cultures believed the heads were "from another star, a gift from above."

"There are some who are skeptics and say that they're all fakes. That's what the Smithsonian said," says Aykroyd. "But I can't quite believe that because the Navajo spoke of them, the Aztec spoke of them, the Maya spoke of them. And they spoke of them as a very integral part of the tribe's responsibility."

The decision to connect vodka with the heads was natural, he says. After his friend and renowned artist John Alexander designed the bottle based on their shared loved of the Mexican Day of the Dead, Aykroyd decided to put something pure in it to be "enlightened" drinkers and then trade off the legends of "positive thinking and self-empowerment."

Although it's only coincidence, the release of supernatural-themed booze couldn't be timed more perfectly considering the popularity of scripted entertainment like *Paranormal Activity* and *2012* and the glut of reality-TV shows such as *Paranormal State* and *Ghost Lab*, which are all dedicated to ethereal matters or paranormal investigations. However, even though he says there's a big difference between mediums, channeling, and other Spiritualist beliefs he holds and "ghost hunting," Aykroyd thinks the overall effect of such shows is positive.

"I think it's great that people are employed. It's giving work to people; it's enlightening the public and it's opening the subject up to discussion and debate." He also adds there is a parallel between the current paranormal trend in the mainstream and how Spiritualism was especially *en vogue* in the late-19th and early-20th centuries.

"Well now, with the digital cameras and all the electronic voice phenomena (EVP), people now have a lot more tools to go out and hunt this stuff. You know, virtually every county in America has a ghost hunting society."

"But you know, as my dad's book points out, there's always been an interest in it because ... it's always been a part of our existence."

If there is such a thing as a mashed-up meta-pop culture irony, it definitely applies when talking to Aykroyd, a true believer in ghosts and maker of supernatural spirits, yet also the alter ego and creator of the fictional Dr. Raymond Stantz - one-third of the most famous paranormal investigation team in history. It only seems more meta after watching Aykroyd and his Spiritualist father appear on *Larry King Live* last October alongside "real- life" busters Jason Hawes and Grant Wilson of *Ghost Hunters*, and medium Chip Coffey of *Psychic Kids*.

For his part, Aykroyd sees a similarity between the gadgets, the special vehicles and the team dynamics of the reality-TV ghost shows and his own *Ghostbusters* characters. "No doubt they're inspired by us; I think so." But as far as his own foray into the reality-TV ghost genre, Aykroyd will confine his work to fantasy, so there will be no guest spots on the shows.

Still, the entertainer isn't done with ghosts yet and he confirms there will be a third installment in the adventures of Stantz, Venkman and Spengler. While mum on plot details, he will admit, "It's happening."

"We're closer now than we ever have been it's a matter of a script and a screenplay." Aykroyd even affirms "everybody's on board" for *Ghostbusters 3* and he thinks Ivan Reitman will return to direct.

In the meantime, Aykroyd remains busy as an actor. In addition to voicing Yogi Bear in the upcoming live action/animated film ala *Alvin and the Chipmunks*, Aykroyd made a cameo in an October 2009 episode of *Family Guy*, reprising his role from *Spies Like Us* with costar Chevy Chase. He also popped up in an *SNL* skit in February as US House Minority Leader, Republican John Boehner.

Most recently, he appeared as Jimmy Carter in the Ron Howard- directed FunnyorDie.com advocacy short also starring Will Ferrell, Jim Carrey, Dana Carvey, and Chevy Chase aimed at encouraging the creation of a consumer financial protection agency.

"Like in so many of my entertainment experiences, I was awestruck by the talent in the room," he says. "To be in that company was a real honor."

But acting aside, Aykroyd has his Crystal Head Vodka, which he promotes through bottle signings much like the one in Iselin. And so far, he's pretty amused with the reactions he is getting about the spirit. He jokes his father is a "big consumer of the vodka" because he can "have six shots and not get a hangover." And as far as nonfamilial reactions, "we've gotten the full range of emotional responses to it. People have hated it. It's banned in two areas of the world. It's banned in Idaho, and it's banned in the province of Ontario. They will not sell it."

That's only half correct. The vodka has actually been doing well in Idaho; Bill Applegate, the product manager with the Idaho State Liquor Division says the brand has been quite successful and done much better than he ever expected it would. He adds that, even though the vodka isn't inexpensive, it "apparently has quite a following."

However, Chris Layton, a spokesperson with the Liquor Control Board of Ontario, confirms they won't sell CHV because consumers might find the skull bottle's "symbol of death" imagery offensive - and that it runs contrary to the LCBO's mandate and brand vision of social responsibility.

Still, even if powers-that-be in his home of Ontario have yet to embrace the booze, Aykroyd is proud of Crystal Head. He laughs that, "I'm not selling used battery acid here, and it looks really nice in the bottle."

Plus, he thinks it has an "old-time moonshine type of feel," and prefers his with one-and-a-half ounces of the vodka mixed with three-quarters of a cup of fresh-squeezed tangerine juice and a little splash of soda.

And if the crystal skull legends are true, and the world ends in 2012? Dan Aykroyd will take it in stride with his Crystal Head Vodka.

"I'll probably be sitting at home at my farm in Canada with all my friends and we will be drinking it cold off the ice, off the snow - and I'm hoping that the end of the world is the end of just perception as we know it rather than the 'end' of the world."

Rob Zombie: Heavy Metal Musician, Film Buff ... And Superbeast?

(June 2010)

Rob Zombie is not the devil. At *Revolver* magazine's April Golden Gods Awards in Los Angeles, his stage presence was that of a long-haired, bushy-bearded heavy metal headbanger in an inverted pentagram goat's head tee, but the man speaking now is a calm, soft-spoken optimist and vegetarian. Although he's a musician who has added director, illustrator, and comic book creator to his resume over the years, he's more likely to be rejected by the devil than to become a Superbeast. Still, Rob Zombie is a hell of an entertainer.

It's an exercise of multimedia calisthenics to speak with Zombie about work. Aside from his *Halloween* franchise reboot and its sequel, or the animated "adult/monster/sex comedy" *The Haunted World of El Superbeasto*, Zombie is involved in no less than five projects he can talk about. When he picks up the phone in late March, he's prepping for his "Gruesome Twosome" tour with another theatrical hard rocker, Alice Cooper, that ran for almost two weeks at the end of April, after which he'll tour with the Mayhem Festival until August. His February album, Hellbilly Deluxe2 - the sequel to his 1998 solo album - is still a hot topic, as is the March episode of *CSI: Miami* he directed and a new comic book, *Whatever Happened to Baron Von Shock?*

But before he was Rob Zombie, multi-tasking Renaissance man, he was Rob Cummings until he legally changed his name in 1996. Cummings relocated from Haverhill, MA, to New York City in the early '80s and, in 1985, formed the industrial rock band White Zombie - named after the 1932 Bela Lugosi flick and heavily influenced in sound and lyrics by supernatural and slasher flicks.

Shortly after leading the gritty troupe to success in '92 *with La Sexorcisto: Devil Music, Vol.1* and *Astra-Creep: 2000* in '95, he issued a solo album and broke up the band in 1998. Driven by the visceral sounds of "Dragula" and "Living Dead Girl," the first *Deluxe* was a hit and followed up with three more studio albums and a live album before returning to hellbilly country. In between, Zombie was ready for a bit of the old ultra-violence, and wrote and directed two cult flicks, *House of 1000 Corpses*, and the *Devil's Rejects*, and two *Halloween* installments.

Through it all, the 45-year-old Zombie says he remains unaware of what the popular perception of him is ("I don't know what the hell people think about me") but says he's always just been about fulfilling his two passions of music and movies, which he says he loves equally.

"Working in film, I'm behind the scenes so I love that. You're just creating this entire world from scratch but performing is totally different."

"It's sort of the two sides of my personality. One side that's got to be big and loud and gigantic where you feel you need to explode all over this arena, and the other where I literally just want to be locked away for eight months in a tiny room with an editor."

"Basically, after doing one, I always need to do the other," he says. The sides of Zombie's personality were evident long before his first foray into directing feature films in 2003, and his music has always contained homages to the silver screen. For example, *Hellbilly Deluxe 2* has two werewolf songs, one reference to "Frankenstein," and borrows movie names for songs like "Mars Needs Women," "Virgin Witch," and "The Man Who Laughs." The reason is "every song for me is almost like a movie that doesn't exist."

"Sometimes I'm writing about movies that do exist, but even when I'm not, it's the direction my brain goes. I see all the visual elements in the music as I write it."

For a kid split between two passions, his start in music was natural simply because it was more attainable in a time before Final Cut Pro and YouTube.

"As a kid, I had a Super 8 camera and would make movies but making movies in the backyard seemed like a far cry from going to Hollywood and making movies." He adds, "Obviously, music is an easier thing to do because you can always gather a group of people, your friends, and start a band."

Admittedly, starting a band was a pretty solid choice for Zombie, and his musical success has led to him being able to work with heroes such as Ozzy Osbourne, KISS, and Alice Cooper.

Though a longtime friend of Cooper's who first worked with the '70s shock rocker in 1996 on *Songs in the Key of X*, a CD connected to *The X-Files* TV show, this is the first time Zombie is going on tour with "the coolest guy ever" from his childhood record covers.

"You get numb to it because people are your friends and you just deal with them on that level," says Zombie. "You get used to 'It's Alice, he's 60 years-old, he's your friend,' but then you watch the footage from when he was younger and you go, 'holy shit, that's all him too.' You're kind of mindblown."

Those "mindblown" moments fill him with a sense of contentment about his entire career and contribute to him remaining passionate about his work and staying excited about each new tour.

"You get that feeling like the circle is complete. You're a little kid listening to this music you love, and now jump ahead 30 years later and there you are, on tour, with that same guy doing the same thing. It's such the concrete version of your dreamworld come to life."

At this point in his career, Zombie might be justified being numb to the opportunities that come his way, but says he still finds it amazing to be able to play within the worlds he grew up in.

"Most of the time I don't stop and think about it because it actually fucks with your mind," he laughs. "I grew up with John Carpenter's *Halloween* just like everyone else. I loved it as a kid. To be able to basically be given the reins to the Halloween franchise and be able to do whatever you want, it's pretty wild." The results of Zombie's romp in *Halloween* town were debatable.

Both were critically panned but commercial successes, even though the first installment far outperformed its sequel. But while his time with Michael Myers showed off some of Zombie's cinematic aspirations, it's in *1000 Corpses* and *Rejects* where Zombie-as-auteur can be discovered. Gory, sadistic and worthy of the grindhouse flicks he loves, the final five minutes in *The Devil's Rejects* - the *Firefly Family* vs. police showdown set against Skynyrd's "Free Bird" - is an amazing scene, regardless of genre.

His unique vision continues to land Zombie work as a director, whether for *CSI: Miami*, a gig he took mainly for his mom, a big fan of the show - or as the helmer of the remake of 1958's *The Blob*. While attached to another remake, he says he doesn't know what he'll be filming next.

"It could be The Blob, or it could be a couple other things I'm working on," he says. "It could be something I haven't even thought of yet ... every movie I've done, I didn't think that was actually the next thing I was doing."

He adds, "When I did *Halloween*, I wasn't thinking about *Halloween* on any level."

"I was kind of working on something else. Then I had this meeting, and they were like, 'We're ready to go now, we've got the money, let's do it.' So who knows?"

When it comes to the conversation about remakes and sacrosanct movies, Zombie admits he used to be a purist before coming to the conclusion all movies are fair game.

"If no one ever remade *Nosferatu*, we wouldn't have *Dracula*, and if Hammer [Film Productions] hadn't remade the Universal films, Christopher Lee and Peter Cushing wouldn't have ever been in those movies ... When Scorsese remade *Cape Fear*, I liked that movie, but love the original."

Zombie even allows for a remake of his favorite, *A Clockwork Orange*. But he adds that, "no matter how great the remake is, it can't take the place of the original. The original has history in your life with you; that's why people get so upset."

As for other media, Zombie is excited to be involved in another comic book. Following his "over-the-top monster-fest" *El Superbeasto* - an Image Comics title before it was a movie - he wanted to write a "slice-of-life" story about a protagonist "trying to regain his messed-up life." The result is Image's May 26 release, *Whatever Happened to Baron Von Shock?* Perhaps not surprisingly, considering Zombie's typical subject matter, the main character is a washed-up host of old late-night horror movie fright fests.

Yet with all the connections between Rob Zombie, a man whose career, visual style, and public persona are so influenced by creep shows and the paranormal - and who adopted the name of the walking dead - it's interesting to learn he's resigned himself to being a nonbeliever about the supernatural. But he sounds somewhat disappointed about it.

"When I was a kid in the '70s watching *In Search Of...* with Leonard Nimoy, I sure wanted to believe that there was a Loch Ness monster, a bigfoot, yeti, and everything else." He adds, with an almost disheartened tone, that "my logical mind tells me, 'No, I don't believe in any of that stuff.'"

Zombie's conclusion that he doesn't believe in ghosts or monsters - which he calls unfortunate - and his desire to not look like a jerk, prevents him from accepting offers to appear on paranormal shows.

"I would just be walking around going, 'Why are we walking around in the dark with infrared cameras? This is stupid.' I don't want to go on there and be like the grudge. I get offered those types of things all the time but don't do them for that reason - because I don't want to go on and be laughing about it all."

Still, he says he's always up for a cool paranormal flick and "would like to see a good, serious alien invasion movie," which are often too goofy.

Superbeasts, werewolves, and living dead girls aside, Zombie is a pragmatic professional easily inching into middle age.

"I like to always feel like - even though at some point in your life it's not going to be true - that the best is yet to come and to approach it that way. I feel at this point it's still happening."

What's more, Rob Zombie's aware of his heretofore accomplishments and plans on creating as long as he has forward momentum.

"Once you feel you're going backwards, and it's not as good as it once was - you may not get out at that point because sometimes that dimension returns - because people get old and that's just life. But for the most part, it's nice to feel you can go out there and probably do better than you've ever done before. That's what inspires me."

Master of The Dead George A. Romero On Creating A Genre That Won't Die

(August 2010)

George A. Romero's fans are like the walking dead he's made famous in more than 40 years of filmmaking - namely, they are relentless, move in mobs and often covered in bloody latex.

Except when the legendary filmmaker is in sight, they are not hungry to eat his brain, but rather pick it about zombie rules, zombie apocalypse survival tips, and his take on the great debate of fast vs. slow-moving zombies.

That's the joy - and challenge - of interviewing the director of 1968's horror classic, *Night of the Living Dead*. It may take a few attempts to pin Romero down for an interview, but along the way one witnesses the idolatry shed upon the so-called "Grandfather of Zombie Films." One such attempt was at the May premiere of his sixth zombie film, *Survival of the Dead* - available August 24 on DVD and Blu-ray - at New York City's Village East Cinemas where he was swarmed by a crowd of rotting, zombified versions of Lady Gaga, Marilyn Monroe, Tippi Hedren, a Waffle House server, a hipster, and even a Chihuahua.

Romero is being appreciated by a new generation of fans due to a zombie-genre resurrection to rival vampires, and he eats it all up. "How can you get tired of this, man?" he asks.

At 6' 5", he's an imposing character but a jovial one constantly joking and releasing a cackling laugh. A 70-year-old man with a silver ponytail who continues to wear his trademark utility vest and impossibly thick, black-rimmed glasses, he poses with decaying devotees and gives a zombie growl to the press photographers.

Such a bright disposition may be surprising from the director of Night, one of the best horror films of all time, along with beloved zombie films *Dawn of the Dead* (1978), *Day of the Dead* (1985), *Land of the Dead* (2005), *Diary of the Dead* (2007), as well as non-zom cult favorites Martin (1977), "*Creepshow*" (1982), *Monkey Shines* (1988), *The Dark Half* (1993), and several others. Yet during a conversation a few days after the New York premiere, Romero says he wants audiences to have fun with his work, despite whatever underlying messages his films have.

"Even though I'm trying to say something about the state of humanity, the state of mankind, it's also meant to be funny in large parts," says Romero who likens his zombie films to EC Comics horror titles in the '40s and '50s, such as *Tales From the Crypt*. The "giggle while you barf" moments from those comics inspired him to include "looney tunes moments" in his movies.

"They were terrible stories, but they always had a moral. They were always full of bad puns and silly humor - it's just being able to accept the idea of mixing terrible things with hilarious things."

Romero says that approach continues with *Survival*, which revolves around a group of survivors who end up on an island and get involved with two families, the O'Flynns and Muldoons, feuding for generations now fighting over the treatment of undead loved ones. Although there's plenty of gore and memorable zombie kills, Romero admits to inserting slapstick humor in his tale "about war and enmities that don't die." But he also says he wanted to play with the notion of a quasi-Western genre with *Survival*.

"We really had a ball trying to make this look like an old Hollywood Western, like *The Big Country*," he says before joking, "I don't know, man, maybe having the creative control lets me run amok."

While he may run amok with his creative control, Romero says he always keeps a firm grip on the focus of his films, which are the people. That's why - aside from Night, which he calls a little bit creepy - he doesn't think his "morality tales" are scary. Plus, he adds, he's not even particularly fascinated by the zombies that defined much of his career.

"To me, in those days, zombies were the boys in the Caribbean doing the wetwork for [Bela] Lugosi" in 1932's *White Zombie*," where they were mindless humans, cursed by voodoo magic.

"I didn't even call them zombies in the first film; I called them flesh eaters. I just wanted some sort of game changing event that my human characters could ignore in favor of petty bickering," he laughs.

Even if he didn't call them zombies until Romero altered the archetype of the zombie by creating a hybrid of the classic voodoo-afflicted drone with vampiric ghouls. What he didn't do, was try to make them symbolize social problems. Over the years, a lot of meaning has been associated with Romero's choice of zombies as an allegory for a dozen other things - but not because of his doing.

Romero knows all the suggestions that "Zombies represent the dullness of humanity, how we've become immune and dull, and we're walking around dead, doing what we're expected to do." But he says he doesn't think that way.

"As far as I'm concerned, they're not the allegory. In my stories, it's all about people and how they respond to the situation, or fail to respond, or respond stupidly. The zombies could be anything. I never meant them to represent anything."

Although he's good natured about it, Romero is a disappointed optimist who thinks most of North America needs an anger management session. "To me, they're just the disaster," he says, which could even be a hurricane, but that people still wouldn't be handling it well and would opt instead to shoot each other instead of address game-changing events. In his world, Romero says the villains are the humans and the zombies are intentionally predictable; they can easily be dealt with or escaped if you don't screwup.

This outlook in Romero's work gets to the heart of why he has always been, and will always be, in the slow-moving, shambling zombie camp.

"That's the way they'd be; they're dead. Like in the first film, the sheriff said, 'they're dead, they're all messed up.' If they ran, their ankles would snap so by me, they move slow."

As far as the emergence of the fast zombie, Romero credits video games, and the challenge of "the hand-eye coordination thing: How many can you kill and how quickly can you kill them?"

"Then I think people reasoned that the dead can't move that quickly, so they gave them a Rage virus [as in 2002's *28 Days Later*] or some kind of a bug ... It's become something that is not me."

Romero never intended there to be a reason behind his zombie uprising. In Night, he filmed three possibilities to keep it ambiguous. Because of the need to trim run time, the one that made the final cut was a returning Venus Probe since it involved a lot of production value in his Washington, D.C. scene - it was the only time his crew left Pittsburgh to shoot elsewhere.

Romero scrapped that reason in his next zombie film, but he says, "I've been apologizing for that, sort of, ever since because - even in 'TV Guide' - it says, 'A returning Venus probe causes the dead to come back to life.'"

He adds, "My whole thing is somebody changed the rules: God, the devil, fate, whatever. And the dead are no longer dead, and we need to figure out what to do with it, except we're incapable because we're Just. Too. Stupid."

The reason for zombies notwithstanding, the current zombie renaissance is still going strong with video games such as *Left 4 Dead*, Robert Kirkman's lauded comic book series *The Walking Dead* or the horror-comedy *Zombieland*, " and is partially attributable to the 2004 Zack Snyder remake of Romero's celebrated 1978 "zombies in a mall" movie, *Dawn of the Dead*.

Romero is diplomatic about Snyder's version, but says he's "not particularly" happy about the remakes of his film. He calls the first 20 minutes of the movie "hot" before it loses its purpose, and adds it felt more like a video game than a movie.

He feels the same about the 2010 remake of his 1973 not-quite-zombies protest movie, *The Crazies*, which he says felt like it was trying to be *28 Days Later*.

"We were angry, we were pissed off about Vietnam - It came from a certain place," he says. "It should've remained in that place.

The remake lost its politics ... One of the points we were trying to make is that you can't tell who's crazy: The guys in the Pentagon are just as crazy as the people who are infected."

"But when they have pustules and glowing red eyes, it sort of gives it away!"

Still, although remakes haven't always been kind to Romero's source material (the 2006 film, *Night of the Living Dead 3D*, for instance), he has benefitted from the modern zombie popularity. Land was a successful pre- and post-9/11 commentary from Romero, and the New Media-inspired *Diary* was a low-budget, profitable outing that allowed him to reboot his zombies in a franchise - all the while maintaining more substantial ownership rights. Compared to "Night," which is part of the public domain, Survival is Romero's first direct sequel, and it marks the only time he's been able to use recurring characters.

It looks as if he'll be able to return to that franchise with those characters for two more "... *of the Dead*" pictures, which is a kind of job security he says he's not used to. He's also connected to the iTunes App of the Dead that allows iPhone and iPad users to affix zombie graphics to pictures of loved ones - and then to shoot them - based on makeup from Romero collaborators Tom Savini and Greg Nicotero.

But Romero says you won't see him promoting zombie survival kits, or the theory that a real zombocalypse is on its way unlike his friend, Max Brooks, the author of *The Zombie Survival Guide* and *World War Z*.

"I think Max really does think it might happen!" he laughs.

"Listen, for me, it's all a schtick, right? I've said to Max, 'Max, it's not gonna happen.'"

Romero concedes he's baffled and amused by the trend, however.

"How did this happen? How did it become like this impending apocalypse? Everyone's saying this could really be and there are zombie walks in every major city. What is it? Somebody explain it to me."

Perhaps surprisingly for a filmmaker whose movies typically include some supernatural theme, Romero says he doesn't really believe in anything paranormal.

I'm a lapsed Catholic who lost faith pretty early. I lost faith in the devil - he wasn't coming to my assistance in any way!" he jokes. "I hope UFOs are real, but that's about as far as I go."

This is the voice of the practical filmmaker Romero, who deals with the dictates of reality.

He says he has ideas for non-zombie movies but has learned from experience he doesn't have the energy to wind up in Hollywood for years at a time, "in development hell," trying to get financing for projects that never happen - especially if he can instead get backing for more zombie flicks, which he enjoys doing.

But for anyone who hasn't seen a Romero flick, he'd rather you begin with *Knightriders* or *Martin*, his 1977 vampire deconstruction about a "mixed-up kid" that he started as a spoof then began to take seriously.

"Those are films that are really from the heart," he says. "I like to think these [zombie] films are thoughtful, but they're not me - to some extent they're commercial films and I'm trying to do something with them, but they're not me."

With regards to his zombie movies, Romero recommends starting the viewing of his zombie oeuvre with *Diary* - and doesn't suggest *Night* first except to see where he got his start.

"I didn't know what I was doing," he says honestly. "I look at Night and all I see is sort of the Filmmaking 101 errors in screen direction and just very, very basic filmmaking."

He admits he wasn't thinking about mythology or the development of zombies with. After all, he points out, the ghouls in that movie were eating insects in addition to humans.

Plus, after the acclaim he garnered with his freshman effort, he says he was reluctant to return to the devouring dead.

"When people started to write about it as if it was essential American cinema, I got terrified of making another one - and didn't make another one until I had an idea, I thought would satisfy people looking for the message - which was the shopping mall and the consumer thing."

"Then I started to think in terms of, 'What if there's another one?' and started to think about rules."

Still, mistakes and all, Romero says breaking into moviemaking was easier for him compared to younger filmmakers, even though it's technically easier to shoot a film today. He balks at the idea that there are no new ideas "out there," and instead blames the movie distribution system.

"When I first started ... it was harder to make the films, but it was much easier to distribute them because there were dozens of these independent distributors that would take a little film like *Night of the Living Dead* and actually get it out and put it on the screen."

"It's really harder today to do that," he adds. "There are very few distributors, very few outlets, where filmmakers can go and put their stuff. Distribution companies that matter and can actually get screens are just all looking for the quick buck, the next hit, then something new ... I don't think it's a brain drain and there's no creativity left, it's just that fewer people are buying and what they're buying is the dumbed-down stuff."

Even in terms of his own success, Romero is pragmatic about the chances of having a hit on his hands.

"I always go, 'Thank god for video.' My films usually come out, they sort of get dissed, and in three days they're gone. Thankfully, on video, people rediscover them."

When it comes to talk of him being a legend, or indie film pioneer, Romero laughs it off. He says the comparison is better suited to screenwriter/director John Sayles (*Piranha, Eight Men Out*) and "a lot of guys who have figured out how to do it without selling out."

"John Waters, man. He gets my vote."

Romero says he has "big hopes" for new projects from *Halloween* helmer John Carpenter and his good friend Dario Argento, the *Suspiria* director he credits with making *Dawn* happens because he was the first to bring money into the production. But any time he gets the chance, Romero also mentions a younger filmmaker of Hellboy and Blade II fame.

"My man is Guillermo Del Toro ... He's doing exactly what I would love to do, which is go make one for the bucks, then go make one from the heart," he says. "I loved *Pan's Labyrinth*. It was sensational."

For his part, George A. Romero, the Grandfather of the Zombie Film, isn't too interested in finding a cure to the zombie curse or wrapping up his run with the walking dead. Why? "It's too much fun."

Romero says he figures he'll do a "little set" of his new zombie movies, "then hang it up and go off and do something else." In the meantime, he laughs and says he'll happily continue making films "off in the corner."

"The zombie fad will come and go, and I'll probably still be doing my own little thing with these guys over here."

Quick Bites From George A. Romero

(August 2010)

Reviews:
"So far, it's always mixed with my stuff, so I'm used to it. I spent the first years of my career just ignoring reviews that 'this is garbage' ... As long as some people are getting it, that's fine with me."

Shaun of the Dead:
"I love *Shaun of the Dead*. I've become buddies with those guys. The director Edgar Wright and Simon Pegg were zombies in *Land of the Dead*!"

His zombie survival kit:
"My zombie survival kit is a shotgun and a good car."

His favorite zombie kill:
"It's not a kill but [Tom]Savini did this thing with a real actor with his head down in a table and a real actor's body - it was just some tendrils connecting him to a pulsing brain. It's not a kill but was wonderful makeup and really cool thing. "

Fake blood and prosthetics:
"I love the mechanical prosthetic, on-the-set effect. It's great. Even the actors react better if you're actually pulling something off their face! It looks better. The blood is even interactive; it splashes the right way. All of it is realistic and there's something ... actually

charming about it."

CGI gore:
"I did an effect in *Diary of the Dead* where we hit this guy with acid and you see him, the whole time, walking around and you see the acid eat its way down into his skull and dig a cavity in his brain. An actor will not allow you to do this! ... Computers now allow us to do these silly, looney tunes things."

R.L. Stine, The Man Behind the Boogie Man

(November 2010)

When one enters the lair of a master of fear, it's reasonable to expect a skeleton, perhaps an evil ventriloquist dummy or even posters of creature feature giants like Bela Lugosi. But probably not a cute little pup.

Yet the "lair" of Robert Lawrence Stine - more famously known as children's author and *Goosebumps* creator R.L. Stine - is actually a sunny Upper West Side home in New York City with a gatekeeper in the form of his King Charles Spaniel, Minnie.

Instead of haunting, mauling, or tormenting, she yips, licks, and cuddles in decidedly non-frightening manner. But to get to Stine in his inviting home office filled with books and memorabilia, one must befriend the Minnie beast, which it turns out isn't all that difficult if you're any good at petting.

Stine himself is even less frightening than Minnie. A 67-year-old Columbus, OH, native with a relaxed demeanor who laughs easily and readily shares anecdotes, and earned his other pseudonym of Jovial Bob Stine, he is not what you might expect from a guy who spooked out an entire generation and sold more than 300 million books in the process.

"As you can see, I'm not too scary a guy," says Stine. "Everyone's disappointed! I go to schools, and they go, 'umm, wait a minute. He's not scary, that's somebody's dad.'"

Yet despite his mild-mannered scribe personality, Stine became a ghoulish story-telling crypt keeper to middle-school readers - and incidentally the best-selling children's author of perhaps all time - 18 years ago, when he published the first *Goosebumps* book, *Welcome to Dead House*, in 1992.

Reminded of that milestone and he jokes he needs "to go take a nap." But sleeping doesn't seem to be a priority for Stine who began writing at age nine and hasn't stopped since.

"I wanted to be a comic strip artist - and I had no talent," he says. "I was horrible, so I knew I would be a writer."

With that career track in mind, for two decades after he graduated from the Ohio State University in 1965, Stine worked as a writer and "nobody had noticed." As Jovial Bob, he wrote kids joke books and created the humor magazine *Bananas*, which he worked on for 10 years. As "Eric Affabee," and under his own name, he wrote "Find Your Fate" choose-your-own-adventure type series with Indiana Jones and G.I. Joe characters as heroes.

"I was a freelance writer and never said no to anything ... You're afraid to," says Stine, who adds he would take every project he could, including bubblegum cards and coloring books. Then, in 1986, Stine turned to horror with the teen book, *Blind Date*. The book's success, and his subsequent titles in the *Point Horror* young-adult series, led Stine to creating the teen series Fear Street with his wife Jane's publishing company, Parachute Press.

The horror genre was a natural for Stine, who counts *The Twilight Zone* creator Rod Serling and author Ray Bradbury as heroes, and says he still reads Bradbury's *Dandelion Wine* every year. But Stine also credits EC Comics from the 1950s as an inspiration, and even wrote the foreword for a 2007 hardcover *The Vault of Horror* collection.

"All those stories are really ghastly and hideous, and they all have a funny ending," he says. "That was a major influence on me."

"Once *Fear Street* took off, we knew we had something that was going to last for a long time," and Stine says he found he could start rejecting projects. "That's a big thing in your career when you can say, 'Gee no, I don't want to do that.'"

Fear Street led to *Goosebumps*, which made Stine an international celebrity. The books followed a formula of scaring kids, but not terrifying them. No one died in *Goosebumps*, even though in *Fear Street*, Stine killed off teens all the time.

Plus, the author had a rule to never make it "too real," which included avoiding topics like divorce, child abuse, drug abuse, kidnapping or suicide. While he acknowledges those topics would be good for horror, he didn't want to "ruin the fun of it."

"You're reading it, you're having this adventure, it's very creepy," he explains. "There are ghosts, there's monsters and you don't know who the monster is, but you know you're safe in your own room reading it."

Stine shares that his favorite description of the book series came from a parent who said *Goosebumps* "give my kids shivers but not nightmares." As far as happy endings, Stine followed the Rod Serling example and always wrote happy endings followed by a weird, question-mark teaser at the end of the tale.

The *Goosebumps* popularity was carried over into the Fox Kids hit television show, and while still writing the teen monthly series, Stine also wrote a new *Goosebumps* installment each month, which were then translated into 32 languages.

"Back in those days, when *Goosebumps* was the biggest thing ... I don't honestly know how I did it. I had no life, of course; I didn't get out much." But Stine adds the exhilaration of having people notice his work kept him going.

"It got so big all over the world. At one point we were selling four million *Goosebumps* books a month," he says. "I think we knew that couldn't last." But not unlike his recurring villain Slappy the Dummy, Stine's popularity wouldn't die, and his creative output could not be stopped.

After writing what he estimates to be approximately 330 books, Stine says he prefers the fast pace of writing for a series and hates working on individual books because "it's too slow; it doesn't come out fast enough."

In addition to stand-alone books and new series *Dangerous Girls, Mostly Ghostly, The Nightmare Room,* and the non-horror *Rotten School, Fear Street* begat spin-offs *New Fear Street, Fear Street Super-Chillers, 99 Fear Street,* and seven other related series. Meanwhile, *Goosebumps* spawned *Goosebumps Series 2000* and *Give Yourself Goosebumps.*

Following an eight-year break from *Goosebumps*, Stine is

currently writing 25 installments of his massive crossover serial, *Goosebumps Horrorland*, which is spun off of two earlier books.

Part 16 is a special edition title called *Weirdo Halloween*, and *Part 17*, *The Wizard of Ooze*, was released in September.

Horrorland even has a Wii video game counterpart and there's a *Goosebumps* photograph app on iTunes.

As if the Stine brand isn't powerful enough, The Hub - a children's network from Discovery Networks and Hasbro, Inc. that launched October 10 and replaces Discovery Kids - is airing the original series, *R.L. Stine's Haunting Hour*. And new collections of the *Goosebumps* TV show, *The Blob That Ate Everyone*, and *Go Eat Worms!* are out on DVD.

Considering how much Stine is involved with, how does the guy continue to come up with more material?

After all this time, his trick is to come up with a title for a book first, even though most authors work the other way around, but admits "it's a little more of a challenge" to come up with new ideas after hundreds of books.

"If you've written seven or eight mummy books, it's a little harder to find another mummy story ... somehow they always come."

Though Stine says it's his audience who deserve sympathy for having to write so much.

"Kids have to write more than any living humans," he points out. "No one else has to write reports, book reports, essays, and about their vacation, and kids have to keep a journal."

This connection with children is a frequent topic with Stine. But he says the hard part of his job - "especially the older you get" - is staying in touch with youth culture and putting himself in his readers' minds.

"You don 't want to sound like some old guy trying to sound young; It has to be very real."

At the height of the *Goosebumps* craze, he did this by keeping an eye on his son Matthew and his friends, who were at the right age for the books. He listened to their language, paid attention to what they wore and how they hung out. But Matthew is a married composer and sound engineer, so Stine has to look elsewhere.

"Now I have some nephews that are the right age and do a lot of school visits and talk to kids and try to keep up with pop culture."

He adds that when it comes to scares, the kids are the same even if their language changes.

"What they're afraid of is the same; the fears are the same from when I was a kid - afraid of the dark, afraid someone's waiting for you under your bed waiting to grab you, that kind of thing."

Stine also says that while he always thought of himself as conservative when it came to the intensity of scares he wrote about - and that publishers always begged for him to turn it up a notch - he doesn't think pop culture violence and scares have much effect on kids.

"Kids are very smart, it's the one thing I've learned all these years writing for kids ... if they see a movie and people are having their heads blown off and horrible violence, that's one thing. And if they go outside and see somebody beat up on the street, that's a totally different experience ... It's a totally different kind of violence, and kids know the difference. "

Although he does admit with a chuckle, he has lots of 20-something Twitter followers who tell him, "I can't go in a garage at night now, thanks to you; I'm terrified of ventriloquist dummies thanks to you ... I get that all the time."

This highlights an interesting aspect to Stine's legacy. The kids who read *Goosebumps* in the early '90s are now graduating college, beginning careers or starting families of their own. There is an entire generation of Stine's readers who have entered adulthood.

Last May Stine gave his first commencement speech, at Macaulay Honors College of the City University of New York, to a group of students who grew up with *Goosebumps* - and he naturally entertained them with a ghost story.

"These are my kids," he says, which is why he likes the microblog Twitter. Although he says he had to ask to stop being called a "blast from the past," he enjoys continuing to communicate with the audience that made him so popular - an audience that includes a few famous faces, such as *Late Night* talk show host Jimmy Fallon who said he wanted to frame a tweet from Stine.

The scribe's acceptance of new technology extends to e-books, and he doesn't share the opinion of alarmists in the publishing industry who fear electronic media will be the downfall of books.

He travels with a Kindle - on which he reads "beach reading" all year long - and also reads from his wife's iPad.

Says Stine, "It's the words that count, and not the way you get the words; a scary story is going to be just as scary on a Kindle."

But Stine doesn't necessarily think all is well with the book business, and is disappointed that inexpensive, monthly series have fallen out of favor.

"I think largely because of *Harry Potter* and the *Twilight* books and Lemony Snicket books, publishers would rather do hardcovers, and have them come out not as series [but] one a year. Bookstores would rather have hardcovers because they charge so much more."

"That's a very big change," he adds, "I'm sorry to see the change from paperback to hardcover because I like for kids to be able to afford books ... nice, cheap paperbacks kids can buy."

Even *Goosebumps* is now a bi-monthly, Stine points out, but is still only $5.99 per title.

But if Stine is not particularly scared for the industry's future, what is the spookmeister afraid of?

Aside from typical adult fears, he says his one irrational phobia isn't that interesting: Stine can't jump into a swimming pool.

"My nephews think that's just hilarious; the scary guy can't jump in the water."

When it comes to the monsters and ghosts that lurk in his creative mind, Stine says he's unsure about their existence. He hasn't had any paranormal experience and lacks evidence. But he says he's always looking, because "this is what I do."

"Whenever I go to schools, I always ask, 'Have any of you seen a real ghost? Not a TV ghost, but a real ghost,'" he says. "And at every single school, at least two, three, four kids raise their hands and have stories of things they've seen, which I think is pretty amazing."

Despite Stine's interest in the supernatural, it's unlikely he'll have much time to seek out evidence any time soon. With new projects arriving all the time, R.L. Stine will be haunted by deadlines and not the creatures at his disposal to spook kids with. He jokes that if you need to find him in the next year, he'll be chained to his keyboard in his office. Thankfully, Minnie will be right there with him, guarding the lair and cuddling away any goosebumps that might arise.

Generation Z: Zombie Superstars Robert Kirkman And Max Brooks Living It Up Among the Undead

(January 2011)

If George A. Romero, iconic director of 1968's *Night of the Living Dead* and the five follow-ups, is the king of the modern zombie movement, then Robert Kirkman and Max Brooks are the deans of the dead.

In October 2003, comic book scribe Robert Kirkman's Image Comics series *The Walking Dead* debuted as a monthly title. The celebrated title follows a growing, then declining, group of survivors from Kentucky to Georgia to Washington, D.C., as they attempt to survive and rebuild lives after the dead refuse to die.

Kirkman was already an accomplished comic book creator before *Dead*, but only 78 issues in - with no end in sight, he says - *The Walking Dead* is Kirkman's legacy. Alternating between occasional uplifting moments and many depressing, disturbing scenes, the ongoing story presents a world where no main character is safe.

Kirkman's success with *The Walking Dead* led to Marvel Zombies in 2005, where he was given the freedom to turn superheroes Spider-Man, Iron Man, the Incredible Hulk, and others into flesh-eating versions of themselves. On October 31, the televised adaptation of *The Walking Dead* premieres on AMC with a pilot directed by Dead fan/executive producer Frank Darabont (*The Shawshank Redemption*) and is perhaps the most eagerly anticipated show to premiere in the fall.

Not a month before *The Walking Dead* was introduced, Max Brooks' *The Zombie Survival Guide* was published in September 2003. Although previously an Emmy-winning comedy writer for *Saturday Night Live*, after Max Brooks wrote the critically-acclaimed bestsellers *Guide and World War Z: An Oral History of the Zombie War in 2006*, he became known as an academic of the slow-moving undead. Far from being in the shadow of his father, comedy director Max Brooks, the 38-year-old is a zombie historian and lecturer who gives presentations on recorded living dead attacks throughout history and offers suggestions on how best to survive an impending zombocalypse.

With the *World War Z* being turned into a summer 2012 film, starring and executive-produced by Brad Pitt, and the *Guide* having been spun off into the *Recorded Attacks* graphic novel and zombie scanner iPhone app, Brooks has become a zombie superstar - all because the shuffling, rotting corpses from horror movies haunted his dreams.

Along with director Edgar Wright and actor Simon Pegg (*Shaun of the Dead*), Brooks and Kirkman are the Gen-X caretakers of the house that Romero built. Like Romero, both artists treat zombies as terrifying, slow-moving disasters - but it's the humans who play key roles as heroes, villains, and troublemakers. The current fascination with the traditional living dead genre (fast zombies need not apply) which has bitten pop culture is directly related to the work of these two. It is perhaps, no small coincidence that my interviews with both were independently set up and scheduled back-to-back with them.

As a result, the responses from Kirkman and Brooks to the same questions ParanormalPopCulture.com asked them are presented here, together, as one interview.

What celebrity/historical figure as a zombie would you like to encounter?

Robert Kirkman: As a general rule, I would not like to encounter any zombies in real life. But, if I were to pick a celebrity, it would probably be someone like Shirley Temple or somebody who's manageable. I'm not gonna be picking the Abraham Lincoln zombie or anything. That guy is far too tall and formidable. But, yeah, just somebody you know. Some kid that - what celebrity kids died of an early age, because I could probably pick them as zombies. I could probably handle that. I don't want to get bit. That's basically my problem ... I would probably just run away. You know, picking a child zombie was probably not the best idea.

You know this is going to be the headline for the story: "Robert Kirkman Wants to Kill Child Zombies."

RK: It's really just because of self-preservation. And that's not out of any kind of desire to do that.

Max Brooks: What celebrity or historical figure would I like to encounter? [French painter Henri de] Toulouse-Lautrec because he's short and couldn't move very fast. [I would take him out] like I take out every zombie: with a shot in the head. And with Toulouse-Lautrec you just have to angle down instead of up.

What's the weirdest, off-the-wall question you get from people about zombies?

RK: As far as zombie related and stuff like that, I get the question a lot, "How do I think I would fare if there were an actual zombie apocalypse?" And I think people expect me to be like, "Well, I think I'd do really well because I write this comic book and there' s this TV show coming out." I obviously know a lot about this. But I would jump off a bridge pretty quick just because I don't think I would last very long. And I wouldn't want to get eaten. It doesn't seem like the kind of world that I would want to live in for very long. So I would check out pretty quickly ... take the coward's way out.

MB: Probably "What celebrity or historical person would you most want to meet as a zombie?"

So I have earned a place in the odd interview question hall of fame.

MB: I think you nailed it.

Are zombies actually your favorite horror genre? Or is there something you like more but you sort of fell into zombies?

RK: I just want to say that I'm glad this question isn't getting me to talk about my desire to commit suicide or kill children. So I appreciate that. As far as like a horror sub-genre, I guess, yeah, I really do like zombie movies quite a bit. If I were going to pick my favorite, I would definitely rather watch a zombie movie than a vampire movie any day of the week ...

MB: I'm just a zombie nerd who happens to think about this stuff ... I'm a zombie fan before I'm a zombie creator.

Why write these stories that are so focused on the people that survive horrific events?

RK: I put a lot into *The Walking Dead*, but it's not really just a horror thing. There are a lot of different characters; it's a very human story. I try to do just basically a straight drama that has zombies walking around in the background.

MB: The reason [George A. Romero] is the godfather of zombies - it's basically his world, we're just living in it - I think the reason that he is The Man, is because his movies are about people. And they are all about social commentary.

Why did you write the stories, then?

MB: I wrote them for me. I didn't expect anybody to really be into this stuff. My books are just answering my own questions. I went looking for zombie survival guide, believe me. I wanted to read this thing, and nobody had written it. And so, I wrote it for me. When it came time for "World War Z," all the zombie books and all the zombie movies and stories in general, comics and video games, they are all micro. They're all one story of one person - which is good, I'm not dissing that - but zombies in nature are big, they are global. I wanted to read a big, global zombie story with survivors from all around the world. And I couldn't find it. And I'm like, "you know what? I'm going to do it." I'm going to answer my own question. I am going to feed my own need. I think that's the thing with me: If I'm going to do it, anything with zombies, it's gotta be because I can't stop thinking about it.

There are people who actually believe the zombie threat is real

and are preparing for it with guns and bunkers. Is the appeal of zombies - and for some, and actual belief - that it's easier to discuss how to defeat the undead than it is to figure out how to solve the healthcare debate or financial crisis?

RK: Exactly. You can't just shoot the healthcare crisis in the head. It's a much more manageable threat.

MB: I think you have just nailed it right on the head. 100%. I think why zombies are successful in general is because we live in very uncertain times, and I think we are constantly being assailed by crisis after crisis. I think most of these crises are really hard to get your brain around. How the hell did our economy suddenly melt down over night? And why is the planet melting? And what do these terrorists really want? I think there are so many complex issues with so many complex solutions. Something like zombies is a very manageable way of dealing with our apocalyptic anxieties. Because in a zombie story, the world still goes to hell, like it would in any other scenario. But a walking corpse I can shoot in the head. I get it. I think it calculates our fears and gives us literally and figuratively a magic bullet.

At what point do you want to take people aside and say, "Yeah, I believe it's real but p.s., it's not real."

MB: I think that the reason the book is successful, honestly, when you take away all the compliments, I think the reason it works, is that when you take away the zombies, it's still a disaster preparedness manual. Which is exactly how I went about it. I went about it very realistically. I thought, ok, if zombies were actually real, forget movies, forget plot devices and gimmicks and drama. How would you really survive? So all the knowledge in there is knowledge that you would need in an earthquake or a riot or any kind of disaster. So the nice thing is there's nothing in there that is zombie specific.

RK: I don't want to believe that zombies are real.

[To Kirkman] Have you read Max Brooks' work?

RK: I was given the *Zombie Survival Guide* as a gift, and I just flipped to one page looking through it to see how it was formatted and stuff because I didn't really know how the book was done. It was a page about how you can fortify an apartment building by destroying the stairs on the first level and living on the levels above the first level - zombies wouldn't be able to get up there - but you've got a rope ladder so if you needed to get down or up, you could. I was like, "Oh my God, I could totally do that in Walking Dead; that's totally a practical thing that the characters could do and it's totally cool. And I can't do it now because it's in this book. Damn it!" So I closed the book and I decided I was never going to look at it ... I didn't want to feel influenced by it, so I just avoid his work.

MB: [Responding to Kirkman] The poor guy is so paranoid about that. I met him once. The first thing out of his mouth is, "I didn't read it." And I'm like, dude. First of all, I don't care if you did.

And I don't care if you do rip me off. George Romero would be the first guy to tell you he ripped off Richard Matheson ... I don't care if you do rip somebody off. As long as you do something cool with it. Isn't that how it's supposed to work? I'll be the first person to tell you I ripped off Studs Terkel - shamelessly. He wrote a book called, "The Good War." It's an oral history of World War II where he interviewed survivors of World War II and he was a big influence on me, and I shamelessly ripped him off.

When does the zombie work end?

RK: I don't really have an end in mind for Walking Dead. I could say, "Oh, it'll take 10 years or 15 years." But I could see it going 20 more years. I really, I set out as a young man to get into doing comics and writing comics for a living, and to get to tell stories for a long period of time over a number of years with the same characters and have complete control over those characters in that book. And I have exactly that. So with Walking Dead, I'm doing exactly what I set out to do. And I'm having the time of my life ... I think I'll be able to keep the book going for a good long while.

MB: There's definitely zombie projects that I think of - not necessarily novels or stories but there's definitely elements of zombie survival culture that I've been thinking of. And there's one I've been kicking around ... Not a novel, not another big World War Zombie project. Nothing like that; just a little side thing. We'll see.

Comic Creator Mike Mignola and His Supernatural Son Hellboy

(April 2011)

Hellboy is not your typical superhero. Aside from the fact he doesn't have a secret identity and eschews spandex and a cape for a trench coat, he is a red, horned demon and "Beast of the Apocalypse." Not to mention, he was summoned to Earth by an evil Russian mystic and Nazis.

Still, Hellboy is one of the most recognizable superheroes ever and belongs in the comic book pantheon alongside Batman, Superman, and Spider-Man.

But behind the Hellboy character and the eponymous book is creator Mike Mignola. The 50-year-old artist and writer began his work in the comics industry as an inker for Marvel Comics on *Daredevil* and *The Incredible Hulk*, then as an artist for DC Comics on *Gotham By Gaslight*, before launching his hero for publisher Dark Horse Comics in 1993 with artist/writer John Byrne scripting Hellboy's first adventure.

"I was just never good at drawing the regular, mainstream superhero stuff," says Mignola about his decision to leave the big two comic companies of the early '90s. "I just did the book I wanted to do, and I got lucky."

If it comes down to luck, Mignola has it in spades. In the 18 years since Hellboy's debut, Mignola's creation has become a pop culture mainstay, appeared in two live-action films, two animated movies, three video games, and several anthologies and novels.

There are action figures, backpacks, keychains, and spirit

boards.

The popular character's title has even spun off more titles - not all of which Mignola writes - including *B.P.R.D.*, surrounding the continuing adventures of Hellboy's team; *Sir Edward Grey, Witchfinder*, about a Victorian-era occult detective a la Van Helsing, is another. It is difficult to quantify how much his creations appear across Dark Horse's lineup since they exist mainly as miniseries, but in the first half of 2011, there were two *Hellboy* minis, two *Hellboy* one-shots, three *B.P.R.D.* series and a *Witchfinder* miniseries.

So why does Hellboy's creation resonate with audiences? "It's a funny name? He's red?" he asks. "I have no idea,"

"I'd like to think it's a little different than other stuff that's being done. One of the things that is frustrating to me about so much stuff in comics is everybody seems to be doing a slightly different version of Batman, Superman or one of the X-Men."

"For whatever reason, the thing I did worked."

The reason it "worked" might have something to do with Mignola's kinetic and gothic art style, famously described as "German expressionism meets Jack Kirby," by comics legend Alan Moore of *Watchmen* and *V for Vendetta* fame.

The other reason Hellboy, as well as Mignola's other creations, have become successful is because he returned to his childhood for inspiration. Born in Berkeley, CA, on September 16, 1960, he is the eldest son of a "tough and leathery cabinetmaker" with a personality remarkably similar to the red hero.

As a 12-year-old, he discovered Bram Stoker's Victorian-era *Dracula* and became absorbed with monsters, ghosts and the rest of the supernatural - elements that continue to fuel his work.

Over the years, secret sects, fairy tales, myths and folklore were also added to his influences.

"I have so little interest in the real world," says Mignola, who adds he works with old movies playing in his studio. Favorites like Universal Pictures' *Bride of Frankenstein* influence his creative process.

"I cannot get enough movies about cursed families and crumbling castles with vampires in the basement ... there's a real charm to that old school, gothic, horror stuff."

It shows. A typical Mignola story might find a nefarious

creature of yore, a hidden society, or occult-obsessed mad scientist gathering in castle ruins to unleash a world-devouring creature from the bowels of some Lovecraftian realm.

Now might be a good time to point out that for a guy who is happiest drawing monsters, Mignola isn't a dark personality; he actually has a pretty sunny disposition and calls his work "harmless " fun despite any darker elements that may appear.

"If I was really nuts - and I'm sure some people must think I am because of the stuff I write - I think you'd recognize it in the work," he says. "But I know a lot of guys who draw monsters and very few of them, do I think, are crazy."

"A lot of people might look at them and go, 'these guys draw axe murderers, and headless bodies, and a guy posing with a bunch of human heads leaning on a fence; this guy is clearly crazy.' Well, I know that guy. He's not crazy, he just thinks this stuff is fun."

Although he admits his work attracts some "weird letters " where people notice patterns and messages in his work - which he believes says more about the letter-writer than his work - he has largely avoided controversy with occult and supernatural themes.

"I stay away from a lot of the stuff I find kind of icky and gross, so it's kind of a fun monster book." He adds, "If guys are performing a black mass, they're probably the bad guys. People don't mind that stuff in there as long as we know which one's the good guy and which one's the bad guy."

As far as his own beliefs in the paranormal, Mignola says he largely thinks in terms of fiction, but that "there's probably ghosts." He describes a time in London, promoting the film *Hellboy 2* with director Guillermo Del Toro and composer Danny Elfman. Del Toro, "a believer" in the paranormal, came up with the idea to get a haunted hotel room and have each spend time in the room alone.

"That I wasn't too keen about," says Mignola. "Maybe I do believe in this stuff a little bit because as much as I don't mind hanging out in a haunted hotel room with two other guys, an hour or half an hour, in the dark, in a hotel room that is supposedly haunted? I got enough imagination that that's not the most appealing thing I can think of."

While somewhat on the fence about ghosts, Mignola does acknowledge that the secret societies he mentions in his comics are often based in fact.

"These groups are real, [but] I suspect none of these groups are nearly as interesting as they sound when you read about them," although he adds the experiments and "science" of groups like Nazis shows how reality is often more absurd than fiction.

"As weird as it made some of those groups sound - or my version of those groups sound in the Hellboy books - I keep stumbling into cross references of these guys in my various research and think, 'Wow, the stuff I made up was stupid; the stuff that they're doing was so much more far-fetched.'"

Still, while Mignola says his work is often based on some research, he's not "writing these stories for historians." He takes bits and pieces from mythology and folklore and has an aim towards making his stories generally accessible without being dumbed down - or without taking away the fun.

"I want to be as accurate as a 1940s movie about Jack the Ripper would be," he says. "If I can get that level of authenticity, it's good enough for people who don't know anything about the subject."

This creative philosophy perhaps sheds light on his approach to moviemaking, and the changes Del Toro made to the cinematic portrayal of Hellboy. Though resembling Mignola's first Hellboy miniseries "*Seed of Destruction*," the 2004 film strayed from the source material. *Hellboy 2* was a complete departure from comic book canon.

"The first thing I thought" about the movies, Mignola says, was "I've done it my way, you do it your way." "It's a radically different medium."

He adds that changes make sense to gain a wider audience and cites the example of The Joker being the murderer of Bruce Wayne's parents in Tim Burton's 1989 film *Batman*.

Mignola admits the movies were great for selling comics, and helped keep a spotlight on his characters, but that he has no control over the films and can't be concerned about them - although a *Hellboy 3* seems unlikely, he says.

"I won't say there's no possibility, but certainly, there's no talk of a *Hellboy 3*."

However, with the 20th anniversary of Hellboy fast approaching, Mignola has big plans for "big red" and his other characters without dealing with a movie. The creator has always contended there is an arc to his most famous character, and there is an end. While he remains silent on details or timelines, he has crafted a history to his universe and it's one of permanence where people stay dead, and actions matter.

"I don't ever want to be Marvel or DC comics," he says. "Batman's always going to be Batman no matter how many times you break his back or do whatever the hell else you do to him."

For instance, in the comics, hell is literally breaking loose (*B.P.R.D.: Hell on Earth*) and *Hellboy* has lost an eye. Mignola says those things happened for a reason and won't just be undone. He says he's excited to be taking his universe in a certain direction, and the end result is an altered Hellboy because "Hellboy is meant to change."

But for those worried about a drastic 20th anniversary gag, Mignola says that will never be his approach.

"We won't turn him into a robot that year," he says, but does hope to be drawing the *Hellboy* comic for another 10 years - then teases it can be a comic without the Hellboy readers knowing.

In addition to his goals with his creations, Mignola has his own character arc. While he has done covers, he laments that he has focused primarily on writing and not art for some time.

"I just don't want to have a full-time job writing," he says, "Which is almost what I've been doing for the last five years."

He says he realized how long he'd been away from the art while writing an afterward to this July's release, *Hellboy: Library Edition, Volume IV*, which collects other artist's drawings of Hellboy. Fortunately, he is back at the drawing board and readers will see his art return to the books by next year.

"I was not supposed to be gone this long. I'm actually very disgusted with myself and very embarrassed; I feel like I've got a lot of time to make up."

Mignola has that time at his disposal. He says he's surprised he has never tired of Hellboy and is still having a hell of a lot of fun with the iconic character.

'Being Human' Stars Strive For The Normal Within Paranormal

(April 2011)

Three young 20-something roommates sit around the kitchen table of their rented fixer-upper house. They don't eat the food in front of them, mainly because one isn't interested and the other two can't; they commiserate about life - but mostly death. He is undead and she is dead, and the cursed third wishes he was.

This is what it's like *Being Human* for the vampire, ghost, and werewolf characters on the Syfy network's newest hit, a remake of a British show, and if you think living a normal life is hard, try a paranormal one.

It's a gimmick: three supernatural roomies trying to get along in the real world. It is the kind of gimmick likely joked about over horror movies and booze, but which then coalesces into a serious idea.

"That's what makes our show different from all the other genre of vampires/werewolf/ghost shows," says Meaghan Rath, who plays ghostly student/fiancée Sally.

"Our characters aren't necessarily embracing their supernatural powers. And it's, like, you can take away that element of the show, and the story will still be as compelling because it's about these people trying to retain their humanity."

OK, so it's an effective gimmick.

After all, when British TV channel BBC Three premiered the series in January 2009 with more than a million people viewing, the resulting success led to two more seasons (Season Three concluded its run in the UK March 13 and on BBC America tomorrow night). After the show made the leap across the pond to BBC America in July 2009, it garnered a fast following stateside for being, to quote horror website DreadCentral.com, "a powerhouse of good old-fashioned horror that played like a completely supernatural version of *Three's Company*." By October the same year, it was announced Syfy would be remaking it.

Part horror, angsty Gen-Y drama, and dark comedy, the series revolves around the trio as they attempt to regain their lost humanity while also struggling to evade the forces that took it in the first place. But neither "remake" nor "re-imagining" quite captures Syfy's *Being Human*, which premiered in January with an impressive 2 million viewers. Now set in Boston, the show is Americanized and tweaked, but stands on its own as an equal - and is for some, superior - to its predecessor.

Rath - who previously starred in the Canadian sitcom *The Assistants* - views her version of the show as an "homage" to the original, although she only saw a few episodes to avoid being too heavily influenced by her British ghost counterpart, Lenora Crichlow. But Sam Huntington (*Cavemen, Superman Returns*), who plays dropout pre-med student and werewolf Josh, agrees with Rath's sentiment.

"I think the world of the British cast and thought about that every day - and how to honor them and respect them - but I think ultimately what we're doing is exactly that, is honoring them."

Sam Witwer (*Battlestar Galactica, Star Wars: The Force Unleashed*) is the male nurse and 257-year-old vampire Aidan - named after Aidan Turner, the Irish actor who plays the vampire on the BBC - adds he hopes the show is part of what he jokes is the "circle of television" where "whatever we end up doing honors what they've done and brings a bigger audience to them, and in turn perhaps their audience supplements ours, and it's a big happy family."

"Big happy family" is an apt choice of words for Witwer since the three actors have a remarkably sincere chemistry with one another. They often finish one another's sentences and instead of trying to one-up, they joke, poke fun at, and support each other as close-knit roommates might.

"Every single day I go to set, I am so excited to be there working with these guys," says Huntington, who adds that his castmates and crew elevates his own work."

"We like being around each other," says Rath, and Witwer chimes in that they get along so well they've "actually gotten the comment from directors to tone down our chemistry, which I've never heard that comment before."

Also part of the *Human* family is Sarah Allen as recently turned vampire Rebecca, Alison Louder as Josh's sister Emily, and the show's recurring heavy, head honcho vampire Bishop, played by the same Mark Pellegrino who played the godlike Jacob in *Lost* and Lucifer in *Supernatural*. These characters vary slightly from the BBC series; Josh never had a sister onscreen and Rebecca stuck around longer than her British version Lauren.

"In the beginning of the first episode, I inadvertently turn a girl into a vampire," says Witwer, before joking, "Hey, guys, you can't blame me. She's beautiful."

"But that character is a lot larger of a character and has much more influence on my character than the British version. She's like a legitimate love interest, whereas in the British version, from what I understand, it's not quite that way."

Huntington says the changes, which may upset some fans of the original, is a good thing and "helps the audience kind of understand his [Josh's] journey. And it informs who he is."

Witwer goes on to say the variations from the UK *Being Human* is both necessary and beneficial for the new series to stand on its own.

"There's a lot of things where we'll take maybe an idea that they have and expand it into entire plotlines. And of course, there are other things that go in completely different directions because they didn't have the screen time."

For instance, the vampire world became more diverse. In addition to the inhuman *Human* family of Pellegrino's Bishop character, Rath lets slip "they're introducing this new sect of vampires that wasn't in the British one."

The vampires here are stripped of a glamorous veneer and are themselves very Americanized - and quite different from the fangers of *Twilight*, *True Blood*, or the *Vampire Diaries* who are prone to wearing leather dusters. Executive producers, showrunners, writers - and married couple - Jeremy Carver and Anna Fricke (who worked on *Supernatural* and *Everwood*, respectively), say they were aiming for "urban, working class" New England vampires, which is part of the reason Boston was chosen as the show's setting.

Bishop turned Aiden during the Revolutionary War and Bishop himself came over as a settler originally from Europe to basically make his way in the new world as a vampire, you know, seeking sort of new territories to hunt," says Carver. "So Boston has proven very well to sort of tie into - sort of tying our vampires coming over to the founding of America."

"If you're familiar with the sort of New England mindset which is sort of a more hardscrabble, modest mindset, that is very much the sort of way our vampires assimilate into society," and is why they hold down day jobs and interact with humans.

As far as Witwer's vampire goes, he's a reformed sociopath trying to break his bad blood habit by not feeding off the living. The character is the latest in a line of dark characters like Davis "Doomsday" Bloome from *Smallville*, and both Darth Vader and a Sith apprentice in *The Force Unleashed* video games.

"I get a lot of guys who have damaged psyches, I guess."

Witwer then jokes the casting directors for the damaged psyche characters must say, "He just looks like he's a guy with problems. Let's hire him. He's got problems, right? You have problems?" To which he'd reply, "Yeah, if it gets me hired, sure."

However, he adds, more seriously, that the common element of all his "dark" characters is that they are good people by their nature but have been put in circumstances that take that out of them.

But Witwer has clearly had deep thoughts about his role as recovering vampire.

"The fun about the character, I think, is he's rediscovering his humanity," he says.

"He's seen everything ... but the fun about it is if you were in kind of a drug haze for a long formative period of your life and you came out of it, the world would seem like a very, very scary place, and you would have emotional reactions in the most unexpected circumstances."

If Witwer's Aidan is the damaged psyche of *Being Human*, Anna Fricke says Huntington's werewolf Josh is the heart.

"He is the most human," the producer says. "He sort of has the most to lose. We really needed someone to have that vulnerable and heartbreaking quality but who was also funny, you know?

And Sam really brought that to the floor. He was really - you feel for him immediately."

For Huntington's part, he embodies the character's odd sense of humor, but enjoys how introverted Josh is. Fairly new to the werewolf curse, Josh is afraid to change and hurt others, so he runs from humanity.

"He turned into a werewolf two years ago, or got turned into a werewolf two years ago, and he's going through a little bit more. Obviously, he hasn't come a long way in those two years; he's just kind of biding his time ... he really doesn't know what's going to happen."

As far as the metamorphosis, a werewolf transformation has always been a point of special effects pride in Hollywood and *Being Human* doesn't disappoint. The character goes through exceptional pain while changing but begins with the actor nude in the woods.

"It's really, really disturbing to watch the transformation." Adds Huntington, "The wolf itself is very different than anything you've ever seen" and he says there was much discussion about what was taking place internally during the change, which informs his performance. Still, he says, the nudity makes the viewer feel bad for Josh.

"When he's turning into a werewolf, he feels so exposed," says Huntington. "He's so, so, so scared, and I think that the nakedness really, really hits that home. You know what I mean? It really makes you feel uncomfortable for him."

Unlike the centuries-old Aidan, Rath says Sally is coming to terms with loneliness, her death, and her journey towards resolution, instead of "running around haunting people." Rath thinks Sally is more like Josh because her character is also in a new situation - which is why she didn't feel compelled to research ghosts.

"As far as research goes, I really was experiencing everything for the first time with Sally. She died six months ago at the beginning and doesn't know what's going on, and so it's appropriate that I too am now finding my way and figuring out what I am. So I was just sort of going through it as she was."

But the ghost says, "They could not have picked a better person." "I'm so into that. I love everything with spirits and ghosts." Rath even claims to have her own background with ghosts from her childhood.

"I used to live in a really haunted house, the first house I ever lived in - I left when I was three years old. We had this ghost, and there was a grave in the backyard and my parents would tell me that every night they would hear someone walking up the stairs at the same time ... But it was a good energy. It wasn't threatening."

The ghosts hanging over *Being Human* have also been kind so far, but any time a popular show is remade, the specter of the original haunts the new version - especially when the original is still on the air with a devoted fanbase. Huntington jokes that if anyone questions "how dare he" remake their beloved show, he'll throw it right back at them.

'Tm going to make them feel really uncomfortable. I'm going to throw it right back at them and be like, 'Those pants don't match that shirt.'" He adds, though, the American show is different and awesome, but "I'm a fan of the British show, you know what I mean?"

"So I understand that ... it's a lovely, amazing, original incredible show. So I want to say, like, I'm with you. I love that show too."

Having also appeared in the remake of *Battlestar Galactica* as "Crashdown," Witwer says both shows can be enjoyed on their own after a "burn-in process."

"No one talks anymore that when *Battlestar* came on, that there was this huge fan backlash because Starbuck was a girl and all this crap," he says. "Now we just remember, 'Oh, everyone loved *Battlestar*. It's like, 'No. No, we didn't' They didn't. So I'm fully prepared for whatever they want to throw at us."

So far none of the actors have met their counterpart but would like to because, as Witwer puts it, "We owe them a debt of gratitude in a big way. Huntington adds he'd love to meet British werewolf Russell Tovey and the others to "just like, Skype with them or at some point just talk to them - even if they hate the show, I would still love just to hear and meet them."

Meanwhile, Rath jokes the two teams could either fight - "Meaghan wants to fight everybody," says Huntington - or "there would be a tear in the time-space [continuum]."

Huntington suddenly agrees and offers, "a hole might open up in the universe."

Witwer's take: "Just fight them."

Although a fight between these paranormal characters might be expected, it's obvious watching the actors portraying them that, on and off camera, the show has a lot to offer about *Being Human*.

Bruce Campbell's B-list: 'Burn Notice,' 'Bubba,' Books and Back To 'Evil Dead'

(July 2011)

He is Ash, the wisecracking hero with a chainsaw hand from the *Evil Dead* movies. He is Autolycus, the comical "King of Thieves" from the *Hercules: The Legendary Journeys* and *Xena: Warrior Princess* television series. He is an aging mummy-battling Elvis Presley in the horror-comedy *Bubba Ho-Tep*. And among nearly 100 other characters, self-proclaimed B-movie actor Bruce Campbell is now retired Navy SEAL Sam Axe from USA Network's hit spy show, *Burn Notice*.

Instead of gaining fame as a pretty marquee face in blockbuster movies, Campbell's notoriety is the result of years spent in the blue-collar world of acting. Originally from the suburbs of Detroit, he is a work-for-hire performer who just happened to appear in enough movies and TV shows that he got to be well known. It didn't hurt that his roles in the aforementioned cult favorites (not to mention his turns in *Maniac Cop, Escape from LA., The Adventures of Brisco County Jr.*) made Campbell a pop culture stalwart. Campbell has even traded in on his working-class cult actor status in those Old Spice commercials, a meta movie *My Name is Bruce* - where he played himself - and two books, *If Chins Could Kill: Confessions of a B Movie Actor and Make Love! The Bruce Campbell Way*.

But it is getting more difficult for the 53-year-old to claim "B" status.

Since the show's premiere in 2007, Campbell has appeared in *Burn Notice* on Thursday nights at 9 p.m. as Sam, a beer- drinking, ladies' man who uses his espionage knowledge as a do-gooder private investigator in Miami alongside disavowed spy Michael Westen (played by series star Jeffrey Donovan) and former IRA operative Fiona (Gabrielle Anwar). A fan favorite, Campbell's character received the stand-alone treatment in the TV movie, *Burn Notice: The Fall of Sam Axe*, and the fifth season premiere of *Burn*

Notice netted 5.2 million viewers. His current success also involves appearing as the voice of "Torque" Redline in *Cars 2*, in theaters now and an upcoming appearance at Comic-Con International in San Diego.

While taking a break from filming the sixth season of *Burn Notice* in Miami, Campbell discussed his work on *Burn Notice*, as well as involvement with *Evil Dead* and *Bubba Ho-Tep* sequels, and more books.

You've lived in Oregon for some time but have also been filming Burn Notice in Miami for a few years now. What's the big difference between the two areas?

Everything. In Oregon, you're just going up a hill or down a hill. It's green but it's a really different kind of green. It's really lush here in Miami. It's all very lush ... And I guess, driving etiquette.

Driving Etiquette?

It's sort of lost here in Miami. It's a strange combination of collision of cultures here. It's different in Miami with driving. In Oregon, at four way stop signs, we'll go, "You go. No, no. You go ahead. No, no. You go ahead." In Miami it's. "Can I just blow the stop sign?" It's a whole different mentality. But the air is spectacular in Miami. It's fresh air. It's fresh sea air. So that part is awesome ... And about everything else is different. I crawl out of my home in Oregon, all pasty and white, and then I have to become the guy who is too tan. It's a life of contrast. But that's kind of the fun, I guess.

What is the appeal of Burn Notice compared to other spy franchises out there?

Here's my take: If you're trying to be cool, you fail. In the case of Burn Notice, we're not really trying to be cool. We're a bunch of middle-aged, former spies, former Navy SEALs, former IRA terrorists, former housewife. Burn Notice is the story of a behind-the-scenes version of spies. You get to hear what they're concerned about, what they're bored with - all while saving the average person's life. I think the appeal is that we're just people, and the kind that hopefully you'd like to go out and have a beer with. If you don't like these people, you won't care if they're in a life-or-death situation. My problem sometimes with either spy shows, or spy movies is that the kind of the lead guys are too cool and they're more concerned about being cool than being well-rounded characters.

It isn't a downer of a show, either.

The end of every week, it's not a jaded show. The bad guys are going to go down. We may take them down from the inside or the outside or both. They will not succeed. Every week, we just help innocent people. That's the main thing with what we do. I think the average American can relate to that.

Burn Notice also has something of a blue-collar approach to spy work, which is a theme with your acting career.

Yeah, we're very old school. Fiona has a line [in the Season Five premiere] where she says, "I could have done the same thing with a little olive oil on the engine block." Sometimes you don't have to have these big, practical operations. Sometimes you just have to go out and conduct old-fashioned surveillance.

In The Fall of Sam Axe movie, which is being released on DVD and Blu-ray July 26, you have a scene where you hurl a chainsaw. It's very Ash-like. Who came up with that idea?

It was the writer's. I usually try to avoid any reference to anything I've done in the past. They even had a couple of other lines and I told them I couldn't say it. They were just too on the nose. I think it was their fun little nod to my past.

You've done so many characters that people know and love, but do you want to retire them?

No ... you know, people want another *Evil Dead* movie, but

272

they should be careful what they wish for. I remember when *Army of Darkness* came out. It was not some great salvation that was going to save all the *Evil Dead* fans. It got generally lousy reviews. It did horrible at the box office. It wasn't until literally 20 years later that it's now hailed as a cult classic. It's on American Movie Classics for God's sake. And now, it's got 17 versions of it on DVD.

So folks caught up to it. But not only was it not a hit with people right away, it took *Army of Darkness* 20 years to become a successful movie.

Were they difficult films to make?

Without a doubt, those were most difficult shoots I've ever been on. Those three movies. There's no other. Nothing else compares with anything I've ever done before or since. And I doubt I'll ever be in a situation like that. And I doubt I'll ever let myself be in a situation like that again. These are really grueling movies to make.

So is "No" the final word on any more Evil Dead movies?

I'd actually like to just do another really cool, scary horror film that actually isn't Evil Dead. Just make it a scary horror film. I would be into that even more than a sequel. Sam Raimi [director of Evil Dead and Spider-Man] happened to have been launched into the A-leagues of directing. So I think he would only do another Evil Dead movie if it was the funnest thing ever - which they're not. So, you know. Who knows? None of us has ever said, 'Never.' But I don't know that the word will change.

And what of the rumblings about an Ash vs. Jason vs. Freddy flick?

That's another big one. We had a conversation about a new one. But once you find out Ash can't kill those two characters, then what are you there for? ... And creatively, the only thing we had control over was the character Ash. So, OK. What does that mean? They trade zingers and one liners and beat each other up for 90 minutes? For me, it's all about, what's going to satisfy the audience?

But seeing Ash back on screen may make the audiences happy, right? To see the character back in action.

Here's the truth of it: Evil Dead comes out, some people really like it, some people hate it. We make another one. A lot of people say, "Oh, it's not as good as the first one." But a lot of people watch the second one. Army of Darkness comes out and people say it's not as good as Evil Dead II. From a filmmaker's side, we always hear what the fans have to say - and it's not always positive. It just means they want more of the same stuff. They want more cotton candy, but it might make them barf at the end. It might make them sick if they get too much.

When you do fan conventions, people come to see you as Ash, Autolycus, etc. Are you noticing more people showing up for Sam Axe?

A fair amount. I kind of monitor when I go to conventions. Just to kind of take a poll and see what people are into. And I'll have a photograph that comes in front of me on the table. You're going to have, 80% will be Evil Dead, 10% will be Burn Notice because it's sort of filtering in and it takes time for it to really settle in ... You always get the current stuff to work again, and some people always bring that for you to sign. And then it's about 10% of miscellany. They range from Brisco to Bubba Ho-Tep to Herc and Xena - that sort of spattering.

Do fans surprise you with obscure favorites?

The other day, a guy came up with Man With The Screaming Brain. I was like, "Wow. Not many people bring that up." And the kid goes, "Oh God, I love that movie." I'm like, "Wow. I've never heard that. You love that movie?" "Yeah, it's so bad." It's such a terrible movie that he just loved it. I guess whatever gets you to buy something.

You've done so many projects with connections to monsters, zombies, ghosts, demons, etc. What is your personal take on it? Do you believe in anything within the paranormal?

No. No, but I'll go with UFOs. Because I think it just makes sense for them to be out there, and they shouldn't be called UFOs but beings from another planet. I'm all over that. I'm pretty sure that's happened. And you know, we could use a little help here, frankly, so I hope we do get invaded or discovered or whatever you want to call it. If someone could actually come to our planet, then we need their technology.

When you live in that big, open sky, up in the Pacific Northwest, have you ever seen anything?

We get great stars up there. But no, I haven't seen anything worth telling anyone about.

There's a big summer movie that came out that reminds me of you: Super 8. It's a movie that has younger actors, not really a ton of A-list stars and it revolves around kids playing with a Super 8 camera like you used to. Have you seen it? Did you feel any sort of personal connection to it?

I actually want to see it mostly because of that. It'd be fun to see how accurate they are about the cameras. How they had to do stuff.

Did you enjoy the process of providing the voice of "Torque" Redline in Cars 2 and then seeing how it's animated?

You try to figure out what they're going for, try to get what they're looking for, mostly. He's a spy, a hot rod kind of tough guy. It's funny when the animations just come alive. I haven't seen the finished Cars 2 because I've been working down here in Miami but it's fun to see what it becomes. You're in a studio recording, then when you see it, it's a huge, digital creation.

Think we'll see another book from you, or the Bubba Ho-Tep sequel Bubba Nosferatu (where Elvis fights vampires)?

You won't see Bubba Nosferatu unless something drastic happens. [Ho-Tep Director] Don Coscarelli and I cannot agree on a script. So that's kind of a fundamental thing. We realized it's not worth doing if we don't agree. I have to speak with my publisher about a third book called, Vagabond: An Actor's Gypsy Life. It's really just the kind of things I've been doing when I wasn't filming. It's a sort of travel book I guess you might say with a movie slant.

Are you working on anything for a post-Burn Notice career?

I've been working on some material before I realized that if I'm working on a TV show seven months of the year, it limits what I can do with my off-season. So what am I doing developing all this material? [But] I got an action movie that I just had written, and then I'm working on a little Western - so a couple things. I'm getting ready for when Burn Notice ends.

Would you ever want to do another meta type of movie, like My Name Is Bruce, where you played yourself?

Well, that movie was pretty savaged when it came out, so probably not. People - it's so funny how they react when you basically say that it's you. I think there's probably somebody out there the really thinks that I feel my dog whiskey based on the movie. It's hard to say. And that movie was weird ... I said, "Yeah. A chance to make fun of everybody. Myself and fans included. " I thought it was a fun opportunity. I don't think I'll do it again. It's probably some of the worst reviews I've gotten.

I happen to like it.

Twenty years from now it'll be on American Movie Classics!

You turned 53 in June but look great. Is it true you lost 20 pounds? For The Fall of Sam Axe?

Well, I had to play Sam Axe five years younger and [Jeffrey] Donovan [who directed the film] was like, "So, dude. What are you going to do?" I'm like, "Well, I'll dye my hair." He's like, "No, you're still active. So you got to get active." So I went home on the last break. And we got mountains that are up to 7,000 feet. So I just hit the mountain to get back at it. You know, you get the eye of the tiger back. And this time, I'm doing my darnedest, because I just turned 53. Now I'm just doing it for me. Years past, I would get ready for a movie. You work out, you work out, you work out. All that training and all that crap. Really living in a gym. You get tired of it and I did that for about 10 years. Then you're like, you know, I'm just going to do my own thing now. Now, I'm just going to maintain it for me, now.

Speaking of books, comedian and The Daily Show correspondent John Hodgman was your first literary agent, correct?

Yeah. John was the first guy to send me an email and say, "Hey, How about writing a book?" He was an assistant to a literary agent and then he became a literary agent. And then he became John Hodgman. The son of a bitch gets more residuals than I do!

Do you guys stay in touch?

We're tight email buddies... I'm so glad. He's always been the smartest and funniest guy in the room. And it's just great to see a guy just take off. He's an incredibly nice, hard-working guy, so I just think it's awesome. There's an origin to everything, everybody.

So Hodgman helped make If Chins Could Kill happen?

Yeah. That was the first Chins book. It's not an A-listers book. It's a book about, sort of, the working stiffs of the film industry. I give him a lot of credit for making it happen.

After becoming so well known, and now being on Burn Notice, are you still a "B" actor?

Look at it this way: Burn Notice is "B" television. We're cable. It's a B-TV show and is technically a genre TV show.

So you still classify yourself in the "B" role?

I do. The funny thing is, ironically, I'm known as a cult actor. But currently, I'm working for two Fortune 500s. You've got NewsCorp which owns Fox, which produces the show, and you've got USA, which is owned by GE. So I work for corporate types even though I may make my living doing off-kilter stuff - but then they wind up selling it to big corporations!

Are you going to be at San Diego Comic-Con?

I will be at Comic-Con, I think, on Thursday or on Wednesday and do the panel on Thursday. Then I'll just still be roaming around on Friday doing various things. So Wednesday, Thursday, Friday. You got to go to Comic-Con. You got to!

Zombies vs. Vampires: Celebs of The Supernatural Weigh In
(October 2011)

The undead vs. the walking dead: We spoke to celebrities who have built a career around the supernatural about this undying debate ...

JOHN CARPENTER
Director, Halloween, Vampires, Big Trouble in Little China

"They're both great. Vampires go way back to when I was a little kid. And back even more to my parent's generation - and back even before them. The zombies are a little more recent. One of my favorite directors and close friends is George Romero and I think he transformed the horror genre with *Night of the Living Dead*. And it's everywhere today. Everywhere. That movie has influenced everything here, all movies that are made. It's unbelievable - and ripped off and ripped off, again and again."

ROBERT ENGLUND
Actor, Nightmare on Elm Street, Zombie Strippers!

"Well, I'm kind of partial to some of the Hammer vampire films. Because I saw those when I was a teenager at the drive-in movie. So they were all wrapped up in my memory with making out in the back seat with a surfer girl, trying to get to third base and looking through the windshield and watching Christopher Lee or Peter Cushing bite Barbara [Shelley]'s neck and the blood would run down in her cleavage. That's all a very hormonally confused memory for me! But right now, as we speak, right now I think that my two favorite vampire films are the Klaus Kinski Nosferatu [Nosferatu the Vampyre] and also, the Swedish film, Let the Right One In ... My favorite zombie film is I Walked With A Zombie and Romero's *Dawn of the Dead*. The one in the mall, right? I love that. I love the original and the remake. I love both."

ELVIRA
Mistress of the Dark; Host, Elvira's Movie Macabre

"Of course, I have a soft spot in my heart for vampires, because they are dark and sexy like myself. But lately zombies are taking over, man. I love zombies. My premiere show [for new Macabre episodes] was *Night of the Living Dead* and I haven't seen it in so many years, but I think I've seen it 10 times in the last three weeks. I realize how much I love it, and how good zombies are.

There's been so many great zombie films out recently. Zombies are kind of taking over for me right at the moment."

GEORGE A. ROMERO
Director, Night of the Living Dead, Dawn of the Dead, Martin

"I'm not particularly fascinated about zombies. I sort of backed into it. I didn't even call them zombies in the first film; I called them flesh eaters. I just wanted some sort of game changing event my human characters could ignore in favor of petty bickering ... My favorite film of mine is Martin. It's not quite a spoof, but started as one, and during the course of making the film I started to take it a little more seriously. It's my sort of vampire spin."

TOM SAVINI
Makeup artist, Director, Actor (*Dawn of the Dead* (1978, 2004), *Night of the Living Dead* (1990), *From Dusk Till Dawn*, *Machete*)

"I had stayed away from the *Twilight Saga*. 'Amber-eyed, sparkly, homosexual vampires' was the catchphrase people were handing me. I had never seen it, so I didn't know what it was about, but I watched *Vampires Suck*, which was a parody of those movies and that made me want to see a better version of it. I started watching *Twilight* and I really liked it. I really like the treatment; I realize it caters to teenage hormones, but I really liked it. I've seen all three of them now. Zombies: Romero's original *Night of the Living Dead* of course, but I thought the best zombies were what we did together in *Day of the Dead*. That's Romero's favorite *Dead* movie and mine too ... But what [friend and fellow makeup guru] Greg Nicotero has been doing with *The Walking Dead* [the show based on Robert Kirkman's comic book, premiering on AMC on October 31], these are the best zombies I've ever seen. So vampires or zombies? To me they're such a huge gap between them. It's like, is it Edward or Jacob from *Twilight*?

Vampires can be elegant and sophisticated, beautiful ... but zombies are ugly, dead people continuing to be dead and rot, and not become superhuman like in the remake of *Dawn*. It's a huge gap, but I think I prefer the elegant, witty, gorgeous vampire."

ZAK BAGANS
Paranormal investigator, Travel Channel's *Ghost Adventures*

"Vampires ... they're darker. Zombies have just been infected by some kind of virus. Vampires can do things that zombies can't do. Zombies are just slow kind of slow walking, and just people that moan and groan and just look ugly. Female vampires are sexy as hell. They're just cool, man. They're awesome. They suck blood and make it look cool. They're attractive, powerful, immortal, you know. Vampires are immortal. Freakin' zombies you can kill with a freakin' spitball, and they're infected, sick, ill. Vampires are not. And vampires are creatures of the night. And I'm a creature of the night. That's why they're cool."

DACRE STOKER
Great Grandnephew of Bram Stoker Author, Dracula The Un-Dead

"Vampires ... I do like the Coppola movie [*Bram Stoker's Dracula*] but I also really like the 1931 Todd Browning original - just because it's the first one ... I can't speak with any quality or any conviction on zombies. I just don't do those."

R.L. STINE
Author, Goosebumps series

"I have to say, I'm not a zombie fan at all. I've never written a real zombie book. I would love to see zombies go away because zombies are so limited. As a writer, there's so little you can do with zombies. I like surprises and twists, and fooling a reader, but you can't fool anyone into thinking a zombie isn't a zombie.
What can they do? They stagger."

DANNYTREJO
Actor, Machete, Halloween (2007), From Dusk Till Dawn

"I love them all. I just finished a vampire movie, *Rise of the Living Dead*, but [favorite vampire movie is] *From Dusk Till Dawn* ... Zombies? Anything that Rob Zombie does!"

Bruce Campbell's Secret Blood Recipe and Other Horrible Makeup

(October 2011)

Whether you prefer the shambling or sprinting camp, there's no excuse to be a shoddy zombie at a Halloween party.

Sure, retail stores have stocked up on fake blood and latex applications this October, but those are the same pre-packaged apps anyone could buy and use. That's not good enough for a dedicated nerd who wants to take their effects to the next level.

So we've assembled a few movie magic tips from makeup gurus who know how to make you look horribly awesome this Halloween.

BRUCE CAMPBELL (*Evil Dead & Burn Notice* actor and erstwhile low-budget filmmaker who had to work on his own effects)

Nobody has any excuse to not have a recipe for good makeup; it's all online. All you have to do is Google 'special effects makeup' and you'll probably get a dozen or more 'how-tos.'

What you need to do is get into latex to make your skin look different. You need to get into some colors to make yourself not look normal. Derma Wax [also known as Mortician's Wax] is good for bumps and lumps. Between latex, Derma Wax and clown white, you're halfway there.

A good blood recipe is critical.

Most people don't know how to do good blood. It's a corn syrup base, the Karo corn syrup. Get the clear kind, not the dark kind. You mix everything in that bottle; you don 't even change the bottle. Take the lid off and pour in some coffee creamer that's already been mixed up, like Coffee-Mate.

Blood is opaque, so you need a little bit of white opaque mixture in there. It could be milk, but it'll go bad on you, so a non-dairy creamer. Mix that up, get the lumps out, pour a little of that in. Then take one of those red food coloring things you get in the store - not the four pack, but a separate red food coloring and pour the whole thing in. Mix that up really well, and test it on a white surface like your sink or bathtub

You might need a drop of blue food coloring to keep it from getting too pink or too red. But don't put in literally more than one or two drops because it will turn it to make it purple.

Coloration is key. It will stay extremely sticky. A note to everybody: It will get on everything. Whatever you touch, it will get on it. Be judicious with it, or don't care about it. Blood is one of the main things that if you get it wrong, you blew it.

TOM SAVINI (*Dawn of the Dead* and *Day of the Dead* makeup special effects master, *Machete* actor)

My zombie tip would be to be skinny. Skinny helps. Although there are heavy zombies, I prefer the skinny ones [so you can look like you emerged, decomposing, from a grave].

And of course, you want to get rid of your healthy flesh tone by using a gray makeup. You want to accent your skull by accenting your cheekbones - put shadows underneath the cheekbones - and your optical bone around your eyeballs. Another good technique is to highlight the actual bone beneath your nose.

Halfway down your nose you start creating a shadow, or even darkening the tip of the nose a bit and then highlight the bone above it.

If you can get some false teeth - some horrible, ugly false teeth - that make your lips protrude, that would help. But do anything to make the skull look like it's protruding - like you're emaciated.

There's only so much you can do to the face to make it scary. A lot of people put wounds on, but they forget to make up their neck, their hands, and arms. That kind of destroys the illusion.

But there's prosthetic appliance kits you can get in costume stores that are beautiful. They didn't have those back then. I wish they did. We had to make our own and sculpt it, mold it, produce it in rubber, attach it, paint it. It was pretty complicated. Now you can just buy it in a store.

MCKENZIE WESTMORE (Face Off host on Syfy, makeup and beauty expert, daughter of makeup effects artist Michael Westmore)

You can use egg whites on your skin. On the beauty side, it's a little-known secret that some women will put it on under their makeup because it's an instant lift to the skin, and it tightens the skin.

But if it's put on in a little bit more of an amount, it will crackle. If you put some red paint (like the devil makeup) over the skin, and put the egg white over it, it will crackle the makeup. It gives a really interesting texture to the skin [and works as an old man makeup]. There's also black eyeliner on the lips. You can line your lips, fill it in, and make really great, scary-looking lips.

Use black and brown and blue eyeshadows to create really great colors under the eyes. But as far as really trying to make it look good, and pass as fairly decent makeup, I've done a lot better to go buy some simple pieces from a local Halloween store. The instructions that come with them are so simple and so easy to do now than they were way back when. You couldn't even find this stuff ... there's so many stores now that do cater to that person wanting to take it to the next level. That would be my best advice to someone really wanting to make it look good. So many stores have come so far with what they sell.

CLEVE HALL (Star of Syfy's upcoming reality series *Monster Man*, Hollywood creature creator and makeup effects specialist)

The techniques go back to Godzilla days and making a creature out of foam rubber. For that you usually work with anything from one inch - to one-half inch, depending on what you're making - of a light mattress foam you get from an upholstery place.

The best way is to order it from a place that just sells that. And then get contact cement. It's a similar process to clothing fabrication except you don't have to sit there worrying about sewing or seams. You're sculpting with the foam. It pulls its own shape when you bend it and curve ... this is the way of making a very simple creature body.

The texturing is a matter of finding latex - which is sold in any art store as a mold-making product - that you coat it with. Then you cut into the foam and glue the edges, and pinch texture into it, or burn it in with a soldering iron.

But don't breathe (the burning latex smoke), because it's dangerous. Or you can actually texture the surfaces with oatmeal, corn meal, stucco, all sorts of things.

For a simple gore effect, my favorite requires liquid latex, a large piece of glass or mirror or something smooth. Spread some colored latex - colored with a little bit of acrylic paint, red paint with spots of blue and kind of blend it - in an even, thin layer on the glass. Let the latex dry, and it will stick to itself when it dries. Put a piece of thick yarn in the center and start on one edge and -

kind of like a Fruit Roll-Up - roll it around that cord or yarn in the center.

You don't have to be even with it because it looks more natural when it's not. Just keep rolling until basically you've got a long pinkish, bluish, purplish rubber tube.

Then you force it against itself into a squiggly back-and-forth shape, and you've got perfect intestines. Dip those into some fake blood and it's just awesome.

Movies That Scare the People Who Scare Us

(October 2011)

A chill is in the air, dread spirits are walking the earth and, as Halloween approaches, everyone from the most diehard horror geek to the casual fright fan is filling their queue with horror films to celebrate the season.

To be sure, there are plenty of options.

But while the masses may have flocked to see *Paranormal Activity 3* last weekend (its $54 million made it the strongest September/October film opening ever) genre fans were no doubt dwelling in the gooey viscera of more underground fare.

To help you out of a potential celluloid jam, we talked with some of our fan-culture favorites, asking them for their recommendations on potentially obscure (and sometimes absurd) horror flicks you should check out this Halloween.

BRUCE CAMPBELL (Actor, *Evil Dead, Burn Notice*)

The Tenant by Roman Polanski because it only uses your head. There are no special effects, there's no monsters, there's no digital. It's awesome. It's scary as hell. It's creepy - the anti-monster movie. There's no giant creature that's been bit by a radioactive spider, nothing stupid like that. It messes with your perception of reality, and to me, that's way scarier than a creature...

Or I would go with something like *Frankenstein 1970* just to see how horribly outdated the movie was. It was made in 1958.

What, did they think 1970 would never come? *Frankenstein 1970* is a pretty bad one if you just want to see a kitschy, bad horror movie.

JOE HILL (Author, *Horns, Locke & Key*)

I think you have to look abroad, for starters. You have to get over that hump where you say, 'foreign films are hard work, foreign films can't be fun.' I just saw one that's out of Ireland called *Isolation* that has to be one of the most absolutely revolting specimens of horror cinema ever put to screen, and I mean that in a very affectionate way. There is more cow afterbirth in this movie than there is in all the horror films made in the last decade

It is about genetically modified cows creating this kind of cow-cockroach spawn that spin out of control in this mucky, muddy, nasty-looking Irish farm. It sounds like a joke. Just talking about it I can feel the urge to start spitting out cow puns - it was udder-ly disgusting - but it's actually played very seriously. It is real dark, and real grim, and very affective. And very, very nasty. It's not for the squeamish ...You're just kind of like, 'Did someone

slip me something before I sat down to watch this film, which is like the most outrageous thing I've ever seen.' But it's great.

MAX BROOKS (Author, *World War Z, The Zombie Survival Guide*)

I don't know if it's scary, it depends on your tastes, but it is a cultural imperative. It is called *Wild Zero*. It is Japanese and it is the story of aliens trying to take over the planet by raising the dead. So there's an alien-engineered zombie plague, and the only people that can stop it are a young Japanese man, his transsexual girlfriend and a Japanese rockabilly band called Guitar Wolf.

That is a real movie. I have no idea what the intention was. I look at this movie and think everybody has to see this movie.

I don't know what to make of it to this day. I love it. I just keep watching it   I showed it at a screening in London in 2006 as I was hosting a zombie film festival there, and the kids just went crazy for it. There's incredible violence, there's gore, there's weapons. And the band Guitar Wolf? It's a real band.

DANIELLE HARRIS (actress *Hatchet II, Halloween* franchise. Director, *Among Friends*)

The first time I saw *The Descent* [about a group of women who spelunk into a cave of hungry humanoid bat creatures], it wasn't a big movie in the theater. I just got it from someone on DVD. It didn't have a whole big to-do about it, but that was something I thought, 'this is really rad, I love this kind of stuff ... I tend to gravitate toward the female-driven, kind of sick, twisted ones. There are not enough female serial killers in films so movies like *The Descent* are the closest thing to the f-ed-up chicks who are manipulative but are still in the horror world. They're a little bit more realistic but are kind of like crazy women ... The movies I'm writing and making; I've got those elements. I want to have the underground, very cultish movies that are chick flicks for messed up girls.

MIKO HUGHES (Actor, *Pet Sematary, Mercury Rising*)

Well, there's one that's a cult classic that has kind of gotten more awareness in recent years. I don't know quite how underground it's still considered, but it's a Japanese film called Audition [about a scorned maniac actress]. I love that one. It doesn't present itself as a horror movie and is only crazy in the last 10 minutes. It is really suspenseful and has a great slow build, and you kind of forget that what you're seeing is a horrible incident because you get lost in the story.

So, when events take a turn, it really takes you by surprise. It is hard to sum it up without giving away the twist, but it is definitely a Japanese film; the pacing is a bit slower. It is a movie worth paying attention to, because when it does twist, it just reels you in.

Formative Gifts of Geek Celebrities

(December 2011)

For an emerging nerd, the holidays can be a formative time of year. In the yuletide, when gift-giving is at its peak, family members and friends see us for the geek that we are, the geek we will become, and embrace us for it.

Even in this day and age, when geek is chic and images of nerds are all over pop culture, that kind of honest acceptance is rare. When loved ones give us gifts that speak to our true nature without attempting to judge or change us, it leaves a lasting impact.

In that spirit, I reached out to a few famous nerds to share their fondest geeky gift memories - and to also share how becoming accomplished members of the nerd herd has affected the kinds of goodies they now receive.

NEIL DEGRASSE TYSON (Astrophysicist and director of the Hayden Planetarium at the American Museum of Natural History)

"By far, my first telescope. It was a tiny refractor. I was, this would have been 1970, so I was turning 12   I used it throughout the whole winter. And the difference between that telescope and the telescope most parents buy for their kids, is that I had already expressed interest in the universe. So, this gift was feeding a preexisting urge. Often, a lot of hopeful and wishful parents buy the chemistry set, or they buy the telescope, or the microscope on the expectation that the child will then show interest in it. I don't know how successful that tactic is."

"Now, people see that I have a lot of ties that are cosmic. What they don't know is that I have an aesthetic threshold, below which I will not drop. They just think, 'Oh! A novelty cosmic space tie!' My threshold is that I have no hardware on my ties. I don't have the Starship Enterprise. That's not on my tie. There's no pictures of Spock. People are thinking that that's space and that's fun space, so let's just do it. No. No, it's not."

ASHLEY ECKSTEIN (Founder of Her Universe, a clothing line for women geeks; *Star Wars: The Clone Wars* voice actress)

"When I was a girl, I was not into Barbies. Instead, I got the He-Man and She-Ra playset, the castle, the whole shebang. And my brother and I would play with it. I was so excited. Forget the Barbie Dream House, I wanted He-Man and She-Ra. I got a Karate Kid uniform as well. I was really into the Karate Kid. That was where it was at for me. I cherished that Karate Kid uniform - including the headband. So, when it was time for school pictures, I would not wear a dress, and would not wear anything girly. I wore my Karate Kid uniform for my school pictures."

"One of the best *Star Wars* gifts I've gotten was a Hallmark Ahsoka ornament (the character she voices on 'Clone Wars'). Hallmark came out with an Anakin and Ahsoka; they were two separate ornaments that came in the same box, and Hallmark sent me one. They had no idea how much that meant to me. I actually talked to them later and said, it was so nice because I also bought one and sent it to my dad. At that moment, I think I had finally made it, in my dad's eyes."

SAM HUNTINGTON (Actor, *Being Human, Fanboys, Superman Returns*)

"Remember Sega Game Gear? It came out a little after the Game Boy. It had a color screen with lots of games, and it was just awesome. I wanted one so bad. My mom drove me to the electronic store to buy one on my birthday. I get there and the chick working there comes up and goes, 'Hey, so I'm so sorry. We got a whole shipment of Game Gears in, but they were all defective, so we had to send them all back.' So in the middle of the store, I literally crumble. I was dying. I was too old to be as upset as I was. I don't think I actually cried but I was visibly, wicked upset. My mom felt so bad. My mom had called the store ahead of time and told them to make up this lie, this ruse, to get me. My mom was going to take it through to getting home but felt so bad that she ended up giving it to me in the store."

"I recently went to this, Metropolis, IL, Superman convention. In Metropolis, there's a giant Superman statue in the middle of the town, and it's this crazy thing. This guy gave me a pop art painting of me as Jimmy Olsen. When he gave it to me, I was like, 'This is so cool.' I bring it home, thinking it is so cool. And my wife looks at it and goes, 'What do you want me to do with this? It's a picture of you; you can't put this up.'"

DR. LEROY CHIAO (Former NASA astronaut, commander of International Space Station Expedition 10)

"When I was probably 8 years old, 9 years old, in addition to building models, I was always fiddling with wires and lights and switches and playing around building. Back then, electronic kits were quite popular. You could solder these little kits together and make radios and stuff like that. I was always going through batteries, so my mom, unbeknown to me, had a friend of hers at work who was a hobbyist build me a power supply. It was one of those grey metal boxes that you can probably still buy. He had built the power supply that you can plug into the wall, and you can change the voltage of what was coming out. It had two meters, a voltmeter and an ammeter. That was just the coolest, geekiest gift I think I've ever gotten, and I still have it."

"As for recent history, the most memorable or gratifying Christmas gift was when I was in space. We were on the international space station at the end of 2004 and the previous crew, the Expedition 9 crew, had gotten into our food. So we had a food shortage. We had to ration food for about four to five weeks and ended up losing about 5 to 10 pounds each. Then, on Christmas Day in 2004, the resupply ship arrived, and we got a new load of food and goodies. That was a very nice Christmas present."

TODD MCFARLANE (Comic book creator; founder of McFarlane Toys and co-founder of Image Comics)

"One Christmas, Mom and Dad gave me a drafting table because they knew I wanted to be an artist. And I got that, probably when I was 16. I used that drawing table literally up until only like two or three years ago. I remember telling people that every page of comic books I've done in my career has been done on this same table, and it's the table Mom and Dad gave me. It sort of was an important gift because a lot of parents sort of look at art a little bit down the nose. Even dads, to some extent, say 'Son, you gotta get a real job.' But my mom and dad never had that attitude."
"Unfortunately, as you go on in your career, and you get more successful, everybody just assumes you've got everything you want … That's why they invented gift cards. I think those are way smarter. If you have any hesitation on what you should be getting somebody, just get them one of those."

BILLY WEST (Voice actor, Futurama, Ren & Stimpy)

"I grew up in the '50s, and one time my family got this space helmet. There was a TV show called *Men Into Space*, and it had a colonel of the spaceship called Col. McCauley. They had these Col. McCauley helmets and [my parents] got me one and I wore it all summer. I think I was hyperventilating because I was so excited to be Col. McCauley that I forgot you're supposed to be able to breathe. They didn't have the cool gear down yet, so they didn't put air vents in it. You had the sun visor and it just clamped down in this helmet. You couldn't breathe in it, but I didn't care because I just felt so cool."

"Now my mom keeps sending me these giant stuffed red M&M dolls (because West is the voice of 'Red ' in the M&M commercials). Like this is in case I forget what I do for a living? I don't know what the message is. The law of displacement is wrecking my house. The closet can't hold anything except these M&M candy dispensers. I told her the company gives me stuff like that! "

JOE HILL (Author, Locke & Key comic, Horns)

"In my comic, *Locke & Key*, there's a door, the ghost door, with sinister supernatural powers. My ex-wife and a Maine artisan, Israel Skelton, conspired to make a replica of this door for my office; looking at it is like looking at a panel from the comic brought to life. For sheer mind-melting awesomeness, I doubt I'll ever get a Christmas gift to match it (I'm also lucky to have a relationship with my ex that's better than some guys have with their wives - a gift in and of itself."

"This one time, after a signing, a dude came up to me with a dark, peeling, black leather bag, that reeked of formaldehyde. It had belonged to his great-grandfather, an early twentieth century mortician. He figured as a person who writes ghost stories, I'd love it. I mean, the dude meant well - he really did. But the thing was a big bag of death. Touching it made my skin crawl. As a rule, just because a guy writes horror doesn't mean he wants a scalpel for Christmas. There is such a thing as carrying it too far."

Steve Niles 'Remains' In His Chiller Movie

(December 2011)

Forget zombies or vampires, but when it comes to microwave ovens, horror novelist and comic book writer Steve Niles has a scary problem. It turns out that the creator of *Remains* - the supernatural zombie comic adapted for a December 16 movie on the Chiller Network - cannot run the microwave while also on the phone. Much like a walking dead uprising throws a monkey wrench into someone's everyday life, the microwave obliterates the phone signal when Niles is conducting an interview.

Kitchen appliance disruptions aside, Niles is having a pretty good run. After bringing elements of the Frankenstein and zombie mythos to the worlds of Batman and Superman (in *Simon Dark* and *DC Infinite Halloween Special*) - as well as creating his own originally scary stories like *30 Days of Night*, *Wake The Dead* and *Criminal Macabre* - Niles is credited with a crafting a horror renaissance in comics. Niles is also a horror pundit and personality, appearing on Spike TV's "Zombie Vs. Vampire" *Deadliest Warrior*.

Now, his story Remains is the basis for Chiller's first original movies. Starring Grant Bowler (*True Blood*), Lance Reddick (*Fringe, Lost*), Miko Hughes (*Pet Sematary*), Tawny Cypress (*Heroes*), and Evalena Marie (*Are We There Yet?*), and produced by Synthetic Cinema International, Remains is about zombies in post-apocalyptic Reno, NV, who make things exceedingly challenging for survivors as they grow steadily stronger, smarter and more aggressive by the minute.

Niles spoke with me about the new movie, which airs Dec. 16.

Were you involved in this production beyond creating the source material?

You know they kept me very close to it. Basically, I guess the best way to call my role was, I supervised a lot. They ran the script by me, and I did set visits and I was in constant contact with the folks at Chiller and Synthetic and they kept me involved at every stage of approving makeup and like I said, the script. But part of it is these guys really knew what they were doing, and I felt perfectly comfortable being on the coast while they were working on it.

As an author what do you look for when you're approached by someone who wants to turn a graphic novel of yours into a movie or a series?

Honestly, enthusiasm for the material means more to me than a big option ... [This is when the signal breaks up due to the microwave] I don't even want to - this is so embarrassing to tell you what that was. My wife forgot you can't run the microwave when I'm on the phone ... So yeah, the bidding war for 30 Days of Night is the perfect example of - the thing was I really didn't care. There were three studios bidding, they all had a lot of money, but I went with the one that had Sam Raimi, you know, attached to it. because I know Sam knows horror, and that was very similar with the guys from *Remains* ... A lot of times what happens in Hollywood is people will come to you and say, "Oh my, God, I love your book. Let me tell you our take on it." It's like, "But the book is the take." And that didn't happen with Chiller and with Synthetic Cinema. They wanted to do the comic book; you know? They wanted to capture the spirit of it.

Why do you think zombies are so popular right now?

I think horror always reflects our general fears and anxieties in society. And right now, without getting too serious, right now we're actually afraid of other people. We're afraid of disease, we're afraid of being invaded by people who look kind of like us, so you know the way we sort of express those fears are through what better than this mindless zombie hoard that wants to eat us. You know, these - our neighbors. I mean, they're our friends and neighbors who want to kill us and eat us. So, I think zombies are a very, very basic way for us to confront those fears too, because the reality of it, it's the real-world stuff is so horrifying and zombies are a great way for us to sort of work through those fears, and that's just something I feel about horror in general. I always feel like it's a relief and we use it to like I said, to illustrate what we're afraid of, and then shoot it in the head, you know?

How is it having the first original movie on Chiller?

You know this is really exciting for me because I really like TV movies. I grew up with TV movies. Dan - I don't even know if this name will mean anything to anybody on this call, but Dan Curtis, a hero of mine, he wrote the show, the *Night Stalker* shows and *Dark Shadows*, and I mean he was behind so much of these great things and he used to do all these great TV movies. And also, it used to be Richard Matheson used to write tons of ABC Movies of the Week during the '70s and they're these really wonderful, pretty much exactly this kind of stuff.

What are you more partial to, vampires or zombies?

That's a tough one. I have to go with vampires and let me qualify that. The - my kind of vampires ... Mean, nasty vampires that don't want to seduce you; they want to take your blood. I just - I've been writing them for a long time, I've developed an affection for them, and as a writer there's slightly more you can do with that particular monster. Zombie stories are great for telling stories about humans, oddly enough, while vampires are great for telling stories about vampires because they are technically still human and have brains, and lives, and emotions, and things like that that you can play with. So, I'd have to go with vampires.

For those who haven't read the Remains graphic novels, what separates your zombies from others?

Well, really, I mean that's a big thing I wanted to bring up - or I want to talk about too, because I know a lot of people right now, *Walking Dead* is so popular and that's sort of the current version of what people think zombies are. When I sat down to write *Remains*, you'll - you remember this, it was the time when *Walking Dead* was just starting to get strong as a comic, *Land of the Dead* was out. There was just sort of - there was a zombie surge building.

The Paranormal Pop Culture Collection

And when I sat down to do *Remains*, I wanted to do something different, and I wanted to do something that was a little bit bigger than the - do they run, or do they shamble? And for that it seemed it like I had to come up with something that could put the audience and the characters on edge, because let's face it, now especially, everybody knows how to deal with zombies, you know? You board up in the house and you wait it out. You shoot them as they come to you, you know?

But, in *Remains* that doesn't necessarily work because of the event that creates these zombies there's actually two different kinds. And one of them was slightly more advanced and they're eating the others and they're evolving, and there's - so you can't - in *Remains* you can never sit back in your boarded up house and be comfortable, because the zombies will sooner or later figure out how to either climb in or pull the boards off, so I had a lot of fun with that. I had a lot of fun playing with zombie conventions, because there's not just the *Walking Dead* zombies, there's the George Romero zombies, the (Fulci) zombies, there's the *Return of the Living Dead* zombies, there's the remake of *Dawn of the Dead* zombies, and I really tried to kind of have fun with all of them, you know?

What were some of the biggest production challenges, you would say, bringing the Remains comic book in front of the camera and then on to the small screen?

In a comic book you have no budget. I can do anything I want. If I want 10,000 bikers coming out of the horizon, I can do that. The artist will be mad at me, but it's not a budget issue.

So, the first thing we had to do was go through the comic and there were a few set pieces that would have just been impossible, and if - people who read the comic, there is a biker scene in there that it just would have cost too much money because it literally is hundreds and hundreds of bikers approaching through the desert not realizing that they're about to hit an entire system of wires and so they all get sliced like deli sandwiches as they ride into the city. The budget to shoot that was just way over the top, so we had to come up with other ways to do it.

I'm really happy with Synthetic Cinema because the budget was a TV movie budget, I am absolutely shocked at how much of the comic that they actually got on film, you know? They did such a good job of figuring out a way around all the - I don't want to give too much away, but there's a scene involving a circus prop for a sort of Cirque du Soleil-type casino, I assumed that it would just be cut because it's so over the top and so silly, and they found a way to do it. And not only did they, they found a way to do it so that it's really effective. So, I've been really happy with this. I have always been a fan of low-budget horror.

As a matter of fact, I think in the history of horror most of our best films started with kids with not much money trying to figure out a way to make the best movie possible. And I will point to the greatest zombie movie of all time, which is *Night of the Living Dead*. It was shot for what, $70,000 on the weekends because they were making industrial movies at the time.

You seem to have a knack for figuring out or anticipating what the next wave of the genre is going to be, so you manage to do that with vampires with 30 Days, with zombies with Remains, and even now the Frankenstein book that you're doing ... What do you sort of use as your guideline, in terms of what sort of things you want to write?

I was just going to say I'm just a fan of this stuff. Everything I've ever done has - you know *30 Days* came out of I just wanted to do something - I mean I didn't get paid. When we did that comic, it was for free. So, Ben [Templesmith, Niles' artist collaborator] and I had an opportunity to do a different kind of vampire.

It's just I'm a huge, huge horror fan. I mean I don't think there's, especially with the classics, I don't think there's anything I haven't seen 10 times. And so I have that thing in me where I want to do my versions, but nothing in me wants me to - I have a complete aversion to just doing what somebody else did before, so I always want to try to come up with some sort of fresh new take to - but that's coming - it really is coming out of the spirit of fun. I know I - for a horror writer I use the word fun a lot, but that's really what it comes from, you know? The Frankenstein book is - I carried Bernie's [Wrightson] Frankenstein book around, the first one, when I was kid, and now I've grown up and I'm working with him on the sequel, you know? I mean, I'm the luckiest kid - monster kid on earth.

And it really is just enthusiasm because I genuinely love this stuff and I would be doing it whether they were being made into movies or comics, I'd be doing it anyway. And that's what I did my whole life, I had this reputation of being very prolific, when in fact I'd just been writing my whole life and I just have a lot of material piled up, you know?

So, I have never felt like I'm predicting anything or I'm ahead of any curve, that's a dangerous road to go down, trying to predict trends. So, I just do what I like and just do what I love and I happen to love Frankenstein, vampires, and zombies.

Are any plans to do anything with Cal McDonald [from Criminal Macabre], either for the small or big screen?

Well, he is spoken for. Right now, Cal is being developed at Universal Studios for a feature movie. And after being through multiple studios we finally have - Universal really gets it. And they're letting us do it as an R, because for years people wanted me to do it as a PG-13 movie and I was like, "Have you read the comic?" Like there's really not a lot of PG-13 stuff to Cal. As a matter of fact, I had breakfast with Mike Richardson from Dark Horse yesterday and we discussed it, and we will hopefully have some really good news in, I'd say, the next six months or so, but I'm continuing with the comics. As a matter of fact, I turned in the latest installment of *Criminal Macabre* yesterday, and so we're keeping the comics going, we're going to bring the novels, we're going to reprint those, and keep all that going.

Most zombie movies are usually completely post- apocalyptic in so far as we don't know how it happened, it's so much of a 'fait accompli', so to speak, why devise such a specific way to get the ball rolling?

I hate to give a really simple answer, but in the comic I did it because it was funny, you know? I mean it was the - I really wanted to go for the absurdity of the situation that, here we are finally figuring out that we're going to disarm and it's Peace Day and something goes wrong, and Peace Day winds up being the end of days. So, it really was - I was going for something and I was trying to do something a little different, because most zombie movies don't explain it, so I wanted to try to explain it. And I needed to because I knew that I was going to try to do this thing with different varying degrees of zombies. You know that there are different ones, depending on who was closer to the event, what happens, you know, what kind of zombie you turn into. So that kind of came out of just trying to do something different.

Sam Witwer Is 'Being Human,' A Vampire ...And 'Walking Dead' Zombie?

(January 2012)

As the vampire character Aidan in Syfy's 20-something horror drama *Being Human*, actor Sam Witwer breathes new life into the undead. Sure, Aidan can walk in the sunlight, but aside from that, he's an old school vamp- a sexy, dangerous, super cool American cousin to that famous Transylvanian Count.

Being Human - which begins its second season on January 16 at 9 p.m. - is based on the BBC drama of the same name about a vamp, werewolf and ghost who live together as paranormal roommates trying to regain a sense of their normal lives. Rather than a direct facsimile of the popular British show, the stateside *Human* has become its own beast. Not only have plotlines diverged greatly from the source material, but Witwer and castmates Sam Huntington and Meaghan Rath have made the show theirs.

However, with all the vampires sucking up audience attention in pop culture lately, the 34-year-old Witwer may have the largest hurdle to jump as an actor on the show. Not only has he been required to break from the character of Mitchell (the vampire played by Aidan Turner on the BBC show), but the actor from Glenview, IL, had to develop a vamp that withstands comparisons to Bill and Eric, Stefan and Damon, Lestat and Louie and more.

But after crafting unique characters on popular shows such as *Battlestar Galactica, Dexter, Smallville, Star Wars: The Clone Wars* (and the *Star Wars: The Force Unleashed* video game), Witwer has proven he has a talent for creating identities.

Instead of making Aidan a self-loathing romantic a la Robert Pattinson's Edward, or an unrepentant bloodsucker like Colin Farrell's Jerry in *Fright Night*, Witwer has done this by utilizing shades of both to create a nuanced character. He plays Aidan as a man with an addiction, and as a monster who is trying to rediscover his humanity.

Witwer recently spoke about the direction of Aidan in the second season of Being Human, as well as opening up about his role in those other well-known geek culture franchises. He even breaks big news about his involvement - and non-involvement - in *The Walking Dead*, reveals his thoughts on the firing of Frank Darabont and talks about the zombie plotline that never was!

We've spoken before about the addictive nature of your character. Some addicts end up being train wrecks. They are on the rails, then go off the rails. What's the end game for him? Will it just keep going downhill until he takes everyone with him?

It very might. I can't tell you what the end game is because that would be huge spoiler material, but I will say that the addiction theme is absolutely more present than it was in the first season. Things get really ugly pretty quick in the second season. So we've been shooting some very uncomfortable stuff - while at the same time, we're still maintaining the humor and all of that.

But yeah, it's absolutely there. As we've talked about, that's what I was most interested in, in terms of playing this character. I was so happy to expand on it in the second season. We get to see different sides of it, too, and where it takes him - what he's willing to do. There's also very defined - god, I'm trying to think what I can say without spoiling it - there's very defined personality changes that come out because of him indulging in certain things. It's pretty cool.

Has there been a decision-making process with the roles you've chosen that are so diverse?

Some roles you choose, others you get chosen for. I can't say I chose *Dexter*. That is something I just went in and auditioned for something called *Dexter*, and they wanted - as they described it - a squirrelly computer nerd. I really wanted to play the character even though I didn't know he was going to turn into Kevin Spacey from *Seven*. But it wasn't until I got the part that I was shown the pilot and was like, 'Oh, oh, OK. Yeah, let's do this show.' Things like *Battlestar*, actually, were kind of my choice in that I asked my agent to seek out a role on that show. The later you get in your career, the more people actually ask you to do things.

In terms of *Being Human*, I was stupid. I cracked open the script, got to page three, and I was like, 'I don't want to play a vampire; there's too many vampires out there, why do we need another vampire show?' I only read like three pages. It wasn't until a friend of mine said, 'You should really think about doing your job and reading the script! You are an actor, right? You can read, you are literate.' So I read the script and realized it was an absolutely irresistible character, and that it was very fresh and original, and had some really provocative things to say.

As far as roles go, I think you look for - for me - if it's a role where I'm afraid I'm not good enough to do it, that's the role that I want. The role that's going to keep me up at night, losing sleep - which this role definitely has. Ask my producers about 4 a.m. emails. Suddenly I'm lying in bed, wake up and go, 'Going to write an email about this and have you thought about that?' It's all because I really like this to be good. Yeah, you want to be challenged as an actor and hopefully rise to the occasion.

Between choosing to take it and actually completing it and hoping you made your mark, there's a lot of stress in between. But that's not worth it if you don't have some level of that stress - if you're not worried that you're not quite up to the task, then you're probably not trying hard enough.

Is Battlestar your favorite role, and is that why your band is named the Crashtones?

Battlestar is significant because it taught me all my bad habits, and when I say, 'bad habits,' I also mean good habits. *Battlestar* taught me to be ridiculously outspoken, and to take the initiative a lot. On *Battlestar*, those guys ran that show like no other. You've got a lot of green screen stuff, right? A lot of special effects. For shows like that, it takes a tremendous amount of planning. So what do I get told my first day on set? David Eick says to me, 'Hey, OK, here's how it's going to go: Give us one as written, then say whatever you want.' What? 'Yeah, yeah, yeah – ad lib, do whatever you want.' What are you talking about? That's a suicidal way to run a show, is what I'm thinking. He goes, 'No, we hired you because we trust you. If you go too far, the director will pull you back but we want performances to be unpredictable.'

That sort of created in me the sense that actors should really be a little bit more aggressive and really should bring as many good ideas to the table as possible and then let someone else sort out which of the ones we're going to keep. Some shows they don't like it. I remember on *Smallville*, I was at some event for the show and one producer comes up to me and goes, 'Um hey, you know what, you're doing a great job just do exactly what you're doing.' Then another producer came up right after that and goes, ' Hey, if you could keep it just more to the script, that would be great.' No matter who I talked to, it was a different story. I was like, well, I'll change a few things here or there if it makes something better.

Even on my first day [on *Smallville*], I changed a few lines. These people had been on the show for, I don't know, seven years. We were on the eighth season. They were writing things familiar to them, but my character was an outsider. So I'm like, 'He doesn't know about meeting your people, he doesn't know about Krypton, he doesn't know about any of this stuff.' So I thought he would say it like 'this.' Let's remind the audience that this stuff is weird. This is strange phenomena; not everyone is familiar with it. They let me get away with it. They were gracious about it.

But the rule is, as an actor, if you're ever going to deviate from what someone tells you to do, it has to work. If it doesn't work, you've wasted people's time and money. So you have to be really picky and choosy when you decide to stick your neck out.

But *Battlestar* taught me all that because we were all going nuts on that set. We were all going crazy and coming up with crazy things to say. I mean, I didn't show up that much in the first season until the end and most of the things I said were some modification of an ad lib and they encouraged me to do that. The discovery of Kobol in the first season was very much like, 'Oh we found a planet. It's got Oxygen and water. Cool. Awesome.' As it was written, it was like we found a planet. Cool. And Crashdown was cracking jokes and being snarky and I was like, 'No, he needs to be mindblown.' Ron Moore wrote in the series bible that space is a cold, desolate place with just asteroids and nothing. It's just Big Empty. You don 't find habitable planets. Because of that, I ended up just not saying a bunch of lines but having this moment of 'I can't believe this ' and then going in and being snarky but having a moment of [angelic] 'Ahhh.' When you see the episode, they actually put in the music of 'Ahhh.'

What character of yours do fans most approach you about, and do you gauge the popularity of Being Human based on how many fans come up to you to talk about it?

You know what's strange? You go to conventions and stuff and people are happy to see you, but when *Being Human* happened, that's when you couldn't walk through a convention anymore. It used to be you would walk and you take a picture. Then with *Being Human*, we tried to walk the Comic-Con floor and couldn't go anywhere.

The interesting thing is, when they come up it's sort of like a critical mass and they want to talk about *Smallville*, they want to talk about *Star Wars*, they want to talk about any number of things. I get more *The Mist* attention now than I did when the movie came out. Same with *Battlestar*, oddly. I keep going, I can't believe anyone remembers that character. But I get people on the street coming up to me going, 'Hey *Battlestar Galactica*.' I don't even look like that guy, it's weird. Obviously, I'm extremely happy when people offer their support for *Being Human* because it's what I'm doing right now, and it's where my focus is, but I'm really happy the *Star Wars* character [of Starkiller] caught on. I love that kids are coming up and going 'Starkiller.' I love people expressing what that meant to them because for a lot of people, that was a *Star Wars* movie experience. I just think that's great that I hit that. The movie win-win where my character shows up in that basically as a rallying cry for the leads, which is great. I also love that it's led to more Lucasfilm work. They've been extraordinarily kind to me and continue to be.

Look, I'm a geek myself. If anyone had told me when I was a kid, I was going to be working on some *Star Wars* projects, and furthermore, if you want to stay at Skywalker Ranch - not just know where it is but actually stay there - you just need to make a phone call and this will happen by the time you're 31, I wouldn't have believed it. But they've been so generous and open with everything they're doing and I occasionally get to go in and do some really fun stuff. I wish I could tell you some stuff because there's an announcement coming soon about another character, I'll be doing for the *Clone Wars*, and I'm just very excited about it and can't talk about it. It sucks.

Because of your collaboration with Frank Darabont on The Mist, was there any talk of you getting on The Walking Dead before he was fired?

I was already in *The Walking Dead*. You guys have heard what's happened, recently. I'm furious at them for this, because Frank is my friend; he's my buddy. Not only is he my buddy, but he's a guy I'm extremely loyal to, because he gave me a shot with *The Mist*, when I didn't have a hell of a lot going on. Here's a guy who gets his cast and crew together and gives AMC a show, packages it all together, which is way cheaper than anywhere else because everyone is working way under their pay grade. Why? Because they want to and love working with Frank Darabont.

He has shared with me what kind of pay cuts people were taking, and I am also friends with other people on that set in other departments. He said to me, 'Look, I think it would be really cool to tell a prequel story about how Atlanta fell, do *Black Hawk Down*, but with zombies, have a few main characters pass through, but the lead will be you. You're a soldier and all these horrible things happen, and the chain of command breaks down, and, eventually, you have to take out your superior officer. Then, eventually, in the end, you get bit.' He's pitching me this. 'You're crawling and you crawl into this tank, and you have a grenade and you're going to blow yourself up, but you set the grenade next to you and you die. Then, we reprise the scene from the pilot, where Rick gets in the tank and there's a zombie there.'

If you look closely, I played that zombie, because we were setting up this prequel we were going to do. If you watch the pilot of *The Walking Dead*, that's me in the tank as the zombie, and then Rick blasts him and he gets deafened, and he gets that grenade which saves him at the end of the season.

It's not happening now. Why? Because AMC wanted to save a few bucks. That is just one example of the kind of cool, awesome forethought, this guy has put into this show, that is now absolutely written off. For me, it doesn't matter much because I'm busy doing *Being Human*. We were going to schedule things around. I'm not lamenting the loss of a job; I'm lamenting the loss of an amazing idea. And there are dozens and dozens of amazing ideas just like that, which are now gone.

Kristen Hager Talks Non-monstrous Job Of 'Being Human'

(January 2012)

So, you think transforming into a werewolf is ugly business? Try joining a new series as a recurring love interest/lycanthropic character originated by another actor on the British source material. As if that's not quite enough of a challenge for an actor, add in the fact that the showrunners for this re-imagined series plan to go in a completely different direction than the original show, and your character could get a silver bullet in any episode.

Still, as tough as that seems, Kristen Hager isn't concerned. Already an accomplished actor with film and TV credits including *I'm Not There, AVPR: Aliens vs. Predator - Requiem, Wanted*, and the MTV vampire show *Valemont*, Hager is loving her new digs on the Syfy network's *Being Human* - werewolf changes, threat-of-death and all. Though she hasn't quite moved in and begun paying rent on the house of werewolf boyfriend Josh (Sam Huntington), vampire Aidan (Sam Witwer) and ghost Sally (Meaghan Rath), she is the show's fourth roommate as nurse Nora.

Similar to actress Sinead Keenan, Hager's counterpart on the

British version of the show, Hager plays Nina as a suffer-no-fools smart-ass who manages to fit in with the menagerie of monsters quite well as a formidable foil. But Hager ups the level of sexy toughness with Nora, and her character arc in Season Two appears to focus on her anger and reluctance to join the crowd of the cursed - while also dealing with the joys of a supernatural pregnancy.

Paranormal Pop Culture caught up with Hager to talk about her role as Nora and joining the trio of actors for a second season filled with beastly action, as well as how she has managed to spend so much time in the paranormal world with aliens, zombies and cute vampires.

One of things about the show is how much chemistry there is amongst the actors. We're initially introduced to the three (Sam Witwer, Sam Huntington and Meghan Rath) and then you kind of join in. Was it daunting to join this tight group as sort of the fourth roomie?

The moment I first met Sam Huntington, he gave me a big hug and was like, "it's so great to meet you." It was the exact same thing with Meghan, and the exact thing with Sam Witwer. I've never worked with such open, inviting, fantastic actors. From day one I felt like I was immediately part of a family, which is unlike any other job I've ever had. It's such a special, special group.

During the second season you're hanging out in the house a little bit more, so is there a sense of sort of a girls vs. boys now we've got two women and two men?

Yeah, there's so much excitement when I can finally see Meghan. And when Megan was on, she was like, "I'm doing a scene with another girl!" because all her scenes have been just Sam and Sam.

The Sams seem like the typical nerdy boys, and Megan seems to kind of tolerate it and go along with goofiness a lot of times. Is that sort of the dynamic?

Oh yeah. Everyone's always taking the piss out of each other and making everyone laugh and definitely, you know Sam Witwer likes the *Star Wars* stuff. But Meghan as well is super funny and they're just three incredibly dynamic individuals. I don't know, I just think that they play so well off each other that they're so excited and happy, but I am so excited and happy, too to be able to play along with them. You definitely do have that sense when you're around them that are always on and engaging.

Is that a good challenge for you because it keeps you sharp?

Yeah, exactly, but also more than that. It makes the days go by quickly and it makes me really love going to work.

Is that typical for most of your jobs, or is that kind of unique?

No, it's so unique. I've been fortunate that most of the sets I've been on, everyone's always been very friendly and easy to work with, but this is by far the exception. It is like I literally got home at night and can't wait for it to be 5 a.m. the next day so that I can get back to work because it's so much fun working with them.

Since this is a reboot or re-imagining of the UK show, what choices did you make to sort of not mimic or not be too closely compared to your British counterpart Sinead Keenan?

I chose to go into this entirely on my own. I've never seen an episode of the British series. I just decided to do my own thing, so I have no idea how similar our characters are. I know nothing about the character arc. I didn't want it to influence me, and I felt like it would.

So then, at what point did you find out that you would become a pregnant werewolf?

There were some whispers on set, but I literally found out when I got the script and saw the line that says, "Josh, I'm pregnant."

As far as the werewolf part, you got the scratch at the end of the first season ...

Exactly. People talk and I obviously knew without having had to have seen the British series - I knew that Nora turns into a werewolf. So, there was always that at the back of my mind that that could potentially happen. And then there's the scratch.

Nothing is set in stone at the end of Season One, but I was like 99.9% sure I'd be a werewolf and sure enough we start with a bang in episode one.

Was there ever a thought process like, "I got this job, I like it, I like my coworkers, but I'm sure they're going kill me off because I'm the obvious choice, and the love interest"?

That thought was always there, too, at the back of my mind. But you know what? If there's one show you should die on, it's this show because you could always come back as a ghost. I'd be like, you have to bring me back. But you'll find out in Season Two that a lot of people may or may not show up again at some point later in the season. I think you can figure it out because of that. So yeah, of course I was always worried that they could kill me but dying on the show is not the end. [laughs]

And of course, it would seem like you're referring to Mark Pellegrino's character, Bishop?

Of course. Yeah. Well, him and others.

And is Mark going to come back as a zombie or a ...?

Wouldn't that be perfect? To mix it up with more, bring in more of the supernatural element?

Back to Nora. The show is very sexy, but vampires always get to be sexy. Is there anything sexy about being a female werewolf?

I re ally had to wrap my head around this and really try and find out what's sexy about being a werewolf. It is like becoming a vampire: your senses are heightened, and you feel incredible in your body, and are connected to nature and very grounded and very powerful. So therefore, yeah, it is sexy. It makes you feel sexy, and so I really had to, you know, embrace that part of it because physically - turning into a dog is not the sexiest of transformations!

With Sam Huntington, he can tear off his shirt and then kind of do the incredible hulk thing and writhe on the ground. But you, as a woman on TV, have to cover things up a little bit more. So whose transformation is more difficult?

The best man, Sam, hands down. He wins because of the fact that you can't really have me busting out of my shirt or ripping my shirt off all of the sudden, so even though I literally spent four hours with a prosthetic - with the prosthetic people ahead of time doing all the casting - I actually have the chest cast, and the back, and the face, etc. but because it's less exciting without my clothes ripping off, I really didn't have to wear as many of the prosthetic pieces as I got made. So he has it worse than me because he had to spend hours, and hours, and hours. Whereas I just really had cheeks, claws, and then the dots on my face when they do the CGI. That was pretty much the extent. I don't even know if I'm allowed to be saying this, but that's the extent of my transformation - which is great for me, but a lot of waking up in the nude in the forest. They definitely compensated by there being many, many wakeups [after changing back]. Which is something they can show because you can place appropriate leaves in appropriate places.

What about this new kind of breed of werewolf that you guys encounter?

I could definitely tell you that they come in as powerful werewolves, like none we've ever encountered before. And even though I immediately dislike them, I may end up liking them more than I think I will because I feel like they have a lot of answers to a lot of questions that I have.

Nora is so outwardly pissed off about what happens to her, so is there any potential for her to go off on her own or, instead of being a love interest, becoming more of a rival to the other roommates?

In theory, but Nora's got a good journey this season. There'll be a lot of surprises, I think, and a lot of struggles trying to figure out what this means to her. I'm going to have some difficult decisions to make. That's probably all I should say for now.

You did attack, and maybe kill, a vampire in the second episode. Do we see you get a lot more action?

I definitely have a lot of action as you put it. Yeah, there's some good action sequences that's going on in there, for sure.

What was your interest in this kind of genre before this job came along?

My career has gone off in this direction. I've done a lot of sci-fi stuff, so I felt very comfortable in this world.

Do you enjoy watching those kinds of shows and movies and stuff, like vampires, werewolves, ghosts?

Oh yeah, definitely. Since I was very young. I loved *The Lost Boys* as a kid, and then *Bram Stoker's Dracula*. I've always loved the genre. You know, I think every girl, like every adolescent girl growing up has a vampire thing. I don't what it is. There's something weirdly romantic about them, hence the reason why *Twilight* is such a success.

And you just completed a movie called A Little Bit Zombie?

Yes, I did. It is a Canadian independent film, that's actually premiering at the Gala Canadian opener of the Victoria Film Festival in a month? Actually, not even a month, maybe in February? Two weeks? And so yeah, I'm heading up there. I haven't seen it yet, but it's a really funny, zombie romantic comedy. I'm a human; my brother turns into a zombie, and it's like he becomes infected with some sort of virus. We're trying to figure out what's wrong with him, and it turns out, it's a zombie virus.

Anything else on your horizon?

At the moment, I'm auditioning and waiting to hear what's happening with Season Three of *Being Human*. I have another Canadian film coming out called *Servitude* which is a comedy coming out March 30 across Canada about a bunch of waiters taking over a restaurant, the system fighting the system.

The Joe Letteri Effect: Visual FX Wiz Talks Creating 'Apes,' 'Tintin,' 'Hobbit'

(January 2012)

Pull back the curtain on much of today's movie magic and you're likely to find the wizard is visual effects master Joe Letteri.

The resume of Letteri's effects work reads like a list of some of the most popular, and biggest banking, films of the last 20 years: *The Abyss; Star Trek VI: The Undiscovered Country; Jurassic Park* (recently released on Blu-ray); the 1997 special edition of *Star Wars*; *The Lord of the Rings* (*The Two Towers* and *The Return of the King*); the highest grossing film ever, *Avatar*. Even films that look great but aren't remembered as great films, like *Van Helsing, X-Men: The Last Stand* and 2005's *King Kong* survive because of his talents.

The strength of Letteri's work isn't just that he brings the visions of directors Steven Spielberg, Peter Jackson and James Cameron to life, but his creations impress the movie biz' toughest boss, the audience, and has earned him five Oscars.

But Letteri keeps upping his game to keep all parties happy. In 2011, he created the super intelligent apes of *Rise of the Planet of the Apes* (now out on DVD and Blu-ray), a movie that was initially met with skepticism by fans until that initial trailer showed off the expressive eyes of Caesar - which was courtesy of Letteri. He is also behind the performance capture effects in Spielberg and Jackson's The *Adventures of Tintin* and is currently at work on *The Hobbit* series, the first installment of which is one of the most anticipated films of 2012. Moreover, it's a good bet that Apes will net Letteri another Oscar nod for best visual effects.

Letteri spoke with us about *Apes*, *Tintin*, and *The Hobbit*- as well as some of his past work - and opened up about the relationship between technology and actors.

What is the first thing you wish audiences would understand about being a visual effects supervisor?

Boy, that's a good question. What we are always looking for is that moment when it works. And it's kind of intangible. For me, the thing that interests me the most is, working on characters and creatures that are the kinds of things that you can identify with on the screen. So, for example: Caesar. Just being able to create this character that you can look in his eyes and understand what he's thinking and how that fits with the story - and given the whole experience that you're watching. To try and answer your questions, it's more about, for us, all these things are not real, yet we have to make them appear real. It is always a constant question of, 'how do you do that?' It's an ongoing dance between science and technology. Looking at story and looking at character, and looking at lighting and just everything that you can think of in the real world that actually has to come together when you roll a frame of film. We have to create by thinking through all that because it's all virtual to us.

Is it best when people don't recognize your work, or that you've been there? Is that what you're striving for?

Not necessarily. For me, it's always more about the - I want to say the unbelievability of it. I remember working on the dinosaurs in *Jurassic Park*. As a kid, drawing a dinosaur was always a really great thing. But to see a dinosaur on the screen and have it run across the screen and look like you were running film on that island while this was all happening, that's, to me, the stuff that I like. It looks like it couldn't be real. But your brain is telling you that it is real. To me, that's the most interesting stuff.

It's fascinating because you've created these indelible images. If we had a T-Rex on the streets of New York right now, we

would sort of expect it to look like creatures that you've created. So you've had this larger cultural impact. Have you ever thought about that? That's you've created the images that people expect if they were ever to be introduced into reality.

Only from the point of view, we kind of give that thought building into it. You want people to get it right away, what they're looking at, and to not question even the smallest of choices. In a way you kind of do try to arrive at a consensus at what people do expect to see. It was the same thing when we created Gollum. Everyone has read those books. What is he going to look like when you see him in front of a camera? Really, just try to hammer out the details to make sure that that's actually the case. In a way, I guess that's what we're shooting for.

Speaking of Gollum, or even Caesar, or the characters in Tintin. How important is the role of a human in these films? And what do you say when someone sees these creations and says actors are doomed?

I'd say the opposite. What we're really doing here is bringing actors into the center of all these fantasy characters that there would be no other way to do. I don't want to say there's exactly no other way. You could have done Gollum with Andy Serkis in makeup. You wouldn't have had this big impact. He needed to be this creature the way Tolkien described him. Take Caesar, for example. He needed to be a real chimp, from a baby to an infant. But you needed to understand the beginnings of his intelligence and how his feelings of rejection by society, by the human society that he thought he was part of, motivated this desire for freedom. These are things that we all kind of deal with ourselves as humans. There would be no other way to really convey that unless it felt completely real to you. You'd be taken out of it.
You'd be questioning it too much.

Is there a component when you're working on these films that you dread having to deal with? Like hands? Something where you are just like, 'OK, we have to do this.'

All those things that we are used to seeing that are in so much detail, that just take infinite amounts of detail to get right are exactly those kinds of things. Hands are a really good case in point. They are really difficult to understand what's going on with all the muscles and bones and skin and everything that actually happens with the hands. Obviously, people are so used to seeing what hands look like. Seeing an ape hand is not that big of a leap from seeing a human hand. So it has to be just perfect. So those are the kind of things that we just spend a long time going over the details, hoping we got it right.

When you look at a film like Planet of the Apes, what is an example of your work that you think really shines?

A moment that makes you really proud. Also, is there a moment that you 're kind of like, we can go back and do that a little bit better?

For Apes, there's a shot that got used in the very first trailer, where you are seeing Caesar in his cell and a guard passes by in the foreground and you see his eyes just kind of follow him. You can see from that one shot that he is thinking, and he knows what he is about to do. He knows that he has to do it and he's just waiting to make it happen. To us, that was the key moment. That was the first shot we did of Caesar. We thought you need to see that on the screen and understand all those things just from that one beat. If Caesar can deliver that one performance - because we saw Andy deliver that performance - if you saw Caesar deliver that performance, then we knew he could do anything else he needed to do for the film. So, in a way, that was kind of the highlight of the thing that kickstarted it. There's not anything in the film that I would think we'd want to go back and redo. We constantly do that through the filming process, as the character evolves, and we get to know the character better. We always go back and look at the film, and go back and watch it over and over again and say, 'OK, do we know more now here? Could he do that bit a little better?' And we had a chance to go in and make all those changes so that Caesar was the character that he needed to be through the whole film.

You've worked with guys like Lucas, and even Spielberg, who

has gone back and re-tweaked effects on films years after they were released. Is that something you would want to do with your films - as years pass, go back and apply modern technology?

Personally, I wouldn't. To me, they live in the era when they were created, and I'd rather just leave it that way. Plus, I have very little interest in going back and redoing something I have already done. But I understand for a filmmaker like George, where he's got the *Star Wars* legacy - where he's also got to think about audiences who are seeing films for the first time, like young kids growing up who are seeking more modern and much more realistic effects. He's going to want them to - I'm just speculating here; I haven't talked to George about this - but I'm guessing that he's going to want them to not be thinking that they are old- fashioned. The stories are not old-fashioned. So he's not going to want any element of the film to take that route. As a director, he's got a different way of looking at this than I would.

What's something with The Hobbit, specifically, that you are excited to introduce. Something you are excited to work on?

Actually, for us, it's really simple. It's just going back and working with Andy again to do Gollum. In a way, nothing new there other than we've been able to go full circle now. This technology that we've created, starting with Gollum: The idea of using motion capture and performance capture, and having an actor on set. We are now able to put Andy on set and capture everything he did right at the moment. When we started with Gollum, Andy would perform with the other actors but then he'd have to re-perform his bit on the motion capture stage. We'd have to go back and fit it all in, after the fact. So, it was quite a bit of work in doing that. But with Caesar, we were able to take all this motion capture technology that we created for Avatar and figure out a way to bring it to the stage and do it with a lot of action right there. So Andy's performance was the performance, in the moment. Being able to do that with Gollum, it's nice because it has come full circle.

What are some of your favorite special effects from other people's movies?

I'd have to say Davey Jones was a good one [from *The Pirates of the Caribbean* franchise]. I tend to like character pieces and I thought that was a really good one. That would have to be a highlight of the last few years.

Even stretching a little further back, anything really old school, maybe old monster movies?

Old school, obviously *King Kong, Harryhausen, Star Wars, Blade Runner, 2001*. Even *Planet of the Apes*. All the old classics; all those things introduce you to the world in a way that you're not used to seeing. But they are still stories about our world. These fantasies, they get you to think about things in a way that you may not have thought about them before.

With all the technology we have you can put together an entire movie like Tintin with performance capture, but do you long for those old Harryhausen, stop- motion animation or man-in-rubber-suit effects?

No, because the realism of what we can do today. With all those old movies, there was a suspension of disbelief that you were required to make when you first saw it. Like, when audiences first saw King Kong on Skull Island, you could see all the thumbprints and the fur moving in every frame. I don't think people thought they were looking at a real gorilla. Yet, they knew the story was, 'This is a real gorilla,' and there was no questioning it. Now, I think, as we do with Gollum, he has to look like a real 'gorilla.' You have to make the leap now to where your eyes are totally involved with what you are seeing on the screen.

In just in the last couple of years, so much has changed. Avatar was a game changer. Planet of the Apes changed the game again. What, in your mind, is that next leap - that next big hurdle to tackle with technology?

You know, I really don't know because it depends on the story. Technically, anything that you see in the world is something we are interested in creating in one form or another, whether it's architecture, or clouds, or a smile, or hands, or fur. Anything like that is interesting because, anything like that can make a really good photo, and a really good image, and a really good story. But where we put the focus really depends on the script of the story.

If you're to look at the last couple of movies that you've done - you personally - what are the things that you felt raised your game? From Avatar to Planet of the Apes, to Tintin, to Hobbit. Do you look at it and say, 'I have now raised my game to that next level?'

I think *Avatar* was really the film that did that. For me, there were breaks where these things happen. *Jurassic Park* was really the first one because we're putting an organic character on the screen for the first time. And you kind of saw a lot of that for a while. Then the next step for me was Gollum because now you are putting a speaking character, driven by an actor's performance, on the screen with other actors that has to hold his own. Then you started to see a lot of that for a while. With *Avatar*, then, Jim Cameron just set out to break down the barriers between live action and digital filmmaking. That caused us to rethink everything that we know from a technical and science and performance point of view - and start all over again because you have to build the whole world not only inhabited by these creatures but influenced by the back-and-forth that happens with the environment and the people living in it. So that kind of cracked everything wide open.

You said the job sort of dictates what you create. But still, as an artist, what is your dream creature or dream thing that you would love to one day create on screen?

That is a good question because I've got to do a lot of them so far. I've gotten to do dinosaurs, gotten to do a human-like character like Gollum. Alien characters like the Na'vi. Doing realistic, like *Planet of the Apes* was kind of a dream because I love the old movies but now you can do this with a realistic chimp and actually see the intelligence evolving. Really, I've had a chance to do these things that I've been really interested in thus far, so I'm not really sure what else would be out there. I guess *Tintin* was a surprise to me. I've never really thought about doing a character coming out of a cartoon page. But when Steven started talking about it, you could see all the possibilities, and that was interesting as well. I guess somehow, I just like to respond to what's out there.

Mark Pellegrino Of 'Being Human' Gets 'Lost' In Gods, Monsters
(February 2012)

If the apocalypse does occur in 2012, it's a safe bet that Mark Pellegrino is somehow involved.

As an actor, he has played multiple roles so significantly tied to the survival or obliteration of humanity one can't help but wonder if his agent is reading the Book of Revelation in between scripts - or if Pellegrino might actually perform on a stage at the end of the world.

Pellegrino is not a god, but he has played a few memorable ones on TV. He is respected for notable roles like Rita's wife-beating ex Paul on *Dexter*; Gavin Q. Baker, a flamboyant attorney to cops on *The Closer*, a character worthy of his own spinoff; Tom Dempsey, an old-school mobster on *Castle*. But the actor is better known as Jacob, the godlike protector of the Island on mythology-heavy Lost.

Other viewers know him better as Lucifer, the fallen archangel-cum-devil on another mythology-heavy show, *Supernatural* - a role he just returned to on the February 17 episode "Repo Man" as a vision to Sam Winchester.

Still others might know Pellegrino best as Bishop, the undead (and later very dead) leader of Boston vampires on Syfy's reboot series *Being Human*. In *Being Human*, which airs Mondays at 9 p.m., Bishop is yet another character in Pellegrino's rogue's gallery with a god complex. Bishop has designs on wiping out much of the human race and turning the remainder into slaves.

And because death can't keep a good bad guy down, Bishop returns in tonight's episode of *Being Human* to torment his vampire son Aidan (Sam Witwer), who is experiencing a bit of parenting problems himself.

Mark Pellegrino joined us over the phone to discuss Bishop's return, his career as angels and demons, and even his love of video games, zombies and a possible role on *The Walking Dead.*

So I've spoken with your Being Human cohorts, and I heard you're a big gamer with your vampire son, Sam Witwer. Is that true?

Oh yeah. I'm kind of expanding my horizons a little bit in that realm. I used to be just the zombie apocalypse guy, but I'm starting to go outward into horror games and even shooter games, in general. I'm quite a fanatic about it.

What kind of zombie apocalypse games do you really enjoy?

Well, Left 4 Dead is my favorite. I like the first one the best because the characters are just pretty damn cool. I've been getting into the second one. Me and Sam play versions that are downloaded. There are these special games you can play on Left 4 Dead 2 that incorporates Left 4 Dead and those characters, and that's always really fun. [laughs]

Are you a big fan of sort of the zombie genre in movies or just video games?

I do like the zombie movies! In fact, I'm wearing a shirt right now my son gave me that says "Z-E-A: Special Agent, Zombie Emergency Agency." It looks like an FBI logo, but it's got all the bells and whistles of zombies. Yeah, I do like the zombie movies quite a bit. I know there are purist zombie guys that don't like the running zombies, but I dig the infected thing. I think that's a scarier incorporation of an element into the genre.

Well, it's funny. I could see you actually fitting in well with The Walking Dead folks. Has there been any talk of that?

Well, you know, first of all, I read every single one of *The*

Walking Dead graphic novels. Twice. And Sam Witwer, is friends with Frank Darabont. So one evening, I was over at his house, we were playing zombies, and he said, "Come on, I want you to go to dinner with me." He took me to dinner, and in walks Frank, and we all sat down and ate together.

You know, it seemed at the moment at that time that there was a possibility of me going in to work for the show, but you know, of course, things happened with Frank and the show. Who knows where I stand now? I have a good friend who works on the show, too, so maybe one of these days I'll get to be a survivor.

Who do you know who works on the show?

It's Jon Bernthal who plays Shane.

Now there are rumors that it sounds like Jon Bernthal is maybe out of the show, right?

Really? I haven't spoken to him in a little while. I saw him at the premiere, but I haven't spoken to him in a while. It looked like the show was going in that direction. I think he knew that kind of from the beginning. I don't think that's a new development, unless you know something I don't.

Everyone seems to like zombies for different reasons. What is your connection or theory as to why they are popular?

There's a lot of speculation on what the zombie apocalypse thing means. I have a feeling that it's kind of an expression of our subconscious fears. I think we know that something big and impossible - some enormous crash, equalizing crash, whatever - may be coming around the corner. I think that that is a specter that finds some psychological release in these zombie movies.

I also kind of have a different interpretation than even Romero, the originator of series, would have. I think we kind of live in a bit of a cannibalistic society. Subliminally, the movies show the cannibalism of the many against the few. You know, we kind of have an ingrained, parasitic society. We kind of think it's okay to eat your neighbor.

You've portrayed a few characters that are apocalyptic-minded. What is the appeal of characters like that; these scary guys with a lot of power?

People like that drive a story and test heroic values, so I think just speaking from the literary point of view, they're just phenomenally interesting. But I think people are enamored of power and somewhat fascinated by one who has this quality of amorality. There's something kind of frightening because it's an animal that many of us don't understand - but they're so liberated from so many of the things that hold us back that they also fascinate us.

I think that's what also bleeds over in less literary, less sophisticated ways to some of the reality-TV shows where you see interventions where people are just off-the-hook train wrecks with no regard for the sanctity of anything, let alone their own lives. There's something about that psychology that is interesting, in a way.

Jacob, Lucifer, Bishop: These are all charismatic characters who get people to follow them. Did you ever think, "I'm playing a cult leader here"?

If I looked at it, I think that in fact is what I am. But if I look at it that way from an actor's point of view, I have so many judgments about that kind of character - a cult leader - that are negative that it would make it impossible to act something like that with any sympathy. I usually have to find out the human inside. For me, I relate to what makes me get morally behind my guy.

For Bishop, there were a number of issues that I think any person could relate to. I think what was going on between Aidan and I was very much biblical in the sense of the story: The prodigal son and the father intervening on behalf of his son, who is going down the wrong path and I'm attempting to bring him back into the fold where he'll be happiest. And there's also - on a micro level, on a backdoor level - I think Bishop is attempting to liberate his people.

He's attempting to free an oppressed minority, to come out, to stop hiding in the closets. Integrate is the nice word, but I think he eventually, of course, wants to conquer because he has very, very Darwinian feelings about vampires and human beings. The sense of justice about a more powerful being is that there's something higher up on the food chain that's treating itself with such injustice and disrespect. I think he has such a high regard for his people that he wants to advance them.

So Bishop is a family man with ambition?

I tried to put positive ambition and a kind of family - a sense of family connective-ness into Bishop's character - which I thought was there and is something I could morally get behind. Same with Lucifer. I don't focus so much on the anti-life aspects of Lucifer, but on betrayal from those that he loved and alienation from god, as punishment for an injustice and wanting revenge. Does that sound weird [laughs]?

I mean, it may be weird for somebody that catches this conversation out of context! We know Bishop is going to be back in Being Human after getting killed off by beheading. How do you survive that? Are you coming back as a zombie vampire?

[laughs] Well, you know, I kind of don't know what I am when I come back - if I'm a ghost or a figment of Aidan's imagination. So there's speculation as to whether or not they're going to have me back some more, or under what conditions and circumstances because there's definitely a lot of space to bring me back in.

Do you find it funny that out of all these characters you've played - where many people have died at your characters' hands - that Paul from Dexter is the guy who gets most of the bad-guy attention? I mean, a lot of people have died at the hands of Lucifer and Bishop, but people focus on Paul. Granted, he did awful things, but compared to the devil? Do you ever chuckle at that?

I feel bad everybody kind of sees Paul as this horrific person. You know, again for me, it was about getting my family together and this usurper comes in that is trying to steal what's mine, and you know, I leave it up to the audience to judge. And they have judged harshly whether Paul does it effectively or in an appropriate way.

But yeah, it's very funny. I think the more iconic a character, the more distance there is from their deeds and, in a way, the more acceptable they become. You know Paul's just an everyday, blue-collar guy, and so I think he's much more intimate.

From the perspective of fans, what's the character most people recognize you for?

I've been going to Supernatural conventions, so they tend to be big Lost fans and big Supernatural fans, but it's usually for both of those. Walking on the street, people are really, really into Lost. But on the conventions circuit it's Lucifer.

It's been nearly two years since the series ended (the finale was May 23, 2010), so are you still getting questions about Lost that people expect you to answer?

Yeah! They expect me to explain the entire show to them. And it's a little bit shocking to them when I tell them, "You know, it's anybody's guess." Nobody believes I'm as informed as you are about things. You're just going to have to come up with your own solutions the way I did. [laughs]

Checking In With 'Innkeepers' Director Ti West, Star Sara Paxton

(February 2012)

Ghosts are scary, but not as scary as the growing awareness that you're expected to do more with your life beyond just working the desk at the local haunted hotel. So naturally, the best way to distract yourself from your personal crisis is to hunt for ghosts.

That's the setup for the new horror movie *The Innkeepers*,

directed by Ti West and starring Sara Paxton which hits theaters on February 3 and is already available On Demand. Although West has previously dealt with Satanic worshippers in the lauded horror movie *The House of the Devil*, and Paxton has battled creatures of the deep in *Shark Night 3D*, they agree the general malaise that sets in during the 20s is more unsettling than monsters - but that ghosts are still freaking creepy.

The film, shot and set at the supposedly legitimately haunted Yankee Pedlar Inn in Torrington, CT, follows desk clerks Claire (Paxton) and Luke (Pat Healy) who decide to seek proof of the hotel's ghosts in the final days before it closes for good. In between goofing off, drinking on the job, and harassing a spiritualist hotel guest (Kelly McGillis), the pair play with an oversized audio recorder to capture EVP evidence - which works out a little too well for Claire. The film is scary with its patience; West isn't above toying with his audience and takes his time with the jumps, but when he does unleash the scares on his character, the result is a scary fun flick that's like *Clerks* meets *The Shining*.

In an interview in New York City, West and Paxton revealed exactly how personal *The Innkeepers* is for both of them, both for normal and paranormal reasons. In fact, while both claim to be skeptics about ghosts, they also are viewers of ghost hunting shows and are eager to join a television crew for an investigation - and even want a reading from one particular famous psychic.

The movie is as much about Luke and Claire having this mundane job as it is a ghost story, so what are your past mundane jobs?

Ti West: I've had them all and that's why it was a huge part of the reason for making the movie. I'm qualified to direct movies or be like a busboy. I don't have any career skills or talents or trades or anything. So I worked very hard at having that all on the page. What's it's like to be at a minimum wage job, and sort of stuck there? And it may not be digging ditches, but in your own world, it's your own bourgeois problem. It's those own little worlds you create with your work friends, not your real friends and things like that. So I've been like a busboy, or a cook. I've mowed lawns, I've sold shoes, I've worked at a video store - I've done all those things.

I did it for like 10 years. So I'm in no hurry to go back. But I wanted to make a movie about the charmingness of it all.

Sara Paxton: I've never had a real job. [laughs]

TW: Have you met anyone who's worked?

SP: [laughs] Yeah. I can really relate to the Claire character. Just because I haven't had real job, you know what I mean, I get her. I mean, I've felt like that.

TW: Struggled?

SP: Yeah, I mean I've felt like that - not to that extent where I'm in a dead-end job, but we've all sort of been there, like, "Uh, now what?! What next? Where am I going with this?"

TW: I think everyone has their own weird, existential crisis about, like, "Should I be caring more about this than I do?" I don't know, but like in the movie, it's sort of like "What do you do?" "I work in a hotel." "But what do you really do?" "I work in a hotel, is there something wrong with that? " I never thought about it. I was just going along with my life, feeling good ... sometime in your 20s, you start to get introspective and neurotic.

SP: Youth crisis.

TW: And I think it's weird, like this personal anxiety. So that's what I tried to put in this movie because I went through all that stuff. Like I said, "Not good enough to just be having this job."
"What's wrong with this job? Maybe nothing, but now I feel weird about it."

So that part is very relatable, but ghosts? Have you also gone through that?
TW: In a way. I think what I wanted is, I wanted to do just a very traditional, old-fashioned ghost story, like an 1800s kind-of ghost story - but with these modern nerves in it because I thought it would be interesting to see how they would react in a ghost story

versus the people in the 1800s of this period. Now, the actual hotel is a real place. When we made our previous film House of the Devil, we lived there. We make a Satanic horror movie, but some weird stuff would happen back at the hotel.

Such as?

TW: Everyone in the cast and crew thought it was haunted. The staff thought it was haunted. One of the guys who was there had a ghost hunting website about it; the whole town thinks it's haunted. The building is this amazing 1800s historic building with bad 1970s renovations on top of it. Like, there's 20- somethings working at the front desk. It's this really weird place. So it was a very personal movie, and we went back to the same exact place and filmed there. I'm a skeptic, I don't believe in ghosts, but as close as I'll ever come is doing two tours at the Yankee Pedlar Inn.

What is something unexplained that you experienced at the Yankee Pedlar?

TW: Well, I mean, certainly doors opened and closed by themselves, lights turned off and on by themselves, my phone would ring, and no one would be on the other line - which is something they say happens all the time. I can tell you the vibe just feels weird. We are staying at the Ace Hotel now, and I don't feel weird at all. But at the Pedlar, something's just off. You have very vivid weird dreams - I don't know what that's about, it could just be weather.

I'm a skeptic, so while I don't know what any of that stuff was, I don't necessarily jump to ghosts as the number one option. But the other thing that was weird was the room in the movie that's the most haunted room, the Honeymoon suite. I only picked it because it was on the third floor at the end of the hallway and big enough to do a dolly shot. I was like, "That'll work, we'll use that one." And then after we wrapped the movie, I found out that that's the most haunted room in the hotel, in real life. I don't know if it means it's haunted, but what a weird thing to go through, you know? But Sara had ghost things happen.

SP: I don't know if they were ghost things. It was the same stuff: my door would just violently fly open when I'd be sitting in my bed watching TV. It would just burst open. And I was like, "yeah, hmmm, it's the wind" but my windows were closed. Just weird stuff like that.

So do you believe, or don't believe?

SP: Well, I mean, there's definitely a creepy vibe. I am a baby, so I would kind of get scared, but I don't know. I've never seen ghosts up close and personal, so ...

You're shooting a haunted hotel movie in a haunted hotel, so do you think that influences your imagination when you lay your head down on the pillow at night?

SP: Just being there, period, was weird. From even before we started shooting, which was like one day, I just walked in there and it was weird. Even the town is just off. Everything is just...

TW: It's a strange place.

SP: It was a really weird place, yeah.

Luke is an amateur ghost hunter, so do you watch any of those shows?

TW: I've seen a lot of them, yes. I'm fascinated by them. They're pretty popular shows, but they fail every episode. These are the absolute experts, no one is better at finding ghosts than them, and they haven't found any ghosts. So in a way, I feel like they're almost counter-productively proving that there is no such thing as ghosts. Yet they keep getting more seasons despite not finding ghosts. I find that to be kind of amazing.

And also, I just think it would be funny if they did encounter a ghost, then all the expertise would go out the window, and they'd be like, "Ahh! Let's get the f--- out of here!" That's a big thing in the movie. They [Luke and Claire] are fronting like they know more about something than they do, and when your covers are pulled, that's really how you reacted? So I think it would be funny to watch an episode of those ghost hunter shows and just watch them lose their mind when a ghost shows up.

Have you gotten feedback from people within that ghost hunting community?

TW: I would love to talk to them, to experts about all this. It is fascinating to me. I don't believe in ghosts, but that doesn't mean they aren't real. It isn't that I don't want to believe in them, but when I see a ghost, I'll believe in a ghost. Until then to say this recording is like a door opening is like, "I don't know what made this exact noise, but I'm not sure it was a ghost." [But] that doesn't mean there's not a ghost.

Sara, has anybody reached out to you that's like, "I'm a ghost hunter and I think when you do this, you should...?"

SP: No! I wish they would.

Really?

SP: Yeah, in fact one: The one on Travel Channel [*Ghost Adventures*]. The guy's like, [in a masculine voice] "come here, ghosts! Come out, come out! Stop being so scared!" He taunts the ghosts, but I wouldn't do it like that.

TW: I like Chip Coffey.

SP: Yes!

TW: I'd like to do an interview with Chip Coffey. That'd be fun.

SP: I want to have a reading with Chip Coffey. I want to pay him money. He's the most entertaining person -

TW: I would love to talk to Chip. I mean, the funny thing is I make fun of those shows, but I'm also totally legitimately intrigued by them. But I do think it's funny because I do think it's counterproductive, but I would just love to talk to people about it, to really find out what keeps it going, you know what I mean?

Obviously, there's the intrigue. The interest is obviously something very important to them.

One of the ghost characters [in the movie] is based on an experience I had with someone. I'd never want to believe in spiritual healing, or any of that stuff too, but the closest I ever came was with someone with a pendulum talking to me about stuff that kind of came true. I was like, I just intrinsically don't believe in this, but that was pretty spot on, and it freaked me out a little bit. And that's what Kelly McGillis' [medium] character is based on. It was like the kind of stuff that happens to Sara and Kelly in the movie. That happened to me at the Pedlar in real life. That's why I think Chip Coffey would be interesting. A friend of mine had a reading with him for her birthday and he said some stuff that kind of came true, so I'm fascinated by it.

Where the movie succeeds is that a lot of people outwardly may be a skeptic, but there's the old saying "there's no atheists in fox holes," so maybe there are no skeptics in a haunted house. Was that something you were intentionally trying to tap into?

TW: Absolutely and I think it was important for me to have two very clear viewpoints you can take away from the movie ... You can make a very strong case for the movie that there are no ghosts and it's all in your head. Or you can have the believer's approach and be like, "the stuff that the characters in this movie were saying was real and it wasn't avoidable, and this is something that is real" ... I like it if people see the movie and when they drive home, they're in the car, and they're thinking about it - and that makes it worth making a movie, to take it beyond just an escapism experience.

Instead of using modern ghost hunting equipment like night vision cameras, your characters go old school with this giant audio recorder. What was the decision behind that?

TW: Well, for one, those *Paranormal Activity* movies have got this sort of night vision thing. I felt like to do that was just so "that" and I didn't want to go and tread on that territory. I also found I wanted to do something with EVP because I think it's more compelling for me and I've never seen that in a movie where you kind of go into the character's point-of-view from an audio point-of-view. I thought that was interesting and just scarier to me. Like, what you don't see, but what you hear. If you're hearing something, but you don't see it, that to me is scary, and that's more like believable as a ghost. It is like this idea that electricity is just always here. We didn't know it until we discovered it. That to me is interesting about the EVP part of things. I also liked that Luke's camera is broken and he doesn't have money to fix it, you know?

Talk more about the website Luke creates in the movie.

TW: I always liked the idea like he means it about his [Pedlar Inn ghost] website, but his website is not very good. He is mediocrely talented at doing what he's doing, and I'm always charmed by that - someone who's not really that good, but it's the best he can do. And that's what I feel about the movie, is that the camera is broken - I've got this microphone and this old-ass thing. Like, we're doing the best with what we've got!

Sara, as an actor, is it better to work with that low- tech, big microphone or would you have liked to play around with the...

SP: Yeah, I know. I felt like dorky or something when I was holding this big, chunky thing, walking around with the mic. It just worked. I instantly felt like nerdy. It would be a little weird if it was like, black ops night vision goggles.

Have friends or strangers started coming up and telling you their ghost stories yet?

TW: In town they did. People always try to tell their Yankee Pedlar stories while we're in town.

SP: [Local] paramedics told me a lot and said so many people died there at the Yankee Pedlar. They told me all their little ghost stories.

329

TW: I mean I'm so fascinated by it I spent two years making a movie about it. [Ghost stories] are interesting to me and something a lot of people are fascinated by because it does relate to everybody - because we'll all die, and we all know people who died. And so unlike maybe other horror themes, it's very personal for everybody. It also seems to be the most believable, and so it's just like there's this quest. Like if we just get a little bit more proof, then we could relax about it. It's interesting that it's been so hard.

Sara, was this the kind of role you had to do any research for? Did you look into this world at all?

SP: No, I mean, I'd already watched all those ghost hunting shows. I was already a fan of those, and I didn't do any research into ghost hunting or whatever. As for the character, I could really relate to Claire.

TW: I did a lot of that stuff. I think that was in there. I mean, technically, I probably know very little. I think I know a little bit about EVP and things like that, but I don't know if I know a lot about some of the denser equipment and the way it works. But I hopefully did enough so that it's not too cringeworthy for people who are incredibly interested in it. Ultimately, this movie really isn't about that. It is about these characters, so it seems like it's a movie about ghost hunting, but that's kind of secondary. So that's why I backed off on a lot of the extra technology and all the specifics about it. Because had I gone that route, then it really is just a ghost hunting movie, which is not really what it's about. It is kind of about being stuck in a place in life and things like that.

Is there a good ghost hunting movie out there, in your opinion?

TW: I think there is a good "just ghost hunting" movie to be made, but I also remember in *Poltergeist* like a really good scene with the expert. (Anytime an expert comes into a movie is always really satisfying for me because they know what they're doing, and they seem so confident about it.) But in *Poltergeist*, they get the experts to come, and they're in over their heads. When an expert is in over their head, we're all screwed. And so that's a little bit what happens to Luke. He knows everything, then you realize he's scared and it's like, "but he's the guy! He knows the most in this whole movie and if he's gone, we're screwed now." And I think that's an interesting dynamic.

What about scary movies? Are there any great scary movies that you kind of go back to maybe each Halloween or ...?

SP: The Exorcist scared the shit out of me, and I'm still traumatized. I'm Jewish, and I still sleep with a rosary next to my nightstand because of *The Exorcist*. I'm scared; can't do it. I don't f--- around with that shit.

TW: I agree, *The Exorcist* is scary. I think The Shining is scary. I think *The Changeling* with George C. Scott is one of the best ghost movies. And recently I saw one which was kind of strange called *Lake Mungo*, which is a ghost movie. It is great. It is this found footage-ish documentary-type movie and I highly recommend it. Not a lot of people have seen it, which is a shame. It is about a family whose daughter goes missing, and they find out she's dead, and they think that she might be haunting them. They sort of set up stuff to try and find out if they can get proof of it, and then they do, but it ends up not being what they think it is - which, of course, makes you think of some other ghost film, but it's not. There are all these weird twists that happen in it, and it's really well made ... It actually creeped me out. And movies don't do that to me anymore. So I was watching it like on Netflix and instantly was like, what's happening? It actually affected me.

Sara, there's a scene right at the beginning of the movie where your character is with Luke and we're doing something pretty mundane, and he pranks you with a good jump. Do you think it kind of sets this tone that "we're gonna play with you a little bit"?

SP: That was real. It scared the shit out of me.

TW: Yeah, I wouldn't show it to her until we did the take.

And to put the word out there right now, if Ghost Adventures is looking for a celebrity investigator, are you going to go on?

TW: It was brought up. I got asked to do a Pedlar episode with me for one of those shows, and I'm like, I would love to do it. I don't know what's going to happen, but I am 100 percent all in.

SP: Oh yeah, I'm in. Can I be your sidekick?

TW: Yeah! I'd love to do it. I was so excited when they asked, because I was like "dude, absolutely!" But the Pedlar's in foreclosure, so there's not a lot of time left. But I, yeah, I'm all for it.

IronE Singleton Talks T-Dog's Fate On 'Walking Dead'

(March 2012)

For two seasons of *The Walking Dead*, IronE Singleton has just been trying to fly under the radar. While he has been part of key, intense scene during the zombie drama - and become a beloved fan favorite - as showrunner Glen Mazzara puts it, Singleton's character of T-Dog is aware of his outsider status as the only African American character on the show and is trying to be a team player who doesn't attract too much attention.

Conversely it is hard not to pay attention to IronE Singleton. A native of Atlanta, GA ("born and raised ... a Grady baby!"), Singleton is a laid back, convivial guy who doesn't hold back with a laugh. I caught up with Singleton at the Atlanta Run For Your Lives zombie 5K race and obstacle course and tried (really, really tried) to get him to open up about the fate of T-Dog.

What resulted was a funny, but still informative, interview where we learned more about an actor caught up in the midst of a hit show where anyone can die at any moment. Read ahead - and very closely between the lines - to determine if T-Dog will survive tonight's season finale, as well as what it was like to shoot the infamous Sophia scene and deal with the zombie gore, and if T-Dog might get an appearance in Robert Kirkman's comic book.

Would you survive the zombie apocalypse?

Definitely. I'm always optimistic. I'd probably get with a pack. That's the best way to survive. You have to stay with a group of people in order to ensure your survival. You can't stay by yourself.

I can't help but notice you let your hair grow back in, but don't you guys go back into production soon.

You guys? That's a general 'you guys?' You're skillful (laughs)! But hey, I can't say, I don't know if T-Dog survives or not. People have to tune in to see.

Is your razor sharp for cutting off the hair any minute?

Not any - I don't know [laughs]! You want answers, don't you? I did this for another role, to soften my look. I'm playing a police officer for a movie I just shot with Neve Campbell in Toronto a couple weeks ago. I play Officer Rupert Nichols. That's why I grew out my hair, but if I have to take it off, I'll take it off. IF!

[Before the episode aired] we got some information leaked about Shane's (Jon Bernthal) death...

I heard about that! My agent was just telling me about that. That's crazy. I don't know where they got that information!

So, if indeed the leak is true about Shane's death [which we know now it is], what do you think about that character? Is that a good thing for the survivors?

He's going to be a major loss. A major loss. We need Shane. The group needs Shane.

Is T-Dog going to step up? Does he have leadership material?

I think he has leadership abilities, and whatever needs to be done for the group, I think T-Dog is willing to step up to do that?

What do you think his task or expertise should be? Glenn (Steven Yuen) is good at scouting, Rick (Andrew Lincoln) is a leader, etc. What do you think is a job he could own among the survivors?

T-Dog could do all of that. He could do anything that needs to be done. He's really versatile, but right now, the leader of the group is Rick. He acknowledges that and accepts that. It's a general consensus. But if Rick goes down, and T-Dog needs to step up in a certain area, that's what T-Dog is going to do.

Aside from a moment of doubt when he cuts his arm and is delirious at the beginning of Season Two, he's been loyal to Rick and the group. Will that continue?

If he lives, I think so. T-Dog is an even-keel type guy. He just goes along with the program, as long as it's not ridiculous to where he thinks it's going to endanger the lives of the group, he's for it.

Right now, up through this point, I think he sees Rick as the rational one. He wouldn't do anything that would endanger the lives of the survivors. So yeah.

Neither T-Dog nor Norman Reedus' character Daryl were in the comic, but we expect he's going to show up in it. So have you had a conversation with Robert Kirkman about T-Dog appearing in the comic?

That would be a cool thing. But now Daryl is a - what can I say? The women love Daryl! Have you seen his following on Twitter and Facebook? This guy is a stud. So I can't argue with that! [laughs]

But you have a following too. So you haven't said to Kirkman, "let's make this happen"?

Not formally, but we've had quite a few informal conversations and who knows? We'll see what happens, but until T-Dog attracts the type of attention that Daryl attracts, then I think it'd be a pretty hard thing to do to convince Kirkman to do something like that. But I don't know. T-Dog is pretty popular but he's no Daryl. I just have to keep it real and be truthful about that.

We recently heard about the announcement of David Morrissey as The Governor - actually, have you read the comics?

I haven't gotten through the compendium. It's about this thick.

Oh, yeah it is. But you know how bad a guy The Governor is.

Of course. He's menacing. He's bad.

So how is T-Dog going to do against him? Are you worried you might be a casualty of The Governor?

The Governor - I don't know about the - if T-Dog makes it that far, then [laughs] ...

I'm trying. I'm trying. You're like Fort Knox here. You' re good! I'm always trying to get information out of you!

I can tell! (laughs) If T-Dog makes it that far, that's a good thing. But like everyone else, we've got to fight for our survival. So just like Merle Dixon (Michael Rooker), it's just another opposition there. Business as usual.

The show is pretty violent, but do you ever think you're going too far?

I've never thought we're not going far enough. I've never thought that. I think you'll agree with me on that - this thing is as gory as it can get. It's a bloody mess at times. I think we're in a good place. It's a fine line. I think we're doing a great job of incorporating key moments and highlights from the comic book into the show, but at the same time, doing enough to keep people guessing. Like you! Constantly trying to figure out what's going to happen next!

There have been some great intense moments that weren't in the book, like the Sophia (Madison Lintz) scene where she shows up after being searched for through six episodes, then Rick has to put her down.

Yeah. I think that was the most intense that we've done from Season One all the way through. It was tough because Madison Lintz who plays Sophia had become part of the family. That's how we look at it. There's so much love. The vibes are so great. And she was a part of our family, so to lose her was like we were losing a family member. It was tough for us to snap out of that. During interviews, people have asked me if I'm able to snap out of it and just start laughing and joking with one another. It wasn't that simple for that. Most of the time, yeah, but not with that scene.

Normally we shoot four, five scenes in a day. It took two days to shoot just that one scene.

Are you going to be at San Diego Comic-Con?

Uh ... with me? If - no, I haven't heard anything about that because I mean, if, if T-Dog survives, then there's a possibility, you know. But if I'm not, then I don't think that T-Dog would be invited.

So, you think you'll be at San Diego Comic-Con?

I don't – [breaks off, laughs]

Think you'll get an action figure sometime soon?

That would be nice! A T-Dog action figure would be nice, right? That's the beginning of our petition!

What Scares Clive Owen Of 'Intruders' About Fatherhood?

(April 2012)

Clive Owen isn't the leading man actor normally described as dashing and ruggedly handsome when he enters the room.

Sure, the movie star charm and warmth are there, but when Owen sits down with a group of reporters, it's as a father who knows terror.

After being introduced to American audiences in 2000 with *Croupier*, Owen has carved out a career in films portraying an intense, if disheveled, man of thought and action in *Children of Men, Closer* and *Inside Man*. He's also shown the ability to be a little less thoughtful with fun, ultraviolent flicks *Shoot 'Em Up* and *Sin City*.

In the new psychologically driven horror-thriller *Intruders*, which opened March 30, Owen plays John Farrow, father to a 13-year-old daughter terrorized by the tormenting being "Hollow Face," who wishes to possess her and might be connected to a family secret. Meanwhile, in another country, a young boy is experiencing the same phenomenon. As the children's stories begin to take shape and come together, the Hollow Face mystery is unraveled, as is Farrow's family unit.

Along with the online sexual predator film *Trust* - and to some degree the single-parent drama *The Boys Are Back* - Intruders seems to mark a new chapter of Owen's career playing fathers who often feel powerless.

Owen sat down with me to discuss his portrayal as a father and his own real-life experience as one. He also talks about what terrified him as a child and as an adult, and the power of secrets in families.

Why do audiences respond to seeing children terrified?

Because we remember being terrified, probably ... Bad dreams and nightmares, when you're very young, are very intense experiences. I remember it, and I've seen it in my own children. I think, over time, you learn to process it, and you wake up very quickly and can figure out what's real and what isn't real. But for a child, it can really throw you off center.

How important do you think family secrets are?

I think that we all have them. I think that's the truth. I think that this is a very personal film to [director Juan Carlos Fresnadillo] and happened to him when he was young and related to secrets that his family had and that's why he wanted to explore them in this film.

Do you think it's important to keep them or is it detrimental?

I think you have to take each one at a time. I think sometimes it is maybe better to get things out in the open.

What scared you as a kid? What scares you now?

I wasn't that sort of a fearful kid, really. I remember having nightmares, but I never had recurring nightmares or got scared at night. I wasn't that kind of child. When people say to me, what scares me now, it's without doubt, the sort of welfare and well-being of my children, really. I think that's the one thing that you kind of don't have much control over - just fearful that they're going to be OK and they're going to be all right.

As opposed to roles where your body has taken a beating, does this kind of psychological role beat up your mind at all when the threat is from within?

That's a good question because it's harder work than you think. You've got to take the audience to quite an intense place and sometimes doing that is as hard as doing a page of dialogue.

Because if you fall short, the thing doesn't work. You have to get to get to a level of intensity. That's why I thought Ella [Ella Purnell, who plays Owen's daughter Mia in *Intruders*] was so good in the movie - because she, in some ways, really holds that together. It's her emotional terror that we're kind of gripped by as the film goes on.

Can you talk a little bit about how your character growing up has unresolved issues with his mother that affected his parenting skills when he became an adult?

I think there's absolutely no question the central theme is that passing on fears to your children is a very real and truthful thing. ... I've got a friend ... and the mother is scared of dogs, and the kids are now terrified of dogs ... That's a very simplistic version, but I think that kids are very sensitive and alive to what's going on within people and specifically, their parents.

Have you passed on any fears to your kids?

Only good things!

When you're dealing with a child actor like Ella in these very intense scenes, do you ever have to step aside with her and just check in on her to see if she's OK?

I think you have to do that before you even start working. I've done about three films in the last few years that have very strong relationships with children and playing a parent, basically.

It's usually important that they feel safe before you begin, especially if you want to push it into areas that are uncomfortable, which is an interesting and good thing to do. But the child needs to feel safe and that everything's OK ... I actually really love working with young actors because I think they are so responsive and instinctive. And it's much less honed a craft they're employing, but it's very real and reactive.

Are you going to veer off from thrillers? Are you going to do more comedy now?

No. I am filming a comedy, which is very exciting actually. It's the first one that I'll do really. I really like it. It really makes me laugh. So, I'm excited about that but that's not for a while, yet.

I think I just instinctively respond to material and, at the end of the day, you look at it, and that kind of shapes a career. There's no question that *Trust, The Boys Are Back*, and this film are obviously related because I'm a parent. I'm a parent of two girls. There are things within that that I thought, 'this is really interesting to explore' ... to do it in a very truthful way is something very exciting to discover.

You've said you're a huge fan of The Exorcist. So why do you love it so much?

I think it's a really well-directed movie. Not just a horror movie, but a movie. I just thought it was extremely well-acted, and it still holds up today. It's disturbing. My 12-year-old daughter has heard about it and says, 'Dad, I want to watch *The Exorcist*.' Sweetheart, you're not watching that for 10 years. Don't even think about it. I had it in the house and got rid of it because I'm paranoid that she was going to think, 'I'll just have a little look,' and get traumatized for the next four years.

The Big Bad God: Tom Hiddleston Brings Mischief To 'The Avengers' As Loki

(May 2012)

Tom Hiddleston aims to misbehave. Unless you've been living under a rock in Asgard - or frozen in suspended animation - you know the English actor is reprising his role as villainous Loki in the biggest superhero flick ever, *The Avengers*.

Directed by Joss Whedon (who incidentally coined the "misbehave" line for *Serenity*), the new blockbuster pits four of the most iconic Marvel Comics heroes, along with help from three other well-known characters, against one god of mischief. Sure, Loki does get help from a few lackies, but in Hiddleston's words, *Avengers* is a "solo villain" movie - and Hiddleston is more than ready to relish the fight.

So, who is the man who can take on the superpowered supergroup of his half-brother Thor, Captain America, Hulk, and Iron Man, as well as Nick Fury, Black Widow, and Hawkeye? Born in Westminster, England, the 31-year-old actor is known more for chewing scenery in theatrical productions and dramas than for chewing up (and spitting out?) comic book legends.

Still, after director and Shakespearean buff Kenneth Branagh hired him as fallen prince Loki in the 2011 sci-fi/fantasy flick *Thor*, Hiddleston showed he could transform a two-dimensional funny page antagonist into a believable, sympathetic and just plain menacing three-dimensional baddie. The *Thor* performance was enough to convince fanboy favorite Whedon - who also penned *The Avengers* - that Loki was enough to support an entire movie's worth of conflict.

In a recent interview at the Disney offices in New York, Hiddleston spoke about the challenges of being the big bad in *The Avengers*, as well as the evolution of his character, his work with Whedon, and the giant group hug that was the Hollywood superstar cast. And in case he ever does need a super- villain group, Hiddleston reveals who he'd assemble for his own legion of doom.

This is the second time you're playing the god of mischief. What are the differences between working with Kenneth Branagh and now Joss Whedon?

The thing about the two of them is they actually share more than you might at first imagine, weirdly. Joss is a huge Shakespeare buff, and Ken's actually a closet comic book fanboy. True story. But also, they both have a kind of pan-literacy about storytelling and mythology and literature and comics. They understand classic tropes of storytelling and narrative arcs. They are both immensely passionate people, and really good at leading, really good at inspiring actors. But everyone has a different artistic fingerprint and, of course, whatever that is - whatever that fingerprint is - it changes as you grow older anyway. Ken has a very classical warmth about him, I think. *Thor* is both warm and classical, in turn. Joss is really interested in comedy, as well, within a sci-fi context. He has this huge canvas where eight superheroes are teaming up to save the world and he's brave enough to make it funny.

How does that affect your performance as Loki?

He changes in that he's definitively more menacing. A lot more. Loki, in Thor, is a lost prince and there's a degree of vulnerability and confusion about his identity. In *The Avengers*, he knows exactly who he is. He's fully self-possessed, and he's here with a particular mission.

Why does Loki need to take out vengeance on Earth?

Like all delusional autocrats, he doesn't see it as vengeance. He sees it as a good thing. Essentially, he's come down to Earth to subjugate it; to rule the human race as their king. His primary argument is: This planet is rife and populated by people constantly fighting each other; if they're all united together in their reverence of one king, there will be no war. I'm not sure he's right about that! [laughs]

But that's his reasoning. There's also a motivation about him ... To bring Hemsworth into it, there's still a jealousy that Thor gets to have a kingdom ... Thor gets a kingdom, Thor gets Asgard and Loki has nothing. So he's going to come and make his own kingdom.

You mentioned Joss Whedon's comedy. Do you get any comedy or are you all hellfire and brimstone?

Literally a lot of hellfire and brimstone, but also Joss had two notes for me: One was "more feral," and the other was "enjoy yourself." I think there's a kind of relish that Loki takes in just being who he is. I hope the audience will enjoy it as well.

You had some awesome physicality at the end of Thor. Will we see more of that in The Avengers?

Definitively.

And are you working alone or do you maybe have some cronies?

There's a lot of working alone and a little bit of support as well.

How do you handle taking on eight superheroes as only one bad guy?

It's all in a day's work, man. [laughs]. There's something about Loki that's been expanded. He is an enormously powerful being. He's the god of mischief, and between the end of Thor and the beginning of *Avengers*, he's evolved. It is as if he's been on three years' worth of military training; like he knows a few extra things - tricks up his sleeve. It's really fun. It's hugely physically demanding for me because there's a kind of lethal, yet sinewy strength he has. Sometimes it is about magic and sort of a supernatural power he has, and other times a raw physicality - which is just me and my body, day in, day out.

Either before or during shooting, did you and Chris

[Hemsworth] discuss what interactions you'd have, or how you want to contrast it with what you did in the first movie - or did you purposefully try to separate yourself?

We sat down with Joss individually, and then we talked about it together. But Joss had such good ideas that it was just sort of following his lead. Because it's not a sequel to the *Thor* film - it's a sequel to the *Iron Man* films and the *Captain America* film, as well - and his idea was just so smart. It is a huge compliment that Joss thought what I did in Thor was okay enough to warrant putting me in the next one. And I think Joss has soft spot for Loki; he kind of likes him as a character and thought he could take both Thor and Loki further down that path and make the sibling rivalry a really interesting element of the clash of egos in *The Avengers*.

So there was no amiable critiquing between you and Chris ... in terms of how you guys interacted without Joss?

I'm so blessed to have such a great relationship with Chris as an actor. I remember our first scene together in *The Avengers* and Joss was like, "you really make each other better; that's a really amazing thing to watch..." We just bring some extra baggage that's good because we've played brothers for so long. It is not an intellectual thing. It's like when you play tennis with someone and you're just evenly matched.

Loki doesn't traditionally have as cool of a signature weapon as some of the heroes, so what prop or weapon are you jealous of from The Avengers, and did you get to play with any of those?

Those Avengers are very protective of their props. There was one day where I managed to slightly mischievously steal Captain America's shield and Thor's hammer. I was parading around the subterranean tunnel with the shield - and one of the producers saw me and was like, "What are you doing with those?" [laughs]. Also, because you know nobody can lift Thor's hammer. But you know, I'm not particularly jealous of them, I wouldn't say. I've got quite a good one in this.

You've got this team of superheroes, a super-friend group. Who would be your evil super friends?

My evil super friends? From like, Marvel?

Anywhere: Literature, Marvel, movies. Put them together.

My evil super friends. Um, that's an amazing question. This is going to take me some time. A little bit of help from Darth Vader if I might want to do this. Hans Gruber from *Die Hard*. Maybe Scar from *The Lion King*. Robert Patrick from *Terminator 2* - the T-1000. Probably Schwarzenegger from *Terminator* one.

Any Shakespearean villains?

Iago, absolutely. That's a pretty awesome group of people.

I think you've given the Avengers a run for their money and probably better lines ... What is that fun little toy you're playing with in the trailer?

It's kind of an evolution of the staff that he played with at the end of "Thor. " But that's Odin's spear. At the end of "Thor" it's Odin's spear, but this is his own makeshift staff of destruction.

How versed were you in Marvel mythology before the movies?

In England we have this game called Top Trumps, and it's a really simple game for kids where you have them for racing cars or fighting planes. I had the Marvel superhero Top Trumps and you literally - each superhero is on each card with their vital statistics - and we'd split the deck. You'd have Thor and I'd have Loki, and you'd say, "height: 7-foot 2," and I'd say, "seven foot," which means you'd win Loki from me. So my acquaintance with Marvel superheroes came from the game.

Did you have a favorite?

Galactus. He's the Top Trump in super villains.

How deep into Norse mythology did you go? And how difficult is it to create a character based off a comic, based off a myth?

In many ways I had to defer to canon, to Marvel. They already had a very clear take on the world they wanted to make. But I really sort of borrowed from both. In Marvel mythology, initial incarnations have him just cackling on the rooftops. He's very much a two-dimensional villain. Really, it was only in the Norse myths, when I went back and read some of them how psychologically complex Loki seemed to be. He's the god of lies the god of deception.

Every religion seems to have an agent of chaos. In Greek mythology, it's Dionysus. In Roman mythology, it's Bacchus. In Norse myths, it's Loki and back in the day, many strange things were going down and people would go, "Loki's around." So, I took the fraternal stuff, the family rivalries - which seemed really based in Norse mythology too ... ultimately those stories are quite similar to other stories in all mythologies of different religions.

He's a kind of Lucifer, in a way. There's an image of Loki who's condemned eternally to the Underworld, and there's a snake with a terrible poisonous venom - and Loki's mouth is forced open - and it drips its venom into his mouth for eternity. The goddess of death, I think Hela, is trying to protect him from the venom with a bowl but she occasionally must empty the bowl, which means the snake's venom goes into his mouth. That seems to me to be a kind of archetypal image from any religion about damnation. You get your comeuppance in the end.

Can you talk about the camaraderie on the set? Did anyone say you're a villain and keep you at arm's length?

No, they didn't. All the Marvel films have a code name to keep things secret. *Thor* was called "Frost Bite" or something. *The Avengers* code name was "Group Hug." There was huge camaraderie on set. Probably because none of us could quite believe we were there making that film - in the beginning. Also, we were shooting in Albuquerque and Cleveland.

Of course, nobody is from Albuquerque or Cleveland and no one has got anywhere else to go. So, you finish up at work and it's like, "Does anyone want to have a beer or something?" And we had some fun houses. Chris Hemsworth had a good table-tennis table. I have to say that Loki beats the crap out of both Thor and Captain America at table tennis.

Did you guys actually go out to bars?

We did, yeah. We actually did. It was surreal and really fun. There was one night where Chris sent a round robin text message saying, "Avengers assemble!" We ended up at a bar in Albuquerque and it's just the place where everyone goes to hang out on a Saturday night. What was quite interesting was your regular Albuquerque bargoer sort of looking around going, "Is that Jeremy Renner doing a lunge on the dance floor? I think it is." Or like, "Why are Chris Hemsworth and Scarlett Johansson in this bar dancing together? I don't know what's going on." But yeah, it was really fun.

Did Samuel L. Jackson go with the patch to the bar?

No, he didn't. He might not have been at that bar; he might have had a big round of golf the next morning.

What is Loki's relationship with Stellan Skarsgard in this movie?

This is where I can sense the dot forming on my forehead from the Marvel sniper in the corner of the roof over there. He's got his eye on me ... He plays the same character in The Avengers, Erik Selvig, who is a scientist. He's employed by SHIELD after his encounters with them in Thor to do some work with them.

How will The Avengers avoid the pitfalls of the multiple villain adventure?

I wouldn't really say there's multiple villains. I would say it's solo villain. It's really like Loki. Loki is the bad guy; that doesn't mean he doesn't commandeer help. But everyone's aware that you have eight superheroes. If you had eight villains as well in a two-hour picture, that's a lot of people to care about and get behind. We don't have that time ... I think Joss' great genius, in the way he put the film together, is that these guys don't find it easy to share the space. It's not an easily functioning team. You see a bit in the trailer of Steve Rogers and Tony Stark sort of bickering about "take the suit away, what are you?" I think a lot of the strength and uniqueness of the film comes in the fact there's a lot of square peg/round hole fitting going on between them.

A lot of actors, when they're prepping for a role, lock onto one line that sort of charges them for the character. With Loki being the big bad of The Avengers, what was that line? When you said it, you felt, "Damn straight, I am Loki."

Oh god, um ... There's so many. There's one in the first scene that I'm trying to remember now. I'm playing it back in my mind ... I don't know if I can tell you because it's a bit of a spoiler.

I think you can tell us.

[laughs] Um ... it's connected to the one in the trailer, which is [in character of Loki]: "You were made to be ruled." And I think that smacks of entitlement and arrogance - and a sort of menace, in way, that sums Loki up. There's more where that came from!

Anthony Bourdain Swears He's A Nerd

(June 2012)

Throughout the years, Anthony Bourdain has been cast as a punk-rock chef or as a food snob who will say anything to stir up a controversy.

For some he is the taste-making adventurer behind Travel Channel's *Anthony Bourdain: No Reservations*, the eight-season strong series where globetrotting is experienced through a cinephile's eye, an audiophile's ear, and a gastrophile's stomach. Still others just think of him as that dude who ate warthog anus that one time.

But actually, Anthony Bourdain is a nerd.

Just as a comic book nerd can obsessively debate the merits of publishing companies, artistic elements, story arcs, and creators, Bourdain is a food nerd who knows his restaurants, ingredients, dishes, and chefs. He is a collector and communicator of food data, and you can add movie, music and, yes, comic book nerd to his list of labels as well.

This isn't exactly groundbreaking news. Bourdain uses his literary confessional *Kitchen Confidential: Adventures in the Culinary Underbelly* and *No Reservations* - along with his blogs, essays, books, writing gig for HBO's *Treme*, and presumably his upcoming weekend show on CNN - as a playground to sate big-kid wishes and hang out with icons like Alice Cooper and Harvey Pekar.

Now he is finally able to pursue a successful fanboy's dream of writing a graphic novel for DC Comics. Published through the Vertigo imprint, Bourdain's *Get Jiro!* is a satirical thriller set in a "not too distant future" where master chefs are mob bosses who pull the strings of power in Los Angeles.

The comic's two ruling "families" are the food-savvy but withholding "Internationalists" (led by an Alain Ducasse-meets-Robert Irvine kingpin) and the hypocritical locavore "Vertical Farms" (led by a pretty obvious Alice Waters stand-in). While the outer rim of the city is loaded down with obese, fast-food-gorging denizens, the inner rim is a place where a reservation at primo joints is a sign of influence. Then there's Jira, a mysterious sushi chef who wishes only to serve his culinary craftsmanship without getting caught up in the politics of the kitchen crime world.

Co-written with Joel Rose (*La Pacifica, Kill Kill Faster Faster*) with art by Langdon Foss (*Heavy Metal*), *Get Jira!* is like *Ratatouille* meets *Kill Bill: Vol.1*, where deliciously gratuitous violence is juxtaposed with painstakingly accurate food nerd details. And Bourdain's commentary about celeb-chefs and our food culture is about as sharp as Jiro's tanto knife.

Bourdain joined me over some blood sausage and a Heineken at Brasserie Les Halles - the Downtown Manhattan restaurant where he served as executive chef and remains chef-at-large - to discuss *Get Jira!* his fanboy bona fides and his upcoming appearance at San Diego Comic-Con.

Why are you entering this world of comic books?

I was a serious comic collector and fanboy as a kid. I wanted very badly to draw comic books for a lot of my childhood and early adolescence. So, when you have an unfulfilled dream like that, when years later you find yourself in a position to make a graphic novel - hell yeah, I'm going to do that.

Let's establish your nerd cred. What comic books did you, or do you, collect?

I was a big, early MAD magazine fan. In fact, even when I was a kid, I would collect anthologies of the MAD magazines in the pre- Comics Code era. So I became fascinated with pre-Comics Code work, because the stuff of my generation was all cleaned up. It had the little seal of approval; there was no blood, there was no sex, no antisocial behavior.

And yet, I quickly became aware there was this whole, nasty world from the '50s, and I hunted that stuff down. Also, Will Eisner's *The Spirit*. When the undergrounds came along, the West Coast stuff, it totally blew my mind. And I liked early Marvel, when Spider-Man was still neurotic and Steve Ditko was still doing him. There was also a period in the '60s where people like Jim Steranko and Barry [Windsor-Smith] were really changing the game. You had four-page splash panels. People were doing psychedelic themes and riffing on various styles. Comics suddenly became really interesting, so I read those on a contemporaneous basis while also collecting dark, violent, antisocial stuff from the '50s.

And my father had turned me on to Will Eisner and *The Spirit*, and the Jules Feiffer collection - so I was reading that stuff as well.

For No Reservations, you've always relied on a cinematic quality for episodes, so you did the same for the comic?

Will Eisner was famous for framing and pacing his panels like early Orson Welles or early noir directors. It was really moody, and he'd use lighting and black-and-white in a way that really added drama to the story, and pace. Obviously, those were influences. I just want to tell a ripping good yarn with lots of blood in it, with food that's ridiculously correct. And a satirical, humorous element was desirable.

You're presenting Get Jiro! to Comic-Con, and that's become a venue where every pop culture entrant goes to sell their wares. Is there any concern that people will think you're just cashing in on the trend?

The minute you emerge from your cellar with a guitar, and play for another person, arguably, you've sold out. I mean, is anything pure? To quote that great man, Omar Little [from *The Wire*], "It's all in the game."

Preying on the hopes and dreams of fanboys is the very backbone of the comics and newspaper industry dating back to 1939 - and certainly the backbone of the music industry. In fact, I can't think of an industry that's not the backbone of. So yeah, I don't have an ideological problem with, "Wow, these people are keeping it real." I mean, there's a 120-fucking-thousand of them out there. I was at a comic-con back in '69, one of the first years, at the Pennsylvania Hotel, across from Penn Station. It was a room about twice this size with a bunch of guys who looked like Comic Book Guy, with some boxes and folding tables. Were those the good old days? I don't think so.

Have you had any stand-out DC Comics/Vertigo moments since you signed on?

Yeah, they gave me a really big stack of very cool books. Swag! At the end of the day, I'm a super nerdy fanboy.

Since the food in Get Jiro! is so accurate, could we expect a spinoff recipe book?

I'm not qualified to tell people how to do the food that Jira makes. I'm qualified enough to eat it, and in a general way, say if it's really good or really, really, really good. But I'm not an expert. It's an incredible testament to the work that Langdon Foss did that he got the artwork so right and so careful.

'Falling Skies' Colin Cunningham Reigns As Pope

(June 2012)

John Pope is not Han Solo. The character on *Falling Skies* is indeed a scruffy-looking scoundrel who - when he's not killing aliens with a rebel force - spends his time cracking one-liners and acting cool. But Han Solo was just waiting to join a resistance group so he could be a good guy and get the girl. Meanwhile, there's a distinct feeling in TNT's alien invasion series, premiering its second season on January 17 at 9 p.m., that Pope isn't a crook with a heart of gold, but is actually only acting good until he doesn't have to.

And that's just the way Colin Cunningham likes it.

An experienced actor who became a sci-fi mainstay with his role of Major Paul Davis in the *Stargate* franchise, Cunningham's street cred within the genre was also helped by work on *The 4400* and *Sanctuary* and several other projects. But it's his portrayal of breakout character Pope that has Cunningham chewing up scenery and spitting out some of the series' best lines (not unlike fellow rascal, Norman Reedus ' Daryl on *The Walking Dead*).

Arriving in the second episode of Season One, Pope could have easily been a throwaway bad guy of the week. But Cunningham's character quickly gained traction as the guy that the 2nd Massachusetts resistance force didn't particularly like but did value in their battle against invading aliens. Throughout the season, Pope performed cowardly, brave, clever, stupid and hilarious acts that all seemed to make sense to him alone. And that kind of across-the-spectrum behavior makes him a thrill to watch.

But if you think Pope's reign as the resident scoundrel on

Falling Skies is over just because he acted heroically in the Season One finale, you've got another thing coming. Colin Cunningham joined us to speak about the upcoming season of the show, and how his character might develop. And Cunningham even offers an opinion about his own chances against aliens.

Just to start off with, what is a thing that you just can't wait to have the fans see with the second season?

To tell you the truth, it's the first episode ... The premiere, the first two episodes, is absolutely off the chart. And I will say I've been doing a lot of ADR (additional dialogue recording) looping at different voice studios and stuff lately, and so I've been able to see a lot of the show. It's absolutely superb. So the hardest part for me right now is to be so excited about something that no one else can see. Even in terms of the press, no one's really seen it yet. So, I guess it's tough to hang onto all this excitement without having a place to really express it.

Since it has been a couple months since you wrapped, do you ever interact with the other cast members and say, 'Man, I was just doing the ADR and this thing that you do, You really nailed it.' Do you ever reach out and circle back on what you're seeing as it comes together?

Yeah, absolutely, because there's also a lot of scenes that you don't see. You'll maybe read the script but you're not necessarily in those scenes. Not that he didn't do a fantastic job in Season One, but I've had to compliment Noah Wyle on his work this season because it is absolutely superb. Another exciting thing about seeing some of the footage or going to see the stuff in the studio is that you finally get to see the contributions of everyone else behind the camera. I mean, we kind of knew what we did on the day, but it is so rewarding and so exciting to see what these incredible, incredibly talented people - whether it be the effects, or how the shows all come together with the score, the editing everything - you really get to see everyone else's contribution to the process and that's incredibly fulfilling.

We all want to see additional growth with characters, to see

them grow in this new world. With that, are you afraid that Pope is going to lose some of that edge, and he's going to become too loveable?

Absolutely, positively not. I know what you're saying. It's like he always had this little spark of light in him and you think it would grow and his heart would get bigger. No. We did not go that direction in Season Two. If anything, it becomes a little darker, a little edgier and a little bit more self-serving. He's still quite the mystery. His motives are still entirely selfish. I think they've definitely done a 'right' thing in continuing down that road as opposed to veering away from it.

Do you feel like you have a real sense of his voice, at this point, that you might interject and say what's written in the script doesn't feel like Pope?

No, if anything ... Well, first off, you're absolutely correct. I do feel, you feel confident going in that you've got a voice for this particular character. But I will say now, after two seasons, I really know who he is, and the voice is just a lot closer. I understand it more now - not that I didn't know it before, but I've got a real sense of who this guy is. That said, the writers are so fantastic on this show. The voice really starts with them. My job can be challenging at first in putting the character together, but we're all sort of on the same page and I think we all understand a little bit more. They understand what I'm bringing to the table, which makes them all the more confident in terms of what they're going to write.

Your character is definitely a fan favorite. People like to see him show up and chew some scenery, and you get a lot of really good one-liners. But when you think about it, the origin, he is a bad guy. When we're first introduced - when we really think about the things that potentially took place at the high school - he's a really bad guy. So, do you think there's some sort of cognitive dissonance with fans that they like the bad guy so much?

When I was putting my own thoughts together, especially as

you mentioned, at the high school, I never thought that Pope was a part of any of that kind of stuff. But, at the same token, he certainly knew about it and turned a blind eye to it. But I think the circumstance of trying to stay alive, your value system becomes a little more tweaked. It's literally about eating and surviving from day to day as opposed to, let's say, lesser crimes.

War certainly creates strange bedfellows. And here you've got the 2nd Mass literally embrace a guy like John Pope because he does serve a purpose. Whereas, if we were in regular nine-to-five civilian peace time, there's no way the two would ever meet. They would be at odds.

So yeah, I don't want to say he's a bad guy, but he's certainly not a good guy. I think the neat thing about the character which, maybe perhaps resonates with audiences, is that he does what he says.

He's very simple in terms of his outlook. He has a very, very simple, defined sense of right and wrong - and it's kill or be killed. There is no grey area with John Pope. You either do it or you don't. It's either right or it's wrong. You don't sit and cry about it. You don't ponder about it too much. This is this. I think he's often baffled because of some of the other, more nobler emotions and values such as compassion and empathy. He just doesn't see any place for it in a world that's gone so crazy. It's literally about survival. I don't think he's encumbered by such a value system. It's literally about survival. So I think him being within earshot of a lot of things that the 2nd Mass discusses, he just finds it absolutely ridiculous. Just pick up a gun and pull the trigger. And that's the end of it.

If he had to put together, not the 2nd Mass but his own kind of, let's say, Avengers-type supergroup, who would Pope want to fight alongside?

[laughs] Oh my God. Jesus, there's a question. I've got no freaking idea ... It could be a good guy; it could be a bad guy. What was the character that Mickey Rourke played in the Iron Man series?

Oh, yeah, Whiplash?

Yeah, he'd hang out with Whiplash, I think, for the weekend.

Well, certainly the hairstyles are similar.

I think him and Whiplash would definitely go out and have a beer every now and again.

How about thoughts on UFOs? Have you ever seen one? Do you believe in them? And why do you think we're so fascinated with this other life out there?

Do I think we're alone? No. Are we the only ones that have ever been? No. Have I seen things that I can't explain? Absolutely. Do I know that they were flying saucers in the sky? I don't know. I've seen a couple of things in the sky that absolutely had me baffled. As to whether people are coming down and stealing people out of their homes in the middle of the night and doing anal probes? I don't know. That might be another subject. But sure, man. I think it's wonderful.

That's what science fiction does. It gets you to ponder these questions and these thoughts. It's a very, very big universe. I'm so blessed to work on such a show that I think, for people, sometimes when you think of alien beings that they would come and somehow be more evolved than us, spiritually and what have you. That may not necessarily be the case. They may not be evolved at all. They may be just as brutal as anything we've ever seen on this planet. There's no telling what's out there. That's why you've always got to fight the good fight.

Noah Wyle: 'Falling Skies A Total Immersion Experience'

(June 2012)

Noah Wyle has built a career portraying thinkers. Whether it was as Dr. John Carter in E.R., Flynn Carsen in the *Librarian* series, Steve Jobs in *Pirates of the Silicon Valley* and, most recently, as a father and college history professor-turned-human resistance fighter Tom Mason in TNT's alien apocalypse series Falling Skies, Wyle has mastered the performance of intellectuals who think before acting.

It is appropriate, then, that Wyle the actor comes across in much the same way. A soft-spoken man with more than two decades of work on his resume, he isn't the badass action hero type who attempts to imbue his characters - or his interviews about those characters - with vein-bulging machismo. Instead, the 41-year- old is thoughtful about his fictional role as a leader of human survivors on Falling Skies, which debuts its second season on June 17 at 9 p.m., and as his role of leading actor and a producer on the ensemble show.

Executive-produced by Steven Spielberg, the first season of Falling Skies premiered June 2011 as a family-friendlier cousin to *The Walking Dead*, except with advanced, insectoid aliens.

These "skitters" appear in ships above major Earth cities and make quick work of upending civilizations. And the humans they don't kill, typically kids, are fitted with a parasitic harness and become mindless slaves. Wyle's Tom Mason comes into the picture as a widower with three sons (Drew Roy, Connor Jessup and Maxim Knight) who joins the 2nd Massachusetts resistance force. Applying his knowledge as a military historian, he quickly established himself as a capable second-in-command under Will Patton's Captain Weaver. Also along for the alien fight was doctor/love interest Anne (Moon Bloodgood), roguish anti-hero Pope (Colin Cunningham), strong silent type Dai (Peter Shinkoda) amongst others.

At the end of the first season, Wyle's 2nd Mass dealt a symbolic blow to the aliens by destroying part of their massive ship over Boston, and by deflecting an attack at their home base. But it also had Tom Mason departing with the spindly, grey aliens who command the skitters to learn more about their mission.

Wyle sat to chat about taking the lead on *Falling Skies*, the series evolution between seasons into a darker show - and avoiding problems from the first season - and the toll a show of this magnitude takes on him.

It's been a few months since you've wrapped, so in that timeframe, what are you thinking about with the show? Are you going back and rethinking the choices you made about a character or do you just sort of pack it up and set it aside?

Of all the jobs I've worked, this one is a particularly hard one to decompress from. It took a long time to get my feet back under me and feel normal again once I got home. Probably because of the survival instinct, I did put it to bed. I said, 'Well, I did the best I could and I'll revisit it when I have to sell it.' So I really haven't thought that much about it. As I get closer and closer to air date, and I talk about it more and more, I'm in the anxietal stage of going back and rethinking all my choices. So it's both.

Why is it a hard project to decompress from?

It's a pretty total immersion experience. Four-and-a-half months away from your comfort zone and your family - living in a hotel room - and working 17, 18, 19-hour days in a fairly bleak world, and having to maintain that headspace is a tough undertaking.

Plus, it's a physically tough show to both produce and to execute. We identified a couple of significant flaws last year; one being that the show doesn't work as well during the day as it does at night. So that meant that we were going to be shooting mostly on a split schedule of going to work midday and working until sun up. So you were keeping vampire hours and living on a different time clock than your friends and family.

And the other is that the show doesn't work as well when the group is stationary and holding a position. It works much better when they are on the move, being hunted - which means that we were going to be doing a lot less interior work and a lot more exterior work in the elements in Vancouver in the winter; all of which made for exciting TV and fairly arduous experience. It's always tough to regulate coming out of something like that.

Are you able to bring your kids while in Vancouver?

It's harder and harder. We shot the first season in Toronto and they were two years younger than they are now, and I brought them every two weeks for two weeks at a stretch. Which seemed to work out but my son's got soccer and my daughter's got ballet, and they both have school and they both have friends and lives.

Sometimes, it feels a little selfish to pull them out of their comfort zone and routine to live in a hotel room where I'm working 18 or 19 hours anyway - and not really able to spend that much time with them. So we struck a bit more of a balance this year. They came up. I came down on weekends when I could. They came up for longer weekends more often. It's tough. It's not like they can come and be with me the whole time.

Because of the experience you've had in the business, in a lot of ways, you're the elder statesman on the cast. Do you find that you have to take on that role?

That's an unintentionally loaded question because it's one I'm still grappling with. E.R. I sort of inherited, over the years, and moved up the call sheet as other characters left the show. So I never really felt that was my show as much as it was a communal effort. This was the first time I started Day One on the call sheet, at the top of the call sheet. I was excited to tackle that challenge to see if I could carry an ensemble - and a young ensemble, at that - and how I want to do it, and who I thought did it really well, in my experience, and who I could pull and draw from to make that an easier experience for everybody.

But in practice, it's a tough thing to do. Everybody comes to the table with varying degrees of experience and different work ethics. Sometimes, it's an unenviable place to be when you feel like you're a hall monitor and telling people to show up on time and know their lines and hang up their costumes and whatnot. And other times, it's a pleasure to have a creative seat at the table, and for the first time in my career, really feel like I've got a creative stake and sense of ownership in the material I'm involved in. So, it's both.

In your career, you've played a doctor, a librarian, a historian. You've done wonders for higher education within popular culture.

[laughs] Having not gone to college, I think I'm atoning for the

end of a mission.

Do you find that your character Tom's biggest weakness is that he is so much of a thinker? Is that his strength and weakness?

Well, that was what was appealing about the arc. Again, there's an analogy to be made with E.R. in terms of what attracted me to the project. When I looked at the pilot script for E.R. and I saw that John Carter was having his first day on the job in the pilot, I realized very quickly that he had the largest arc ahead of him.

Because everybody else had to start off with a high level of proficiency and confidence, and that I would get a really juicy landscape to be able to play.

Similarly, you take a character that's lived a very cloistered life in the realm of academia, an intellectual - and throw him into a situation where that skill set seems totally useless and esoteric - seemed like it was going to provide another good arc as he had to become more physically adept, come to terms with feelings of inadequacy, a real reluctance to step into a leadership role that he doesn't feel he's adequately prepared for. And then there's the learning curve of discovering, because he taught history, that a lot of times there are historical precedents that could inform present-day decision making on a tactical level, that was a significant turning point for him. The realization that because he was a teacher, he's, in a lot of ways, better served to lead a civilian army than somebody that has a military background would be because he's used to conveying information and instilling a sense of confidence and inspiration in kids, in particular.

So it all makes for a nice well-rounded arc of a guy who starts confident and gets incredibly unconfident and starts to build himself back up again. Having a character like Captain Weaver played by the incomparable Will Patton, who starts off ideologically on the opposite end of the leadership spectrum and getting to play this sort of transference that occurs of the course of two years between them where he adopts more of the humanistic side of Tom, and Tom adopts more of the militaristic side of Weaver, seemed like great storytelling.

Do you believe in aliens? Have you ever seen a UFO?

Never seen one. Don 't really know anyone who has. But who am I to argue with Stephen Hawking?

Hawking says that if we were to encounter aliens, they' re going to be nasty. They're going to be like us: Conquerors. We see that reflected in popular culture. Even Steven Spielberg, his early alien stuff was kind of friendly, cuddly, benevolent. As his career has gone on, it's sort of shifted to malevolent, nastier creatures. What do you think that shift says about us?

I think, historically, science fiction is a genre that seems to come into fashion on the heels of some great technological advancement that creates a divide of opinion as to whether this is positive or negative for us. You saw it, certainly, with the advent of the atomic bomb, with the moon landing. And I think we're experiencing it now with our increasing dependence on technology for basic survival and communication. It sort of makes us schizophrenic in a sense. It seems that we're either on the brink of utopia or our own version of the Roman ruin. That's why these things are sort of back in the zeitgeist again.

Can Tom spend so much time away, with these aliens that he spent an entire season killing, and then come back and not have gotten too close? Will he be tainted because he's been embedded with them?

I think it will be an easy transition. I think he gets off that ship inexplicably and suspiciously let go, but with a very clear understanding that there is no negotiation to be had. And there's no peace to be brokered. That this is going to be a fight to the last man and to the last stand, and that whatever sort of hope he retains about the kind of society we might be able to rebuild, needs to be shelved for a while until the threat is eliminated. So, I think he comes back pretty focused - and a lot more amenable to adopting a pretty strong dogmatic approach to dealing with them. A Skitter in a Mech suit.

The show is a family sci-fi show, and we know that it tends to be going in a darker direction this season. Is there no going back to sort of a, by comparison, lighthearted Season One?

Well, every episode we try to show advantage, disadvantage. The disadvantages are obvious. We're living in a high state of deprivation, under a constant level of threat, on the move, zero creature comforts, danger around every turn. But there's certain advantages that we try to showcase as well.

In the midst of all that, the quality of the relationships becomes a lot more authentic, and Tom is a far better father post-apocalypse than he was pre-apocalypse. He's, out of necessity, forced to negotiate with and comes to terms with very desperate personalities who he probably would've had nothing to do with under normal circumstances. A celebration is a true celebration. A birth is a real ritual. Things that we sort of take for granted now become extremely significant then.

I think that allows the show to retain a sense of hope and optimism. In the face of it, people are still going to be people. They're still going to need to laugh and to love and procreate, and all the rest of it. And we did pretty well balancing that, I think.

When you wrap the season, are you happy to go back to a clean-shaven face? Or is this just part of your lifestyle now, rocking the beard?

There were periods of time when I was really excited and I had fantasies about, on the last night of shooting, as soon as they called, 'Wrap,' going right to the makeup trailer and shaving. But then you get producers, of which I am one, saying, 'Wait a second, we might need to reshoot something; don't shave yet.' And then, we came back and there were press photos they wanted to do, and promo spots for the network where they wanted us in character so I had to keep the beard for that. Eventually, I just got sick of it and shaved it off.

And I guess you've got a little bit of time before having to grow it back. Do you know what the prospects are already for Season Three?

Well, confidence is high. We did pretty well last season. I think we'd have to have a significant drop off in our numbers to not justify it given the level of investment the network has put into it. If everything goes as planned, we'll be back to work around September. But we won't get the official pick-up until we start airing a couple of episodes and see how they're doing.

You mentioned to me before you were hoping to do Shakespeare in the Park at some point. Are you really aiming to do more theater?

I would love it. I would love it. You know, all my ambitions are mitigated by fatherhood and theater is the one casualty that I haven't quite been able to reconcile because nighttime is daddy time. I run my own company in L.A., I would very much like to do a play as sort of the gymnasium for me. But I haven't been able to do it for a little while so I'm sort of chomping at the bit to do it.

Is there a show in particular that you want to put on? And would you also star in it?

Yeah. I don't have one identified yet. I don't have my star-making piece of material [laughs]. I just recently, actually, took part in a benefit for the Ohio Valley playwright conference, which I do every year. And every year we honor another playwright. We've done Terrence McNally. The year after that we did Jon Robin Baitz, and this year we did Bill Cain.

I'm not sure if you're familiar with Bill Cain's work, but he's an extremely prolific, and growing in popularity, playwright. And he wrote a play called, Equivocation, which was a really wonderful comedy set in Shakespearian England and is about Shakespeare and his acting troupe, which I thought was very funny. I read the Shakespeare part and just had a ball doing it. So it's the one that jumps to mind.

And finally, what other apocalypse scenario would you like to visit as an actor?

I feel fairly sated on that front, at the moment! [laughs].

A Tale of Two Comic-Cons
(July 2012)

It was the best of cons, it was the worst of cons, it was the age of fan celebration, it was the age of crass commercialism, it was the epoch of true believers, it was the epoch of sell outs, it was the season of the nerd, it was the season of Hollywood.

Never before had I felt such a sense of belonging accompanied by one that I was out of place.

San Diego Comic-Con 2011: After a day of conducting press interviews and covering panels, I hit the Con floor to pick up some swag before booths closed. There were more than 130,000 attendees and I think I bumped into every single one of them. My eyes were in constant danger from too-close interactions with passing wings, lightsabers, claws and more than a few Dalek protrusions - and I had no Nick Fury patch to cover any resulting eye loss.

Despite the threat, and claustrophobia, I was with my people. With a newly acquired foam Sword of Omens from *ThunderCats* and an Oscorp Industries ID badge from Sony's *The Amazing Spider-Man* display, I headed to the Hard Rock Hotel across the street from the convention center in pursuit of a Her Universe *Sharktopus* tee from the Syfy shop.

People lined up outside the Hard Rock club, and my finely tuned instinct to pursue free food and booze (when not pursuing swag) kicked in. An SUV limo pulled up, the very important posse of a very important person filed into the club, and the nerds outside were left with a snapshot of a celeb and an encounter with the superhero of the Con's party circuit - the Velvet Rope Guardian.

The message is clear: This is not for you, you don't belong, return to your area.

When Hollywood started showing up at the Con a few years

back, it brought exclusive happenings that your average fan wouldn't be invited to, or likely even hear about. Nerds who complain they liked the Con before it was cool often mention this; the celebs show up to shill and court fan buzz but don't really want anything to do with them after an hour-long panel or autograph session.

However, another nerd contingent is fine with that. They argue the pretty people should retreat to their swanky soirees and do their thing because they'd prefer to hang with fellow geeks at multiple open-access joints, like last year's "Cowboys & Aliens" saloon or the Cafe Diem from *Eureka*. There are enough events like the masquerade or zombie walk to keep Comic-Con a nerd event. To focus on the celebrity culture and crave insider status is to miss the point of the Con anyhow.

Then there is the hybrid celeb/fan event, like this year's "Con of the Dead," sponsored by horror network and website FEARnet. By distributing tickets to 300 participants of the zombie walk, and then giving away more through genre co-sponsors like DreadCentral.com, the party creates an exclusive-to-fans vibe. Not everyone will get in, but those who do will be able to mingle with horror personalities and get a chance to feel important.

So is SDCC a tale of two cons - or maybe two and a half? Has it become too much for the famous, or is it still for the fans? To answer the question, we reached out to some trusted nerds and Con regulars for their take.

ADAM GREEN (*Holliston, Hatchet*):

"If my name is on that list and I can't bring in friends that aren't, I won't go. That's where Comic-Con starts to get a little disgusting to me. One of the things I'm most proud of is the 'Con of the Dead' party - FEARnet and Dark Sky Films are doing everything they can to make sure fans get tickets ... so that it won't just be a bunch of people that see each other in the business.

You're there for the fans ... why do you need every agent and manager from Hollywood in there to drink their free drinks? Get the fans in there; that's how you're going to sell your product and make those relationships."

SAM WITWER (*Being Human, Star Wars: The Clone Wars*):

"The parties for me are just, 'I can see people that I haven't seen for a while' ... that has nothing to do with any kind of weird elitism or anything. There are people there you have relationships with. They congregate at these parties. I don't like the loud music and all the fancy stuff about it, but I like seeing the people."

MORGAN SPURLOCK (Comic-Con *Episode IV: A Fan's Hope, Super Size Me*):

"I meet people who end up getting into parties all the time. I think if you're somebody who can get your hustle on, you can get into a lot of things ... As a geek, as a fan, to get to meet people that you idolize and put up on some sort of pedestal is fantastic."

DEBORAH ANN WOLL (*True Blood*):

"I think part of the fun of Comic-Con is it's an opportunity for the fans to become involved in what would usually feel like an insider, entertainment-industry world. It does feel like, sometimes there are the two worlds - but then there are people like me who are actually part of both worlds and actually prefer the geek world. I don't go to any of the parties, really. I've never been very comfortable at parties, so I much prefer the panels and dressing up in costume."

LEVAR BURTON (*Star Trek: The Next Generation*):

"It's less about the fan experience. The marketing machinery of Hollywood is really the engine driving the train in San Diego now (and I understand the same is true of Jacob Javits Center at New York Comic-Con). Look, I believe in the free-market economy and I get that Hollywood has finally recognized the value that fan culture, and specifically geek culture, represents to them, in terms of a demographic that they can market to. And unfortunately, it's an atmosphere and an environment that isn't as much fun as a fan-run convention. I try and make every encounter with a fan a positive one because that's my point of view on being a celebrity."

BRUCE CAMPBELL (*Burn Notice, The Evil Dead*):

"The city of Los Angeles empties out for Comic-Con. They're conducting show business that's around some other kind of crazy theme. It's a way for studios to see if people are really interested.

Then, on the geek side, if you will, they still have a ball because they get to see everything bigger than life. They get to see movie stars talking about [some stuff]. They get to see more now than they ever did ... I do think it's too commercial now because

Hollywood has muscled into our little convention world and started elbowing us in the face. And I'm like, ' Hey, why don't you eat it, man? ... Sometimes it takes a little bit of the fun out of it."

KEVIN SMITH (*Clerks, Mallrats*):

"It's like when anything gets discovered, man, and everyone starts to embrace it. The world that builds up around it is bigger than the world that created it ...

Comic-Con itself hasn't changed. It has changed over the course of the last however many years because they doubled in capacity, but it's the same commitment to programming, it's fucking free, it's nonprofit. There's not some person upstairs going 'Aaaaah,' just bathing in money. They put it right back into the con itself ...

There are some people that want to market on the backs of that, which is fine. You bring in money to the geek community? I got no fucking complaints. I'm not one of these cats that go, 'Leave us alone, go the fuck away.' I don't have the garage band fan mentality where it's like, 'Oh, this shit is less cool because more people like it.' Bullshit. It doesn't matter. I'm one of those cats that's like, the more the merrier. I know people who are of the mindset that the more people that like it, the less cool it becomes.

But those cats have to let that version of the Con go. It's never coming back. It is only going to get bigger and bigger ... As you see on all the banners coming through, it's no longer a simple comic- con. It's no longer just about, I'm going to find back issues I don't have.' It is celebrating the popular arts ...

It's beyond fandom. If you want a fandom con, I can point you in the direction of plenty. You can sit around and do time like this with me, even if you're not a journalist. Wonder Con is also run by Comic-Con International and they do a hell of a job in terms of intimacy. It has always been referred to as the creator's con or the fan's con - because there is more intimate time. But if you're looking for intimacy or one-on-one, forget it. This is the circus.

This is Lollapalooza. It is just massive at this point.

It's cool for me as a fan. I'm not one of these people that's like, 'I wish the fucking whores would get out; why can't we throw the money changers out of the temple.' It's not that holy of a place."

Big Troubles in Little 'Haven': Emily Rose, Eric Balfour, Lucas Bryant On Season Three

(September 2012, with Erin Lilley)

After nearly a year since new episodes aired, it's time to return to Haven. But don't let the name of the fictional town from the Syfy supernatural series fool you, there are more troubles than ever in store for Season Three, which begins tonight, Sept. 21 at 10 p.m.

Based loosely on Stephen King's novella, *The Colorado Kid*, the series focuses on FBI Agent Audrey Parker (Emily Rose) as she discovers the idyllic small town, she's stumbled into is plagued by "troubles," various super-powered afflictions with often deadly, or at the very least, dangerous effects. Adding to the mystery, Audrey finds that this may not be the first time - or even the first lifetime - she's visited *Haven*. Aiding Audrey's investigation, for the most part, are Nathan Wuornos (Lucas Bryant), the chief of police, and Duke Crocker (Eric Balfour), an ethically challenged boat runner.

Debuting July 2010, the show saw a five percent rise in viewership over the second season and became a hit for the network. Both seasons are now available on DVD/Blu-ray, and the third season of the mythology-driven show marks a new chapter of Haven as the summer series moves to the fall schedule. Although that ups the pressure on the show, cast and crew feel a sense of validation and say the move signals confidence from Syfy.

Rose, Bryant, and Balfour and executive producer Lloyd Segan joined us for an interview to discuss the show's movie, as well as a third season that they promise will answer long-standing questions (including last season's cliffhanger "Where is Audrey Parker?") as well as offering new mysteries to unravel, new faces, romance, haunted houses - and time travel? As if that's not enough, the cast even opens up about ghosts, and throws a challenge down to Kris Williams of *Ghost Hunters International*.

I've been seeing the Escape to Haven hash tag promotion and the video and it makes me wonder if the troubles become more organized this season like they tried to do at the end of last season and how that might affect your characters?

Eric Balfour: I think the coolest thing about what we're trying to do with the Twitter stories and the online sort of interactions and storylines is really to enhance the experience of the show for everybody. It's not necessarily something that nobody else is doing at this point.

But we're really trying to, I think, do it in the unique way that makes it exciting for the viewers and makes it exciting for the fans to feel like they get a little bit extra and a little bit more than just from watching the episodes on television. And then hopefully, also enhance the experience of watching the episodes.

Lloyd Segan: Yes - well, that's - I couldn't have said it more eloquently than Eric did. I think what's neat, what this initiative is, and it is unique in that we were the first people to really take social media and take it to another level last year with Vince and Dave's experience and interaction with our audience.

This year we're going way beyond that and integrating these opportunities for our audience to interact and sharing with them gems that are going to be happening over the season. And also helping people who have never seen the show before and getting them excited about possibly joining our community.

One of the big things on the show is obviously kind of the love interest and everything going on and Nathan's now starting to open up and kind of tell Duke what's going on and everything. Can you talk about how all that's going to kind of develop throughout the season?

Lucas Bryant: Yes, I guess. Nathan is now in a place where - in the second season we saw him sort of uncomfortably thrust into the position of police chief. And in the third season he's kind of manned up a bit and he's accepted his position and taken more - I think, taken more initiative. And our - Duke – and my relationship with Duke this season takes a number of turns, doesn't it? I guess it comes - it goes - we fall in love and then we break up again.

But, you know, the cool thing about - I guess it shows many sorts of love stories and Nathan and Duke are sort of arch enemies or each other's nemesis in many ways. But what really is under that is a great affection for each other and I think both of them really care about each other and rely on each other.

So when they get to occasionally team up, we have a blast doing that and we get - we did get an opportunity to do more of that in season three and I think they do - they work better together than against each other.

Eric Balfour: I like to think of Nathan and my character's relationship as sort of like When Harry Met Sally. And I think now we're sort of in the second act of When Harry Met Sally when I think they've probably slept together at this point but it was a little awkward and they're going to have to now realize how much they actually mean to each other.

No, I think, you know, the show obviously has this really exciting element of the troubles and every week you have these fantastic scares and mysteries. But, at the core of this show, it really is about this love story and this triangle between these three characters and about the different relationships that Emily's character, Audrey, has to these two men. And they sort of represent different components of her own personality, if it's okay for me to say that.

And I think what the writers even told us at the beginning of the season and what was most exciting for me and I think is going to be incredibly exciting for the viewers who tune in this year is that this love triangle is really going to just be like a rubber band. And it's going to expand and contract and move and grow and cause rifts and strife and it really is dynamic this season.

And I think that's what's going to be ultimately I just think the most exciting part for the fans of this show because we really do get to take the audience on a ride this year with the love story that goes on between these characters. As friends, as lovers and it's my favorite part of the show this season.

What did you guys each learn about your characters this year as - without, of course, spoiling too much?

Emily Rose: Well, it's interesting. I think Audrey, the first season she just kind of is curious when she finds a connection with the place of Haven, that there's something there about herself. And then by season three, she's facing some really, really dark, dark, dark questions regarding who she is and there's a - sort of a clock in play. So, it's really, really hard and I think she's in a really, really hard place all season. It's not a fun place for her to be in mentally.

And I think - it was interesting, we filmed the second to the last day yesterday when we were finishing up the season and there's this one scene at the very, very end of the season where Audrey is able to kind of ask all of those questions that she sort of dealt with and it's just neat. It's neat to have posed a lot of questions to the audience for so long and then finally have a season where some of those things are addressed or directly asked and to see what kind of answers are given is really, really interesting.

Eric Balfour: Yes, and, I mean, for Duke this season, Duke is going to have really decide who he wants to be in this world and he's going to get pushed to the limit and has to make some really tough choices about who he wants to be in this town and in this world and to these two people in life.

Lucas Bryant: And for Nathan, I learned that Nathan has a lot more ability to find his private parts and strap them on then he might've necessarily known. That's maybe a crude way to say it but, it's the truth.

Haven has generally been a summer series but this year it's moving to a fall premiere. What was the motivation for this and do you think it will help or hurt the show?

Lloyd Segan: Well, I can give you what is the total honest answer without posturing whatsoever. I think it shows the strength of the show and the franchise to the network and that the network sees great growth potential in the fall. And they are very excited about the two-hour block that now has been created with our marriage to WWE and obviously our connection to that is even deeper now with the role of Dwight played by Adam Copeland a.k.a. Edge.

And so, I believe, as they believe that there is greater opportunity for us now to reach an even more diverse audience. And so that is the goal and aspiration and I think it's a pretty wonderful vote of confidence for the show.

Eric Balfour: Yes, and I think from a - just from the standpoint of the cast we were both excited and nervous about the prospect of this. I think on the one hand what Lloyd just expressed, we all felt. I mean, it felt like we'd been sort of been validated that they believed in us enough to put us on the fall schedule.

The challenge of that, obviously, is in the fall there are more shows, there are more options for people to tune in to, there's more competition. And so there is - with great risk there is great reward and I think that's what we're facing right now.

So I think the one thing I would just like to express is that that's why it is so important - given the hiatus that we've had, you know, whereas normally we would be on in the summer a few more extra months, we really, really need journalists like yourself, fans of the show, everyone who loves the show and wants to see it continue to really get out there.

What in the new season are you most excited for fans to see?

Lucas Bryant: Well, I think the season just feels like the show's really got its game on. Everything the scripts this year are hugely ambitious and I think succeeded in producing hugely ambitious storylines. The stakes are that much higher. Like, everything's just kind of juiced up a bit.

For people that enjoyed following the first two seasons felt like it's been a sort of steady increase on intrigue and it - and it's like the lid gets blown off a lot of it this year. And so I'm excited to see how people react to that. A lot of big questions and big mysteries are answered in a way that they haven't been up until now. And I think just each show is bigger and better than ever before.

Eric Balfour: Yes, I'm most excited about the fans getting to see just how deep down the rabbit hole this show goes this year. It really goes - it really just sort of opened Pandora's box and it kind of lets everything out of the bag, it's pretty cool.

Emily Rose: Yes, I think that's the neat thing about the genre of sci-fi is that a lot of things are possible and this season with the methodology of this show, we actually go into a lot of those questions and see some of those answers sort of face to face. I'm really excited about the finale, we just shot that. And I think that by the end, people are going to be like what the heck, you know. So that's exciting to me to have shot the finale and to feel like it's a strong, strong season. You know, looking back and going oh, that was a cool episode.

Then that was that episode. Oh, and that was that episode. You know, it's like it's really neat to feel like you have a - like a very large, large amount of very strong episodes. That's exciting for a cast, to look at their season to see that.

Each of you have gotten much more of your backstories as the show has progressed, coming into the show and as time has gone on, how much have each of you have known about your character's history? Have you found it out when we found it out or did you come in kind of getting a bible on your character to know what was going to be filled in?

Emily Rose: No, I think I said this before in interviews, so I hate to say it again but it is true. I've never in my life ever played a character where I didn't know the backstory on her where that was the story, was filling in the blanks. Like, I have very, very basic things and then at the end of Season One, I was told all of those things weren't real. So I've never - in every acting class you ever go to, your questions that you're asked are: Who are you? Where do you come from? What were your parents like? What kind of social status do you have? All these things. And a lot of those questions were unanswered mysteries for Audrey and then she finds out she may not even really be Audrey.

So it's - it wasn't anything that - I mean, we had some discussions about, you know her training as an FBI agent, those things that were kind of inherent to who she was and to - for the day to day of the show to work. But when all that gets thrown out, it's mainly just been a discovery of who she is and just living in the unknown and discovering that on a daily basis. Did you guys have a bible?

Lucas Bryant: No bibles allowed. I mean, nothing not like that. Bibles are welcomed but show bibles for this show, I don't think they exist and if they do, they don't tell us. I know that the writers have plans about where they're going, and where we're going, and where we've come from and what we'll learn as we move forward. But initially, I was like tell me what's going on and then they said no. And then I said, please and then they said no. And then I realized that I liked that situation because I am as clueless as my character, just discovering what's going on as he does. So that's all I get.

Eric Balfour: Yes, that's actually really interesting because they told me everything about my character. They said Duke lives on a boat and that was all I needed. And I've been pretty much going off that for three years now and it's worked out, I mean, pretty well in my opinion.

What can you tell us about your Halloween episode coming up?

Emily Rose: It's very scary and we were actually warned before we filmed in the location that it was a haunted location. Nothing really happened to us while we were there ...

Eric Balfour: That's not true ... I got knocked on my ass at that house and had a bruise the size of my face on my left butt cheek.

Emily Rose: That is true and you took me out in the process.

Eric Balfour: Yes. The ground underneath that house literally sucked my leg out from underneath me, threw me on the ground, and then took out Emily with it. That wasn't my fault.

Emily Rose: It was really cool because we opened up a closet and in the back of this closet were all of these really old - what were they called ... piano scrolls. And our art department had to put them in there, so it was a really eerie, weird house. Jason Priestley came back and directed that episode, which is always fun to see him again and have him working with us. But we were really happy to get out of that house.

Lucas Bryant: Yes, it was claustrophobic.

Emily Rose: Yes, it was creepy.

Eric Balfour: And also, the Halloween episode is amazing because we have the amazing Iain Glenn from *Game of Thrones* in the episode ... And this location was an old - I think it was like an old brick - like an old railway hotel and ...

Lucas Bryant: It was a brothel.

Eric Balfour: Yes, perhaps maybe a brothel.

Lucas Bryant: It was a whorehouse ... this place was in Nova Scotia's most famous whorehouse.

Eric Balfour: There was a mass murder that actually took place in the house ... I don't know.

Lucas Bryant: We don't know about that.

Eric Balfour: I'm making this up as I go.
Lucas Bryant: But I - but you could - you know, it was

definitely a creepy joint and we did get a visit from the paranormal society that tried to warn us off shooting there but we don't take any advice from anyone. And we risked life and limb to bring you this...

Eric Balfour: Yes, apparently, the cast of *Ghost Hunters* International, another Syfy show, wouldn't even come to this house, they were too afraid. So, I'm just throwing it out right now, I challenge you guys. Bring it ... Bring it Kris [Williams] ... I know Kris is on that show.

What was your most memorable moment filming this year?

Eric Balfour: My most memorable moment was there is an episode where a woman is trapped in a car that is sinking under water and it was a huge stunt. And it was, you know, the first time where our show felt really big and we have the car over this cliff, in the ocean, waves crashing on it, paramedics and stunt guys and cranes. And that to me was probably the most memorable moment. I mean, I felt like we were making a movie. It was really cool.

Emily Rose: I felt that way too about episode - I'll say this all the time - but episode 309. We - it's a time travel episode and watching our entire - every single department show turned out like completely to the nines, like this era. I mean, it felt like a film. I mean, I felt - you walked on set and *Haven* was still *Haven* because it feels classic and sort of timeless, but yet it was getting to see it like it all of it's like shine and glory from that '50s era. And it was fan-freaking-tastic.

Eric Balfour: Yes, it's true. That was - that's probably my - one of my highlights from this year too is that whole episode was - it was like doing a, you know, period film. The production value was just amazing. Hair and makeup and wardrobe and the art department was really - did a phenomenal job and we had such cool locations and scenes. It was really exciting to be a part of.

Lucas Bryant: Yes, I think it's one of the funnest parts about this element of this season is the moments where we got to see

Haven at the turn of the century and other centuries and in other decades this. And we've always sort of known these different incarnations of Audrey exist but to kind of go and see some of them in different versions is going to be - it's going to be really fun for the fans.

Tim Burton's 'Frankenweenie': Weird Kids, Childhood Pets, Monster Mashups

(October 2012)

They are movies where normal is not to be trusted and weird is celebrated; where quirky characters possess the heart of the story; where colorful, yet dark, settings are the delightfully freaky-deaky playground of the macabre and comedy. Everyone knows what a Tim Burton movie looks like.

Ever since the director emerged as a feature film director with 1985's *Pee-Wee's Big Adventure*, followed by *Beetlejuice, Batman, Edward Scissorhands, The Nightmare Before Christmas* and so on, the "Tim Burton" style has been a signature brand of moviemaking that married the mainstream with horror nerds and goths.

Meant in the most complimentary way possible, his is the kind of off-center, but mass consumable, product that Hot Topic was made for. This actually makes a lot of sense. Burton, 54, was a weird outsider of a kid who grew up in sunny Burbank, CA. A young artist influenced by Charles Addams and Roald Dahl, he eventually went to work at the most mainstream place on Earth, The Walt Disney Company, as an animator before striking out on his own to harness his style.

Of course, the problem with having his own style is that a lot of people try to duplicate it poorly. And over time, Burton himself has been criticized for striving too hard to be Tim Burton-esque (See: *Dark Shadows, Planet of the Apes*).

But by and large, the same is not being said of Frankenweenie, Burton's new stop-motion animated, black-and-white 3D film opening today. Based on a 1984 live-action short about a science-minded boy who reanimates his dead dog, Burton recently told the audience in the packed Hall H of San Diego Comic-Con that the movie "stemmed from having a dead dog as a kid," and a love of *Frankenstein* movies.

Originally designed to be released with an animated film like *Pinocchio*, Burton revealed that Disney executives "got freaked" the short would be too scary. But he said Disney movies are actually scary movies with heart, and that half the audience of kids watching *Pinocchio* ended up screaming. With that in mind, he called *Frankenweenie* "the perfect Disney movie."

The updated *Frankenweenie* fleshes out the story to include more characters - such as a class of weird children and a Vincent Price- inspired teacher (voiced by Martin Landau) - and a monster mash-up approach straight out of old Universal flicks which combined several creatures. He said it also was born from a feeling that everything was strange in school - so much so that he said he still gets freaked out when he goes to a school because it "reminds me of horrible memories."

But the origins of *Frankenweenie* and the Burton style extends beyond his old classroom. Tim Burton joined Paranormal Pop Culture and a group of reporters to answer questions about his work immediately following his Comic-Con panel.

Your first go-around with Frankenweenie was done on the sly, and the story goes you got in trouble for it - until Disney released it on DVD. So is this something of a great revenge for you that they authorized a feature film version?

Revenge? I don't know if it's a good word. I mean, it's a project that always meant something to me and the opportunity to do it with stop-motion, black and white, sort of expand on it with other kids, monsters and characters - it just seemed like the right medium and project. Even though it's revisiting something that I did a long time ago, it feels new and special.

As you started to expand the story, how many things were ideas lingering in your head that you didn't have a chance to do versus what was brand new?

Well, there were always characters I sort of had, but sometimes you do characters and don't know what it fits into. There were always some little characters it's kind of playing around with. Also just going back - not only the thing with the boy and the dog -

but going back to school and remembering some of the kids I had in school, and some of the weird teachers. And also, growing up with those kind of Universal horror films, I was also a fan of House of Frankenstein or *House of Dracula* - or *Frankenstein Meets the Wolfman* where they combine them together. A lot of it had to do with those kinds of things that I loved.

At Comic-Con, can you describe the feeling when you walk on stage at Hall H and feel the love. Is it daunting?

It's amazing. I wish my family treated me that way. I walk in the door and nobody says anything! I remember coming to this back in the late '70s at the Holiday Inn in San Diego; it is amazing what this has turned into ... it is just fun to see Halloween in July. There is something that is very special about this place.

It seems like you bring back a dog of yours in almost every movie; what's the background on that?

When you're young, it is the first kind of pure relationship you have - if you're lucky enough to have a pet that you love. It is something that connects right to your heart. I was lucky enough to have a special pet that I had that kind of relationship with.

Now the whole *Frankenstein* element is wish fulfillment in that kind of way. I always found those movies like *Frankenstein* quite emotional. So, it seemed like a fairly natural connection to combine the two.

Over 20 years ago, with Batman, you were one of the first modern filmmakers who dug into that superhero world. What do you think about the current state of that genre?

I recall back to when we were doing that, and how worried they all were that it was too, too dark. Now it looks like a light-hearted romp - Batman on Ice! It is interesting because it was such a struggle to get that at the time.

Why stop-motion animation?

I do love stop-motion. These things always take time to get done. It is a rarefied medium; it is a slightly lost art form - although there is more being done now than there was in the past. There is something so beautiful about it, just to be able to touch and feel the puppets and move them. There is something magical about it; you kind of wish everybody could experience it. It is hard to talk about it, but if you felt these things - just the intricacy of the movement - it is quite a beautiful art form.

Will there be any Frankenweenie characters in the Disneyland Haunted Mansion attraction (which is transformed into The Nightmare Before Christmas mansion every year), and what is your favorite Disney ride?

Aaah Sleeping Beauty's castle ... No. Is that still there? I'm a Space Mountain man, myself, but the Haunted Mansion is - that was such an honor. I grew up loving the Haunted Mansion and that they turned it into Nightmare was an amazing thing for me. That's like one of those weird "dream come true" kind of things, a very special moment for me.

Is this the most detailed film of yours, with regards to the puppets and backgrounds? And this is the second time you've worked in black and white after Ed Wood.

Well, it was a real pleasure to do it in black and white. That was part of the reason for wanting to do it. And any stop-motion film is intricate. We had a slightly smaller crew on this than we usually do because we wanted to show the stop-motion. On *Corpse Bride*, a lot of people thought the puppets were so good they were computer animation. So, we went back and did it a little bit more low-tech so you felt the stop-motion ... also, the black and white draws out textures more. It made the film a bit more emotional, and makes you feel like you're there. It does a strange thing, and it's hard to put into words, but it definitely affects the way you watch it.

How has the technology changed with stop-motion?

That's the thing we love about it; it's still the same. It goes back to the beginning of cinema. It is a technique that still basically is an animator moving a puppet 24 frames per second. That's, I think, why we all love it. As much as you can do anything with technology, there's something about going back to the simplicity of that. And the excitement - you see somebody move it, then see it come to life. It is very magical.

We see the science teacher, voiced by Martin Landau, looks Vincent Price-esque. Is this your ultimate fanboy character creation for you? And are there other character shout outs in the movie that are your own personal valentine?

Well yeah, everything. You don't try to put references in for people that don't know *Frankenstein* movies. It is not something that is necessary to see the film. But yeah; from remembering kids I went to school with, to the teachers, to Vincent Price - throw Christopher Lee in there. Also, just basing some characters on Boris Karloff, there are things in there that always meant something to me.

What are the challenges of adapting a short into a feature-length film?

It wasn't too much of a stretch. The heart of the story is the same. Having these other characters that were rattling around, it doesn't make seem like it is a different thing. That's why I feel proud about it; it doesn't feel like a short that we're padding out. It gets to explore kid politics, and the way kids are to each other, and weird teachers. To me, it didn't feel like a padding or stretching thing. It felt quite natural. If it hadn't felt that way, it wouldn't have been worth doing. It is important it works as its own thing.

Looking at all the films you've worked on and created over the years, is there one that stands out as your favorite. It must be hard to pick ...

It is hard to pick. You spend so much time on each thing. I think things like *Scissorhands, Ed Wood,* or *Nightmare.* This one is up there. You have to connect to everything, but these are ones that are probably slightly a bit more personal.

Was 3D always part of the plan with Frankenweenie?

The idea of black and white, and 3D, was always something I was interested in. There was a lot of talk about 3D: "It's too dark, it's too muddy, it's this and that." This was an opportunity to kind of, with the black and white, keep it crisp. When I watch it, I just love it because you see things in a different way. The idea of stop-motion in black-and-white 3D seemed like a really good combination.

'Walking Dead' Actors Morrissey, Gurira On Michonne And the Governor

(November 2012)

How about a twofer for *Walking Dead* fans today? With all the crazy stuff happening this year, this is still the season of Michonne and The Governor. The two characters have brought so much to the table, along with some astounding scripts, that *TWD* is better than it has ever been.

We've been lucky enough to catch up with Danai Gurira and David Morrissey, who play the characters, and we wanted to pass along their thoughts about joining AMC's zombie drama.

I spoke with the duo before the season premiere as they look forward to having fans see their take on Robert Kirkman's characters.

Danai, how was the adjustment to the katana? Did you enjoy taking that up?

[laughs] Are you kidding me? Yeah, I lived with it. I'm sleeping in the same bed with it ... They gave me a great guy in L.A. I was working with and had an amazing time. I broke into it, and it was hard. Different muscles started to cry that you didn't know existed until now. It's been great, and a continual process. And finding her [the character of Michonne], and what are her movements? She uses it very practically, and effectively, and efficiently, and economically. She's not trying to be flashy. So, it's really finding that balance as well.

David, can you discuss stepping into the role of such a famed character?

I came to the show as a fan; I really loved the show. And when there was an opportunity of joining it, I was over the moon. It's just been great. I was really nervous before I arrived. I felt a lot of pressure before I started because I was inside my own head with it. Then I met the rest of the cast and crew, and that pressure went off me because they were all so welcoming.

Have you read the comics?

Yeah, I've read quite a few of them. After I got hired, I got a whole slew of them. I got really addicted. The beauty of how this has all worked is the graphic novel is such an amazing, original piece of work. And the TV show is its own amazing, original piece of work. So, as we've seen, their adaptations are very free and they pull from the graphic novel in very specific ways you could never predict.

The character is so visually different (from the comics), what did they tell you about why they chose to not give you the look of the comic?

We didn't have that conversation, really. It was very much about, 'This is the character, and how we're going to do it, how we're going to interpret it.' So it was starting with what the writers came up with for the show, it wasn't about the iconic, classic look of the character in the comic book. So I think those decisions had been made before the casting happened. But once they cast me, they were very happy for me to look like this. Also, I think the spirit of the character is very much there. Whether the look isn't there, the psychotic side is there.

Would you dread them saying they're going to add an eyepatch to your repertoire?

You know what? With how the show goes on, I'm never surprised by anything. That's the beauty of it; as we get the scripts, we're as surprised as much anyone else. I don't think too far ahead of it, but I wouldn't be surprised with what they do with him. And you know people really care about the show, so anything they do is coming from a great place.

What was the biggest adjustment to joining the show, whether it was the Atlanta weather or something else?

When I came in, they go, 'you're going to have to deal with ticks.' I go, 'Noooo, I won't, I refuse to have to deal with ticks.' But, lo and behold, that is just going to be part of your reality in this job. It was an interesting adaptation at first. People are trying to make TV. Usually, it's glamming you up, but it's 'no, no, you need more shine, dirty nails, dirtier nails.' So it's very interesting. There's all sorts of different grime that you really have to start embracing. That's kind of refreshing, honestly."

The other thing about coming into the third series, for us, is it's not like we watched the first two series and thought, 'Oh great, we're going to be walking into 'Downton Abbey.' You sort of knew what it was by where it was. Things like that - the heat and ticks - they're tough but at least at the heart of it, you're telling a great story. You're loving it, you want to be there. So that's the bit you have to deal with. Sometimes you have to deal with the traffic in an inner city, or you have to deal with the rain in London. The work, at the bottom of the day, is what you love doing.

I think it adds to it. I'm watching it and there's something so visceral. I was watching the first two seasons, and it's so visceral - that heat, and seeing how they're navigating this rush into rain. That's exactly what you literally are doing as you shoot - and you feel so alive. It's a character in itself.

In the comic book, the characters are a little more "comic booky." How did you balance that on the show?

Given the writing that's gone on in Seasons One and Two, they fit in a sense that the writers are writing for us in such a wonderful way. They gel into the spirit of the show; they are very much a part of this world. The important thing for an actor, you have the comic book and you read that - but our duty is to the scripts that land on our doorstep every time we go onto an episode. That's our character. Our characters are there, not in the comic book. It's up to us to sort of interpret those characters, not the other ones.

'Walking Dead' Leftovers: Lingering Questions with Cast
(December 2012)

With tonight's midseason finale of *The Walking Dead*, fans are expecting showdowns between The Governor and Rick, Merle and Daryl, Michonne and Andrea, etc. Both the living and dead will likely be mutilated and beaten up pretty bad, and at the end of the hour, more questions will be left over.

In that spirit, we wanted to present *Walking Dead* leftovers; that is, bits and pieces from interviews with cast members - Andrew Lincoln, Norman Reedus, Michael Rooker, Steven Yeun, Lauren Cohan, and creator Robert Kirkman - that we've just not gotten around to using yet. They cover a wide range of topics, but thought you might need an appetizer before tonight...

ROBERT KIRKMAN

On how the show has evolved:
"I couldn't be more proud of what we've been doing on Season Three ... I'm constantly shocked by what we're able to pull off."

On being tempted to hold back on killing/maiming a character:

"Yeah. I know Glen [Mazzara] has spoken publicly on how Hershel was going to die at the end of the second season. That was something we came up with in the room, and really liked and how it laid out the story and factored into the Shane/Randall scenes. It was very much involved with how Randall escaped and Shane went after him. But as we got into the scripting process and developing those episodes, it just wasn't working. It was something where we kept going, 'We can't lose this guy.' This guy represents a lot of different things ... and so he gained a reprieve. It happens in the comic a lot."

On seeing Danai Gurira dressed as Michonne the first time:

"I like to think of myself as kind of a mellow, low-key kind of guy, but when I arrived on set and saw her walking around in costume between scenes - she stays in character so she storms around, looking grumpy - it was really great. I just had this stupid grin on my face and had to concentrate, like 'Hey, you're doing that dumb smile again.' It was a big moment for me. It's crazy going from Season One to Season Three. I was there when Andrew Lincoln and Steven Yeun met for the first time. Steven came onto set when we were filming the pilot. I got to stand there and watch Rick Grimes meet Glenn for the first time. It was crazy. I have all these kinds of moments, like the first time I walked into the prison. I got to go inside a cell and tour the hallways by myself. It's a lot of fun to have the comic book brought to life."

On The Governor's future:

"He doesn't look like the comic book Governor but we're going to start him at a certain point and evolve him to a certain extent ... we're definitely going to see the violent and dark Governor you got in the comic."

ANDREW LINCOLN
On how the show has changed his life:
"I call America and Georgia [where the show shoots] my home now. We have a very extraordinary life now where we live more in America than in London, and I love it ... it's changed my life in as much as I don't want to do any other job. From the outside of it, and meeting you guys and doing this, I'm very private. I go to the same coffee shops. Nothing's changed ... But there's something about working in Atlanta - not really an industry town - that's really amazing. People see us down at the coffee shop, and they come up, and it's like they've embraced us. We're like their show down south ... It's because they were with us before we were *The Walking Dead*, when we were just scruffy and wearing a hat."

On Norman Reedus and Daryl Dixon:
Norman "went to cool school" and is definitely "the wing man" and "strongest warrior of the group."

On what scares him:
The Omen, which "completely traumatized" him as a kid - and Jaws or all sharks

On The Governor:
The Governor is the "evolution of Rick ... further down the line"

On Rick as a leader:
"I think his [Rick's] humanity is intact but his ruthlessness has moved into a Shane point of view."

NORMAN REEDUS

On the evolution of Daryl:
"Growing up with a big brother like Merle, you'd probably assume he's constantly being put down, and constantly having to fight to be heard. With how things have gone with the apocalypse, he's kind of begun opening himself up to people and being respected in other ways and finding reasons to fight for certain people and be part of a group. It's a big deal for him. With Shane being gone, some of those responsibilities are on Daryl ... but

Daryl doesn't want the responsibility of taking over a group. He's just trying to fit in ... I try to think of him as a wet coyote in an alley; he's starving and you want to pet him, but he'll bite you. Not because he hates you, but that's how he's grown up."

On reuniting with Michael Rooker's Merle:

"It's not what you think. Daryl and Merle are always looking for each other and hope the other one's out there. But there's a lot of toes being stepped on. There's a lot of 'whoa, whoa, whoa, no, no, no.' It's so complicated and not what you think at all. I know both things you can think, and it's not either one of them."

On Daryl's love life:

"If it happens, I hope it happens in a way that's not very smooth. I don't want Daryl to have any game whatsoever. He's not a 'throw you up against the wall' type of 'taking you now' guy. He's more of a 'what are you doing - stop, cut it out.' He wouldn't be the aggressor, I wouldn't think, unless the situation called for it. But I don't see him as a smooth operator in regard to that, at all ... I'm not sure Daryl's emotionally up there yet."

On his crossbow vs. Michonne's katana:

"Crossbow's still cooler. I wouldn't trade it for the sword."

MICHAEL ROOKER

On the most exciting part about being back:

"Getting paid! [laughs] - very exciting, a lot of fun. No, you know, I made friends with a bunch of guys down there, and it's always fun to work with everybody. And when you come back, you get to have a meeting with the writers, which is kind of cool."

On the reunion with Norman Reedus' Daryl:

"I think we [Daryl and Merle] have always dealt with baggage, even before the zombie apocalypse. There was baggage between big brother, little brother. Big brother running away and leaving little brother; little brother being pissed off because big brother went out and didn't take him with ... I taught this guy how to hunt, trap, track. He saw I wasn't there; he could track me down!"

On his bayonet arm:
"It gets a little hot and sweaty, but other than that it's fairly comfy. I can do a lot of stuff with it. I'm very adept at using it. I can cut apples and stuff with it. It's a real blade; when I get angry, I stick it in the wall! ... we have rubber blades for when we have a real hard, rough-and-tumble, hand-to-hand kind of stuff."

On other arm attachments:
"What I have is pretty good, but I was thinking a mace. A little chain, mace - pop your head off, just like that. Go into a horde of zombies, and just start swinging."

On a Merle action figure:
"It's coming!"

STEVEN YEUN

On Glenn's fate in the comics:
"Isn't it just so twisted? He [Robert Kirkman] could have just killed him, but three pages of mush?!"

On Glenn and Maggie as the heart of the show:
"What was cool was in the first season, for Glenn, he kind of plays the hope role, in a way. He's a naive kid that wants to believe everything is still good in the world. But in the second season, it's two people actually coming together to create that and to be that lasting, working image of that."

LAUREN COHAN

"Maggie and Glenn's relationship is, you're always looking for someone who is more courageous than you in some aspect. Or someone who thinks like you or believes the things you do. It might be the apocalypse but Maggie and Glenn have this because it works. They were supposed to find each other. People talk about the parallels between this and the Rick and Laurie relationship, and it's like they offer complete different things."

Chad L. Coleman Joins 'Walking Dead' As Fan Fave Tyreese

(December 2012, with Larissa Mrykalo)

Sunday's mid-season finale of AMC's uber-hit *The Walking Dead* gave readers of the comic book series a long-awaited treat when it introduced Tyreese, a fan favorite and all-around badass character, now played by actor Chad L. Coleman.

An Atlanta Falcons football player in the pre-apocalyptic world, - which, no doubt, gives him a physical advantage when it comes to fighting off the walkers, he's a central character in the books and becomes Rick's right-hand man after the death of Shane. While there was no mention of this plot point when Tyreese and his crew make their way to the survivor's prison, he did rock his signature hammer for some effective melee action.

So how else is TV Tyreese going to be similar to his comic book counterpart?

Previously seen as the reformed criminal "Cutty" on *The Wire*, Coleman is a Virginia-born actor who says he strongly identifies with Tyreese's strong convictions and value for human life and that the character is "fighting for a new world."

Coleman spoke over the phone to share more about his take on Tyreese and appearing in five of the season's remaining eight episodes.

What can you say about the character of Tyreese and how he's different from the comic book version?

Well, I'm not an inside-out student of the graphic novel. When I came onboard, I was told if you need to reference it, we will. as we need to reference the graphic novel, we'll give you some insights from that perspective we will, but just, you know, ride it out with us script for script kind of deal.

So in as much as I would say the humanity of the man is very much akin to what was done in the graphic novel [and] I believe his kind of lack of skills as a marksman ...

Can you talk a little bit about getting cast in the show?

Well yes, unbeknownst to me, my agents had been speaking to Robert Kirkman for a little while about the possibility of me playing this role. So, whenever you have the creator kind of pulling your card and saying they want you to be a part of it, you're in a pretty good position.

Does that add pressure for you or do you kind of welcome that, that everyone would think of you for that role?

I'll put it to you like this, so Michael Jordan is shooting the last second, three quarters to win the game, I think he relishes it so I relish it. Every actor wants to be relevant and every actor wants to be held to a high standard and this allows me that opportunity, it keeps me sharp, I like it.

When you were up for this role were you aware that it was a big fan favorite character?

Yes, as soon as I went online ... that's the icing on the cake just to be able to create an original role before but to have something that was already present in another form - and to have to be able to honor it in a way, to be able to live up to that, that's huge.

Can you tease and do some forecasting for us about where the relationship between Tyreese and Rick might be like?

Well, that's a dangerous question ... Forces collide on some level is what I would say.

We saw you jumping right into zombies, running around. You kind of get thrown right into the cast, right into the mix of things, so can you talk about your first days of killing zombies? Did you have fun?

Yeah, a complete and absolute adrenaline rush, that's what it is - it's like electricity running through my body like crazy. And also the technical aspect of it, you know, I won't give away but was equally as compelling for me, like, 'Oh wow, this is how you do it, oh, okay cool' ... Zombies are so real so it's really no acting required; you just see the amazing work that's being done. It's just so real, it's just eerie, but the most eerie part of it is to see them just doing regular things like in-between takes or going to lunch break - just to watch a guy getting the salad dressing - and he's all made up, all zombied out. It's pretty hilarious.

For the rest of Season Three we're going to see no shortage of zombie killing and action for you as well?

No doubt about it, no doubt about it - the man has a hammer and he knows how to use it, so.

Do you feel like you're in adequate shape to do all this running from zombies in the Georgia heat?

Oh, of course. I grew up in Richmond, Virginia, so it gets a little sticky in that area as well and I spent a lot of time in Georgia - I have two sisters who live there as well - so yes, oh yes, bring it on. I love running in the heat.

If there's anything to the Mayan Calendar predictions or a zombie apocalypse, how would you like to spend that last day of yours?

Family. I know that sounds corny. I was going to be selfish and say, you know, a significant other but I would hope with a significant other and family surrounding me, just circling the wagon with each other and just trusting that wherever we're going at least while we were here, we loved and we loved fully and we stayed together.

What does Tyreese value in a post-apocalyptic world?

Life ... human life and the preservation of it and humanity and normalcy - family like (truly) can we just wake up for one day and not have to anticipate living like this? Can we just have some safety, some security, you know?

If you were in the zombie apocalypse, what would be your weapon of choice?

Wow, you know, I mean honestly, I love the crossbow but would have to stay true to the hammer.

Crossbows are heavy - hammers are more portable.

Exactly, exactly ... well you can see I can do a lot of damage.

Are you a fan of zombie movies?

Yes, 28 Days Later. I do the genre. My daughter's a huge fan. I'm into gore and all that good stuff - even the funny ones like Shaun Of The Dead and stuff like that. I know I haven't hit on an absolute American one but *The Walking Dead* covers that. But yes, I do enjoy the genre and I'm becoming more and more of a fan every day of it ... but I've never been a straight student of it.

In the scene where Carl had locked the door and wouldn't let you out, you said you heard the man. Does Tyreese see something different in Carl?

Yes, I would say so, and I love that. Also, it speaks to his ability to read a situation, read it clearly and communicate in an effective manner to try to get the objective taken care of. So he read the situation really quick; he could see something in this young man, in the way he handles himself with that weapon and just his whole presence and stature was very clear to me - or, you know, Tyreese - of what he was dealing with. And he was going to handle it as diplomatically as possible and he in no way, shape or form was going to take for granted who this young man was.

In the comics, Tyreese becomes Rick's second-hand man. Any hints about that in the series, and do you think Rick needs one or is Tyreese just destined to become another Shane?

I, Chad Coleman the actor, would love that just for the opportunity to mix it up, go toe-to-toe, to be in the scene with

Andrew Lincoln, so that's the selfish aspect of it. From the story, I think it would be compelling; I think it would give the audience a lot of meaty exchanges. I can't say that I know that that's going to occur, but I put my vote in for it for sure.

Has the regular cast welcomed you with open arms or like your character, do you feel more like an outsider who needs to earn a place in the established order?

It's quite the opposite. This is an amazing, extraordinary cast of human beings and I don't exaggerate at all. Andrew Lincoln has to be the nicest, egoless lead actor that I've ever met in my life and I'm not exaggerating at all. And his energy and his temperament just, you know, falls over everyone and it's just a one big happy family...
This is special, it doesn't happen often so it's only the second time in my career where in a television endeavor that I feel this sense of family and open-arm kind of 'come in and we want to see you shine' attitude - and it really for me starts with Andrew Lincoln.

One of the things that fans of color have been waiting for is some black characters who will stick around on the show for a while. Can you give us hope that, as they add black characters on the show, they won't kill them off like they've been doing?

I can't say anything there but slow down, be easy, you're going to be incredibly proud. Glen Mazzara, all of these folks, have the highest of integrity and character and they know we matter as much as anyone else, so you're going to see that played out on the show. I don't think there's any kind of agenda on their part, it's just how story telling unfolds at times, but you guys are going to be incredibly proud of Michonne and Tyreese and Sasha [who is his sister on the show].

Tyreese and his group may end up in the prison and they feel like they're safe but little do they know they have the entire threat of Woodbury The Governor descending on them fairly soon. How does Tyreese respond to being thrown in the middle of this conflict between the prison and Woodbury?

Now that's a loaded question. You'll be having the same experience at the time this is happening as I - wide-eyed and discerning and just taking it all in, trying to process and trying to find a safe haven ... You'll be on the edge of your seat and in that journey with me.

Actress Jenna-Louise Coleman Talks 'Doctor Who'
(December 2012)

Batman had Robin, Holmes had Watson, Han Solo had Chewbacca; iconic heroes have iconic sidekicks who keep their main man sane and humanized, while providing the audience with a proxy. But whereas the Lone Ranger only had one Tonto, "The Doctor" from 50-year-old British series *Doctor Who* goes through a lot of "companions" - so much so that new arrivals are met with fan anticipation and anxiety.

Enter Jenna-Louise Coleman, the 26-year-old actress who officially steps into the role of sci-fi sidekick on the popular BBC America show's Christmas Special. Known to American audiences from the April 2012 ABC miniseries *Titanic*, and for a brief role in 2010's *Captain America: The First Avenger*, she joins *Doctor Who* as Clara/Oswin, a companion to The Doctor, a mysterious, human-looking "Time Lord."

Played by Matt Smith, he journeys through "Time And Relative Dimension In Space" in his ship the TARDIS - which looks like a blue British police call box on the outside and is as iconographic a vehicle as the *U.S.S. Enterprise*, Millennium Falcon, or DeLorean. Launched in 1963, change and evolution is part of the show's DNA. When a lead actor steps down, The Doctor essentially dies and is regenerated into a new body, but as the same character with a new actor portraying him. Smith is the 11th to do so. However, over five decades, the more than 30 companions have been unique characters with their own back- story. The Doctor invites them on adventures across the "time vortex" to face monsters and save worlds. As they retire or die, fresh ones are needed to keep the Doctor company.

Although she is only the latest of companions, Coleman's debut comes during a unique moment during *Doctor Who*. Gracing the covers of *TV Guide* and *Entertainment Weekly* as a fan favorite, garnering a cover mention in Rolling Stone as a best fall show, ranking as iTunes' most downloaded TV show in the US, packing the house at San Diego Comic-Con International, Coleman arrives as the global brand has become a bona fide hit in America - and immediately following the death of popular predecessors Amy Pond and Rory (played by Karen Gillan and Arthur Darvill), Smith's first companions.

Coleman played a surprise role in last September's season premiere - as Oswin, a different character from Clara, but one connected to her - and takes on full companion duties in "The Snowmen" Christmas episode, airing December 25 at 9 p.m. ET. A mysterious woman with a secret, Clara is a feisty, flirty foil to a grief-stricken, apathetic Doctor.

"We see him having just lost the Ponds, and he's not in a great place," said Smith. "He's lost his mojo a bit, and his sense of adventure, and I think this season certainly looks at him rediscovering that fire with Clara."

Smith added he is excited for fans to see the developing chemistry between him and Coleman, as well as the "real intrigue" behind the mystery of Clara's identity. And just as the nature of *Doctor Who* is change, Smith said fans will also embrace Coleman's Clara.

For her part, Jenna-Louise Coleman has already embraced her role as a companion. During a recent interview at BBC America's Manhattan offices, she offered insight about her character and her relationship with The Doctor, and weighed in on Clara's soufflé obsession, driving a spaceship, her Bond Girl moment and Christmas traditions.

Can you share a moment when you felt the enormity of stepping into this popular world?

You see "it" everywhere and you're used to it, like I was used to seeing Matt's face all over the place. But, when I was auditioning, being sat on the Tube and you see the posters, and it was always like he was pointing at me ... (But) there's not very much time to analyze as you go. It is only now that I feel like I've just been playing with all my mates for the last couple of months, and then suddenly, I'm like, "but people are going to see this," you know?

What would you like to add to the legacy of the show as Oswin/Clara?

I like that it's not plain sailing. Like (executive producer Steven Moffat) was saying, it's not very interesting if you come in and it's like this friendship straight away. He's been very clever in creating a mystery, because, no matter what, it's always going to be hard to bring in somebody else into the show, when Matt, Karen, and Arthur started out together, and you're used to seeing them on screen together.

How would you define your character's relationship with The Doctor?

I like that she holds her own. You know, The Doctor's this amazing man, and she's like, "You know, cool. I think you're amazing, but so am I." So, it's a nice double act.

Has Karen offered advice on joining the show?

She's been really supportive ... She came to the screening in New York City with Matt, and when Oswin was on screen, she texted me saying it was great. (But) from interviews I've seen of Karen, she was saying she didn't want to, because she wanted me to have my own experience. I did want to be like, "What do I need to know? Tell me everything!" But she's been really cool about it.

There was never a realized romance between The Doctor and Karen's Amy, but your character gets flirtatious straight away, right?

It's been interesting how it's changed Matt's Doctor. There is a natural bounce between them, and a flirtation, and attraction. But, again, they've always got this friction because they're a bit magnetic and drawn to each other, but she can't quite figure him out. He's got loads of secrets and he's always looking at her, trying to figure her out.

Can you tell me about the first meeting between you and Matt?

He's with the same agency as me, so my agent said, "You're going to be reading with Matt and he's lovely. He'll take care of you." I walked into the room and he's just like, "Heeeeyyyyy," and gave me a big hug. He really helped me out in the audition. I've read with other actors in auditions before, but Matt really got involved so it was like we were both auditioning together almost.

This is an iconic franchise, but are there other big franchises you'd want to step into?

Totally! I'd love to be a Bond Girl. I did have my Bond Girl moment - well, what I thought was going to be, but it was very much a *Doctor Who* version. Like being on the back of a motorbike, but then we've got the goggles and the hat, so it was like *Doctor Who's* take on James Bond.

Have you played with any cool sci-fi gadgets on the show, like the TARDIS?

There are certain parts of the TARDIS which I love. We've got these new kind-of rally balls, which is my favorite. But my character got to drive the TARDIS at one point!

In the long list of Doctor Who monsters, who's your favorite?

The Weeping Angels. It's the concept (that they only move when you aren't looking at them). But there's one at the end of this season it's a new monster, and I'd say you have to wait and see that. That one is my favorite, so far.

One of the things we know about your character is her love of soufflé. Have you tried making one?

I had to be baking one in a scene recently. So, I got the Google up and tried to figure out exactly how to do it, take it kind of really seriously to make sure I've got, like, the whisking right. But maybe that's what I should do over Christmas.

Is it odd returning to a "normal" world after living in The Doctor's?

"This" life is so exciting on a daily basis. Everything's so dramatic every day, and it's the end of the world every week. You're either running or there's a snow machine or rain machine, or you're in a harness and you're on wires ... On an off day, I find that I get bored quickly, like, "Where's the Cybermen?"

The Doctor Who Christmas Special is something of a tradition - do you have others you'll keep?

There are 13 of my family going to a cottage, so we'll be there watching. It's one of my grandmum's favorite shows, so it's big for her. But normally I get home from London and I haven't seen my family for a little while, and me and my mum always wrap the presents the night before with a glass of Bailey's. That's my favorite tradition at Christmastime.

What did your grandmother say when she learned you got this role?

I auditioned for Amy's best mate in it, and was pretty close to getting the part, and my grandma was absolutely devastated I didn't. So, we came back around, and I don't think she can believe it, actually. It is quite surreal for her, and she's quite looking forward to meeting Matt.

What do you anticipate that encounter being like?

My grandma's going to mess up his hair. She's going to be

patting him and hugging him, and Matt's going to have really messy hair for the rest of the night.

Matt Smith's Very Time Lord 'Doctor Who'

Christmas (December 2012)

Every Christmas an ancient time-and-space traversing visitor swoops in on his flying ride to give a gift to the children of the world. But instead of a jolly elf with reindeer, this one is a Time Lord with a TARDIS.

Yes, it is time again for the "Doctor Who Christmas Special," a holiday tradition as special to nerds as Towel Day (and maybe even Life Day). Airing tonight on BBC America at 9 p.m. ET, "The Snowmen" is 11th Doctor Matt Smit's third special but marks an important first for him - the arrival of a new companion.

Following the untimely departure of the Ponds, The Doctor is out of the saving-the-world business, and has become a curmudgeonly Scrooge in Victorian London. Though he keeps company with allies Strax, Vastra, and Jenny (who comprise something of a Sherlock-esque sleuthing team), The Doctor has largely separated himself from humanity, but things change when he encounters Clara. Played by Jenna-Louise Coleman, who we met as "Oswin" in the Season 7 premiere "Asylum of the Daleks," Clara is a smart and saucy woman with a double life. When she stumbles into The Doctor at Christmastime, and onto a race of monstrously animated Snowmen controlled by Doctor Simeon (Richard E. Grant), Dickensian England gets interesting.

Unlike some other Christmas Specials, "The Snowmen" plays an important role in setting up the second half of Season 7 - and ranks as one of the best specials in the rebooted show. The grief-stricken Doctor is still coping with losing the Ponds and is living with his head in the clouds. Meanwhile, it introduces Coleman as new companion Clara and sets up a mystery for her character.

Moreover, we get to see glimpses of a new TARDIS and are

treated to a few surprises.

But for Smith, the Christmas Special is integral to seeing The Doctor get his mojo back. In a recent conversation with Matt Smith at the BBC America offices in Manhattan, the actor discussed the Christmas Special, having Coleman join him on the TARDIS, and how the holiday action impacts the rest of this season.

To begin with, I recently just re-watched "The Next Doctor" Christmas Special with David Morrissey and wondered what you thought about an unofficial Doctor becoming The Governor on The Walking Dead.

I'm a huge fan of *The Walking Dead*, and it's exciting to see him in that sort of badass villain. He's a fabulous actor.

What was the biggest challenge in transitioning to a companion since this is the first change in companions for you?

Change in Doctor Who is always slightly resisted, but that's what the show is based on - change and evolution and embracing that. Whether it be with The Doctor or a companion. In story terms, The Doctor, we leave him having just lost the Ponds, and he's not in a great place. He's kind of lost his mojo a bit and his sense of adventure and I think this season certainly looks at him rediscovering that fire with the character of Clara. For me and Jenna, as actors, it's kind of like the show in many ways. You develop a chemistry and a work ethic together as the season goes on, you know?

What sort of thing are you excited for the audience to see with Jenna?

Well, it's the mystery that surrounds her that, I think, will be of real intrigue this year. I think it's cool, because we kind of have this gang with us this season, as well, Strax, Vastra and Jenny- who are brilliant and funny, and one's a lizard assassin, one's a sort-of ninja from Victorian times and the other's just a complete psychotic war-monster. You sort of add that into the mix. And Richard Grant [in "The Snowmen"] is in fine form as a villain. So, there's a lot coming up.

Are Strax, Vastra, and Jenny going to be sticking around for a good portion of the season?

Yeah, they're around. They'll be back. And [River Song, played by Alex Kingston] is always swooping in.

How is that going to work? This seems the character of Oswin is directly more flirtatious, and it seems like there's more romantic spark right away, which is never quite realized with Amy.

No, because she was sort of in love with Rory, wasn't she? And there was always that. The Doctor was sort of like their weird granddad/ child.

You're a married man and kissing another woman!

I know! I mean, he's still ... you saw me and the kiss. I'm flailing around like a wombat. He still doesn't really know what to do.

That's certainly the one area where The Doctor always falls apart, when it comes to the romance and the feelings. Feelings are kind of a weird, icky kind of thing ...

It's the human stuff that he doesn't really know how to compute or deal with.

Let's bring up another quintessentially British character, James Bond. Bond and The Doctor always seem to get their friends - and girlfriends - killed off. What is it that about the British sensibility?

I don't know! It's funny, isn't it? Everyone that comes with us ends up taking the fall at some point. I think it's very interesting for both characters, if you look at the bloods on their hands. But, actually, James Bond and The Doctor - they'd probably get on - but

I think The Doctor would just be like, "Let's talk before we shoot, and why do you keep kissing everyone? What is that all about? Let's go. Let's move on." I like to think they'd get on quite well. Maybe The Doctor would just think he's really cool. I don't know.

He does wear bowties.

He does wear bowties and has cool one-liners.

Are there still moments where you just think, "This is so freaking cool that I get to do this"?

Oh man, every day playing that character, because it's limitless. It's boundless. I'm more so very fortunate that I have Steven Moffat at the helm of it, who, in my eyes, is a complete genius. So, I mean, honestly, not sounding too happy about myself, but it's every day that I'm grateful for it because it offers you so much opportunity, especially as an actor.

Do you like being able to go in a darker direction than you have before, in the Christmas Special? And is that going to resonate?

I think so. Over the three seasons I've done, I've always wanted there to be a slight variation, so you look back on each season and go, "Yeah, I look back, seeing The Doctor in 'The Eleventh Hour,' sort of like a newborn lamb - and now, he's a bit slower." But still, he'll get his mojo back. He's got to; he's The Doctor.

You see that mojo come back a bit in the Christmas Special, right?

Once the bowtie is on, he's like, "Okay, game time again," you know?

Would you ever want to do the evil twin Doctor?

I love the idea. Watch this space is all I can say to that.

So we're going to see "evil" you?

You might be, you might not [laughs].

I've talked to you so many times from when you first came presenting The Doctor in America to now; how is the fandom transitioning even further? Evolving even further?

That's been one of the most exciting parts of my tenure, really, is seeing the growing evolution of the show in the States - and just the general awareness of the show. I think the viewing figures - it was the biggest selling show on iTunes last year. TV Guide, Entertainment Weekly - things like that are real big steps for the show, and I feel very proud to be a part of it. It is nice to work on something that feels like it's in a moment, or of a moment, you know?

Where are the American fans right now? We know that they're younger. You get a lot of Gen-X fans and a lot of old-school, Tom Baker fans. Where do you see the American fandom going?

Interestingly, I think more children will come on board. I was talking to Alex Kingston who says when she goes to pick up her kid from school, the kids go, "River Song! River Song!" I think it would be interesting - and good! - because it is right that it's for children, as well. So, I think the audience may get younger. But what do I know, you know?

So, the new TARDIS: I like it but miss the kind of Steampunkiness ...

Of the old one? Yeah, yeah.

That sort of fit your sensibility.

All the bits? Yeah, I know. I miss certain bits of the old one, as well. But like with everything on the show, I think you've got to just go with the change. Otherwise, they'll leave you behind.

They've kind of gone more traditional, like more back to Jon Pertwee, Sylvester McCoy- like, if you look back at it, it's a definite nod to an older version of the show and the TARDIS.

I appreciate you calling back to older Doctors. It's a lot of homework to do. Do fans ever try to quiz you on it?

Yeah. Interestingly, in "The Doctor's Wife" - the previous Neil Gaiman episode - there's a scene where he builds a TARDIS out of old TARDISes. He's in the TARDIS junkyard, and there was a guy on set who could name - just from the wall - what TARDIS, what era, what episode. So, for any Whovians out there, if you can name what TARDIS, what era, what episode, then you know your stuff.

I've watched the show a long time, but I don't know how I would do in a trivia game.

Do you think you'd do well?

No, because I know it, but I'm not an encyclopedia like some fans.

And there's so much to know!

Could you ace a game of Doctor Who trivia?

You know what? I wouldn't want to say yes. I don't think I could. Steven could. Steven knows it like finite. He knows everything about it. He's a complete nerd.

Keep It Weird and Keep In Touch

Thank you for reading the Paranormal Pop Culture Collection. Please stay in touch, and follow Aaron Sagers' further adventures, dog photos, and tiki recipes on Instagram, Twitter, Facebook, and TikTok. Listen to the NightMerica podcast wherever you download your favorite podcasts. And join in on the cocktail classes, livestream interviews, and general tomfoolery with Aaron at his Geeky Creepy Tiki Travels Patreon.

Patreon.com/AaronSagers
Instagram.com/AaronSagers
Twitter.com/AaronSagers
TikTok.com/@AaronSagers
Facebook.com/AaronSagersPage
Subscribe to NightMerica podcast: Spotify, Apple Podcasts, Stitcher, Amazon Music

www.AaronSagers.com
www.ParanormalPopCulture.com
Contact: Publicity@AaronSagers.com

Made in the USA
Columbia, SC
18 August 2022

65051385R00252